INTERNATIONAL ECONOMIC LAW

*General Editor*: John H. Jackson

# THE STRUCTURE OF REGULATORY COMPETITION

## Corporations and Public Policies in a Global Economy

# *The Structure of Regulatory Competition*

## *Corporations and Public Policies in a Global Economy*

DALE D. MURPHY

*Walsh School of Foreign Service*
*Georgetown University*

OXFORD
UNIVERSITY PRESS

OXFORD
UNIVERSITY PRESS

Great Clarendon Street, Oxford OX2 6DP

Oxford University Press is a department of the University of Oxford.
It furthers the University's objective of excellence in research, scholarship,
and education by publishing worldwide in

Oxford New York

Auckland Cape Town Dar es Salaam Hong Kong Karachi
Kuala Lumpur Madrid Melbourne Mexico City Nairobi
New Delhi Shanghai Taipei Toronto

With offices in
Argentina Austria Brazil Chile Czech Republic France Greece
Guatemala Hungary Italy Japan Poland Portugal Singapore
South Korea Switzerland Thailand Turkey Ukraine Vietnam

Oxford is a registered trade mark of Oxford University Press
in the UK and in certain other countries

Published in the United States
by Oxford University Press Inc., New York



First published 2004
Published new as paperback, 2006



British Library Cataloguing in Publication Data
Data available

Library of Congress Cataloging in Publication Data
Data available

Typeset by Hope Services

Printed in Great Britain
on acid-free paper by
Biddles Ltd, King's Lynn

ISBN 0–19–926751–0 (Hbk.) 978–0–19–926751–4 (Hbk.)
ISBN 0–19–921651–7 (Pbk.) 978–0–19–921651–2 (Pbk.)

1 3 5 7 9 10 8 6 4 2

*In memoriam:*

Robert W. Murphy 1921–1995
Ruth C. Hetherston 1900–1997
Dora H. Murphy 1923–1997
Gene H. Hetherston 1927–1998

# General Editor's Preface

The Oxford University Press is again pleased to publish an interesting and topical book as part of its series dealing with subjects of International Economic Law. This volume, by Professor Dale D. Murphy, of Georgetown University, Walsh School of Foreign Service, has taken the subject another big step forward, by choosing a new, effective, and highly empirical approach. He follows an inductive method, for which he quotes Nobel prize-winner George Stigler's reasoning, 'the truly intended effects should be deduced from actual effects.'

In pursuing this approach, the author examines six specific cases in depth (his Chapters 2 through 7), to evaluate the factors that led to one of three possible outcomes of 'regulatory competition': lower common denominator, a higher common denominator, and a mixture in between. The author proposes an original theoretical explanation for the diversity of international rules and national regulations that are affected by international trade. The explanation bridges studies of law, economics, political science, and business strategy. It is a fascinating study which closely examines the real world, and is an important contribution to the literature of international economic rules.

Professor Murphy successfully challenges several orthodoxies in international political economy and law and offers a new theoretical understanding based on firms' regulatory preferences. Chapters 2 and 3 demonstrate that regulatory competition-in-laxity is not a myth, as some allege, and that it has occurred in such fundamental industries as shipping and banking. Chapters 4 through 7, however, demonstrate that higher regulations may also result from increased trade and foreign direct investments, contrary to other critics, as well as reactions against greater interdependence. Unlike earlier works on interjurisdictional regulatory competition, this book predicts the circumstances under which each outcome is likely.

These case-studies—some familiar, some new—also illuminate controversies over 'globalization' and responses to them such as corporate social responsibility and public-private partnerships. The compelling historical narratives draw on the author's work experience in the private sector (Citibank), government (U.S. State Department), and development agencies (World Bank, United Nations, USAID) in over 30 countries, as well as his academic training.

Braving provocative questions, the book shines light on the black-box of policy-making and analyzes the fundamentally important role that firms play in shaping regulations. It makes a significant theoretical contribution to the field in the analysis and differentiation of firms' varied regulatory preferences, rather than treating these as monotonic. Not content with vague generalizations about 'market forces' or 'the private sector', the book burrows beneath superficial press releases and digs deep into firms' strategies and the political process by which regulations emerge. This painstaking research pays off both in the insights it generates and the robustness of the arguments.

As discussed in the final chapter, the theoretical model leaves room for wise choices, strategy, and leadership, building on a new intuition. The conclusion draws on these insights to offer advice for practitioners of law, business, and government.

JOHN H. JACKSON*

* *University Professor of Law*, Georgetown University Law Center (GULC), Washington, D.C.; *Director*, Institute of International Economic Law, GULC; *General Editor*, International Economic Law Series, Oxford University Press; *Editor in Chief*, *Journal of International Economic Law*, Oxford University Press.

# *Preface*

As formal trade barriers fall, what were once domestic policy matters become issues of international concern. This book identifies cases in cross-border trade and investment with the potential for competition among regulatory jurisdictions. The policy outcomes of this competition vary: one sees convergence toward a lower common denominator in some cases, convergence toward a higher common denominator in others, while in still other cases national differences persist. The book proposes three (related) causes of these divergent outcomes. First, national regulations on production processes yield laxity; conversely, regulations on the market access of products or services yield stringency. Second, industrial structure affects the strength of the process *versus* market-access distinction. Concentrated markets facilitate collective action and regulatory capture. Powerful producers push for market-access and process regulations that reflect their particular interests. Third, the asset-specificity of firms' investments affects regulatory 'convergence' on a given issue. Firms with low asset-specific investments facilitate a competition-in-laxity. Firms with high multinational asset specificity seek homogenous regulations to lower their transaction costs. Firms whose asset-specific investments are domestic seek heterogenous regulatory protection. In prose accessible to lay readers, this book explains six cases in detail using these propositions, two for each policy outcome. The case studies suggest the model is necessary to understand general outcomes, although not sufficient to fully explain individual cases.

This book is the product of many years of research. To thank all those who helped along the way would be an impossible task. Without certain individuals, however, it never would be finished and they deserve special mention. First among these was Kenneth A. Oye, whose inspiration, assistance, and research collaboration provided the foundations on which this book is built. Initial funding was provided by a research grant from the V. Kann Rasmussen Foundation, through the MIT Initiative on Environmental Leadership. Funding from Georgetown University's Edmund A. Walsh School of Foreign Service allowed me to research and complete the chapter on offshore banking, for which the London School of Economics provided an invaluable base. At Georgetown University thanks go in particular to Theodore Moran, John Kline, Robert Cumby, Carol Evans, Lola Brown, and others in the Karl F. Landegger Program in International Business Diplomacy for providing a stimulating and collegial home, to Dennis Quinn, Michael Levy, and John Mayo, in the McDonough School of Business, John H. Jackson in the Georgetown Law School, and to George Shambaugh and other supportive colleagues and students in the Schools of Foreign

Service, Law, and Business who provided valuable insights and helped me build bridges across academic disciplines. David Vogel, Maria Green Cowles, Dan Flanagan, Nathan Foster, Robert Kagan, Ethan Kapstein, David Lake, Giandomenico Majone, Katherine Murphy, Pierre Rinfret, Susan Strange, Kenneth Thomas, Joel Trachtman, Daniel Verdier, William Wechsler, Oliver Williamson, Yuqing Xing, and two anonymous reviewers all made helpful suggestions. Gwen Booth offered much helpful editorial advice. Kelly Miller, Horacio Martinez, Daniel Dellaferrera, Rebecca Regan-Sachs, and Sarah Knight provided valuable research assistance.

I was fortunate to have many outstanding teachers and colleagues on this path who deserve mention here. These include Hayward R. Alker, Jr., Suzanne Berger, Lincoln P. Bloomfield, Donald Blackmer, Lael Brainard, Nazli Choucri, Charles H. Ferguson, Peter M. Haas, Thomas Homer-Dixon, Rudiger Dornbusch, Ellen Immergut, Judith Layzer, Richard M. Locke, David Marks, James Maxwell, Stephen Meyer, Mario Molina, Lucian Pye, James Rosberg, Richard Samuels, Judith Tendler, Inger Weibust, Myron Weiner, and Sanford Weiner at MIT; and James E. Austin, Abe Chayes, William C. Clark, Richard Cooper, Peggy Duxbury, Stephen Haggard, Samuel P. Huntington, Robert O. Keohane, Tyn Myint-U, Joseph Nye, Jr., Aye-Aye Thant, Glenn Tobin, and Robert Putnam at Harvard University. Essential was the long-distance support of Alan Murphy. Thanks also to colleagues at ETH-Zurich, including Renate Schubert, Stefan Saladin, and Regula Venzin. Others include Al Leventhal, David Rosenberg, Ruthie Newman, Milt Yanicks, Mary Lindquist, Harry Leavitt, Sanford Petersky, Charles and Linda O'Connor, and Marianne Fellows. It pains me not to be able to thank individually the many other friends, relatives, colleagues, and students who supported this work, but the list is too long. As always, any errors in writing or logic are my own responsibility. For all those who asked 'How is the manuscript?' and responded with encouragement to my laments, I can only say 'Thank you'.

D.D.M.
Washington, DC

# *Summary Contents*

# Contents

# *List of Figures*

# *Abbreviations*

| | |
|---|---|
| AALL | American Association of Labor Legislation, 1905–1943 |
| AAP | American Academy of Pediatrics |
| ACLU | American Civil Liberties Union |
| API | American Petroleum Institute |
| BCCI | Bank of Credit and Commercial International |
| BIBF | Bangkok International Banking Facilities |
| BIS | Bank for International Settlements |
| BOLAM | Bank of London and Montreal |
| BOLSA | Bank of London and South America |
| CEA | US Council of Economic Advisors |
| CFC | chlorofluorocarbon |
| CIA | US Central Intelligence Agency |
| CITES | Convention on International Trade in Endangered Species |
| CSR | corporate social responsibility |
| EC | European Community, 1967–1993 |
| ECSC | European Coal and Steel Community, 1952–2002 |
| EEC | European Economic Community, 1958–1967 |
| EEI | Earth Island Institute |
| EPA | US Environmental Protection Agency |
| ERT | European Roundtable of Industrialists |
| ETP | Eastern Tropical Pacific |
| EU | European Union, 1993–present |
| FATF | Financial Action Task Force |
| FBI | US Federal Bureau of Investigation |
| FBSEA | US Foreign Bank Supervision Enhancement Act |
| FCEA | US Foreign Credit and Exchange Act |
| FDI | foreign direct investment |
| FDIC | US Federal Deposit Insurance Corporation |
| FDICIA | US FDIC Improvement Act |
| FDIRP | US Foreign Direct Investment Restraint Program |
| FOC | flag-of-convenience |
| FOE | Friends of the Earth |
| FOO | flag of origin |
| FRB | US Federal Reserve Board |
| FRBNY | Federal Reserve Bank of New York |
| FSA | UK Financial Services Authority |
| FTA | free trade agreement |
| FTAA | Free Trade Agreement of the Americas |
| GATT | General Agreement on Trade and Tariffs |

| | |
|---|---|
| GDP | gross domestic product |
| GMO | genetically modified organism |
| HCD | higher common denominator |
| HCFC | hydrochlorofluorocarbon |
| HET | heterogenous regulations |
| HFC | hydrofluorocarbons |
| IBF | International Banking Facility |
| ICFTU | International Confederation of Free Trade Unions |
| ICI | Imperial Chemical Industries Ltd. |
| ICIFI | International Council of the Infant Food Industry |
| IET | US Interest Equalization Tax |
| ILO | International Labor Organization |
| IMC | International Monetary Conference |
| IMF | International Monetary Fund |
| IMO | International Maritime Organization, formerly IMCO |
| INBC | International Nestlé Boycott Committee |
| INFACT | Infant Formula Action Committee |
| IOSCO | International Organization of Securities Commissions |
| IRS | US Internal Revenue Service |
| ITC | US International Trade Commission |
| ITF | International Transport Workers' Federation |
| *JAMA* | *Journal of the American Medical Association* |
| LCD | lower common denominator |
| LDC | less developed country |
| LOT | load on top (oil tankers) |
| MARPOL | Convention for the Prevention of Marine Pollution |
| MAS | multinational asset specificity |
| MMPA | US Marine Mammal Protection Act |
| MNC | multinational corporation |
| MRA | Mutual Recognition Agreement |
| NAFTA | North American Free Trade Agreement |
| *NEJM* | *New England Journal of Medicine* |
| NGO | nongovernmental organization |
| NIS | Norwegian International Ship Registry |
| NMFS | National Marine Fisheries Services |
| NOAA | National Oceanic and Atmospheric Administration |
| NSC | US National Security Council |
| *NYT* | *New York Times* |
| OCC | US Office of the Comptroller of the Currency |
| ODCCP | UN Office for Crime Control and Drug Prevention |
| OECD | Organization of Economic Co-operation and Development |
| PPM | process or production methods (GATT) |
| SEA | Single European Act, 1987 |
| SEC | US Securities and Exchange Commission |

| | |
|---|---|
| SME | small and medium-sized enterprises |
| SOLAS | International Convention for the Safety of Life at Sea |
| STCW | Standards of Training, Certification, and Watchkeeping |
| TABD | Trans-Atlantic Business Dialogue |
| TAED | Trans-Atlantic Environmental Dialogue |
| UNEP | United Nations Environment Program |
| UNICEF | United Nations Children Fund |
| USTR | US Trade Representative |
| VERs | 'Voluntary' Export Restraints |
| VLCC | Very Large Crude Carrier |
| WHO | World Health Organization |
| WIC | Women, Infants, and Children food program |
| WIPO | World Intellectual Property Organization |
| WMO | World Meteorlogical Organization |
| *WSJ* | *Wall Street Journal* |
| WTO | World Trade Organization |

# PART I
# INTRODUCTION

# 1

# *The Puzzle and an Explanation*

The competition of nations in the trade of the world, and the community of interests proceeding therefrom, makes it impossible to create successful institutions for the benefit of working men of one country without entailing that country's power of competing with other countries. Such institutions can only be established on a basis adopted in common in all countries concerned.

Otto von Bismarck[1] (1890)

Over a century ago, Otto von Bismarck, the Iron Chancellor and *Realpolitik* architect of German unification, voiced fears that domestic regulations were undermined by the flow of goods and capital among nations. Today the extent of world commerce has once again put economic regulations at the forefront of international policy debates. So-called 'Anti-globalization' protestors have echoed Bismarck in their rallies for and against a wide variety of causes. These groups' goals were inchoate and sometimes incompatible, but their one unifying theme was political in nature, not economic: they protested against 'plutocracy' and the political power of large corporations.[2] Meanwhile, government officials and business executives sought to liberalize trade and foreign direct investments (FDI) and to promote economic growth while reconciling conflicting interests within and between rich and poor countries. Officials, executives, and protesters alike claimed to speak on behalf of impoverished peoples across the globe, many of whom depend upon foreign markets, goods, and capital for their livelihood.

In the rhetorical heat of street demonstrations and the corresponding political and corporate media spin, few observers impartially understood that firms vary in their preferences for regulation. It is not possible to understand the contemporary international political economy without analyzing these variations in preferences, their origins, and impacts; nor is it possible to achieve the policy goals which various sides seek. This book explains

[1] Cited in Moss (1993) from 'Instructions of Prince Bismarck to the German Ambassadors and Ministers, 8 February 1890, Inviting the Powers to a Conference at Berlin, March 1890'. Students of German history will note that Bismarck was struggling both to defeat the Socialist movement and to prevent his imminent ouster by the 'Labor Emperor', Kaiser Wilhelm II. Bismarck privately opposed the labor conference as a weak concession to Socialists. He resigned under imperial command on 18 March 1890, the very month of the conference.

[2] The protesters were not alone. Three-fourths of Americans surveyed thought large corporations held too much power (Pew Research Center, 21 February 2002; and *Business Week* cover story 11 September 2000).

firms' preferences, and helps predict regulatory outcomes. Much has been written about the normative implications of international regulations, which involve significant but idiosyncratic issues. An underlying concern over the undemocratic nature of corporate power should not be equated with the one-sided view that corporate interests are inimical to broader social interests. Conversely, a concern for economic efficiency and growth in output should not mask the fact that large firms use public policy as part of their strategy, often at the expense of competitors and occasionally at the expense of broader social goals (Chandler 1990; Oster 1994; Vietor 1994; Lizondo 1995; Kogut 1998; Doz 1999; Dunning 2002; Birdsall 2003). The goal of choosing an analytical and predictive approach over a normative one is to reach insights useful to all parties in these debates.

As formal barriers fall for foreign trade and investments, what were once domestic policy matters become issues of cross-border concern. Preferences for regulations vary among and within countries. There is little agreement on the assessment of risks associated with economic activity, the assessment of the costs and benefits that would result from restrictions, or the preferences for levels and types of regulation. Despite two decades of trends toward deregulation, many business managers now spend more time on regulations than previously. Pfizer's CEO, Edmund Pratt, noted: 'The biggest single change in management during my career has been the increase in time that managers spend dealing with government officials' (Paine 1995).

Virtually every form of economic activity is subject to regulation. In the international arena, there is no overarching authority to resolve what legal scholars refer to as the 'conflict of laws' between different regulations (Esty and Geradin 2001). States whose economies are open to foreign trade and investments create opportunities for firms to seek the most favorable regulatory climate, either by relocating production elsewhere or by voicing their interests to regulators.[3] Open economies thus increase incentives for states to achieve a 'comparative regulatory advantage' for their producers. In some cases, firms in states which adopt the least stringent regulations may prosper at the expense of firms in states adopting more stringent regulations. In other cases, convergence on higher standards may be reached. In still other cases, firms may benefit from national regulations that discriminate against foreigners. As a consequence, one observes significant variation in state-by-state policies, as well as some coordinated policies among states. What is the pattern in this variation?

[3] This book uses the legal and international relations term 'state' which Margaret Levi (in Katznelson and Milner 2002: 40) defines as: 'a complex apparatus of centralized and institutionalized power that concentrates violence, establishes property rights, and regulates society within a given territory. . .' Depending on the context, this organized geopolitical unit encompasses both countries in the international system and territories within federated systems such as the USA.

## 1. The puzzle

Over the long term, cross-border variations in initial sets of national policies may generate any of the following three basic trajectories or outcomes for a given issue:

— movement toward a lower common denominator (LCD) via competition-in-laxity;
— movement toward a higher common denominator (HCD) via more stringent regulations; and
— persistence of diverse regulations allowing a heterogenous (HET) regulatory climate.

What makes this investigation particularly interesting and complex is that all three trajectories occur simultaneously. These three outcomes constitute the dependent variable of this book: that is, the puzzle to be explained. The main goal is to explain the necessary causes of each outcome, thereby providing policymakers and managers with a foundation from which to act.

The remaining sections of this Chapter further explain these trajectories and offer three related propositions that help predict when each will occur. The locus of regulations (on production processes rather than products' market access) explains regulatory movement toward stringency or laxity. How a particular industry is structured explains the degree of change. The specificity of assets explains how homogenous the regulations are among states and it also affects movements towards or away from laxity. Chapters Two to Seven offer six detailed case studies: two for each of the three outcomes LCD, HCD, and HET.

Figure 1.1 (the dependent variable) maps out the stylized trajectories that regulatory outcomes can take. The horizontal axis marks the commonality of policies among states. Do states adopt homogenous regulations (common among some group of states with competing industries) or heterogenous regulations (in which national differences persist)? The vertical axis marks the stringency of policies: most simply, does economic activity occur under more stringent or more lax regulations? This two-dimensional dichotomy is for conceptual clarity. Stringent is defined as 'marked by rigor, strictness or severity, with regard to a rule or standard', from the Latin *stringere* or to bind tight. 'Homogeneity' and 'commonality' are similar terms and preferable here to 'harmonization' or 'convergence'.[4] Regulations here are defined broadly as 'direction from a competent authority'. Therefore, regulations

[4] 'Harmonization' has benign normative overtones, as opposed to 'disharmony' (Bhagwati and Hudec 1996). 'Convergence' has teleological overtones and references to broader socio-political studies on modernization or macro-economic policy such as Berger and Dore 1996; Heidenheimer, Heclo, and Adams 1990; Skocpol and Amenta 1986; Goldthorpe (ed.) 1984; Kerr 1983; Inkeles in Attir 1981; Garrett 1998; and Garrett and Mitchell 2000.

*Figure 1.1*: The dependent variable: Trajectories of regulatory competition among competing states

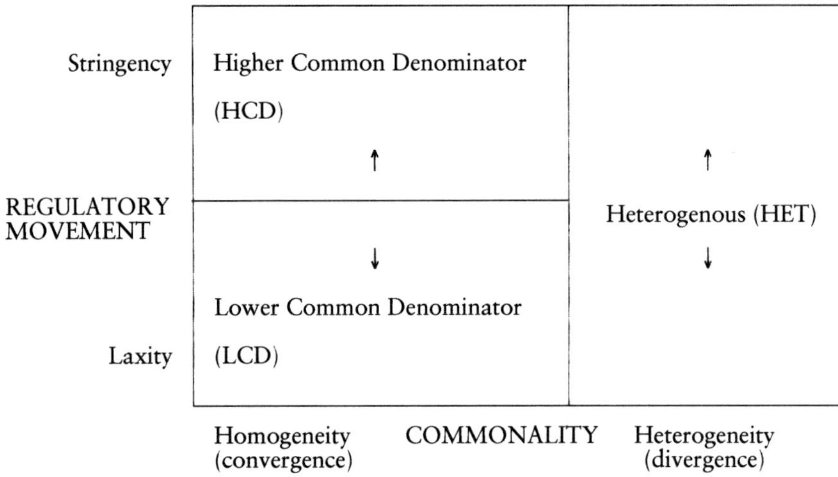


include a wide variety of policies, including laws, administrative guidelines, bureaucratic regulations, codes, and other standards. The emphasis is on *de facto* implemented standards, and not simply *de jure* laws on the books.

## 1.1 Lower common denominator (LCD)

Competition among jurisdictions may lead to a competition-in-laxity down to lax outcomes (LCD), which David Vogel (1995) has dubbed the Delaware effect. In Switzerland it would be called the 'Zug effect'. Both states deliberately wrote their regulatory codes to attract domestic industry. These outcomes are not new. Supreme Court Justice Louis Brandeis used the phrase 'race of laxity' in *Liggett Co. v. Lee* (1933). During the debate over Delaware, 'race to the bottom' was picked up by William Cary (1974) and Ralph Winter (1977). US Federal Reserve Board Chairman Arthur Burns described the US federalist financial system as a 'competition in laxity' in his 21 October 1974 address to the American Bankers Association Convention.[5] 'Competition-in-laxity' is more analytically useful than the colloquial 'race to the bottom', as the latter implies some nonexistent

[5] Moss (1994) uses the phrase 'degenerative competition'. Law and policy journals use the phrases 'interjurisdictional competition', 'regulatory arbitrage', and 'competitive deregulation', and the general subject falls under legal conflict of laws studies. See also hearings before Congress, 'Corporate Rights and Responsibilities: Hearings Before the Senate Committee on Commerce', 94th Cong., 2d Sess., 241 (1976); including a statement (pp. 343–6) in which 80 law professors argue that US state law suffered from a 'race for the bottom'.

extreme condition and is often meant pejoratively or as a straw man to confute.

Competition-in-laxity implies a change in negotiating power between firms and states where one state offers lower regulations. Firms who take advantage of these regulations may gain market share and create incentives for other states to follow suit to maintain or regain market share. Firms may engage in regulatory arbitrage, playing off one government against others.

This competition-in-laxity may manifest itself in four forms:

(i) *de jure* competition-in-laxity occurs when states actually lower their regulatory standards in response to competitive trade and investment pressures (this is the most extreme form of a 'race to the bottom');

(ii) *de facto* relocation competition-in-laxity occurs when domestic firms relocate production to countries with less-stringent regulations (this form is also striking and may attract headlines);

(iii) *de facto* market share competition-in-laxity occurs when firms already operating in countries with lax regulations increase their market-share of world production or trade. Firms operating under stringent regulations would then gradually lose out, even though no laws are changed and no relocation of production occurs. A 'race to the middle' is one variation of this form, in which standards in a developing country are raised, but not as high as in the wealthy country from whom they gain market share;

(iv) regulatory chill is a fourth form of competition-in-laxity that occurs when states stay 'anchored to the bottom', not raising their regulatory standards even in the face of scientific evidence (e.g. climate change) or rising standards in competing states (e.g. US gasoline taxes or British BTU taxes; see Esty and Geradin 2000.) This form is analytically more problematic, though still relevant, as it requires an issue-by-issue judgment as to whether regulations should be stringent.

In the interest of analytic clarity it is useful to focus on the first two, starkest forms of competition in laxity: *de jure* and relocation. Evidence for the latter two forms, market share and regulatory chill, can be elusive. For example, even if a German firm's violation rate (of pollution or labor abuses) in its Chinese subsidiary is double its rate in Germany, this data will not show up in aggregate national statistics on foreign direct investment (FDI) trends in either country. FDI is determined by a myriad other variables. Arik Levinson (1996: 440–2) reviews the literature and explicitly concludes that using 'aggregate trade or FDI data to attempt to discern evidence of industrial flight from pollution regulations' does not make sense. Surveys are inconclusive. Instead, 'it is necessary to use establishment-level data'. Likewise, Kahler (1996: 32) observed that 'existing research is limited by its reliance on aggregate studies; firm-level data on location decision is particularly sparse'. Detailed firm-level case analysis offers more insight here than does aggregate data.

## 1.2 Higher common denominator (HCD)

Regulatory disputes are increasingly resolved by government intervention up to more stringent outcomes (HCD), which Vogel (1995 and 2002) labels the 'California effect' or a 'race to the top'. In the European Community, Globerman (1993) noted: 'The experience of the EC suggests that when environmental standards differ across countries, convergence of standards will ultimately take place in the direction of the more restrictive set of standards.' Although competition-in-laxity has received more media attention, in part because it serves as a focal point for those who protest against corporate power, it is less common than critics suggest. This seems to hold especially true for environmental regulations.

Public interest concerns (for health or the environment) may be bolstered by powerful producers who modify regulations to their advantage and use them as a barrier to entry against competitors. In this vein, business strategist Michael Porter (1990: 585–6) exhorted firms to raise their environmental standards voluntarily:

> Establish norms exceeding the toughest regulatory hurdles or product standards . . . Find the localities whose regulations foreshadow those elsewhere. Some regions and cities will typically lead others in terms of their concern with social problems such as safety, environmental quality, and the like. Instead of avoiding such areas . . . they should be sought out. An advantage will result as other regions . . . modify regulations to follow suit.

Porter noted that a complete view of competitive advantage looks forward to the long-run, not merely short-run cost advantages. These races to the top may lead to homogeneity, but can also be heterogenous.[6]

## 1.3 Heterogeneity (HET)

In the international arena there is a third outcome of competition among jurisdictions: heterogeneity, or divergent regulations among countries. These may serve to restrict cross-border trade (protectionism) or to promote exports (regulatory subsidies) or both. Firms may seek more stringent domestic regulatory environments for prudential reasons of security as well as for barriers to entry and other more parochial reasons (e.g. Kane 1987; Bhagwati 1988; Salvatore 1993; Bhagwati and Hudec 1996; Khor 1999). Protectionism is a frequent response to 'squeaky wheels' in domestic politics, notably firms and unions who lobby for measures to restrict trade or

[6] Jaffee *et al.* (1995) were critical of Porter's conclusions.

limit outward FDI. Coalitions with 'anti-plutocracy' groups may increase these pressures. So, too, will an economic recession or diplomatic and military hostilities.

There is no US state after which to name this effect, because the 1887 Interstate Commerce Act forbids heterogenous barriers to trade among US states. Internationally, however, such heterogenous or unilateral regulations are common. One might call this the 'Japan effect' after Japan's chronic trade surplus and low rates of inward FDI or the Smoot-Hawley effect after the USA's iconic trade-restrictive measures of the 1930s.[7]

Despite the ardor with which these issues are sometimes framed, this book imputes no normative judgement to any of these trajectories, stringency or laxity, homogeneity or heterogeneity, nor to the Delaware, California, or Japan effects. The descriptive term laxity does not imply the normative term 'undesirable' (see Winter 1977; Swire 1996). The consequences of 'globalization' on domestic regulations are varied (Rodrik 1997). The fundamental goal here is to posit necessary conditions that explain which regulatory outcome occurs and when.

## 2. An explanation

As a rule, regulation is acquired by industry and is designed to operate primarily for its behalf.

George Stigler 1971

The answer to the puzzle described above lies in differentiating private sector interests and state responses to them. Powerful firms exert influence but they do not seek a monotonic goal; one must identify each firm's different interests. Over time, these preferences will shape state regulations.[8] To lower production costs firms may seek deregulation in some cases. However, in other cases they may seek policies to restrict market entry by rivals, restrict substitute products (highways *versus* mass-transit, for example), offer direct or indirect subsidies, reduce the cost of inputs, or raise the price for finished goods.

[7] Singling out one country after whom to name this trend invites conflict over proof of non-tariff barriers or subsidies.

[8] This does *not* imply that the state government apparatus is irrelevant or merely an instrument of leading industry. As Stigler notes: 'The state. . . is a potential resource or threat to every industry in the society . . . [It] can and does selectively help or hurt a vast number of industries' (1971: 114–141). The state has the power to coerce, seize money via taxation, control the movement of resources, and constrain economic decisions. Nor does Stigler deny that public interest groups may influence regulations. Further, as Schattschneider (1960) pointed out, if firms had all the power and government had none, government would try to bribe or influence firms and not vice versa. (See also Levine and Forrence 1990.) Nonetheless, over the long run concentrated producer preferences are reflected in state regulations.

This answer links private economic incentives to government decisions. Changes in regulations depend on the incentives and strategies of private sector firms and governments. Firms face three options in regard to a potential change in regulations:

(i) relocate production to a new location ('exit');
(ii) lobby, educate, and litigate regulations that reflect their interests ('voice'); or
(iii) mutely accept whatever regulations come their way ('loyalty').[9]

Firms seek a regulatory environment to maximize their value. Each firm calculates its interest, with bounded rationality and opportunistic behavior.

Governments respond to firm behavior, as they balance the interests of their constituencies (and their own interests). There is opportunistic competition among governments, as with firms. Government policy options are also threefold; they can:

(i) unilaterally relax regulations to lower production costs for domestic firms (deregulation);
(ii) exert pressure on foreign countries to change regulations (influence, diplomacy); or
(iii) erect regulations that protect domestic firms against foreign rivals (protection).

Both influence abroad and protection may depend on governments' ability to use access to their domestic markets as a club to bring about the desired regulatory outcome.[10]

This approach follows Nobel economist George Stigler's inductive method: 'The truly intended effects should be deduced from the actual effects' (1975: 140). This approach avoids problems of strategic misrepresentation, spin for the media, and counterfactual projections. Nonprofit organizations deliberately place issues on the public agenda via the mass media and often claim success whether they had an impact or not. Governments must similarly legitimize their decisions publicly. By contrast, firms are far more discreet in their regulatory agendas and successes and often have incentives to conceal or disguise them. Bhagwati noted this trend in the NAFTA debates: '[US businesses] were definitely interested in investing in Mexico, contrary to their coached denials of such intentions once they began to be burned on the issue in the public domain' (Bhagwati and Hudec

[9] Hirschman (1970: 257). 'Exit' is a common economic means of expressing preferences: consumers and workers vote with their wallet or feet. 'Voice' is the political process for influencing outcomes; it involves dialog, persuasion, and sustained organizational effort, including voter drives and democratic elections or referenda. 'Loyalty' in this context might be in the expectation of future political 'goods'.

[10] On the use of economic threats to create co-operation, see Hufbauer, Schott, and Elliott 1990; Martin 1992; and Shambaugh 2000.

1996 v1: 34). Stigler was a pillar of the free-market Chicago School of Economics. His work is largely critical of the inefficiencies caused by firms who 'acquire regulations for their own behalf'.[11]

Avoiding such normative conclusions, this book offers three related propositions that explain the observed outcomes. First, the locus of regulations (on production processes *versus* products' market access) explains movement toward stringency or laxity. Second, industrial structure explains the degree of change. Third, asset specificity explains commonality among states; it also affects movement toward or away from laxity. These are explained below.

## 2.1 Proposition 1: Process regulations *versus* market-access regulations

The first proposition concerns the locus of government policies. States may limit or prohibit manufacturing or service-industry *processes* within their jurisdiction. These are called 'process restrictions'. Or they may restrict the *market access* of particular products or services. These are called 'market-access restrictions'.[12] The distinction between process and market-access regulations goes beyond the different interests of export-oriented and import-competing industries and the different political resources available to producers and consumers. Firms seek regulations that improve their competitive position.

Conventional American wisdom holds that firms seek less government intervention. This 'wisdom' may disguise more than it reveals. While firms often want 'the government off their back' (via lower taxes, less red tape, less government scrutiny), each firm wants the government off its back in different ways and each lobbies to get its own way at the expense of competitors. Further, firms occasionally seek a ride on government's shoulders. In specific instances, firms may seek more stringent government regulations. These regulations can function as a barrier to entry against competitors or a barrier to substitute goods, or they may shape consumer demand in desirable ways, or reduce suppliers' power, or break up competitors' alliances, or increase the firm's power over buyers, or gain the firm subsidies and other government supports. As a simple example, upscale shop owners may support stringent zoning laws which allow them to exclude a fast-food restaurant from their street. Understanding and differentiating firms' preferences for regulations turns out to be a necessary step in understanding government policies. What shapes firms' regulatory preferences?

[11] Stigler 1971: 114–141. See Johan den Hertog (2000) for an overview of economic theories of regulation, including critiques of Stigler and rejoinders, as well as other approaches.

[12] This distinction is adapted from the traditional product-process distinction. See e.g. M. Porter 1990; D. Vogel 1992 and 1995; Murphy 1993; Ogus 1994; Murphy and Oye 1995; Swire 1996; and Casella in Bhagwati 1996.

*Heterogenous national restrictions on manufacturing* 'processes' *may spawn competitions in laxity.* Process regulations restrict the way in which a good or service is produced. Without regulations, firms would generally seek the lowest cost method of production; hence, process regulations are likely to increase the cost of production. Domestic business and labor in a state with costly restrictions on manufacturing processes tend to operate at a disadvantage with respect to competitors in less highly regulated nations. In the absence of common international action for a common higher standard, both export-oriented and import-competing sectoral interests will fight for lax national restrictions on manufacturing processes to improve their competitive position. In cases of costly regulation or inexpensive relocation, firms may move manufacturing to less highly regulated states. The threat of industrial relocation and the resultant loss of jobs and tax revenues may convince governments to keep process standards lax.

*Heterogenous national restrictions on the* 'market access of products and services' *may spawn protectionism.* Simply defined, market-access regulations restrict the sale, consumption, distribution, or disposal of products and services. Restricting access to a market is an effective barrier to entry against competitors. Domestic business and labor may push for a market-access restriction to the extent that it reflects their parochial interests. Domestic market-access regulations are likely to give them an advantage with respect to foreign competitors. In the absence of common international action against market-access restrictions as *de facto* trade barriers, sectoral interests may seek to impose domestic product regulations that improve their competitive position.

This definition of market-access regulations is simpler and more encompassing than the definition of product regulations used in the GATT and WTO. The difference is important. For example, all restrictions on imports are market-access restrictions as defined here because they restrict the sale or distribution of products (or services). By contrast, the WTO limits its definition to include only those regulations that address the nature of the product itself (flammability of sleepwear, for example). The reason is that the GATT sought to limit *de facto* trade barriers.[13] The GATT prohibited restrictions on imports that were based on process or production methods (PPMs), with rare exceptions such as forced labor. Internationally, of course, no country has the jurisdiction to impose process regulations on economic activities inside another country. Conversely, the GATT allowed product restrictions on imports so long as domestic goods were treated the same way. Hence, the more narrowly that GATT negotiators could define product restrictions, the fewer the constraints on trade. In applying this

[13] 'GATT' thus refers to the period 1945–1994. The Uruguay Round of 1994 transformed the GATT into its successor, the WTO. On WTO/GATT history, *inter alia*, see Hudec 1993 and 1990 and Curzon 1965. On nontariff barriers see Laird 1989; and John S. Wilson 1998. A study of corrective measures is Nivola 1993; for a review see Lukauskas 1994.

distinction, WTO panelists are thus forced to assess the motivations for a country's regulation (which is a difficult task) and its impact[14] (Farber and Hudec, in Bhagwati and Hudec 1996 v2: 71–76). If the state's motive is to affect processes then the regulation is classified as a process regulation and deemed contrary to the WTO agreements. If the state's motive is to protect consumers because of the nature of the product, the WTO allows the regulation. The WTO's product–process distinction can be contentious. In the Mexican tuna-dolphin case (analyzed in Chapter Six below) the distinction was at the center of legal debate.[15] The phrase 'market-access regulations' used in this book offers the greatest analytical clarity for the purposes of this research.

A major corollary of this first proposition is the importance of a state's market size and access to it. States with large internal markets may use market-access regulations not only to protect domestic industry against imports but also as a club to influence regulations in foreign states. If foreign states do not move toward a common (higher) process regulation or toward fewer discriminatory market-access regulations, their exports may be denied access. Although the GATT/WTO agreements prohibit such activity, states with very large markets such as the USA, Europe, or Japan not infrequently contravene their treaty agreements. Other states with small domestic markets have fewer options to influence international regulations. They have little economic incentive to pursue the WTO's only remedy of authorized trade sanctions or countervailing duties because they might fear retaliation in other arenas. Students of *Realpolitik* have long understood this aspect of economic power (although they do not always appreciate how firms define the national interest). *Ceteris paribus*, the outcome here is a pattern of market-access product regulations moving toward higher standards (heterogenous or homogenous) that reflect powerful firms' interests. The concept of market-access regulations helps explain the California effect, if countries are able to exclude products or services which do not meet domestic standards.

Process and market-access restrictions are likely to have markedly different international consequences and yield markedly different results. The key point is that firms seek regulations that differentially improve their value over competitors. Higher heterogenous process restrictions are likely to decrease competitiveness *vis-à-vis* foreign firms, hence domestic firms will

[14] For example, in assessing whether the US CAFE fuel standards violated GATT precepts, the GATT panel determined that cars which cost more than $US30,000 are 'unlike' cars costing less; and fuel-efficient cars are 'unlike' other cars.

[15] Following the OECD, the WTO began to use a more complicated distinction within PPM regulations: some are 'product-related PPM' requirements which affect the final characteristics of the product. Others are purely 'non-product-related PPMs' which affect the production or processing of the product. On process and product standards and international trade see World Bank research papers by Donald Lecraw 1987; Joel Trachtman 1992 and 1993; Alan Sykes 1995; Alessandra Casella 1997; J.S. Wilson 1997, 1998, and 1999.

generally oppose them. Heterogenous market-access restrictions are likely to increase competitiveness to the extent they reflect domestic producers' interests. *Among states with open economies, this first proposition predicts movement toward more lax regulations in the case of process restrictions and toward more stringent regulations in the case of market-access restrictions.*

## 2.2 Proposition 2: Industrial structure

The second proposition, industrial structure, affects the strength of the first (market-access–process) proposition. It is a well-established axiom in political economy that powerful firms in concentrated markets are most likely to achieve their policy goals. Regulatory movement occurs when the benefits are concentrated among a few powerful firms and the costs are spread diffusely, as is usually the case with protectionism (Pareto 1927; Schattschneider 1935; Grossman and Helpman 2002). Firms' power may stem from their revenues, employment, market share, control of the media, personal or historical ties to top state officials, access to information, national security, and industrial policy relevance. Powerful firms influence states to achieve regulations that reflect their particular interests. That influence can be direct or implicit, or even imputed by governments.

Concentrated markets facilitate collective action and the ability to shape regulations. Oligopolies have greater resources to absorb regulatory costs and to achieve their regulatory goals through lobbying, funding of research, litigation, education, and advertising.[16] Oligopolies also have asymmetrical access to information; indeed, they are often the only source of detailed information available to regulators. Finally, they have incentives to erect barriers to entry, to maintain market share and prices, and to impede (or dominate) substitute goods. Organized firms with concentrated interests are more likely to affect outcomes than inchoate consumers or small firms with diffuse benefits or costs.

States are more likely to respond to powerful firms both as a result of lobbying pressures and to improve their own political survival by boosting employment and economic growth. These findings are well established in studies ranging from free trade and tariffs at the turn of the century, to post-New Deal regulatory bodies to 'voluntary' export restraints in the 1970s and 1980s, to nontariff barriers in the 1990s. Magee, Young, and Stern

[16] Classic economic research on oligopolies includes Bain 1956; Modigliani 1958; Olson 1965; and Chandler 1988, McCraw (ed.) See also Stigler's critique (1968) on mechanisms to achieve collective action; Dixit (1979, 1982) on duopoly; McKeown 1984; Williamson 1985; and Aggarwal, Keohane, and Yoffie 1987. P.G. Porter, Livesay, and McCraw (1988: 270) offer a working definition of oligopoly as a situation in which 6 or fewer firms manufacture 50% or more of the total product value of an industry, or 12 or fewer firms manufacture 75% or more of total industry product.

(1987) concluded that competition by political parties and business lobbies 'causes the role of policymakers to be small relative to the underlying [economic] power variables'. This is specifically true for nontariff barriers: 'The replacement of tariffs with . . . nontariff barriers in the last two decades supports a view that special interests can counter Pareto moves by general interests in sophisticated ways.'[17]

A potential weakness of oligopoly theory is the problem of multiple equilibria: that is, indeterminate prediction. One way around this is to examine several unrelated industries: '[L]ook to the theory in order to find whether there are any (relatively weak) results which might hold good across a very broad class of model specifications. While the detailed specification appropriate to each individual industry may differ, such "robust" results—where they are available—may provide a (game theoretic) basis for certain cross-industry studies . . .' (Sutton 1990: 511). This book adopts Sutton's recommended approach of cross-industry studies and a necessary-but-not-sufficient explanation. Idiosyncratic forces affect the details of any given case but all cases reflect the broader logic. The research yields surprisingly consistent conclusions, across diverse issue areas and actors.

Because firms make strategic production decisions their industry's structure is dynamic, not deterministic, particularly at the product-line level. The decision by a powerful firm to invest in a new process technology (e.g. totally chlorine-free pulp mills) or a new product (e.g. chlorofluorocarbon substitutes) alters the structure of a particular market. These investment decisions also affect regulatory preferences.

Industrial structure points to a possible exception to the process/market access distinction during market shake-outs: as firms compete for dominance, oligopolies may occasionally seek higher process regulations (in a 'bleeding game') so long as the gains from eliminating competition exceed the higher cost of production. The spotlight of intense media scrutiny may force firms to adopt a similar strategy. Conversely, oligopolies may temporarily seek lower market-access regulations to undermine a competitor's protected market. These are important exceptions to the broader pattern. Over time, the process/market access distinction does return. The important aspects are the differential effect of the regulation on various firms and the state's response to them.

A political structure complements the industrial structure. Firms may form lobbying coalitions with each other or in alliance with public interest

[17] See also de Pareto 1927; Schattschneider 1935; Gerschenkron 1943/1989; Huntington 1951; Sola Pool *et al.* 1963; Olson 1965/1971; Stigler 1971; Vernon 1974; Pincus 1975; Gourevitch 1977; Krueger 1974; Tedlow 1979; Weingast 1981; Yamamura (ed). 1982; Cassing, McKeown, and Ochs 1986; Baldwin 1985; Buchanan 1985; Milner 1986; Long 1987; D. Vogel 1989; Peltzman 1989 and 1998; Burk 1990; Hilliard 1991; McCraw 1991; Laffont and Tirole 1991; Frieden 1991 and 1993; Irwin 1992; Campbell 1993; Lawrence 1993; Fields 1995; and Smith 2000.

groups. One expects firms to take advantage of 'Baptist and bootlegger' coalitions, in a synergistic alliance of the 'good and the greedy' (Odegard 1928; Yandle 1982; Noll 1985; Oye and Maxwell 1993). During the American constitutional Prohibition on alcohol (1919–1933) product market-access bans on alcohol led to windfall profits for illegal distributors ('bootleggers'). Those in the temperance movement ('Baptists') unwittingly found themselves in an unholy alliance with bootleggers: both wanted to keep stringent product regulations against alcohol, albeit for different reasons.[18] Politicians who voted for Prohibition (and bans on Sunday liquor sales) were supported by both groups. The phrase serves as a reminder that regulations are legitimized in terms of the public interest. Just because politics makes for strange bedfellows of saints and sinners does not mean those coalitions are somehow in the wrong; they may, in fact, be necessary for social progress. It is precisely because legitimacy is open to differing interpretation that firms and public interest groups can have an impact on regulations. If they can find common ground, public interest groups can play a valuable legitimizing role for firms. Likewise, politicians who support regulations favored by both firms and interest groups can expect support from them both.

### 2.3 Proposition 3: Asset specificity

The third proposition is that *the asset specificity of investments and transactions affects the degree of regulatory homogeneity across countries*. Three categories of asset specificity are offered here: low, international, and domestic. Asset specificity means 'durable investments that are undertaken in support of particular transactions, and that would lose considerable value if the transaction were prematurely terminated' (Williamson 1985; Joskow 1985). The investments may include human, dedicated, physical, brand, and site specificity.[19] Site specificity may be of particular interest in international cases. Williamson observed that a transaction that requires one firm to make an asset-specific investment makes that firm vulnerable because the 'firesale' value of the investment would be low if the intended transaction fell through. Negotiating and implementing this type of transaction becomes

[18] The 'Baptist and bootlegger' phrase is used metaphorically and intends no disrespect. Many of those in the temperance movement were early feminists, who organized to fight physical abuse and child neglect from drunken husbands: see Keck and Sikkink 1997.

[19] Williamson (1985). Site: the buyer and seller are located in a 'cheek-by-jowl' relation to each other. The assets are immobile and their value depends on their location. Human: investments in relationship-specific human capital, such as skills that are imperfectly transferable across employers. This often arises in a learning-by-doing fashion or from team configurations. Dedicated assets: involve expanding existing plant on behalf of a particular buyer on the prospect of continuing sales. Physical: the investments' design characteristics are specific and the equipment would have lower value in alternative uses. See Williamson (2000) on brand specificity as a fifth form.

complex and expensive. Transaction costs are the 'costs of running the economic system'. They are the economic equivalent of friction. *Ex ante* transaction costs are the costs of drafting, negotiating, and safeguarding an agreement. *Ex post* transaction costs include maladaption costs when transactions go awry; haggling costs if efforts are needed to correct misalignments; the setup and running costs associated with the governance structures to which disputes are referred; and the cost of effecting secure commitments (Williamson 1985: 21).

Special contracting or governance structures may emerge as a result. Asset-specific investments are more likely to cause firms to vertically integrate operations into their company or to seek long-term contractual arrangements to lock in their business partners. Arguably, government regulations also function as long-term contractual arrangements, so one would expect firms with asset-specific investments to devote resources to shaping regulations that affect them (Murphy 1993 and 1995; Murphy and Oye 1994).[20]

Assets are specific to the extent they cannot easily be deployed elsewhere (without losing considerable value). *Low* asset specificity means that assets can easily be redeployed; they are not specific to their current use. *High* asset specificity means that alternative uses are much less valuable to a firm. Highly specific assets can be either multinational or domestic. These attributes have profoundly different implications for understanding firms' regulatory preferences. *Multinational* asset specificity (MAS) means that a firm's assets are specific to transactions in more than one country. MAS therefore means durable investments that are undertaken in support of cross-border transactions and which would lose considerable value if the cross-border transaction were prematurely terminated. *Domestic* asset specificity means that assets are specific to transactions in one country.[21]

These different investment patterns affect firms' incentives to respond to regulations in the following ways:

(i) Firms with investments with *low* asset specificity, i.e. assets that are mobile or have valuable alternative uses, may relocate to less-restrictive regulatory environments or uses. The result is movement toward

[20] This explanation received additional confirmation in later work. See e.g. Spar and Yoffie (1999), reprinted in Prakash and Hart (2000); Cerny 1995; Alt *et al.* 1994, 1996, 1999. Alt *et al.* explore the theoretical interplay between endogenous trade theory and theories of factor specificity, and develop quantitative indices of sectoral asset specificity and lobbying preferences.

[21] For simplicity, 'higher' asset specificity here refers to investments that involve both qualitatively more-specific transactions, and larger sums of money. 'Lower' asset specificity similarly refers here to both qualitatively less-specific transactions, and smaller sums of money. Obviously, there is middle ground. Williamson (1985: 73 ff) distinguishes between the two dimensions of investment characteristics (nonspecific to highly specific) and frequency of transaction (occasional or recurrent). This book, however, simply notes movement away from or toward 'market governance'. For this purpose, the single dimension is adequate.

'self-help' governance structures and less regulation. Low asset specificity facilitates a *competition-in-laxity* in which moves by one state to attract (or keep) industry through lax heterogenous regulations are matched by other states. In common parlance, these firms are more footloose. A firm that disapproves of a regulation may close down its operations in one country and contract operations to foreign firms or set up operations abroad. Firms with nonspecific assets can just 'up and leave' so their threats to relocate are more credible. They need only whisper for governments to hear their voice and respond or else these firms may increase production in already lax countries, in a *de facto* competition-in-laxity. Either way, among competing states more production would occur under relatively lax regulations.[22] Both nonspecific investments and process regulations facilitate competition-in-laxity; the variables are collinear.

(ii) Investments with *high multinational* asset specificity (MAS) create incentives for firms to push for common regulatory outcomes across borders. Firms with assets devoted to cross-border transactions seek regulatory homogeneity on issues that affect their asset-specific investments because they seek to reduce transaction costs.[23] Firms oppose divergent regulations that inhibit effective use of those assets and increase transaction costs. Brickman, Jasanoff, and Ilgen (1985: 302–3), for example, conclude that: 'the chemical industry's desire to minimize differential treatment for products across national lines provides a powerful economic impetus for the selection of common regulatory targets.' Gladwin and Welles (1976) observed that some firms used worldwide standards, to save costs through uniformity. Bennett (1991: 215–234) notes that 'Most evidence of convergence through penetration lies in the role of multinational business in successfully securing, for example, a common regulatory framework for its products'.[24] This book delineates conditions under which

[22] Alt and Gilligan (1994: 184) suggest: 'Depending on how far you push the assumption of mobility, it could even be that exit—in the form of moving to another employment, emigration or capital flight—would be a far more common response than lobbying' (also Alt *et al.* 1996: 700). Their analysis emphasizes domestic trade policy coalitions among labor, exporters, and import competitors. See also Trachtman 1993; and Levinson 1996: 452. Levinson notes that pollution-intensive industries may be oligopolies and 'relatively less footloose' because of various industrial costs.

[23] MAS can include assets dedicated to particular export markets or dedicated to greater production than the domestic economy can absorb, as well foreign direct investments and other cross-border transactions.

[24] Bennett (1991) suggests four processes through which broad policy convergence might arise: policy emulation, elite networking, international regimes, and penetration by external actors. The most relevant process here is penetration, defined by Rosenau (1969: 46) as 'a condition in which members of one polity serve as participants in the political process of another'. Bennett does not address the direction of regulatory changes (stringent or lax) and discusses pressures for heterogeneity only in passing. Bennett distinguishes five uses of 'convergence': goals, content, instruments, style, and outcome. This book is concerned with the last: outcomes.

multinational firms are more or less likely to seek that regulatory homogeneity. Detailed process tracing provides micro-level support for broader generalizations about the impact of asset specificity such as those discussed by Frieden (1991) and Cerny (1995).

(iii) Firms with investments specific to transactions only in a given *domestic* market fight against regulatory homogeneity that threatens their investment. They support heterogenous regulations to protect the investment. When a firm has sunk assets into transactions particular to a given domestic regulatory environment, it cannot redeploy those assets elsewhere without the assets losing considerable value. 'Multi-domestic' subsidiaries that operate autonomously would have the same incentives.

Research on asset specificity stems from the study of contract structures. Williamson (1985) distinguishes four types of structures for arranging contracts in rough declining order of hierarchy: unified (vertical integration within a firm), two-party, third-party, and market contracting.[25] For this study's purposes the key distinction is between market contracting and more unified contracting in the form of regulations.

Movement away from lax heterogenous regulation toward stringent homogenous regulation is analogous to movement away from market contracting and toward a unified structure. The firms' underlying incentives are similar. In the private sector, for unified structures 'the transaction is removed from the market and organized within the firm subject to an authority relation' (Williamson 1985: 21). Conversely, with public policies part of the contracting is removed from the market and organized within society; the authority relation is the coercive power of the state. Powerful private sector interests generally support the state's authority relation.

When asset specificity is high, firms need more complex contracting structures to ensure credible commitments and continuity. Otherwise, the parties are reluctant to engage in transactions that would lose value if prematurely terminated. '*The most critical dimension for describing transactions is the condition of asset specificity*. Parties engaged in a trade that is supported by nontrivial investments in transaction-specific assets are effectively operating in a bilateral trading relation with one another. *Harmonizing the contractual interface* that joins the parties, thereby to effect adaptability and promote continuity, *becomes the source of real economic value*' (Williamson 1985: 30, emphases added). Higher homogenous regulations act to harmonize contracts. Firms with high multinational asset specificity support these

[25] In the context of private sector contracts Williamson (1985: 72–78) uses the terms 'bilateral' and 'trilateral' in place of two-party and third-party, respectively. In the context of international relations the diplomatic overtones of these terms can be confusing, hence cognates are used here. Williamson's assumptions apply here: uncertainty is present, transactions are recurrent, and parties to an agreement will opportunistically seek to better their share of the transaction.

regulations. Regulation 'is relatively favored when one is dubious that incomplete contracting will yield desired results and when competitive processes are prone to break down' (Williamson 1985: 328–329). This situation is common for complex public policies.

Regulations are a form of contracting. The contract can be among firms with the government acting as a third-party ('trilateral') enforcement mechanism, or between firms and governments ('bilateral'). In situations of stringent homogeneity, firms and governments make an implicit contract to behave in certain ways. In Williamson's terms, firms and governments move together toward unified governance. (They typically do not reach the level of vertical integration that Williamson addresses.) The goal here is to borrow from Williamson's theory but not to transfer it *writ large* to another domain. His independent variable of 'governance structures' is significantly different from regulatory outcomes but the underlying logic is similar. As Williamson writes (1985: 348, emphasis added): 'Although the particulars differ, vertical integration, nonstandard contracting for intermediate goods, the employment relation, corporate governance, and *regulation* are all, according to the argument developed in this and preceding chapters, variations on a theme.' This book pursues that regulatory theme.

### 2.4 Summary of initial findings

Chapters Two to Seven below apply the three propositions to six detailed case studies. These include not only competition-in-laxity but also higher common denominator and heterogenous outcomes. The initial findings are summarized in Figure 1.2 (summary table). Current debates over economic interdependence tend to select one outcome or another, whereas this book explains the variation.

The three propositions fit these cases well, if not perfectly. Process regulations are associated with less-stringent regulations. Market-access regulations are associated with more stringent outcomes, especially when backed by a large domestic market. Concentrated industries affect the degree of the regulatory shift. Low asset specificity is associated with competition-in-laxity toward a lower common denominator; high multinational asset specificity is associated with homogeneity; domestic asset specificity is associated with heterogeneity.

## 3. Debates over 'globalization' and 'plutocracy'

Questions about 'globalization' and 'free trade' became polemicized and front-page news in the 1990s. Many contradictory normative opinions were given but none explained outcomes. Only rarely did either side in the debates over globalization actually read and rejoin the best arguments of the

*Figure 1.2*: Summary table: Baseline cases

| | 1. locus of regulation | 2. market structure | 3. asset specificity | regulatory outcome |
|---|---|---|---|---|
| *Lower common denominator:* | | | | |
| Shipping registration (flags-of-convenience) | **process** | first-movers = **powerful firms, well-connected** | low | **LCD among competing states** |
| Offshore finance | **process** | first-movers = **powerful firms, well connected** | low | **LCD among competing states** |
| *Higher common denominator:* | | | | |
| CFC-ozone | **market-access** | **concentrated** | **high MAS** | **HCD** |
| 'BIS' Capital Adequacy | **market-access** and process (mixed) | **domestic: concentrated;** international: fragmented but **unifying contracts** | **high MAS** in sovereign debt | HCD (lingering HET) |
| *Heterogeneity:* | | | | |
| Mexican tuna-dolphin | **market-access** | **concentrated** | **domestic** | **HET** (US stringent) |
| US infant formula advertising | **market-access** | **concentrated** | **domestic** | **HET** (US stringent) |

**bold** = conforms with propositions

other side; frequently they relied on straw-person mischaracterizations and *ad hominem* put-downs. More useful is a model to evaluate and help predict outcomes of regulation, regardless of normative or political orientation. To situate this book in the context of these policy debates, a few critics and defenders of 'globalization' are described here, for each of the three outcomes (LCD, HCD, and heterogenous).

### 3.1 LCD and/or 'plutocracy'

These debates are not new. Fifty years ago Karl Polanyi, following Bismarck, vividly cautioned that regulations are essential to society, and not merely in the minimalist form of property protection, contract enforcement, and adjudication of disputes:

Regulation and markets, in effect, grew up together. . . . To allow the market mechanism to be the sole director of the fate of human beings and their natural environment, indeed, even of the amount and use of their purchasing power, would result in the demolition of society. . . . Nature would be reduced to its elements, neighborhoods, and landscapes defiled, rivers polluted, military safety jeopardized, the power to produce food and raw materials destroyed (Polanyi 1944/1957: 68–73).

In Polanyi's view, regulations are necessary for markets, not counter to them.

In the nonacademic press, Ralph Nader often criticized multinational corporations for seeking regulatory laxity:

They demanded . . . that environmental and safety standards be 'harmonized' . . . with the practical result that they would be pulled down toward a lowest common denominator . . . US corporations long ago learned how to pit states against each other in 'a race to the bottom'—to profit from the lower wages, pollution standards, and taxes. Now, through the NAFTA and WTO campaigns, multinational corporations are directing their efforts to the international arena (Nader 1993: 2–6).

Similar accusations were made in Europe about 'social dumping' and *Deregulierungswettlauf*.[26]

The strongest argument these critics made concerned democracy and the political power of large firms rather than the cross-border flows of goods, capital, or labor *per se*. David Korten explicitly made this point:

By focusing on trade, corporate globalists deflect attention away from *the real issue, which is corporate rule*, and direct it to *trade*, which *for most people is not an issue*. . . . The [protest] movement made another tactical error with regard to the term globalization [because] they sound like marginal xenophobic crazies to those who, like Amartya Sen [*sic*], aren't aware that *globalization is a code word for global corporate rule* at the expense of democracy, people and planet. The resulting miscommunication is a dream come true for corporate spin doctors. In truth, *most members of the* living democracy *movement rejoice at the increasing* interaction of people through travel, *trade*, migration, and dissemination of knowledge (2001: 334–5 emphases added).

In his paraphrase, 'It's plutocracy, stupid'. Free trade itself was not the major concern. A variety of popular-press books made similar points that the real issues were corporate power and democracy and not free trade itself.

[26] The phrase 'social dumping' in reference to poor labor conditions was common parlance by 1927, during the World Economic Conference. See discussion of these by Steve Charnovitz, Herman Daly, Lori Wallach, Mark Ritchie, Timothy Weiskel, Janet Chakarian, David Barkin, and David Schorr at a conference on 'International Trade Agreements and the Environment', 29–30 April 1994 at Harvard University. Guillén and Matsaganis argue (2000) that fears of social dumping within Europe have not generally been borne out.

That protesters themselves were rarely elected neither makes nor breaks their case.[27]

Mainstream academics (e.g. M. Smith 2001) have also questioned the increasing political power of unelected business interests. Likewise, British financial historians Richard Roberts and David Kynaston (2001) examined 'how the markets came to rule our world', former-Republican adviser Kevin Phillips (2002) analyzed 'wealth and democracy', and Louis Pauly (1997) asked 'who elected the bankers?' A few peer-reviewed studies have found evidence of industrial flight due to stringent environmental regulations (Xing and Kolstad 2002).

Public relations firms are sometimes more astute to sloganeering than those who take protestors' words literally. A Burson-Marsteller company correctly identified the anticorporate message of protesters in a report to its clients: 'Seattle [1999] was not an anomaly and the consistent anti-corporate message of virtually all the groups who participated there in November is not a temporary phenomenon. Many have traditionally highlighted alleged corporate misconduct . . .'[28]

## 3.2 HCD

Juxtaposed against these 'race to the bottom' slogans, and contrary to hypotheses of competition-in-laxity, one finds many examples in which environmental, labor, disclosure, and other regulations have not fallen but risen to a higher common denominator. Indeed, a growing body of scholarship from the past five years concludes this is the predominant outcome, especially in environmental regulations, and perhaps in labor.[29] Multinational corporations (MNCs) may have a competitive advantage in complying with more stringent regulations than traditional enterprises; hence, they may seek out HCD environments as Porter (1995) advised and Pearson (1987) observed. More recent trade agreements such as the

[27] See John R. MacArthur (2000) on the 'selling of free trade'; Mokhiber and Weissman (1999) on 'corporate predators: the hunt for mega-profits and the attack on democracy'; Palast's (2003) critique of 'the best democracy money can buy'; and Noreena Hertz (2001) on 'global capitalism and the death of democracy'. With the 20-20 vision of hindsight, many people now appreciate a variety of non-elected protest voices from the past, who helped to achieve: the vote for women (Susan B. Anthony), better race relations (Martin Luther King, Nelson Mandela), decolonization and democratization (Thomas Paine, Mahatma Ghandi, Lech Walesa), and environmental quality (Henry David Thoreau, Rachel Carson). However, history is also replete with less-welcome protest voices, including various short-sighted, misguided, racist, parochial, and xenophobic movements.

[28] Gardner G. Peckham, Managing Director, Black, Kelly, Scruggs & Healy, a Burson-Marsteller Company, letter introducing 'Guide to the Seattle Meltdown: A Compendium of Activists at the WTO Ministerial', 14 January 2000.

[29] See Vogel 1995; Levinson, Klevorick, J. D. Wilson, and others in Bhagwati and Hudec 1996; Garrett 1998; Anderson and Kagan 2000; Graham 2000; Garcia-Johnson 2000; Guillén and Matsaganis 2000; Prakash 2000; Sampson 2000; Drezner 2001; Fung, Sabel, and O'Rourke 2001; Inclán, Quinn, and Shapiro 2001; Moran 2002; Vogel and Kagan (eds.) 2002.

US–Jordan FTA addressed environmental and labor issues. Bhagwati suggests races to the bottom 'could be a theoretical curiosity', and Drezner (2000) goes so far as to dismiss them as a 'myth'. Most foreign direct investments (FDI) in the late twentieth century were among the rich, highly regulated economies of North America, Europe, and Japan. The entire rest of the world accounted for less than 25 per cent of FDI. Enforcement of environmental, labor, and many other standards was typically more stringent in the OECD countries, with their open economies, than in the former Communist or developing countries that were less open to trade and investment. Most studies have not found that the erection of more stringent environmental measures reduces business productivity; indeed, some studies suggest a positive correlation (Leonard 1988; Meyer 1993; Porter 1995; Florida 1999). However, not everyone thinks that higher common standards are necessarily a good thing. Bhagwati (1996: 5) warned: 'If the standards are legitimately different, for example, in the poor countries, and if they are "harmonized up" by force of sanctions, including trade sanctions, by the rich countries, that will *ipso facto* harm the poor countries.' Bhagwati *et al.* analyze a variety of normative, efficiency, philosophical, and prescriptive aspects of these issues. This book by contrast helps explain when such cases of HCD come about, including the Montreal Protocol on chlorofluorocarbons and the Basle Accord on banking.

### 3.3 HET

Finally, a wide variety of heterogenous policies exist. Rather than having a 'common' denominator, these outcomes are heterogenous (HET) among countriees. As with the other two trajectories, both detractors and defenders can be found for these outcomes. They may act as nontariff barriers, including 'green protectionism', that benefit domestic industries in one country at the expense of foreign firms. Most economic theories generally support the reduction of barriers to cross-border trade and investments, pointing to greater efficiency. Gains from trade are possible precisely because of divergent circumstances, including natural factors such as variations in climate, geography, resources, and population density, as well as divergent social preferences and risk tolerances. An unusual combination of free-trade economists in rich countries, nationalist economists in developing countries, and World System theorists were critical of industrialized countries who pushed higher environmental standards onto impoverished developing countries in what some called 'green imperialism' (Khor 1999). Bhagwati favored divergent regulatory schemas. He urged the US to impose higher standards on its own firms investing overseas but not on other countries' firms. As he put it (Bhagwati and Hudec 1996–1/5: 33): 'The true and greater crisis that we face in regard to the theory and policy of Free Trade comes . . . from the growth demand for "level playing fields," "harmonization," "fair trade," etc. These demands undermine insidiously the legitimacy and feasibility of Free Trade, since it is virtually impossible to harmonize everything so that playing fields are truly level in every way.' It would be a daunting task to mobilize protestors to support gains from trade for developing countries and to oppose unwarranted protectionism by rich countries.

### 3.4 Toward consensus

One can find some truth in all these perspectives. However, this book's goal is not to evaluate their normative merits but to discern which outcome occurs and when. In many instances lower common denominator (LCD) outcomes may be highly desirable to the extent that they get rid of unnecessary red tape, allow for a more efficient allocation of capital, improve the general social welfare over protected vested interests, offer rewards for innovation and entrepreneurship, and provide employment and income to the world's poorest workers (Revesz 1992; Winter 1997). In other instances, LCD outcomes may result in negative externalities such as environmental damage, financial instability, budget deficits, income inequalities, or degradation of labor standards (Kapstein 1999; Wells 2001; Sachs 2003; Krugman 2003). Certain higher common denominator (HCD) outcomes might overcome free-rider problems, protect desirable public goods or global commons, and be a source of innovation (Silber 1983; M. Porter 1995; D. Vogel 1995). However, HCD outcomes might also stifle economic growth, protect major producers' markets, impose 'not-in-my-back-yard' (NIMBY) constraints, limit the growth of developing countries, and restrain real competition (Bhagwati (ed.) 1996; Khor 1999). Similarly, higher heterogenous outcomes may be protective, protectionist, or, most often, both (Lang 1993). Typically, there are tradeoffs between conflicting normative goals and outcomes. One cannot generalize a normative outcome for these trajectories: this must be done on a case-by-case basis. However, by analyzing the systematic effects on trade of the likely evolution of regulations, this book offers strategic insights for those who seek sustainable policies.

Whatever view one takes, all observers agree on one thing: virtually every form of economic activity remains subject to a wide variety of regulations. This is true despite the widespread cycle of deregulation which began in the USA with Jimmy Carter and Alfred Kahn in 1977 (with airlines, trucking, and railroads) and the two subsequent decades of liberalization, privatization, and free-market discourse. In fact, a great irony of the 'liberalization' and 'market-oriented' policy reforms of the past quarter-century is this: increased commerce among nominally free-market jurisdictions has required ever-greater government intervention, not less (S. Vogel 1996; Shambaugh 2000). Some movement back toward re-regulation was evident in the support for 'transparency and accountability' after the Asian crisis of 1997 and for corporate governance and financial oversight after the business scandals involving Enron, Arthur Andersen, Global Crossing, Halliburton, and others. As Pfizer's CEO noted, business managers now spend more time dealing with governments, not less. One reason is that firms have sought government involvement to help resolve the myriad differences among competing jurisdictions and interests.

Around the world, from Brussels to Tokyo to Washington, governments offer strong support for businesses, albeit with significant cultural variations (D. Vogel 1987; Mazey and Richardson 1993). In America virtually every major firm has lobbying representatives in Washington, DC and belongs to a trade association that also lobbies. From the Reagan inaugural in 1981 to the turn of the century, the number of registered lobbyists in Washington grew tenfold, from a few thousand to roughly twenty thousand. Unregistered issue advocates and 'public affairs executives' greatly exceeded this number. The *Who's Who* of lobbying (or 'public policy management' as practitioners prefer to call it) is the annual book *Washington Representatives*. It contains over 1,400 fine-print pages of lobbying firms and their clients. The overwhelming majority of 'special interests' represented are private sector firms. Firms spend money on these lobbyists because they realize the importance of shaping regulations to suit their bottom line.

Managing the tradeoffs between conflicting interests and values is difficult even within one jurisdiction, where representative democracy has proved to be a robust (if imperfect) institution for achieving compromise. Internationally, however, there is no democracy among countries. There is no mutually agreed process to resolve disputes. Worse, the differences in interests and values between nations are far greater than those within one domestic jurisdiction. Similar cases are likely to grow in number for many years.

In 1991, when this research began, only a small fraction of the population debated the regulation of cross-border commerce. Over the subsequent decade every major newspaper worldwide has run headlines above the fold on these issues. However, many scholars, business executives, government officials, journalists, leaders of nongovernmental organizations (NGOs) and protestors alike have missed a simple pattern in the impact of economic interdependence, and none have explained that pattern. This book fills that void.

## 4. Research approach: Shedding light, not heat

Avoiding polemics, the research method underlying this book is to find a common thread of explanation across diverse cases of regulations that affect cross-border commerce by tracing the historical details of each case. An underlying logic of these cases is similar for all regulatory issues including the environment, finance, and labor. The logic is similar for domestic federalism as well as for international relations. The book's goal is a robust partial explanation of all cases fitting the case selection criteria and not a full explanation of any one case in particular. The conclusions are thus necessary but not sufficient for understanding any one case. This research method goes beyond mere plausibility but does not offer proof.[30] As a *caveat*, the wide diversity of cases that fit the case selection criteria cannot be fully explained by a few variables. It is helpful, however, to begin with these variables as a first cut at understanding. Other variables, perhaps institutional arrangements, norms, or other actors not examined in detail here, might moderate these factors and would be required for a full explanation. These concerns are discussed further in the book's conclusion. The detailed case studies reveal some surprising findings. They lend support to Ronald Coase's (1988) caution about overly hasty abstractions that obscure assumptions such as the role of transaction costs.

### 4.1 Case selection criteria

The domain of cases under study is bounded by three criteria. (1) States are economically interdependent in the given issue area. Goods, investments, services, or externalities cross state borders. 'Cross-border' is a more useful term here than 'international' because it includes cases of domestic federalist competition. It excludes regulations that have an effect only inside one jurisdiction. (2) Regulations significantly impact on some firms. This excludes cases where regulatory costs are insignificant. (3) Initially, no central authority has resolved regulatory differences among economically competing states. These three criteria identify cases of potential regulatory competition.

The empirical case studies are based largely—though not entirely—on industrial democracies during times of peace from the late 1950s to 2002. The model's relevance to other conditions is beyond the scope of this study. In times of prolonged economic recession or depression, governments face greater pressure for heterogenous regulations across the board. In times of military crises, governments may have greater leeway to impose broad policies irrespective of sector-specific interests.

For most major economies most of the time, a wide variety of cases fit the book's selection criteria. Some cases are global, some are regional, and some are domestic (federal). Within each geographic arena they encompass trade, investment, financial, accounting, taxation, technical standards, environmental, and labor regulations, among other issues. Individual cases can have an enormous impact because they can snowball into trade wars involving

30 See Van Evera 1997 and J.S. Mill 1843. In Mill's 'method of agreement', cases with largely different characteristics but similar results are examined. Common characteristics are then nominated, but not proven, as causes of the results.

dozens of industries, hundreds of thousands of jobs, and billions of dollars' worth of exports and investments.

### 4.2 Illustrative examples

Case studies unearth the role of private sector interests. The book examines six cases in detail and mentions some others, but many thousands exist. Readers not already familiar with the dimensions of this problem may be surprised to learn the extent to which regulations affect every imported good, from apples to zinc, even in states whose officials proclaim 'free-trade' policies. (An appendix to this chapter lists some examples.) Whatever the geographic arena or issue area, a common logic underlies all cases. Most economic activity is affected by regulations. Few of these regulations have been 'harmonized' across borders. Most regulations impose costs. These costs impact on some firms more than others. When these differential costs involve cross-border commerce, they create potential jurisdictional conflicts. The scope of this book's implications is therefore vast.

*Global Examples.* A large number of global trade cases have already arisen in disputes before the GATT and the World Trade Organization (WTO) and the negotiations over revising it.[31] These include the much publicized (and little understood) case of US injunctions against Mexican tuna to protect dolphins, analyzed in Chapter Six below. Potential cases rose faster than the institution's capacity to adjudicate them. Governments almost never request a dispute settlement from the WTO without the support of the major domestic firms effected. The WTO specifies that only governments, not firms, may bring a case forward.[32] This bottleneck role gives governments some power over their domestic firms but it also opens up another avenue through which firms can seek government redress.

As extensive as the WTO's trade cases are, they are only the latest focal point for many more enduring disputes. Only a minute fraction of potential trade cases have been raised before the WTO and benefitted from its mechanisms for managing trade conflicts. Of nearly 2,000 identifiable health measures that affected trade in the 1990s, for example, only seventeen were challenged under WTO auspices. The rest were settled bilaterally or remained a source of postponed contention. Many such issues are worked out in firm-to-firm diplomacy, industry standards groups, or mutual recognition agreements (MRAs). Firms may prefer these fora because the lobbying costs are lower and they face fewer retaliatory threats. The politicking

[31] WTO cases are online at www.wto.org. Another useful database is the Trade and Environment Database (TED) at American University www.american.edu/TED/ted.htm, accessed 24 July 2003. Care must be taken in integrating this book with the latter's data, however, as TED uses the standard GATT definition of product regulations, not the market access definition used here.

[32] In October 1998 the WTO began accepting *amicus curiae* briefs.

within such standards bodies or MRAs, however, reveals the same logic of firms' preferences because firms vie for stewardship of key committees (Büthe and Mattli 2003). Bringing a case before the WTO has costs for firms and governments alike, including possible retaliation. For these and other reasons, including institutional capacity, most issues in regulatory competition are not likely to be raised before the WTO.

Relevant examples include shipping flags-of-convenience (Chapter Two below), various global banking deregulations (implicit in Chapter Three below),[33] the Basle Accord to raise capital requirements (analyzed in Chapter Five below), and heterogenous US infant formula advertising (Chapter Seven below). Many other such global cases have received attention elsewhere.[34]

*Regional Examples.* Many regulatory disputes are found within regional trading blocs. The most salient regional examples are the issues involved in integrating the European Union (EU); the US–Canadian Free Trade Agreement, the follow-on North American Free Trade Agreement (NAFTA), and similar regional or bilateral trade agreements. European integration offers both rich cases and some caveats for this research as discussed below. The US and Canada maintain the world's largest bilateral trading and investment relationship. As the world moves toward greater integration of economic and telecommunications systems, and more homogenous demand, Canada and the US offer increasingly salient lessons.[35]

*Domestic (Federalist) Examples.* The logic of this inquiry is found in domestic federalist cases and not just international ones. In countries with strong regional or local governments (states, provinces, cantons, *Länder*), inter-jurisdictional competition is at play. In America, the federalist financial case of Delaware has become an exemplar: over half of all the incorporations in the USA occur in the tiny state of Delaware. Switzerland's canton of Zug has a similar reputation for attracting industry.[36]

[33] The waves of financial liberalization and deregulation which swept the British, American, and Japanese financial markets after 1984 are one example. See Farrar 1981; Pauly 1987; Dollar and Frieden 1988; Benston 1990; Frieden 1991 and 1993; Sobel 1992; Dale 1992; Langevoort *et al.* 1992; Goodman and Yoffie (eds.) 1993; Key and Scott 1994; Andrews 1994; Manzetti 1994.

[34] Scholarly works on child labor include Weiner 1991 and Bhagwati 1996. On international labor see Flanagan 1974; and Charnovitz 1992; Herrigel 1993; Craig Murphy 1994. On Europe's more stringent preferences in the Basel Convention on the Transboundary Movement of Hazardous Wastes, see Hackett 1990 and Logan 1991. Rauscher 1990 emphasizes sector-specific interests such as exporters who lobbied for lower environmental standards. On ocean fisheries see Joseph and Greenough 1979. On endangered species see DeSombre 2000.

[35] For other regional examples, see Commission of the European Communities, 1985; Regens 1989; Nicolaidis 1989; Marsh 1991; D. Vogel 1992, 1995; Majone 1993; Levy 1993; Bernauer 1993; and Erickson 1994; Alter and Meunier-Aitsahalia 1994; Ogus 1994.

[36] On US federalism and conflict of laws see Nash 1957; Skowronek 1982; Fiorina 1986; Buxbaum and Hopt 1988; Gilligan, Marshall, and Weingast 1988; Gilligan 1989; Chayes 1992; Cohen 1992; Vietor 1994; Himmelberg 1994; and Vietor 1994. On Canadian federalism see Cuming (ed.) 1985.

The list of examples is idiosyncratic. Its purpose is to illustrate the breadth of the problem under study. Furthermore, any one of the conflicts can grow into a bigger cross-border dispute in which completely unrelated industries are drawn into a trade war of retaliatory tariffs and countervailing duties. Conflicts of this type are likely to remain high on top business executives' and policymakers' agendas for the foreseeable future.

### 4.3 Research design and measurement issues

The 'puzzle' of when is there movement toward stringency or laxity, homogeneity or heterogeneity emerged from the sources cited above, as did the cases examined in detail. A detailed firm-level case-study approach was adopted, rather than aggregate statistics, for the reasons noted above by Levinson (1996) and Kahler (1996). To avoid selection bias (choosing only examples that prove a point), this research initially selected three cases with a range of values of this dependent variable, so one case each of LCD, HCD, and heterogeneity. This research design permits causal inferences, although not proof or descriptive inferences such as the number of cases falling into each category. King, Keohane, and Verba (1994: 141) argue that this research design 'may help us to gain some valuable information about the empirical plausibility of a *causal* inference . . . if this design is to lead to meaningful—albeit necessarily limited—causal inferences, it is crucial to select observations without regard to values of the explanatory variables'.[37] The three propositions in this book were initially formulated through examination of the flags-of-convenience, BIS capital accord, and US infant-formula advertising cases (see Figure 1.3 below, major baseline cases). These cases were chosen without knowledge of the explanatory variables. The propositions then received affirmation, though not proof, in the consequent examination of off-shore banking centers, Montreal Protocol on CFCs, tuna-dolphin, the many details within each case study, and other similar cases listed at the end of each major section.

The environmental cases are a good trial for these propositions, because they have been cited (Wilson 1980) as least likely to reflect Stigler's approach and the explanatory variables used in this book. If this approach holds true in these cases it bolsters the plausibility that the approach will also hold true elsewhere. This exploratory investigation generates precise and likely hypotheses; the least likely cases add credibility. The details in each chapter greatly expand the number of observations; it is not just the six case studies but the details within them which further confirm the book's approach.

[37] Emphasis in original. See discussion in King, Keohane, and Verba (1994). King *et al.* caution that 'the increased possibility of other problems caused by possible nonlinearities or variable causal effects, means that this procedure will not generally yield valid causal inferences'. On the value of concept formation and its priority over premature quantification, see Sartori 1970.

*Figure 1.3*: Major baseline cases

| REGULATORY MOVEMENT | | |
|---|---|---|
| Stringent | *Higher Common Denominator*<br>**Montreal Protocol on CFCs**<br>**BIS capital standards** | *Heterogeneity*<br>**Mexican tuna-dolphin**<br>**US formula advertising** |
| Lax | **Offshore finance**<br>**Shipping flags-of-convenience**<br>*Lower Common Denominator* | |
| | Homogeneity — COMMONALITY | Heterogeneity |

This qualitative methodology makes sense for several reasons. Transaction costs and asset specificity are difficult to measure. The economists who developed these concepts concede this challenge and defend a qualitative research approach:

> [Both *ex ante* and *ex post* transaction costs] are often difficult to quantify. The difficulty, however, is mitigated by the fact that *transaction costs are always assessed in a comparative institutional way*, in which one mode of contracting is compared with another. Accordingly, *it is the difference between rather than the absolute magnitude of transaction costs that matters*. . . . Empirical research on transaction cost matters almost never attempts to measure such costs directly. Instead, the question is whether organizational relations (contracting practices; governance structures) line up with the attributes of transactions as predicted by transaction cost reasoning or not (Williamson 1985: 21–22, emphases added).

> Measurement tasks [of asset specificity] are not trivial . . . data can be very difficult to obtain. . . . *we are certainly not going to find these numbers written down neatly in a book of industry statistics*. The best that we can hope for is more qualitative information. . . . Schmalensee and I would have been much happier with our analysis if there had been more (any!) empirical support available for the transactions cost perspective that we found so intuitively appealing and so consistent with the historical evolution of the electric power industry (Joskow 1988: 103–106, emphasis added).

Alt *et al.* (1996: 706–709) suggest four possible indicators of specificity: continued excess rates-of-return, lobbying, interviews (including brand-name significance), and indirect measures such as vertical integration, complex contracts, or high research and development expenditures. This book considers rates-of-return and lobbying in the case studies, although not systematically. In general, it relies on discrete comparative categories of 'domestic or multinational', and 'high or low'. This qualitative approach follows the received literature. Efforts to quantify these concepts have improved over the past decade but better analytical tools are still needed to enable such empirical work.[38]

Although the qualitative case-study method has its methodological weaknesses, well-informed concept formation is a necessary precursor to meaningful quantitative approaches (Sartori 1970). As Nobel prizewinning economist Ronald Coase colorfully put it, premature quantification is too silly for words:

> The world of zero transaction costs has often been described as a Coasian world. Nothing could be further from the truth. It is the world of modern economic theory, one which I was hoping to persuade economists to leave. . . . It is therefore hardly surprising that the conclusions reached were often incorrect. The reason why economists went wrong was that their theoretical system did not take into account a factor which is essential if one wishes to analyze the effect of a change in the law on the allocation of resources. This missing factor is the existence of transaction costs. . . . In my youth it was said that what was too silly to be said may be sung. In modern economics it may be put into mathematics (Coase 1988: 184–185).

This book aims to clarify and show the utility of the propositions concerning transaction costs, asset specificity, and the locus of regulations in the innovative context of international regulatory competition.

## 5. Theoretical forebears

> The realm of the conflict of laws is a dismal swamp filled with quaking quagmires, and inhabited by learned but eccentric professors who theorize about mysterious matters in a strange and incomprehensible jargon.
>
> Dean Prosser, 1953[39]

The answers one finds depend always on the questions one asks. As scholars know, these questions in turn depend on a theoretical understanding of the way the world works. This book aims to replace the 'dismal swamp and incomprehensible jargon' Dean Prosser warned about with clear analysis and

[38] Empirical studies on transaction cost economics include: Shelanski and Klein 1995; Wallis and D. North in Medema 1995; Silverman, Nickerson, and Freeman 1997; Dahlstrom and Nygaard 1999; Masten and Saussier 2000.

[39] Quoted in Trachtman 1993b. Legal scholars' despair is social scientists' delight. Many legal studies are descriptive and prescriptive and do not attempt to model behavior. They provide a valuable source of data. See, for example, legal studies on European harmonization by Buxbaum *et al.* 1988; 1991; Bratton *et al.* 1997; Bermann *et al.* 2001.

concrete illustrations. All theories are 'born wrong' because they abstract from the details of reality to offer generalizations (Kuhn 1970). All theories also have forebears. This book gains insight by combining economic theories with theories of international relations, political economy, international business, and legal studies to understand the emergence of policies which affect both commerce and social goals. The book's three propositions build on this literature without bias toward one academic discipline. A few of these roots are mentioned here to illustrate the cross-disciplinary nature of this approach and to situate this study in its broader theoretical context.

As the frontispiece quotation from Bismarck indicates, the potential for trade to undermine domestic regulations is not a new phenomenon. However, no scholarly study offers a general model to explain why competition-in-laxity occurs in some cases, harmonization in others, and heterogeneity in still other cases.[40] As such, one must look broadly for theoretical background. This research began by observing a similar pattern of behavior in international relations, regional integration, and domestic federalism, corresponding to the illustrative examples above. It then offered a model to explain that pattern, building on a variety of earlier studies. That all three arenas should exhibit a similar logic is striking.

Williamson (2000) suggests that neoclassical economics is most useful in explaining firms' short-term (zero to one year) decision-making. Transaction cost economics is most useful in explaining governance structures in the one- to ten-year frame. Broader theories of incentive structures and property rights are most useful to explain the ten- to one hundred-year frame of formal institutions. The chapters below examine cases in the five- to fifty-year frame. They bridge governance structures and formal institutions and also bridge transaction cost economics and other theories based on incentive structures.

## 5.1 International interdependence

Drawing parallels between domestic and international relations runs counter to realist approaches to international relations theory. The fundamental, Hobbesian axiom of *Realpolitik* is that international politics is unique because no over-arching authority can prevent violence among states. (Domestically, Max Weber noted, each state has a monopoly on legitimate violence.) Many international relations theorists therefore debate the nature of an anarchic world composed of states, the impact of interdependence, the sources of power and meaning, the causes of conflict and peace, and the conditions under which co-operation occurs across state borders. Other theorists challenge the primacy of anarchy as a fundamental

[40] For arguments that similar regulatory outcomes are the result of different domestic political processes, see David Vogel 1984; Hoberg, Jr. 1986; and Kagan 1988.

ordering principle, and emphasize the variety of ways in which state preferences are formed and social relations are constructed. One challenge to proponents of realist, liberal, and constructivist approaches alike is to refine their tenets to a more fungible degree.[41] This book helps bridge that gap, permitting a more detailed understanding of state–market relations.

Research beginning in the 1970s and 1980s showed that international regimes and other institutions might facilitate co-operation. One such research path emphasizes the domestic economic and coalitional determinants of international co-operation. Another seminal research program identified states' different domestic political structures as the source of differences in their foreign economic policies. A related approach examined the link between economic and political institutions. This book examines the conditions under which concentrated economic interests seek regulatory regimes, including homogeneity.[42]

This approach is consistent with the 'commercial liberalism' approach described by Moravcsik (1997: 515) that 'stresses the impact on state behavior of gains and losses to individuals and groups in society from transnational economic interchange'. However, it is also consistent with various realist approaches to political economy that emphasize market power and linkage to other issues. This study does not pit the traditional shibboleths of realism against liberalism nor does it prolong perennial debates. The model and the case studies are cross-paradigmatic: that is, they are compatible with serious versions of realism, liberalism, constructivism, and contrarianism among other research traditions. Theoretical research either tests existing theories or constructs new ones. This book aims at theory construction.

Richard Cooper's path-breaking work (1968–1972, 1974) identified this area of international political economy. Cooper noted the conflict created by differing regulatory regimes as international trade increases. He identified five policy outcomes of interdependence: constructive, passive, defensive, aggressive, and exploitative. His outcomes relate to this book's trajectories as follows. Cooper's 'constructive' policies are homogenous ones (LCD or HCD) in which governments frame policies jointly so as to prevent exit by firms from governmental jurisdiction. 'Passive' policies are a variant of homogeneity acceded to by small states; they involve the acceptance of a loss of policy autonomy. 'Defensive' policies are heterogenous nontariff barriers (protection, as in dolphin-safe tuna) that reduce economic interdependence. 'Aggressive' policies move from heterogeneity to homogeneity; they involve

[41] Grieco (1990) analyzes the Tokyo Round negotiations on nontariff barriers from a realist perspective. Among critics of realism, see Alker Jr. (*c.*1985); Wendt (1992, 1999); and Ruggie (1998). An important and clear restatement of liberal approaches is Moravcsik (1997). On the merits and drawbacks of abstract international relations theorizing in general, see Hoffmann (1977/[1987]).

[42] Ruggie 1975; Krasner (ed.) 1982; Lipson 1982; Keohane 1984; Haggard and Simmons 1987. On domestic structures see Katzenstein 1977, 1986. On institutions see March and Olson 1989; North 1991; Alt, Levi, and Ostrom 1999.

the extraterritorial extension of state control to factors of production across borders. 'Exploitative' policies are the heterogenous use of regulatory laxity or subsidies to attract foreign industry. These are havens, as in the cases of flags-of-convenience and offshore banking, mentioned in passing by Cooper and analyzed below in Chapters Two and Three.[43] Cooper's prescience over thirty years ago is remarkable. His analysis did not attempt to explain which policies are adopted under which circumstances but it inspired this author to do so. On more general issues of interdependence, see Keohane and Nye (1977/2000) and Alker, Bloomfield, and Choucri (1974).

Much of the literature on international trade and nontariff barriers (NTBs) has been prescriptive in nature. Many of these trade barriers remain in new forms (Deardorff 1994; J.S. Wilson 1997, 1998, 2002). Some broader studies in international economics assume that factors of production are either perfectly mobile (Heckscher-Ohlin model, Stolper-Samuelson theorem; see Rogowski 1989) or imperfectly mobile across entire sectors (Ricardo-Viner 'specific factors' model, see Magee 1989; Frieden 1991; Irwin 1992). However, to understand regulatory outcomes it is useful to examine variation in the mobility and specificity of investments across firms and even across product lines within firms.

## 5.2 European integration

Another source for framing these issues was analyses of regional integration developments in Europe, and to a lesser extent in North America. Here, however, one must tread lightly. Integration shapes much of the current social science analyses of Europe but it is not among this book's dependent variables. Although the literature on regional integration helps frame this study, homogeneity of regulations need not imply movement toward political integration. Aristotle long ago made this distinction clear:

> It is not the end [goal] of the state to . . . ease exchange and promote economic intercourse. If that had been the end, the Etruscans and the Carthaginians would be in the position of belonging to a single state; and the same would be true of all peoples who have commercial treaties with one another. It is true that such peoples have commercial treaties with one another. It is true that such peoples have agreements about imports and exports; treaties to ensure just conduct; and written terms of alliance for mutual defense. On the other hand they have no common offices of state to deal with these matters; each, on the contrary, has its own offices, confined to itself. . . . Nor would it make a *polis* if a number of persons . . . had a common system of laws to prevent their injuring one another in the course of [economic] exchange.[44]

[43] Cooper mentions flags of convenience, lax disclosure requirements, foreign subsidies, and tax havens in this regard; citing Kindleberger 1960. See also Chinitz and Vernon 1960; Vernon 1971 and 1986; Lindblom 1966.

[44] Aristotle, *The Politics*, Book III, ch. 9: 118–120. 'What [in fact] constitutes a *polis* is an association of households and clans in a good life, for the sake of attaining a perfect and self-sufficing existence.'

What is necessary for a *polis*, according to Aristotle, is the spirit of that intercourse. That communitarian goal is not the scope of this study. However, the convergence/divergence of regulations in the modern global trading system is a subject worthy of study in itself. Thus, the European integration literature is used sparingly. David Vogel's (1992) work on regulatory convergence in Europe was particularly helpful here. The three propositions developed in this book can be applied, refined, and further tested in light of the European experience.

To the extent Europe moves toward a unified political structure, one can expect these propositions to apply increasingly to a federated Europe as a whole.[45] On the other hand, while Europe remains a system of sovereign states, the pressures for regulatory heterogeneity will remain, particularly in subtle forms of implementation and enforcement, and perhaps in semi-voluntary agreements between dominant buyers and suppliers. The EU Maastricht Treaty contained elements of homogeneity and also endorsement of subsidiarity, which allowed for some regulatory competition (Kahler 1996). Considerable heterogeneity remains within European labor regulations, despite European integration (Sapir in Bhagwati and Hudec 1996).

The influence of business on European integration writ large is much debated (Sandholtz and Zysman 1989). Green (1995) argues persuasively that business exercised an 'indispensable influence' on governments in shaping the unified European Community. The European Round Table of industrialists (ERT) itself claims significant credit for the 1987 Single European Act, which bears a striking resemblance to a draft circulated by the ERT several years previously. Moravcsik (1998) downplays the primacy of firms as causal actors yet, even by the evidence he presents, they are a necessary part of the explanation for the shape and timing of European integration, if not the complete picture. The Appendix to Chapter Five below picks up this debate.

From the perspective of international political economy, one strength of many of these studies on Europe is also their weakness: with few exceptions, they offer no comparison with cases of regional integration beyond Europe. This prevents one from holding constant important variables unique to Europe such as commonalities in religion, culture, history, and language; two world wars, proximity to the former Communist bloc, a

[45] Early work includes Mitrany 1943; Deutsch 1957; E. Haas 1958, 1964; Hoffmann 1966; Caporaso *c.*1972; Puchala 1972. See also Hall 1986; Ludlow 1989; Hoffmann 1994a, 1994b; Nicolaidis 1989; Alter and Meunier 1992; Burley and Mattli 1993; Moravcsik 1998; and Majone 1990, 1992, 1993, 1994; Piore and Sabel 1984; Eichengreen 1994. Blankart (in Majone 1990) argues: 'The gap between economic theory of regulation and the policy measures observed can only be overcome if the former is amended by a positive theory of regulation explaining political decisions.'

unique relationship with America, and so on.[46] Because this book's goal is to discover more generalized models of behavior, it looks outside the literature on European integration. This helps avoid the problem of over-explanation. To the extent this model is successful, it is also relevant to events within Europe.

### 5.3 Domestic federalism

Domestic federalism in the American context provides another source for framing this study. State-federal jurisdiction has been contentious since America's founding. As mentioned above, in 1933 Justice Brandeis referred to competition between states to attract industry as a 'race of laxity'. In 1974 Federal Reserve Chairman Burns (1974) expressed a similar critique of the American banking system as a 'competition in laxity' between competing US states. Tiebout (1956) argued on efficiency grounds against harmonization of regulations. His classic article on local public goods is predicated on the assumption of labor mobility where individuals 'vote with their feet', a condition which does not hold in most international domains and requires a number of further assumptions even domestically.[47]

Much lively debate continues over incorporation in the tiny state of Delaware, which is home to 0.3 per cent of the US population but is the incorporation jurisdiction of nearly 60 per cent of all US corporations (including 59 per cent of the Fortune 500). The classic statement of the debate over Delaware was an exchange of articles between William Cary, the former Chairman of the US Securities and Exchange Commission (SEC) and Federal Reserve Board, and Yale University professor Ralph Winter. Cary (1974) argued that Delaware was leading a 'race to the bottom' in its lax provisions for corporate governance. Cary defended a stronger Federal role in regulating incorporation. Likewise, Columbia University law professor Bernard Black (1990: 544) argued: 'state corporate law is trivial: . . . managers and investors together [can establish] any set of governance rules they want. After a century of erosion through competition for corporate charters, what is left of state corporate law is an empty shell . . .' Black mentions lobbying by the Business Roundtable as one source of this change.

It is worth remembering that, in his initial response, Winter (1977) agreed that the Delaware system does indeed reflect a competition-in-laxity.

[46] J. Anderson 1995. A rare comparative series is Cappelletti *et al.* *c.*1985; see also Presser and Kelley 1984; Majone 1991; Buxbaum 1988; European Commission 1978, 1983, 1999; Stith 1991; Charny 1991; Hirschhofer 1990; Kurzer 1993; Eichengreen and Frieden 1994; Sinn 1990; and Cnossen 1990. Also relevant are US responses to integration in Europe, e.g. US International Trade Commission (ITC) 1988, 1989, 1991.

[47] Labor mobility is 'sticky', not only in the current international system, but also domestically, given transaction costs, difficulty in transferring skill sets, and information asymmetries. Tiebout's model makes a number of other market and political assumptions which limit its domain.

However, Winter defended this normatively, on the grounds of efficiency, states' rights, and shareholder benefits. Again, laxity need not imply undesirability. A decade later Winter (1989) had changed his terminology and described this as a 'race for the top' in normative terms. By 1995 Klausner claimed that there was a 'broad consensus' that state competition produced a 'race to—or at least toward—the top'.

More recent research, after 1996, refutes this claim. Bebchuk, Cohen, and Ferrell (2002: 3) suggest: 'The body of empirical evidence on which supporters of state competition have relied does not warrant this claim. This empirical evidence . . . is in fact entirely consistent with the opposing view that state competition provides undesirable incentives . . .' Even if Delaware benefits shareholders more than other states do, 'the overall corporate regimes that states adopt would be adversely shaped by state competition'.

The Delaware debate has focused on the 'law as a product' of competing preferences (Romano). The debate tends to examine who benefits and who loses from particular aspects of incorporation laws, and the response of firms and other states to them. Investors' interests *versus* management's interests has been the focus, largely ignoring other stakeholders. Much research in the 1990s focused on how Delaware became a dominant state for incorporation. (See Romano 1985, 1993, 2001; Black 1990; Ayres 1995; Kamar 1998; Kahan and Klausner 2001.) There is conflicting evidence evaluating the performance of the Delaware system. (See Bebchuk, Cohen, and Ferrell 2002; Daines 2001; Daines and Klausner 2002; Revesz 1992.[48]) A number of authors argue that Delaware has locked in its dominant position and achieved network economies, hence there is no longer a competitive race among states, to the detriment of shareholders. (See Bebchuk and Hamdani 2002; Bratton and McCahery 1995; Klausner 1995.) Bebchuk *et al.* suggest an optional fifty-first federal jurisdiction might be more efficient in some instances than state law, especially if shareholders could vote on the choice of jurisdiction.[49]

This competition between US states to attract industry is also applauded by some business lobbyists (Revesz 1992). For example, the advocacy group 'Small Business Survival Committee' publishes an annual index that rates US states based on taxes, regulations, number of government workers, workers' compensation, pro-union laws, crime rates, and minimum wages. The lower

[48] Thanks to an anonymous reviewer for a number of these sources. See generally related work on corporate governance by Bar-Gil, Barzuza, Black, Breyer, Bratton, Easterbrook, Fischel, Fox, Prosser, Revesz, Romano, Rose-Ackerman, Salop, Slaughter, and Tarullo. Other helpful sources on US federalism include Tiebout 1956; Chubb 1985; Oates and Schwab 1988 and 1991; Dye 1990; Kenyon and Kincaid 1991; McGuire 1991; Swire 1996; J. D. Wilson in Bhagwati 1996; and Kenyon 1997.

[49] Bebchuk *et al.* are rejoined by Choi and Guzmann 2001; Romano 2001; Macey 2002; and Sitkoff 2002. Parting from Winter, Choi, and Guzman (2001: 961) [mis-]characterize the debate over Delaware as purely normative: 'does state competition for incorporations result in a beneficial race-to-the-top or a harmful race-to-the-bottom?'

the value for these variables, the more attractive the state is asserted to be for business. Their report suggested that firms should consider 'making a business investment or location decision' based on the study, and could also use the study to lobby for 'regulatory relief'. They encouraged firms to lobby for fewer regulations and taxes using this state-competition dynamic. If competition-in-laxity were a complete myth, as some argue, it is unlikely that firms would waste their money on such advocacy groups.[50]

This book's approach to trade and investment regulations allows readers to overcome a host of false dichotomies that result from oversimplified studies of globalization. Studies of the business impact on public policy often either sanitize policy to focus on the managerial bottom line or adopt a confrontational and accusative tone. This book avoids these prolonged, polarized, and often antagonized perspectives by using a clear set of explanatory variables to examine the empirical details of concrete case studies. Business executives and policy advocates alike, as well as scholars, can learn from these analytical findings.

The central question is: which of the three outcomes is likely to occur when and why? With few exceptions the academic literature on international political economy did not identify this puzzle in which variation in regulations is the dependent variable. The daily economic decisions that take up the bulk of top decision-maker's time constitute the preponderance of political economy. Studies of the firm must be integrated with policy and legal studies. Theories of institutions must examine who creates institutions and why, and not just treat institutions as an independent variable. The economics literature has successfully applied concepts of asset specificity and transaction costs to the analysis of monopolies; but much work remains to apply these concepts to a wider variety of other regulations in competitive industries. This book fills these intellectual gaps with a firm-based explanation of policy outcomes. Its theoretical findings open a black box in the international political economy literature and clarify a source of regulatory differences and similarities. It extends the explanatory power of transaction cost economics. For nonacademic readers, whichever outcome they seek for a given policy or business issue, it is necessary to properly interpret the world, to facilitate the changes they desire.

The empirical findings in the case material stand alone and are valuable for their historical narrative and counter-intuitive results. For example, who were the first bankers to use offshore dollars at a significant level and what, if anything, did regulators do to stop them? Are offshore financial centers really the result of diminished state power or did powerful states deliberately

[50] From www.sbsc.org, *c.*March 2002. At the favorable top of the SBSC's sixth annual 2001 list were Nevada, South Dakota, Washington state, Wyoming, Florida, Texas, New Hampshire, Alabama, Mississippi, and Tennessee. At the bottom of the list were the District of Columbia, Rhode Island, Hawaii, Maine, Minnesota, New Mexico, California, New York, and Vermont.

support their creation? Or, what best explains why prominent US businessmen created havens overseas for ship registration, in which ships flying the flag of those havens tended to sink three times more often than others? Or, why did DuPont ultimately support a global ban on chlorofluorocarbons (CFCs) when it produced half of the United States' and one-fourth of the world's CFC market? Why did DuPont voluntarily move so fast in phasing out CFCs that the US Environmental Protection Agency requested it to slow down? Or, why did major banks worldwide agree to raise their levels of prudential capital (which arguably raised their cost of doing business)? Or, why did StarKist ultimately support a US ban on the importation and sale of 'dolphin-lethal' tuna? Or, why did US infant formula makers consistently support a code against advertising in the US (even while they opposed it overseas)? This book explains these counter-intuitive findings and counsels a new intuition.

Social science calls for the dual goals of parsimony and good explanation. The approach taken here leans toward Occam's razor and begins with a parsimonious explanation, expanding it only when needed to gain explanatory leverage.[51] The propositions on process versus market-access regulations, industrial structure, and asset specificity explain a great deal of the variance across the cases observed.

One can now turn to those cases. Two cases are analyzed in detail for each of the three regulatory outcomes. The first two cases are examples of lower common denominator outcomes: shipping flags-of-convenience and offshore banking centers. The third and fourth cases are examples of higher common denominator outcomes: the Montreal Protocol on CFCs and the Basle Accord on capital adequacy. The fifth and sixth cases are examples of heterogenous outcomes: US laws restricting the importation and sale of 'dolphin-lethal' tuna and advertising restrictions on infant formula sales in the US. The tuna-dolphin case has received much attention elsewhere, but is rarely well understood. The details of these cases are important because they effectively increase the data under study. A variety of 'sub-cases' can be found in the details, and other cases are mentioned in the Chapter appendices. Each case study begins with an introduction, followed by a description of the market's structure and asset specificity, the case as seen through the lens of this book's three propositions, and a brief summary. The concluding Chapter assesses these propositions in light of the case studies. It goes on to suggest aspects of these cases not explained by the model, further research directions, the implications for social science, and policy and business implications.

[51] See King, Keohane, and Verba (1994: 20, 29–30) on parsimony and 'leverage' in explanations. See also Hirschman April 1970.

## Appendix: Idiosyncratic examples

For readers not familiar with these issues, a few examples are listed here, by region and issue area.

**Global** (including domestic responses to global pressures)

*Finance/business/trade*: offshore bank centers, BIS bank capital accord, corporate disclosure, accounting and taxation; bank deregulation, securities (IOSCO), US responses to EU banking directives, various WTO/GATT cases on nontariff barriers, US Foreign Sales Corporations, patent protection (WIPO), digital privacy issues such as 'Safe Harbor', telecommunication standards, antitrust (competition policy).

*Environment/consumer*: shipping flags-of-convenience, CFCs, Montreal Protocol, infant formula advertising, US–Mexico tuna-dolphin, tobacco advertizing, genetically modified organisms (GMO foods), phytosanitary standards, pollution havens, Codex standards, global warming, fisheries regulations, endangered species (CITES), Basel Convention (haz-mat), European beef hormone, chlorinated products.

*Labor*: conditions at sea, child labor laws, 'sweatshops', repression of unions, occupational safety, phossy-jaw (phosphorus matches), collective labor agreements and corporate relocation, prison labor.

**Intra-regional** (EC/EU, NAFTA, FTAA)

*Finance/business/trade*: various EC Directives such as tax harmonization, business law standards, securities, construction codes, electronics standards, energy efficiency standards, *Cassis de Dijon*; Danish bottling laws, aspects of EU integration itself.

*Environment/consumer*: German recycling laws, pharmaceutical laws, chemicals safety, animal rights, acid rain, toxic dumping (Rhine; *maquiladora*), timber issues, meat inspection (US–Canada), UHP milk (Canada–Puerto Rico), pesticide regulation.

*Labor*: *maquiladora* labor abuses, 'social dumping' (various), Schengen Accords (open migration).

**Domestic** (federal, e.g. within the US, Germany, Canada, Australia, Switzerland)

*Finance/business/trade*: Delaware incorporation, US savings and loan crisis (state competition: South Dakota and Texas); bank branching, regulatory and tax 'holidays', US integration (Interstate Commerce Act), Civil Aeronautics Board, trucking regulations.

*Environment/consumer*: bovine hormone in Wisconsin, Minnesota, Vermont; US state recycling laws, California zero-emission auto standards, state pollution laws (e.g. Louisiana *vs.* Massachusetts), Australian state beer laws, Canadian province pulp bleaching, Germany (Saxony) PVC restrictions.

*Labor*: US phossy-jaw, OSHA enforcement, state labor laws, unemployment benefits, corporate relocation.

# PART II
# LOWER COMMON DENOMINATOR

# 2

# *Shipping Flags-of-convenience*

The ability of shipowners to change the registration of their ship and the nationality of the seafarers on board whenever they wish makes it impossible for this exploitation to be ended by the efforts of any one national trade union.

International Transport Workers' Federation (1992)

## 1. Introduction

Lower common denominator (LCD) outcomes exhibit movement downward, as a result of either co-ordinated action or a competition-in-laxity among competing states. Echoing Bismarck and the International Transport Workers' Federation (ITF), some modern observers criticize free trade and the World Trade Organization (WTO) on the grounds that it will lead to such an undermining of domestic regulations. Herman Daly, for example, wrote: 'Free trade encourages standards-lowering competition [or 'the failure to internalize social and environmental costs'], and shifts production to the countries with the lowest standards of cost internalization . . .'[1] This book's empirical research suggests a more varied relationship between trade and social regulations. Shipping is among the clearer examples of a lower common denominator outcome. Shipping registration (and certain financial services) may be particularly amenable to competition-in-laxity, because of the extreme ease and low cost of relocation.

There are elements of heterogeneity within the shipping case, as first one nation seeks to attract registration through lax regulations. As other nations join in that laxity, one sees a competition-in-laxity among states competing for the same industry. For clarity, ship flagging is treated as one case study here. The fundamentals of the flag-of-convenience (FOC) system were set in place by the 1960s, and have lasted for decades, hence this Chapter focuses on this early period. The trends have largely continued through 2003, albeit with some movement back toward heterogenous Port State control. The

[1] Herman Daly, 'Against Free Trade: Neoclassical and Steady-State Perspectives', paper presented to Working Conference on International Trade Agreements and the Environment, Kennedy School of Government, Harvard, 29 April 1994, p. 8. See also, *inter alia*, testimony before Congress by Ralph Nader, 2 February and 14 June 1994; and related testimony by Lori Wallach.

important point here is not the arbitrary classification at a given time, as heterogenous or lower common denominator, but writ large the overall dynamic movement downward. International shipping offers an archetypical case of competition-in-laxity, thwarting national labor and safety regulations, as a result of location decisions based on comparative regulatory advantage.

What difference does a ship's flag make? It determines most of the regulations by which that ship must abide and it allies the ship with the diplomacy of its flag-country.[2] Generally, only flag states may enforce compliance with labor, safety, or pollution conventions by vessels of their flag. A ship operated with no flag could be confiscated on the high seas as a ship without nationality: in effect, a pirate ship.[3]

Flags-of-convenience (FOCs) are open ship registration systems, outside the beneficial owners' country. The *raisons d'être* of FOCs are low taxes, lax domestic regulations, and little enforcement of international regulations (Lloyd's *Registry of Ships* 1991). FOCs save shipowners' costs in the process of shipping by reducing the number of conventions, regulations, and taxes with which they must comply. These conventions include various environmental conventions, safety, and navigational standards, crew requirements, and labor standards. The FOC system is an example of conflicts that result from location decisions based on comparative regulatory advantage. Ships flying these flags (e.g. Panama, Cyprus) sink more often, lose more lives, and pollute more. The case offers a rich illustration of overall trends toward laxity with some limited movement toward stringency in subsectors, in conformity with this book's propositions.

This case study follows with a summary of the industrial structure and asset specificity of the shipping industry. The third section graphically demonstrates the exit of ships to convenience flag states. The fourth section illustrates the laxity of regulations in those states and, in this case, some negative externalities associated with them. The fifth section shows the role of US private sector actors in establishing the convenience flag system. The sixth section summarizes the supply of convenience flags. The seventh section discusses the emergence of new FOCs and the European response to them. The eighth section is a subcase: it discusses the oil-tanker subsector in which some trends toward a higher common denominator are noted within the broader framework of competition-in-laxity in shipping.

[2] Quincy Wright, 'Etudes des mesures internationales les plus aptes à prevenir la pollution des milieux maritimes', Institut de Droit International, 53 *Annuaire* 255 (1969 II): 'The responsibility of the flag state must be affirmed ahead of that of the coastal state. The stipulated provisions (construction of ships, navigational instruments, etc.) must be applied by the flag state more than by the coastal state' [author's trans. from the original French.]

[3] e.g. various IMO conventions, discussed below. See M'Gonigle and Zacher 1979. IMO is the International Maritime Organization (formerly IMCO). The skull and crossbones flag was originally a warning of plague aboard a ship. It was adopted by pirates for its isolating—as well as intimidating—effect.

## 2. Industrial structure and asset specificity in shipping: 'Assets that float'

The world shipping market consists of both pockets of oligopoly competition between cartels and thousands of independent shipowners, each with only a few ships to their name. Regulatory movement in this case tended to be driven by the more powerful large owners. Within the shipping industry a distinction is made between bulk (or tanker) and cargo (or liner) ships. The bulk sector transports grains, ores, raw materials, and, most important, oil. Shipping in this sector is dominated by multinational corporations. Within the oil-tanker subsector, the seven largest oil companies controlled roughly 20 per cent of world tanker tonnage by the 1970s. In 1977 Exxon was the largest, with 168 tankers, Shell was the second largest with 163, followed by British Petroleum with 107. The industry continued to consolidate through 2002, with mergers between Exxon and Mobil; Chevron and Texaco; BP, Amoco, and ARCO; and Total, Fina, and Elf. The conglomerates' share rose to 30 per cent. Other oil companies controlled another 20 per cent of the oil subsector. Independent owners controlled roughly 50 per cent.[4] Liner shipping carries manufactured goods. A number of shipping conferences or cartels were influential, particularly those from the US, Norway, Greece, and Japan, although the number of independents is also large.

The transaction of re-registering a ship from one country to another has very low asset specificity.[5] Consider an example. An extreme case of convenience-flagging occurred in 1989, when European officials caught an enterprising shipowner falsely 'registering' his vessels in Belize, despite the fact that Belize had no registry. Paint, cloth, and bogus certificates were the only costs. Ironically, the Belize government liked the idea. In August 1991 Belize opened an international ship registry. Within one year forty ships signed up. The Belize registry offered one-year provisional trading papers on the spot, upon presentation of 'seaworthiness' papers from any one of fifty classification societies. (Some classification societies were so suspect that the US Coast Guard had orders to board and inspect any ship registered by them. In 2003 these included a half dozen societies in Panama.)

The transaction of registering a ship is highly nonspecific. It involves discrete, autonomous, 'market contracting' (in Williamson's parlance). Shipowners have no compelling reason to embed contracts in a protective governance structure to promote continuity, or to ensure credible commitments or compliance. They have no interest in the particular identity of registry agents. The fact that there are no durable, transaction-specific assets

[4] Cafruny 1987, and Platts EMIS June 2002. See also Cafruny (1985) for a discussion of power and hegemony in the context of the shipping industry.

[5] ITF, 'Seafarers' Bulletin', 1990/5: 11 and 1992/7: 44; *Business Times*, 10 August 1993.

in ship-registration means that 'hit-and-run entry and exit' is feasible. Williamson noted (1985: 54) that in deregulation of the trucking and airlines industries 'the investments in question here really are "assets on wheels," hence lack specificity'. Likewise, one can conclude that ships are really 'assets that float', hence they lack specificity.

The registration of ships outside the beneficial owner's country inherently involves multinational transactions. In addition, operation of the vessel for trade between countries involves multinational transactions (and cross-border externalities). Hence the case involves low multinational asset specificity. As flag-of-convenience governments seek to attract ship registration, they compete with each other to offer the most flexible (lax) terms to shipowners.

As a result, for most shipowners there is little incentive to establish stringent homogenous regulatory structures across different countries. This is particularly true for the major segment of the market made up of small, fragmented, independent shipowners. The services they provide involve much less specific investments than, say, the services of oil tankers. The assets invested in registration of a ship at a particular registry can be redeployed easily and at low cost if the contract is prematurely terminated or if continuity of the exchange relation is otherwise upset.[6] (A subsector of the shipping industry, led by oil-tankers, is discussed separately below.)

## 3. 'Exit': Industrial flight to flags-of-convenience

Since World War II shipowners have steadily moved their registration to FOCs. They left to avoid taxes, regulations, and union wages. By 1965 more transport ships flew a Panamanian or Liberian flag than the US stars and stripes. Cyprus joined them in 1980, and Malta expanded its registry in 1990. By 1986 more of the world's shipping fleet flew a flag-of-convenience than a flag from the seven largest OECD fleets combined. (See Figures 2.1 and 2.2, share of world tonnage and major merchant fleets.) By 1998 the world's four largest fleets were registered in Panama, Liberia, Cyprus, and Malta. These four alone accounted for 41 per cent of the entire world's registered bulk vessel tonnage. By 2002 over half the world's bulk fleet and tanker fleet were flagged under offshore registries.[7]

Figure 2.1 shows the spectacular growth of FOC fleets and the exodus from industrial countries as a share of world totals, from 1945 onward. Figure 2.2 shows that data in absolute numbers of tonnage, by country (or group). It reveals more detail, notably the decline in European registries

[6] Williamson 1985: 31, footnote 26.

[7] Data are for ships over 100 tons. Calculations by the author from registry and Lloyd's data; and from Minister G. Knudsen, Norwegian Minister for Trade and Industry, Mare Forum Athens, 25 September 2000.

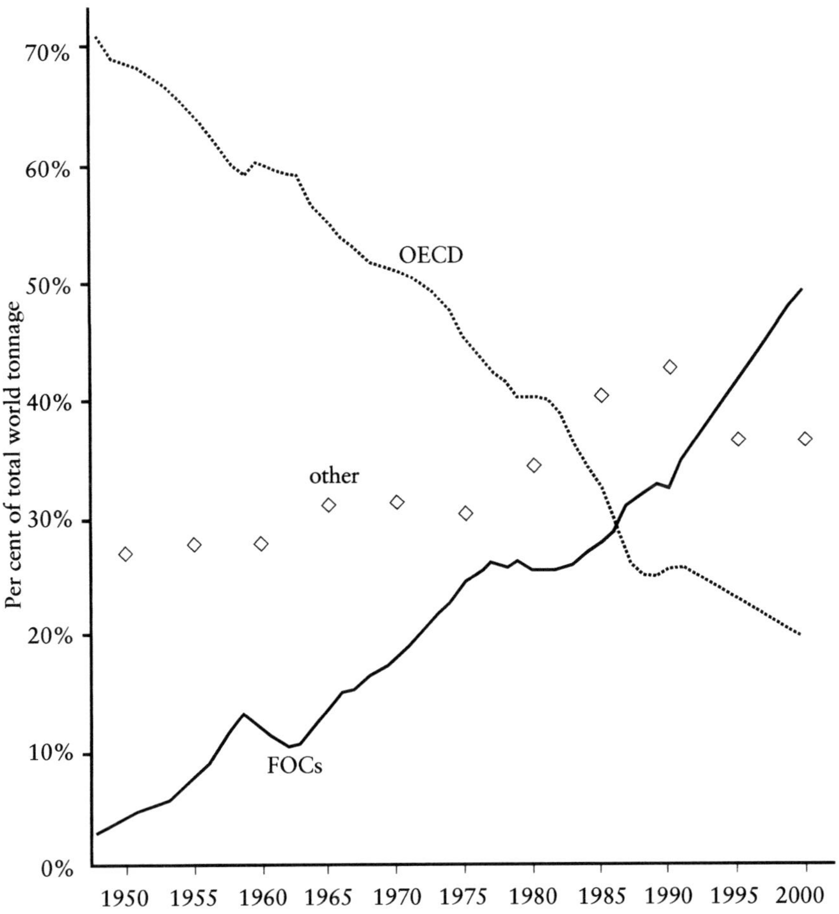


*Sources*: author's calculations from Lloyd's 1948–1992; Norwegian International Ship Registry 1993–2000

*Figure 2.1*: Share of world shipping tonnage, 1948–2000; FOCs *versus* the 7 largest OECD states

from 1980 to 1985, the decline in the Liberian registry from 1980 onward, and the growth in Panama. Further, from 1983 to 1991 it shows the rapid entry and rise of new FOCs in Cyprus, the Bahamas, onshore registries, and elsewhere.

Registration with a convenience-flag poses some costs to shipowners. They may lose the diplomatic support of their own governments during a crisis. The temporary use of US flags and naval escorts in the Persian Gulf during the 1989 Iran–Iraq war is an exception that illustrates the point and

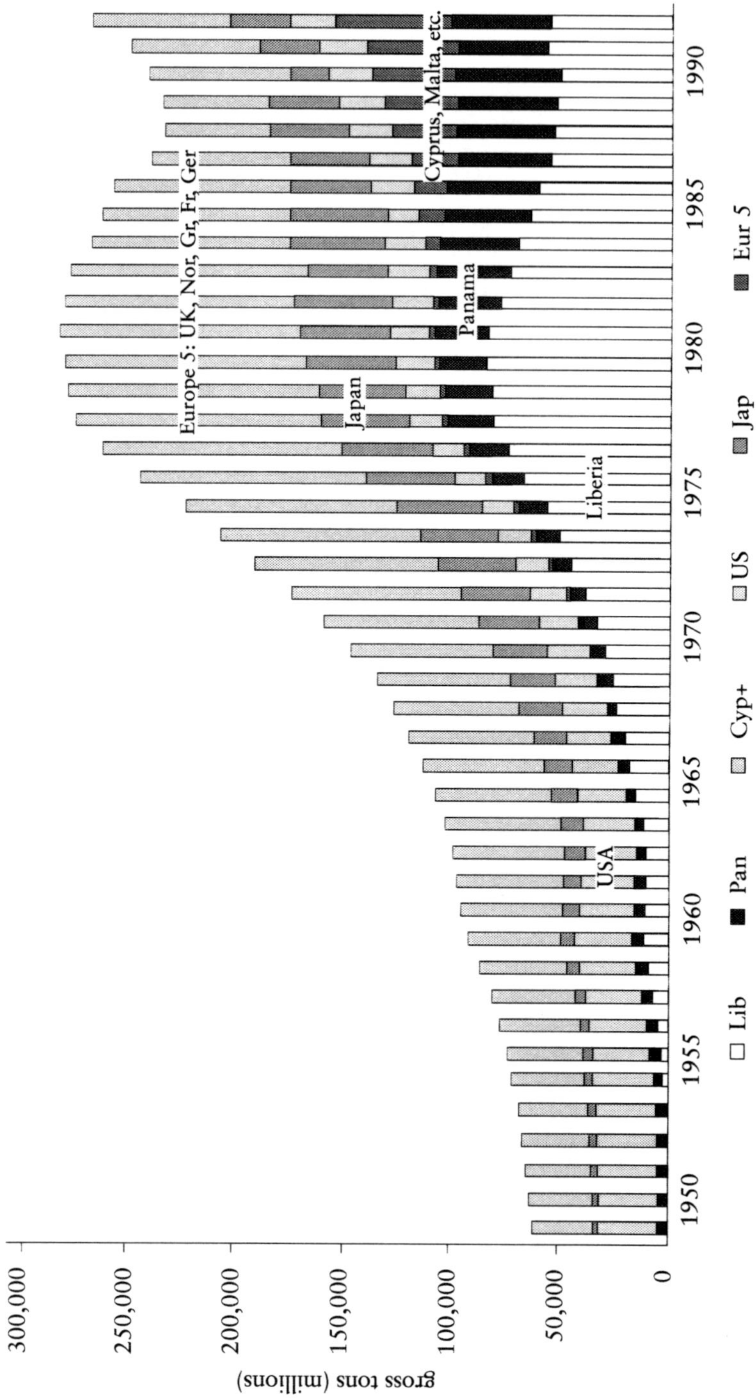


*Source*: Lloyd's

*Figure* 2.2: Major merchant fleets, tonnage 1948–1991

illustrates the underlying support by the US government for the FOC system. The US Navy invented a phony 'Liberian-flagged' ship to draw out Iranian forces for combat.[8]

In the early 1980s shipowners in Norway and other European countries fled the high taxes and stringent regulations of their national countries, and flagged overseas. European governments responded to the exodus in the late 1980s by establishing their own 'international onshore registers' with lower taxes and manning requirements below national levels, to regain their fleets. These trends are discussed in more detail below, following evidence that not only taxes but regulatory standards in FOCs are indeed less stringent.

## 4. Regulation in FOCs is lax

All observers agree that FOCs exist in large part because they offer lower taxes and other fees. The lower costs improve the competitive position of ships flying an FOC flag. Arguably these lower transportation costs facilitate gains from trade, and provide employment for seafarers in emerging markets such as the Philippines. Consumers of shipping services may benefit from the cheaper market prices, although these do not reflect the cost of labor abuses or negative environmental externalities.

There is also strong evidence that FOCs offer less stringent domestic regulation, less transparency to all interested parties, and less rigorous enforcement of international standards. The last includes regulations on various issues such as pollution and other environmental concerns, vessel safety and navigational standards, crew requirements, worker safety, and union and collective bargaining rights. Internationally, these regulations included three International Maritime Organization (IMO) International Conventions. The convention on Prevention of Pollution from Ships (MARPOL) was adopted in 1973. It provides operational procedures to be followed on a variety of pollution issues. The Safety of Life at Sea (SOLAS) convention was first adopted in 1960, revised in 1974, with later amendments such as International Safety Management (ISM). Its coverage ranges from the construction and stability of vessels, to lifesaving appliances, fire protection, pollution, and carriage of dangerous goods. The convention on Standards of Training, Certification, and Watchkeeping for Seafarers (STCW) was adopted in 1978. In some FOCs the relevant question is which—if any—standards are being enforced, not which standards are being avoided.

One indication of laxity is the failure to capture negative externalities.[9] In the shipping case, critics charge that ships flying flags-of-convenience sink more often, are less safe, pollute more, and violate more labor standards,

[8] Newsweek/ABC-Nightline investigation, June 1992.

[9] See debates on capturing pollution costs, inspired by Coase (1960, 1988). This is not necessarily the case and the findings here cannot be extrapolated to other LCD outcomes.

international conventions, and disclosure laws than ships flying flags from national registries.[10] Regulatory concerns include accident rates, labor conditions, and pollution and other environmental concerns. These are addressed below in turn. The data show a considerable divergence in performance between FOCs and national registries, corresponding to the divergence in regulatory stringency.

FOC fleets contain some very large tankers. Panamanian and Liberian ships average 8,000 and 32,000 gross metric tons, respectively, whereas non-FOCs average only 4,000 gmt. The Liberian fleet averages ten times the tonnage per ship of the US fleet. The loss of even one of these tankers (e.g. an Ultra Large or Very Large Crude Carrier) represents a significant percentage of a fleet. It also represents a potentially large oil spill and loss of life. Inertia and momentum could make bigger ships more difficult to navigate. However, size differentials do not explain the variation in accident rates between FOCs and non-FOCs. Size cannot explain why Panama's loss rate was almost four times worse than Norway's given that Panama's average ship was smaller than Norway's from 1970 to 1985. Size also cannot explain why Panama's fleet, with an average ship size one-quarter that of Liberia's, had a loss rate three times worse than Liberia's by the 1980s. It is likely that older vessels which fail national registry requirements as well as larger vessels which face high registration costs will be the first to transfer registration offshore, to avoid costly repairs. (This was the case with Norway: larger vessels began flagging offshore in 1982 because of taxes and regulations.) The International Commission on Shipping (IConS) concludes (2001: 55) that 'cut backs in crew numbers and maintenance effort arising from commercial pressures were blamed as a major cause of accidents with approximately 80 per cent of shipping collisions, groundings and sinkings being estimated to be attributable to human factors'.

## 4.1 Ships lost at sea: A veritable 'race to the sea-bottom'

Compare the accident rates of three leading FOC fleets (Panama, Liberia, and Cyprus) with the largest three national registry fleets (Japan, Norway, and the US). In every single year from 1948 to 2003 the three largest FOCs lost more tonnage as a percentage of their combined fleets than the three leading national registries. On average, they lost nearly four times as much tonnage (0.59 per cent compared to 0.15 per cent). From 1985 to 1990 tonnage losses for Panama and Cyprus averaged five times as much. (See Figure

[10] A national registry refers to the registry in which the ship's beneficial owner resides. An identical term is 'flag-of-origin' (FOO). Data on disclosures merit further study. Stanley Ruttenberg charged ESSO (Exxon) with pushing profits into its tax-free Liberian shipping subsidiary via artificially high transfer prices (testimony, US House Committee on Merchant Marine and Fisheries, SMM, *Energy Transportation Security Act of 1974*, HR-8193, 93d Congress, 1974, pp. 630–680).

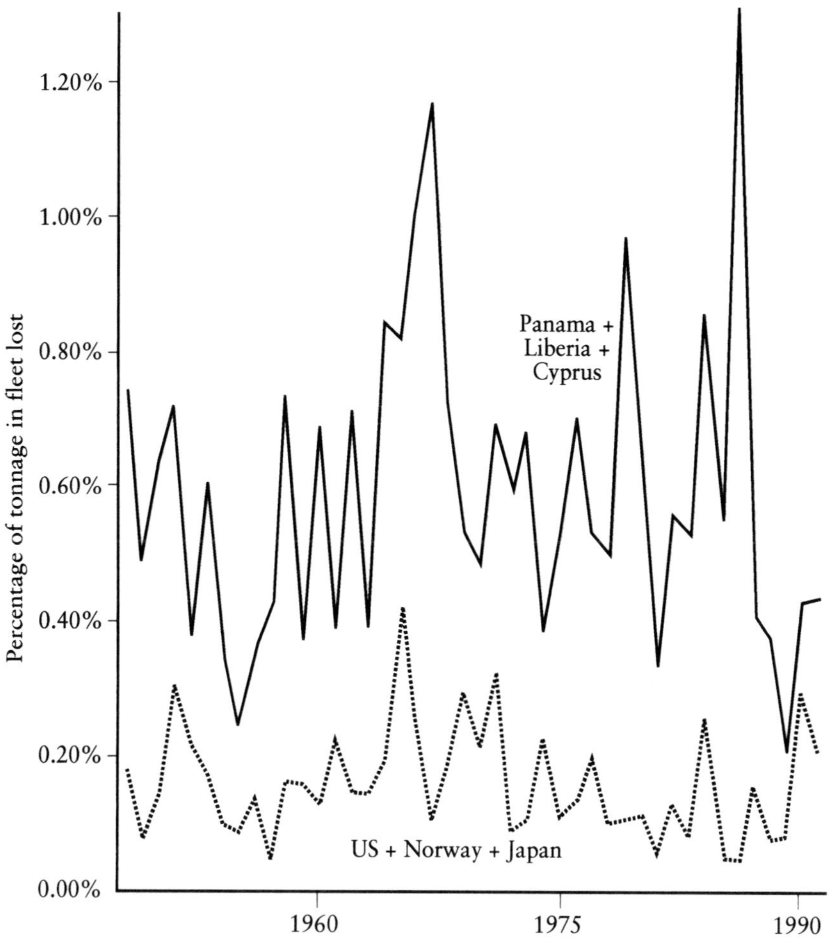


*Source*: Lloyd's Register STT

*Figure 2.3*: Tonnage lost as % of fleet, 1948–1991: Top 3 FOCs *versus* top 3 flags-of-ownership

2.3, Tonnage lost: per cent of fleet.[11]) FOCs also lost a greater number of ships every year as a percentage of their fleets, as well as more tonnage. On average, they lost nearly three times as many ships annually from 1948 to

[11] Data calculated by the author from Lloyd's. The leading FOCs were Liberia, Panama, and Cyprus. The leading national registries (1990) were Japan, Norway, and the US. There was variation within the two categories. Liberia's record improved by 1980 to a level comparable with the US; while Greece's record was often worse than Panama's. See also earlier studies by OECD (1974) and IMCO (1977) cited in M'Gonigle 1979: 21. According to the Institute of London Underwriters the world's worst casualty rates in 1999 were Cyprus, Malta, Vanuatu, Panama, the Bahamas, and St Vincent/Grenadines.

1999 as national registries (1.20 per cent versus 0.45 per cent). In 1999 over half the twenty registries which exceeded the world average loss-rate were FOCs, including Belize, Cambodia, Honduras, St Vincent, Antigua/Barbuda, Isle of Man, Cyprus, and the Bahamas. Most of the remainder were states with tiny fleets, for whom the loss of just one vessel was a significant loss-rate. Just fourteen FOCs accounted for 76 per cent of the world's tonnage lost in 1999.[12] The greater loss-rates in FOCs resulted in greater loss of life and pollution. They reflect general tendencies toward regulatory laxity in FOC registries.

By the 1980s Liberia became something of an exception to that rule, for reasons explained in the sub-case below. Liberia's total loss rate improved to a level comparable to OECD countries, in part due to more stringent enforcement by the owners of navigational and safety standards. Liberia improved the average annual FOC rate to 0.59 per cent from 1985 to 1990, compared to 0.23 per cent for the leading national registries. Interestingly, Liberia also had the highest percentage of ships agreeing to the ITF union's regulations: 54 per cent, against 34 per cent in Panama, 22 per cent in Cyprus, 6 per cent in Norway's NIS, and 0.8 per cent in the Philippines (ITF FOC Report 2000).

Overall, the higher loss rate in FOCs continued. In 1997 46 per cent of all losses in absolute tonnage terms were accounted for by just eight FOC registers. Of the ten registers worldwide which lost the most tonnage (as a percentage of their fleet) five were FOCs with tiny domestic economies: Cambodia, St Vincent, Antigua/Barbuda, Cyprus, and Belize. Thus, 16 per cent of FOCs were in the bottom ten, *versus* just 6 per cent for the large national registers.

## 4.2 Labor standards

The International Transport Workers' Federation (ITF) has protested against poor conditions aboard FOCs for half a century: 'Problems which have only recently begun to affect workers in other industries—international companies moving production and facilities to thwart trade unionism, and pitting one nation's workers against another's—have been commonplace in world shipping for over forty years.'[13] Forced conscription is now rare, according to Lloyd's of London, but some FOC ship captains are guilty of 'genuine grievances of human rights abuses . . . so grotesque . . . that they scarcely permit belief' (Lloyd's List 15 May 1992). According to Lloyds, it

[12] Calculated by the author from Lloyd's (various years), World Casualty Statistics 2000, and IConS 2001.

[13] ITF *FOC Campaign History*, undated mimeograph (received 1992) pp. 1–2. The ITF is the only source available for some of these statistics. See the ITF website, www.itf.org.uk. Also the 'Annual Survey of Violations of Trade Union Rights' by the International Confederation of Free Trade Unions (ICFTU).

is not 'a few losers' who are abused as a routine practice, but a 'sizeable number'. In March 2001 Australia's former Minister of Transport, Peter Morris, released a 266-page study, *Ships, Slaves, and Competition* (International Commission on Shipping 2001) which reported that for thousands of seafarers 'life at sea is modern slavery and their workplace is a slave ship'. Many must pay to land work, in effect becoming indentured servants. The IConS study goes on to say:

> 'Physical abuses include beatings and sexual assault, inadequate medical treatment, substandard accommodation, and inadequate food. Mental abuse arises from isolation, cultural insensitivity and a lack of amenities . . . Non-payment of wages, delays in paying entitlements to families, and even abandonment [in foreign ports] are additional abuses. . . . The crews can go for many months, sometimes years, with no pay and little hope of repatriation (IConS 2001: 57, 29–30).

These poor working conditions also contribute to accidents.

Overcapacity by the early 1980s led to a shipping industry recession and high unemployment, aggravating complaints of labor exploitation. In 1990 471 seafarers died in shipping accidents; 303 of those deaths (64 per cent) were on ships flying FOCs. By 2003 the ITF estimated that 2,000 deaths at sea occurred annually, but robust data was unavailable. Sailors in general have a mortality rate ranging from 200 per cent to 3,500 per cent greater than that in other manufacturing jobs, and four times that of the notoriously dangerous coal mining industry. Most FOCs have an even higher mortality rate, commensurate with their higher total loss-rate.[14] The IConS report concluded that: 'tens of thousands of seafarers in 10 to 15 per cent of the world's ships work in slave conditions, with minimal safety, long hours for little or no pay, starvation diets, rape, beatings, [and] disappearances.' Unemployment was chronic and high: the worldwide demand for seafarers (ratings) in 2000 was estimated at 600,000, whereas supply was estimated at 823,000 (with nearly one quarter of those from the Philippines alone). Conversely, demand for roughly 400,000 officers outpaced supply (BIMCO/ISF Manpower Update, 2000).

The ITF and other labor organizations argue that FOC practices violate basic human rights and frequently involve breach of contract, misrepresentation, and intimidation. They express concern about language problems between mixed crews, inadequate crew size, substandard and aging vessels, lowered standards of training and qualifications, fraudulent certifications, poor safety measures, excessive hours of work (ninety-four hours/week is not uncommon) leading to errors from stress and fatigue, little or no shore leave, indebted advance payment requirements, inadequate medical

[14] The data are attributed to the IMO by British MP John Prescott, Labour Party transportation spokesman, in *The Independent*, 30 January 1993. Lloyds lists 389 total deaths in 1990 and 1,204 in 1991. The ILO 1999 estimates death rates for fishermen between 2 and 21 times the national average. Further reliable comparative data in this regard would be helpful.

attention, death threats against crews who refuse to sail on unsafe vessels, blacklisting of union members, and poor living, sanitation, and eating conditions. Unions file frequent reports of sailors being kept at sea for up to two years with no contract and, after fees and salary deductions, left with almost nothing at the end. They also report cases in which contract terms were nonexistent or were altered halfway through a voyage, wages were not paid, and complaints were met with termination in a foreign port without a ticket home. More than 3,500 sailors abandoned in a foreign port, often without pay, were dealt with by the ITF between 1996 and 2000. Mere involvement with the ITF may result in a sailor being blacklisted from future jobs, in violation of the ILO constitution. Some US cruise ships had contracts which called for instant dismissal if a crew member made contact with the ITF union. Crews from the Philippines, Taiwan, and other countries may be hired with little experience and few language skills. In some of the world's major crew supply regions, one estimate was that 80 per cent of certificates for ratings were fraudulent.[15] All these practices are in violation of long-standing standards in national registries. Labor argues it is easily whipsawed by owners who use competing regulatory systems. Philippine seafarers, for example, have faced competition from even lower-wage Indonesian, Chinese, and Indian seafarers. (These four countries supply 41 per cent of all sailors.) Most courts have denied unions the power to boycott FOC vessels.

Shipowners, FOC governments, and some analysts debate these charges. They argue that the FOCs yield a Pareto-efficient use of labor, creating jobs where they are most needed in the global economy, increasing trade, reducing consumer prices, and cutting through inefficient and protectionist government restrictions. (Larger shipowners are more likely to hire unionized or well paid and trained crews.) They emphasize the distributional aspect of imposing more stringent labor regulations, arguing that it would reduce the comparative advantage of seafarers in poor countries, while benefitting workers in wealthier countries. Anecdotal data from this perspective emphasizes the employment opportunities for those worse off in the global distribution of labor and the remittances to their families.

For this book's research purposes the point is not to evaluate or resolve these labor-management debates, similar to those which Bismarck identified a century ago. Rather, the central point is the consensus that regulation in FOCs is less stringent.

## 4.3 Environmental and safety concerns

Environmental concerns center on intentional behavior such as results from the improper cleansing of ballast or the deliberate contravention of

[15] IConS 2001. On fraudulent ratings, citing Prof. Tony Lane, SIRC public meeting London, 14 November 2000.

fishing regulations, not just the more widely publicized spills from shipping accidents. FOC states have little incentive to enforce compliance with international agreements. They also frequently lack the legal and financial resources. Prosecutions, if any, occur in industrial country ports. FOC ships may rarely, if ever, stop in their port of registration. Violations conducted at sea are unlikely to be detected or prosecuted; little data is available on them. Traditionally, only flag states could enforce compliance with safety or pollution conventions by vessels of their flag (e.g. IMO conventions SOLAS, MARPOL, and STCW). Fishing vessels are a particular problem for the environment, as well as for labor. They frequently engage in flag-hopping: reflagging to avoid compliance with conservation regulations. Effective FOC enforcement is weak, and the US and other OECD countries have begun to exert more unilateral enforcement on ships entering their markets.[16]

While large oil spills capture the headlines and mobilize action, they accounted for only 5 per cent of all petroleum products entering the oceans by 1989. Routine shipping activities accounted for another 20 per cent.[17] Much of this pollution enters the oceans when tankers rinse out tanks or discharge water ballast after return voyages. International conventions have addressed this type of discharge, but enforcement is difficult and weak. A 2003 National Academy of Sciences study assumed that smaller tankers would be only 90 per cent in compliance with MARPOL, for example. Crew members, environmental groups, and analysts agree that FOC ships are less likely than nationally flagged ships to comply with international regulations on discharges.[18]

Another measure of the responsibility of a fleet is its performance at port inspections, for structural, crew, environmental, and navigational safety standards. From May 2001 to May 2002 an astonishing 73 per cent of all 157 ships detained by the US Coast Guard were FOC flagged. Only 18 per cent were from national flags. (Another 8 per cent were from onshore flags such as GIS, or ship-by-ship flags such as Singapore.) Honduras' detention rate was more than 18 per cent, St Vincent's was more than 6 per cent, and Malta's was 3.6 per cent; the overall average was 2.7 per cent. Of the ten FOCs for which data are available, the average Coast Guard detention rate was 9.8 per cent (including Antigua and Barbuda, Belize, Cambodia,

[16] See M'Gonigle and Zacher 1979. SOLAS measures range from construction and stability of vessels, to life-saving appliances and fire protection, to carriage of dangerous goods. MARPOL gives operational procedures. See also Dempsey 1986; Mitchell 1993; IConS 2001.

[17] Mitchell 1993: 183–247, NAS 1975. 1973 data showed that tankers were responsible for 72% of ship-generated oil discharges. Tanker accidents accounted for roughly 10% of ship-generated oil discharges. Tanker non-accidental discharges accounted for 62%. (Non-accidental discharges include deballasting and cleaning of tanks and bilges.) Nonetheless, oil spills focus media attention, as in the coverage of the 1967 *Torrey Canyon*, 1977 *Argo Merchant*, 1978 *Amoco Cadiz*, and 1989 *Exxon Valdez* accidents. See also M'Gonigle and Zacher 1979: 14–38.

[18] James M. Coleman *et al.*, *Oil in the Sea III* (National Academy Press 2003).

Cayman Islands, Cyprus, Honduras, Malta, Panama, St Vincent and the Grenadines, and Vanuatu).[19]

These rates are not new, and not specific to the US. Fifteen years earlier, in 1985, 37 per cent of inspected Maltese ships were detained under the European Port State Control regime. Honduras' detention rate was 24 per cent. St Vincent and the Grenadines had the third worst record, at 22 per cent. National registry detainees in Europe, by contrast, were typically less than 5 per cent. Lloyd's noted that St Vincent and the Grenadines had 698 ships in 1991, 'much too large for the Vincentian authorities to control'. Little had changed by 2000, when the rates for Malta, Honduras, and St Vincent were 12 per cent, 35 per cent, and 16 per cent respectively. The average rate for European flags was only 3.5 per cent. As of 2000, ten out of twenty-two FOC countries were on Europe's black list, as compared with only sixteen out of sixty-two national registries (the sixteen were predominately former Soviet bloc and Middle Eastern countries, as well as Thailand).[20]

While the differential in accident rates between FOCs and nationally registered ships is significant, the absolute level for both is relatively low: half a per cent versus one-tenth of a per cent. At some point the cost of additional safety measures to owners will outweigh the risk of loss and lawsuits.[21] However, such information is not available to all who need it, particularly poor seafarers, small merchants, and citizens of coastal states. A number of principal subsidiary–agent relationships complicate matters. Insurance premiums do not fully capture the externalities, including loss of life, overfishing, and oil spills. Insurance rates are calculated on a per-ship, not a per-flag, basis, but on average are higher among FOC fleets.[22] A lack of transparency and depressed insurance markets led to less differentiation in insurance rates than one might expect. Further, a significant number of ships (estimated at between 5 and 17 per cent) operate without any third-party liability insurance (IConS 2001).

A study by the British House of Lords concluded: 'The development of the flag of convenience system . . . permits a totally incompetent maritime administration to devolve its responsibility for the safety of millions of tons of shipping to a third party.'[23] England's Red Ensign flag has lost a spectacular share of the world merchant fleet, dropping from 22 per cent in 1948 to 1.5 per cent in 1991.

[19] Author's calculations, from US Coast Guard data, accessed June 2002: www.uscg.mil/hq/g-m/pscweb/detentions.htm.

[20] Lloyd's List, 9 June 1992; Paris MOU on Port State Control, Annual Report 2000.

[21] In the absence of regulations, shipowners presumably make a cost–benefit calculation:

risk X ($losses + $suits) = $(safety + navigation + labor + etc.)

[22] Institute of London Underwriters, 1991. Discrepancies from Lloyds' data are due to the inclusion of different states as convenience flags, e.g. Hong Kong. The overall picture is very similar. Thanks to Rex Preston for a discussion of these issues.

[23] UK House of Lords, Select Committee on Science and Technology, study on ship safety, February 1992. Cited in *Lloyd's List*, 2 March 1992.

## 5. American business created the FOC system

The twentieth-century flag-of-convenience system was created by a confluence of private and national interests, with the direct involvement of business executives and high-ranking foreign policy officials. It is no accident that FOCs first arose in Panama and Liberia, two states virtually created by America, with dollar-based economies. Industry led the way in establishing these centers of laxity; the US central government supported those decisions. This section summarizes that history.

### 5.1 Panama: Circumvented Prohibition and higher costs

The Panamanian registry arose in the 1920s with the assistance of W. Averell Harriman, owner of United American Lines, and his attorney, John Foster Dulles. Conveniently, Dulles was also Panama's chief legal counsel in the US and had been the US legal counsel at Versailles in 1917. Prohibition banned alcohol on US-flagged ships. Cruise ships, it is said, run on a mixture of diesel and liquor, so Harriman and others circumvented Prohibition by moving cruise ships' registration to Panama.[24] United Fruit Co. also flagged in Panama (and Honduras) to serve its shipping routes through the region.

Registration in Panama also involved lower labor costs and fewer safety regulations. A freighter company officer clearly stated those reasons for reflagging in 1922: 'The chief advantage of Panamanian registry is that the owner is relieved of the continual but irregular boiler and hull inspections and the regulations as to crew's quarters and subsistence. We are under absolutely no restrictions, so long as we pay the $1 a net ton registry fee and 10 cents yearly a net ton tax.' The savings on manning costs alone for a modest 9,000 ton ship were more than $US700,000 per year (in 2002 dollars).[25]

### 5.2 Liberia: Birth of an FOC empire

World War II left a surplus merchant fleet in US docks. It also left a surplus of manpower among US sailors, and led to increasing union demands. Following the war a second registry was created in Liberia by former US Secretary of State (and former Chairman of US Steel) Edward R. Stettinius,

[24] The US Shipping Board approved Harriman's request to transfer liners to Panama: Carlisle 1981: 14–18. Harriman's motive in evading Prohibition is widely reported (Emery 1970). Harriman also worked for the Union Pacific Railroad Company from 1915 and served as its chairman of the board 1932–1946. He was US Secretary of Commerce 1947–1948. Dulles later helped prepare the UN charter at Bretton Woods, negotiated the Pacific War peace treaty, and was himself US Secretary of State 1953–1959.

[25] W.L. Comyn, Pacific Freighters, *New York Herald*, 1 October 1922, quoted in Carlisle 1981: 11; and author's calculations using producer price index.

Jr. With former Assistant Secretary of State General Julius Homes and Admiral William Halsey, Stettinius jointly owned several ships. American shipowners approached them in late 1947 to enquire about a new registry for ships, to cut costs.[26] In March 1948 Stettinius met in Georgetown to explain his ambitious development plans to a high-level government group: the Secretaries of the Army and the Air Force, the Undersecretary of the Navy, an Assistant Secretary of State, and the Deputy Director of the new CIA. Averell Harriman was then Secretary of Commerce. Six months later the Joint Chiefs of Staff ordered the Chief of Naval Operations: 'In the event the Maritime Commission invites your comments . . . [on a Liberia registry] you interpose no objections to the transfer.' The US Navy supported the system, asserting a US doctrine of 'effective control' over PanLib fleets. The military saw FOCs as an extension of the US presence abroad and a means to prevent lower-cost competitors from underpricing the US fleet, so as to maintain US control over raw material supply routes. They also helped circumvent provisions of the Neutrality Acts before World War II.[27]

Stettinius went beyond Averell Harriman and John Foster Dulles in Panama. He completely drafted the maritime code for Liberia, subject to approval by ESSO (Exxon). Indeed, ESSO expected to be part-owner of the ship registration company. One member of Stettinius' company was Sidney de la Rue, the former General Customs Receiver in Liberia. The Liberian legislature approved the code (although not ESSO ownership) and it became law on 16 December 1948. Within six years Liberia passed Panama as the world's leading flag of convenience. The role of private sector interests here is clear: quite simply, US industry with government support created the shipping registry in Liberia, as in Panama.

The final Liberian law provided for no inspection, no manning requirements, and no taxes on profits. From then on, registry and administration was handled in New York by Stettinius' International Trust Company (ITC).[28]

Liberian registrations leveled off from 1959 to 1963, as labor disputes arose, then grew again.[29] The National Federation of American Shipping

[26] Edward Stettinius had been chairman of the board of United States Steel in the late 1930s; and US Secretary of State in 1945, leading the US delegation to Yalta. Carlisle 1981: 112, 120, 236, fn. 24, 130. Panama reportedly increased its registration fees after the war, leading to complaints by shipowners and the search for a new flag.

[27] Carlisle 1981: 120–121. Stettinius' partner, and former US–Liberian Customs Receiver, De la Rue had recommended (De la Rue 1930) that America write Liberia's commercial law. Carlisle (pp. 199, 202, 205) quotes Joint Chiefs of Staff (JCS) to CNO, US Naval Archives, 21 September 1948. A 1959 JCS memorandum tartly noted: 'these countries are not in a position . . . to dispute US assumption of control . . .' Carlisle (p. 205) cites Assistant Secretary of Defense Perkins McGuire memo to President Eisenhower's assistant special counsel Phillip Arreda. See also Cafruny 1985. European powers controlled those raw material routes prior to World War II.

[28] Stettinius died in 1949; his aide, Fred Lininger, ran the ITC registry for thirty years.

[29] Key legal cases include: *Lauritzen*, *Bobalakis*, *Rhoditis*, *Benz*, *Incres*, and *Hondurena*.

argued in a report to the State Department in 1947 that shipowners 'should not be singled out and barred from foreign investment. It is difficult as it is for our industry to meet foreign competition without accepting additional handicaps.'[30] International competition led to regulatory laxity in this case, as shipowners exited to FOCs. By 1967 Liberia's registered fleet was the largest in the world.

Once set in place by the US, other countries took advantage of the FOC system. By 1999 US shipowners accounted for only 2 per cent of the Panamanian-flagged fleet, whereas Japanese shipowners accounted for fully 40 per cent of Panama's fleet, and other Asian countries another 35 per cent. In Liberia, US shipowners accounted for 12 per cent of the fleet in 1999, followed by Saudi Arabia and Germany with 8 per cent each.

## 6. Supply: Who offers convenience flags and why?

The prototypical FOC states, such as Panama, Liberia, Cyprus, and Malta, have strong historical ties to a flag state, from whom they receive 'soft power' protection while remaining outside formal jurisdiction. Thus, both Panama and Liberia were created by the US, use the US dollar for currency, and follow many US legal traditions. Cyprus depends heavily on Greece for support in its conflict with Turkey, and extends Greek territory in the eastern Mediterranean. Malta has served as an entrepot haven for centuries, for France, Spain, Great Britain, Italy, and Greece. Once these states' offshore flags were legitimized, it opened the door for other small states to follow suit, often with the approval or wink of their former colonial power. Not any country can create a successful registry. Some countries have tried and failed, including Morocco, San Marino, Haiti, Sierra Leone, Costa Rica (closed due to smuggling), Somalia (war), and Lebanon (war). Strong diplomatic protection from a major shipping power seems to be an important requirement for long-term survival. Harbor facilities and a location on major shipping routes are not necessary but help establish international credibility. These conditions allowed for the emergence of offshore flags; the incentives for the offshore state were primarily financial.

The principal benefit to a country hosting a registry-of-convenience is money in the form of hard currency. For example, the shipping registry in Monrovia is the principal dollar earner in Liberia. It produced roughly $US20 million in 1991, two years into the civil war.[31] Panama earned roughly $US45 million per year in legitimate revenues from the operation of

[30] Carlisle 1981: 137, citing US Naval Archives, McCullogh to Longstreet 17 April 1947, Decimal 819.85/5-1547 RG 59.

[31] Other sources estimated the returns to Liberia were as high as $US150 million per year. Liberian rebel leader Charles Taylor filed a suit in the US to stop the rival interim government from gaining access to the funds. Taylor claimed he wanted the money to finance elections.

its foreign register (in fees, tonnage taxes, ship inspections, etc.).[32] Other host country benefits include employment, training, and trade.

The International Transport Workers' Federation (ITF) union classifies countries in three degrees of compliance with labor standards.[33] It listed the following FOCs: Antigua and Barbuda, Aruba, the Bahamas, Barbados, Belize, Bermuda (British), Bolivia, Burma/Myanmar, Cambodia (operated from Singapore), the Canary Islands, the Cayman Islands (British), the Cook Islands, Cyprus, Equatorial Guinea, Gibraltar (British), Honduras, Lebanon, Liberia (operated from New York), Luxembourg, Malta, the Marshall Islands, Mauritius, the Netherlands Antilles, Panama, St Vincent and the Grenadines, Sao Tome and Principe, Sri Lanka, Tuvalu, and Vanuatu. The ITF classifies as second registers (or onshore registers) all ships not genuinely owned by the flagging country nor covered by union-approved agreements. These include the German GIS, Denmark DIS, Norway NIS, French Kerguelen (S. Indian Ocean), Luxembourg (for Belgian ships only), and UK Isle of Man. The ITF classifies on a ship-by-ship basis boats registered in Hong Kong, Philippines (foreign-owned bareboat charters), and Singapore (foreign-owned ships without approved agreements).

## 7. Emergence of new FOCs in 1984 and European responses

Until 1984 Panama and Liberia were the only two FOCs of note, with one-fourth of the world's merchant fleet. Other FOCs were marginal. By 1991 new competitors' share had climbed to 13 per cent. Cyprus' bulk carrier fleet grew tenfold from 1980, to become the sixth largest in the world by 1991, even surpassing the US. By 1999 Cyprus had the second largest bulk carrier fleet in the world, topped only by Panama. In terms of total ships and tonnage it ranked sixth, following Panama, Liberia, the Bahamas, Malta, and Greece. Nearly three-fourths of the Cyprus fleet was made up of Greek-owned ships, along with those fleeing more stringent enforcement in Liberia, Germany, and elsewhere.[34] New registries were also established in several former British colonies. The Bahamas grew from virtually nothing in 1980 to 4 per cent of the world's tonnage in 1991. Malta grew from nothing to more than 2 per cent over the same period; by 1999 12 per cent of the Maltese fleet was Norwegian-owned. Registries also sprang up in the West

[32] In November 1989 a US government fax to maritime administrations around the world reportedly noted that Panama's FOC earnings were $US45 million, plus 'millions more in graft and corruption'. ITF *Seafarers' Bulletin* 1990/5: 16.

[33] ITF www.itf.co.uk, July 2002.

[34] Cyprus grew to 20 million gross tons, the Greek-registered fleet dropped 20 million gt over that same period. See ITF 'FOC Campaign Report', various years.

Indies, and later the Pacific islands. The overall safety record of most of these new registries was poor, as noted above.[35]

Europe responded to FOCs with a variety of policy outcomes. The first round of competition-in-laxity occurred from 1945 onward, as owners registered ships in Panama and Liberia. A second round among European states began in 1985. Norway, France, and the UK saw the exodus of over half of their tonnage to new FOCs in the 1980s. In response, in order to recapture ship registration European countries implemented tax cuts and liberalized crew regulations, adopted some protectionist measures, and lobbied to strengthen FOC regulations.

Consider the following piecemeal evidence of competition-in-laxity, primarily in manning requirements and taxation.

(i) Norway, Germany, Denmark, Portugal, France (Kerguelen), the UK, and Finland have all established second onshore registers since 1985. These act like a free trade zone for shipowners, allowing them to circumvent manning requirements and taxes.

(ii) By 1999 the same countries, along with Greece and the Netherlands, moved to a lower tonnage tax, to bring back ships.

(iii) Norway's NIS offers 'shipowners some of the world's most flexible and liberal operating conditions'. In less than two years the share of Norwegian officers aboard fell from 60 per cent in 1988 to 40 per cent in March 1990.[36]

(iv) In 1992 the Dutch shipowners' association KNRV demanded a $US67 million tax incentive package to stop the exodus of Dutch-flagged vessels. The Ministry of Transport and Public Works backed the proposal. A Coopers and Lybrand study concluded that 60 per cent of the Dutch merchant fleet was likely to turn to FOCs unless provisions were made. Differences in international subsidy systems were forcing local shipowners to relocate.[37]

(v) In 1987 the Netherlands introduced fiscal policies to stem the outflow of ships to FOCs.

(vi) Greece reduced taxes by 50 to 75 per cent on large tonnage vessels in 1990, to compete with FOC registers.[38]

(vii) In Britain, the Labour Party proposed tax breaks for owners and low income-tax rates and insurance contributions for seamen. It also threatened to deny port access to ships falling below British safety standards.

[35] See *The Tanker Register* (London: H. Clarkson); and M'Gonigle and Zacher, p. 373.

[36] *Financial Times*, 15 May 1991, ' "War" on Shipping', by Karen Fossli; ITF *Seafarers' Bulletin* 1990/5: 16. Former government officials stress that safety and environmental standards have not been lowered. Interview with a former Norwegian Deputy Minister of the Environment, September 1993.

[37] *Financieele Dagblad*, 9 June 1992.

[38] *Daily Telegraph* (London), 26 May 1992.

(viii) In other countries registration fees were cut several times in the 1980s, and discounts offered.
(ix) Poland and other former Communist countries rapidly turned to FOCs. Revenues from the Polish merchant navy nearly halved, from 301 billion zloty in 1990, to 167 billion zloty in 1991.[39]
(x) One of the latest FOCs, Mauritius, announced it would not employ any maritime inspectors at all.
(xi) Liberia cut its initial registration fee in 1990 from $US1.20 per net ton to a flat $2,500 per vessel. A Very Large Crude Carrier (VLCC) would save $100,000.

There is arguably some evidence of regulatory chill (aptly termed 'anchored to the bottom'), as well. Amidst the 1970s oil crises (and again after the September 2001 attacks) political cries arose for self-sufficiency in US oil shipping. Various quotas were proposed to boost oil imported on American-flagged ships: 50 per cent (1974), 30 per cent (early 1977), and 5–10 per cent (late 1977). All were defeated. By 1977 only 3.5 per cent of oil imports arrived on American-flagged ships; almost 60 per cent was on Panamanian- or Liberian-flagged ships. Opposed to the bills were the shipowners, the Independent Tanker Owners' Association (Intertanko), and the American Petroleum Institute. Allied in favor were US unions, US-flag shipowners, the American Legion, small refining companies, environmentalists, and shipbuilders.

Interjurisdictional competition simultaneously led to some heterogenous protectionist pressures, notably in the European Community.

(i) Europe created a Port State Control system, to enforce European standards on all ships entering European ports, regardless of flag. Critics call it a nontariff barrier.
(ii) Demands grew for the establishment of a 'genuine link' between ownership and flagging.
(iii) The European Commission proposed the EUROS shipping registry. It would impose European manning requirements and restrict domestic trade (cabotage) to European flags.
(iv) The European Community's Economic and Social Committee also considered a Community flag and concessions to Community shipowners.[40]

[39] *Polish News Bulletin*, 29 June 1992.

[40] European Commission, 'Communication on Maritime Industries: Industrial Policies in a Competitive Environment', *c.*1991. See also discussion in the USA on the Gibbons Bill.

## 8. *Subcase*: HCD regulations supported by large tanker owners

Although the overall story of FOCs is one of laxity, there is some movement toward higher common denominator (HCD) standards within it (albeit not as high or fast as some environmentalists hoped). That movement was led by dominant shipowners, especially within the oil-tanker subsector. This section discusses that subcase within the shipping industry.[41] The reassertion of Port State Control in the late 1990s, given the failures of flag states and classification societies to regulate their fleets, created additional incentives for shipowners who could afford higher standards.

### 8.1 Oil industry created the 1960s load-on-top system

Although public awareness of oil pollution had grown rapidly by 1952, and a 1954 international convention addressed the issue, little action was taken until industry became active. M'Gonigle and Zacher (1979) report: 'The entire 1954 regulatory system was a reflection of the fact that most governments were still not willing to accept any important control costs themselves or even to impose such costs on their industries.'[42] Process standards remained lax, despite the environmental costs. A 1962 Convention similarly showed little policy movement despite proposals to require separation facilities and a discharge limit of 100 parts per million (ppm).

Industry had remained largely silent on the issues, until then. When major oil companies joined in, however, regulatory movement soon occurred. 'The history of the 1969 Amendments is quite different from that of the 1954 Convention and the 1962 Amendments. Private industries (especially the oil industry) were now important participants in the formal negotiation' (M'Gonigle and Zacher 1979: 96). Shell Oil, in particular, decided on the load-on-top (LOT) system as an alternative to the 100 ppm and separation proposals. Shell had developed the LOT approach in 1953, but had shelved it because refineries objected to the costs of desalination. 'After ten years of inaction, it took only a few months until it was "discovered" in early 1963 that both the tanker and refinery operations could be successfully adjusted to utilize the LOT system' (M'Gonigle and Zacher 1979: 97).

British Petroleum and Exxon quickly joined Shell in supporting the system. On 17 June 1964 these three companies announced their adoption of

[41] On the value to research of increasing the number of observations under study by 'making many observations from few', see King *et al.* (1994: 217–228).

[42] This section is drawn from M'Gonigle and Zacher 1979: 81–142. On British environmental concern, see 'Report of the Committee on the Prevention of Pollution of the Sea by Oil' (London: Coordinating Advisory Committee on Oil Pollution of the Sea 1954).

the LOT system of pollution prevention on tankers. Independent shipowners were slower to move:

> The task was now to market the system to [. . .] the independent shipowners. [. . .] European independent tanker owners [were] crucial to the success of the program. These operators accounted for two-thirds of the world tanker tonnage, and it was they who were most intransigent. Unlike the oil companies, competitive shipping was the entire business of these shipowners. [. . .] But the major oil companies had become convinced that it was in their long-run interest to adopt the system.[43]

The LOT system hurt independent shipowners more than it did the oil companies. In fact, the benefits accruing to oil companies were large enough that they agreed to reimburse the independents for any direct costs resulting from the LOT system.

By 1965 the oil companies' LOT system was put into effect, largely over the heads of government:

> At that time, the oil companies could already claim that 60 per cent of all tanker tonnage was employing the system and another 18 per cent was considering it. An important point about the development of LOT is that is was done completely independently of governments and in a very short time. In fact, the oil companies had adopted a system which by their own admission violated both the 1954 Convention (then in force) and the 1962 Amendments then being ratified by many governments. Thus, their actions [. . .] [forced] the hands of governments by presenting them with a *fait accompli*. It was [. . .] because governmental enforcement of the existing regulations was so poor [. . .] that the industry was able to implement its own alternative. (Footnote : [. . .] The preemption by industry of government was so successful that [an expert] did not think that there was a tanker over 20,000 deadweight tonnage in the world complying with the 1962 Amendments despite the fact that they had been law for seven years.)[44]

Oil companies initially circumvented governments, but were later supported by them: '[T]he oil companies had, by now, firmly taken the initiative [. . .] With the greater interest of Britain's domestic oil industry, British environmental policy at IMCO became more sensitive to its views [. . .] [T]he British government now became a strong advocate of LOT and of a new regulatory scheme' (ibid. 99–100). The oil companies 'bombarded' governments with 'intensive lobbying'. Their efforts were rewarded with unanimous government acceptance of Amendments in October 1969 which reflected the industry's position.

[43] M'Gonigle and Zacher 1979: 97–98. The authors suggest that the oil companies were reacting to fears of more costly proposals in the 1962 Amendments. That bears further investigation and analysis.

[44] M'Gonigle and Zacher 1979: 98–99 and their footnote 57.

## 8.2 Supertanker owner support for regulations continued

This subcase study does not attempt a review of all major shipping regulations.[45] Piecemeal evidence suggests that large shipowners have continued selectively to support more stringent regulations than did their independent competitors. That support came no matter where they flagged their ships. But the large shipowners continued to use FOCs to avoid most other regulations and taxes. The Committee for Flags of Necessity (industry's term for FOCs) was created in 1972 by Standard Oil, Texaco, Gulf, ARCO, Mobil, Standard Oil of New Jersey, United Fruit, Alcoa, Bethlehem Steel, and others. They supported continuation of the FOC system.[46]

By 1977 60 per cent of US oil imports arrived on ships flagged in either Liberia or, to a lesser extent, Panama. Large owners contributed to the raising of standards in the Liberian registry. (This partially explains the exodus from Liberia in the 1980s: independent owners were differentially hurt by the higher standards, and left for new—and less stringent—FOCs. By 2001 Panama alone accounted for more than 30 per cent of the world bulk-carrier fleet.[47])

The drop in oil consumption following the two OPEC oil embargoes and the slump in world trade left a worldwide tanker surplus. Owners of large fleets had several reasons to support certain higher regulations: to reduce surplus capacity (and overcome collective action problems), to squeeze out small owners, to increase profit margins, to legislate modernization of the tanker fleet, and to obtain subsidies. Profit motives and environmental concerns worked together. Pollution and safety regulations effectively provided a barrier to entry. In this exceptional sub-case, given the notoriety caused by major oil spills and the backing of the US for higher common standards, the gains to major shipowners of decreased competition outweighed the cost of higher process regulations.

The Federation of American-Controlled Shipping (FACS) was dominated by multinational corporations and supported certain more stringent Liberian regulations.[48] They recommended measures to improve environmental

[45] Mitchell (1993) analyzes several major regulations from an institutional perspective: 1973 MARPOL and 1978 amendments to it; requirements for double hulls, segregated ballast tanks (SBTs), and crude oil washing (COW); and various other IMCO/IMO regulations.

[46] See Naess (1972). 'Convenience' (not 'necessity') is the more common usage. The phrase dates back to 1939, when it was used by the American *chargé d'affaires* in Panama to describe the Panamanian system. See Carlisle 1981: 69.

[47] Other factors affecting the Liberian registry included changes in the Liberian government and policies. The civil war had less of an impact than one might expect, given that few transactions were conducted in Monrovia itself. The war did raise questions as to which was the legitimate government in Liberia, and hence who should receive registration fees.

[48] FACS was the predecessor to the American Committee for Flags of Necessity. Its members included shipping subsidiaries of Alcoa, Amoco, ARCO, Bethlehem Steel, Chevron, Dow Chemical, Exxon, Getty, Gulf, Marathon Oil, Phillips Petroleum, Reynolds Metals, Sonoco, Sun Transport, Texaco, and Union Oil.

compliance, disclosure, safety records, and inspections. These were implemented in 1977 to 1979 under the Carter administration and improved the Liberian safety record. Most requirements on construction of new ships (e.g. segregated ballast tanks, or crude-oil washing capabilities) were also enforced on Liberian tankers.

In a similar vein, Shell Oil in a 1992 report on the tanker industry warned that '80 per cent of world shipping is administered under [governments] whose priority is to make money from shipping and shipping services, while making only a token investment in safety'.[49] Similar concerns over the safety of oil tankers were expressed by Greenpeace.

Erling Naess, head of the association for large independent tanker owners (Intertanko), also supported certain more stringent environmental regulations. Naess welcomed public pressure following oil spills, inasmuch as Intertanko (and later Intercargo) hoped to reduce surplus capacity:

> Intertanko encountered a variety of legal and business obstacles to its various tanker-reduction schemes. [. . .] [M]easures of reduction meant that each individual owner would lose opportunities [. . .] Cooperation was required, but difficult to arrange. [Intertanko proposed] to take advantage of world concern with tanker pollution incurred in tank cleaning and ballasting. [. . .] [T]he US Justice Department [previously] held such agreements [. . .] to be in restraint of trade and illegal [. . .] Thus, in the name of a viable antipollution measure, tankers could be retired to serve as reception facilities in smaller ports. Intertanko lobbied for legislation that would require such facilities [. . .] [and] admittedly planned to turn public antipollution concerns and political pressures to business advantage by securing laws that compelled owners to retrofit tankers with [double hull] measures.[50]

Intertanko capitalized on concern over tanker pollution to reduce surplus capacity and raise shipping profit margins. More recently, IConS noted (2001: 4) that 'Intertanko and Intercargo give some leadership in this regard [for compliance with the standards, eschewing the practices associated with sub-standard shipping]'. It lobbied in favor of government regulation, in part because such activity by the private sector alone would violate antitrust laws.

## 8.3 Market access ensured compliance

The US increasingly acted unilaterally against foreign (as well as domestic) tankers which did not meet the higher industry-supported standards. The US

[49] Quoted in Joel Havemann, *Los Angeles Times*, 26 March 1993. The US 1990 Oil Pollution Act multiplied eightfold the liability faced by oil companies in the event of a spill. It also required double hulls on new ships. An excellent analysis of the politics of pollution control is in M'Gonigle and Zacher 1979.

[50] Carlisle 1981: 183–186 and 190–191. Naess became head of the Independent Tanker Owners' Association (Intertanko) in Oslo. See Naess (1977). See also Mitchell *et al.* 1993; and US Department of Transportation, US Coast Guard (1978, 1979).

enforced certain of these requirements through the law of the port. Threats of market closure, including prohibitions against loading cargo or complete port entry denial, helped ensure compliance on equipment and construction regulations. Market access, however, could not force changes in behavior on the high seas, nor was it typically used to enforce labor regulations.[51] Shipping is the service of providing delivery to a port. US threats of restricting this service led to select higher standards. (Without this market restriction, shipping services tended toward laxity.) The 2001 IConS report concluded that market-access restrictions had led to higher enforced standards:

> Most of the recent progress in tackling sub-standard shipping has arisen when a port/coastal State [. . .] has taken a strong stand in enforcing international or local solutions on foreign ships. [. . .] [T]he likelihood of regional or unilateral [heterogenous] port/coastal State intervention inevitably will increase. The effect will be to commercially marginalise non-performing flags, as the financial benefits to shipowners of operating sub-standard ships are eroded (IConS 2001: 7).

Through various memoranda of understanding, such unilateral actions may spread.

One example followed the Exxon Valdez oil spill, when the US—with its enormous markets—passed the Oil Pollution Act of 1990 which would phase out market access to US harbors for oil-tankers which did not have double hulls. The full ban would not take effect until 2010, twenty years after its passage, giving US industry enough time to amortize its old fleet.[52] Enforcement of other IMO regulations exhibited a similar trend (Braithwaite and Drahos 2000).

## 8.4 Subcase: Conclusion

Within the larger framework of a competition-in-laxity in shipping, this subcase demonstrates that the logic of this book's propositions remains valid when applied to a subsector of the shipping industry. Larger tanker owners supported certain more stringent regulations, in part because they benefitted differentially from them.[53] They agreed to the price of higher process stan-

[51] Mitchell 1993: 218 notes continuing problems in enforcement.

[52] In the latter case, US industry may have acted to forestall even tougher regulations, or to better control their legal and political risks. See Rees 1994 and Brooks and Hoban 1996. Thanks to Robert Kagan for these references.

[53] Improved public relations was one source of value. Oil companies did not merely react to public opinion. Mobil Oil vice president and board member Herb Schmertz used a $US30 million annual public affairs budget and a staff of 85 people to engage in 'creative confrontation' on regulatory issues. Much of that budget was spent opposing regulations of which Mobil did not approve. See Schmertz's 1986 memoir, *Good-Bye to the Low Profile*, with chapters such as 'Confronting Someone Out to Get You'. The 'someone' was *The Wall Street Journal*, which in 1983 editorialized against Mobil's 'campaign of intimidation'. In response Mobil withdrew advertising from the *Journal* from 1984 to 1986 and refused to answer its reporters' questions or send routine press releases.

dards, so long as these were enforced on others. That enforcement came about in part through threats of market closure. Governments were willing to enforce the regulations in part because of public pressure following large oil-spills. In recent years, heterogenous Port State regulations have emerged in OECD countries, especially on marine pollution controls. These have helped stem the downward drift of standards. This movement has been supported by a coalition of wealthy international shipowners and owners of domestic fleets. The confluence of interests between large shipowners and environmentalists allowed a coalition of the good and the greedy.[54]

## 9. Shipping flags-of-convenience: Conclusion

The FOC case shows a pattern of widespread industrial flight to lax countries, where regulations are often nonexistent and certainly enforced less stringently than in national registries. The outcome shifts from heterogeneity to lower common denominator (among competing FOC states) in a classic competition-in-laxity. That trajectory has been fairly constant for more than fifty years.

To review, shipowners relocated in droves to flags-of-convenience following World War II, seeking lower costs. By 2002 one-fourth of the entire world's ships (and half the bulk carriers) sailed under a convenience flag, amounting to over half of the world's gross tonnage. On balance, ships in those convenience-flag states sank several times more often, violated more labor standards, and apparently violated more environmental standards.

An exception to these general trends identified in the text was the subcase of oil tankers owned by major companies and often flagged in Liberia. Here, industry supported more stringent regulation. Large shipowners supported these regulations not only because of their love for pristine nature nor their fears of more costly regulations (although these may have played a role). Large shipowners also stood to gain from the reduction in surplus capacity, which antitrust laws prevented them from doing on their own. With their enormous investments and revenues elsewhere, the costs of regulation were relatively insignificant to them, compared to independent tanker-owners. (The infant formula case, discussed in Chapter Seven below, illustrates the risks to industry when collusive behavior is not sanctioned by formal government regulation.) These instances of higher regulation were created by heterogenous product market-access enforcement, by the US and European maritime inspectors.

[54] On port state control, see IConS 2000: 7, 139–155. See Oye and Maxwell (1993) and Chapter Four below for a discussion of 'green and greed' in the context of DuPont and the ban on CFCs.

Heterogeneity continues to exist in some standards between industrialized countries and convenience flag states (the *status quo ante*) but there was general movement toward a lower common—albeit unstable—denominator among competing FOCs. Many US-owned ships were reflagged in Panama or Liberia, in a clear example of *de facto* relocation. The US did not drop standards for cabotage among its domestically flagged fleet, and some progress was seen in raising labor standards above their worst possible level (although not up to the level of national registries) so the case is not one of the 'uttermost possible lowest common denominator'. But the overall trend is clearly one of competitive pressures and lax regulations—including taxes—enticing shipowners to relocate, and a dramatically increasing share of world shipping taking place under regulations less stringent than those in national registries. Simultaneously, in response to the exit of their fleets several European states (including the United Kingdom, Norway, France, Germany, Belgium, and Denmark) deliberately created international onshore registries with lower taxation and manning requirements. The latter permitted the hiring of crews under conditions which would violate domestic labor laws. They are clear examples of *de jure* competitive deregulation.

The driving force behind the creation of flag-of-convenience havens in Panama and Liberia was American shipowners, with the support of prominent government officials. Process regulations, a fragmented market, low asset specificity, and competitive pressures combined to yield laxity. One sees the creation of new centers of laxity, and responses which combine protection with deregulation.

The shipping case is worth studying for its theoretical as well as policy insights. It offers some support to Bismarck's (and WTO critics') fears of competitive deregulation. The extreme ease of shipping-flag relocation facilitated that dynamic. Similar cases of competition-in-laxity include offshore banking centers, US state regulations on savings and loan institutions, and arguably incorporation in the US state of Delaware. The next Chapter analyzes the origins of offshore finance. The parallels to the shipping case are clear and striking.

# 3

# *Offshore Finance*

We cannot appeal, therefore, to experience to prove the safety of our system as it now is, for the present magnitude of that system is entirely new. Obviously a system may be fit to regulate a few millions, and yet quite inadequate when it is set to cope with many millions.

Walter Bagehot, *Lombard Street* (London: 1873)

In truth, a 'lax' legal system is neither intuitively nor empirically inferior to a stringent one.

Ralph K. Winter, Jr. (1977)

## 1. Offshore finance: The *sine qua non* of liberalization

Offshore finance is financial activity conducted outside the beneficiaries' national jurisdiction, usually in order to take advantage of less stringent regulations and the better rates this allows.[1] The *raison d'être* of offshore finance is regulatory laxity. The incentives generally involve lax process regulations on the 'production' of financial services. Offshore finance allows firms to both circumvent and discourage restrictive national regulations.

The modern offshore financial system is pervasive, unlike its predecessors in turn-of-the-century secret Swiss bank accounts or 1930s tax havens in the Canadian Maritime Provinces or the Caribbean.[2] It is not just the preserve of money launderers, tax evaders, and other shady elements, although criminals do use it. Rather, it is the foundation on which the modern international financial architecture is built, and it is used by virtually every major financial firm and multinational corporation.

[1] Funding for this Chapter came from a Research Fellowship from the Walsh School of Foreign Service, Georgetown University, in the summer and fall of 1999, which permitted essential archival research at the Bank of England, Lloyds Bank, other London City and New York banks, and other financial institutions. The author is indebted to these banks' archivists for their research assistance. The London School of Economics' Centre for International Studies generously provided research facilities, collegiality, and good cheer.

[2] By 1937 Prince Edward Island had 243 American holding companies, Newfoundland had 202, and the Bahamas had attracted 94. Their main purpose was to avoid and/or evade taxes. Panama and Liechtenstein were also named by Treasury Secretary Henry Morgenthau, Jr. in Hearings before the Joint Committee on Tax Evasion and Avoidance, 75th Congress, June 1937. Still, the dollar value and market share of these offshore centers was small. They are an historical footnote, not a cause of the modern shift to offshore finance.

Astonishingly, by 1992 over half of all cross-border assets were accounted for by offshore financial centers. According to one IMF study they accounted for 56.1 per cent (Errico and Musalem 1999: 10 and 18). Roughly $US5 trillion was invested offshore in 1997, more than the GDP of all countries except the United States. Nearly 85 per cent of the assets in offshore centers belonged to banks.[3] Even by the late 1970s much of international finance had in effect become offshore, and there was a grey area between onshore and offshore. Dozens of offshore centers emerged, ranging from nefarious havens such as Nauru to the establishment City of London's international markets and New York's 'international banking facilities' (IBFs). The smaller financial centers often acted as tax havens for non-financial firms as well. Many offshore companies exist for only a brief period, just long enough to serve their role for tax, legal, or other financial purposes. By 1985 tax havens accounted for more than 30 per cent of net income and more than 26 per cent of gross assets of all US corporations' foreign operations (Hines and Rice 1994: 152). For example, when Enron—the fifth largest capitalized US company—went bankrupt in 2002, it had paid almost no taxes for four years and was revealed to have over 2,800 offshore subsidiaries, the vast majority of them legal vehicles with no physical presence.[4] If one added together the cumulative daily sum of all transactions passing through offshore centers, including Eurodollars, foreign exchange transactions, options, swaps, various financial derivatives, and so on, the figure surpassed quadrillions of US dollars per year: a volume that might give Bagehot pause. How did this *sine qua non* of the modern economy and freedom from regulations emerge?

It is a persistent myth that offshore banking was created by renegade financiers or countless, anonymous market forces, using new communications technologies to operate at the edge of the law. For example, a 1998 UN report on 'Financial Havens, Banking Secrecy and Money-Laundering' concluded: 'The origins of "offshore banking" are shrouded in myth and mystification' (UN Office for Crime Control and Drug Prevention, ODCCP 1998). Even the best texts in international political economy tend to shroud the origins of Euromarkets. Frieden and Lake (2000) mention the early roots of Soviet banks but not the role of Bank of England officials turned bankers. Spero and Hart (1997) state only in a footnote that 'there are many theories regarding the origins of the Eurodollar market' and cite Paul Einzig's work from 1970 and Geoffrey Bell's work from 1973.

[3] For this reason this Chapter occasionally refers loosely to 'banks' to denote all major private-sector financial institutions active offshore, including 'non-banks' such as American Express. For the purposes of this Chapter the distinction is not important; whereas in analyzing the overturn of Glass-Steagall, for example, it would be essential.

[4] US Congressional hearings, 6 February 2002; data presented by Senator John Kerry (D-MA).

It is also a myth that these bankers operated beyond the purview of regulators who tried but failed to stop the growth of offshore finance. As this Chapter shows, the truth is that modern Euromarkets and offshore finance were led by major private-sector firms. This is clearly documented in sections 5 through 8 of this Chapter, below. These firms could not write their own blank regulatory checks and balances, but they had a profound influence in removing national restrictions. With striking parallels to the shipping flag-of-convenience case, the search for lax regulations was generally tolerated or supported by high-level financial regulators, through both personal involvement and broad policy measures. In fact, the earliest leaders of the offshore system served both as regulators and bankers, at times simultaneously. This regulatory support overrode occasional conflicts with banks over specific regulations, and bureaucratic turf-battles with other branches of government over tax collection and fighting crime. The details suggest that these offshore markets were not 'inevitable', neither in their existence nor their current form. Overall the story is one of private-sector actors seeking less regulation, and top banking regulators in the UK and US enabling this liberalization. Traditionally, much of the regulation of *haute finance* consisted of a raised eyebrow by central bank regulators; in the case of offshore markets they gave a nod instead. Widespread financial flight to offshore centers was the result.

Top bankers are not surprised by this history. Alan Greenspan informally encouraged the author's emphasis in this Chapter to look in London for the birthplace of offshore finance.[5]

The flight to offshore financial centers from 1957 to 1988 is documented in sections 3 and 4, below. Readers already familiar with this trend might turn to the original research in section 5 on British banks, section 6 on the Bank of England's support, and sections 7 and 8 on American banks and government support, for the historical details which illuminate how this system emerged. Sections 9 and 10 discuss the benefits to offshore governments, and some recent moves to regulate money laundering through the FATF. This Chapter is not a complete account of the creation of the offshore system, but it is remarkable how much of the story can be explained using this book's simple propositions.

## 2. Industrial structure and asset specificity in offshore finance

The industrial structure of banking is similar to that of shipping in that thousands of small firms exist, but a few dozen large firms dominate major

[5] Author's conversation with Alan Greenspan, 13 February 1999, British Embassy, Washington, DC.

markets. Barring unusual governance structures (discussed in Chapter Five below) collective action among banks can be difficult to achieve. Most banks, however, favor lax process regulations on the way they conduct business. Also similar to the shipping case, certain bankers are politically influential, with close ties to their regulators.

Most transactions that flow through offshore centers tend to be very low in asset specificity, despite their high dollar volume. They involve liquid assets which can readily be passed from one faceless dealer to another, the transactions prematurely terminated and another buyer or seller found, without loss of value. Most euromoney transactions, foreign exchange management, swaps, options, and so on are conducted anonymously across computer screens. Furthermore, even for those financial assets with some specificity, the aspect of the transaction involving any given offshore center is typically nonspecific. Firms could move their transactions from one offshore center to another quite readily. There are few barriers, and the offshore centers themselves have very little power over those who use their facilities. Indeed, they advertise their absence of meddling. 'Prematurely terminating' such transactions would impose virtually no cost.

To register an 'international business company' in the Bahamas, for example, costs $US1,500 and can be done overnight. Antigua offered online incorporation through the Internet. Financial transactions in offshore centers are different than the highly specific sovereign-debt negotiations which affected the Basle Accord (discussed in Chapter Five below). By contrast, low asset-specific transactions in offshore banking helped foster lax regulations for those services.

## 3. Exit: Flight to offshore financial centers

This growth in offshore finance was not simply a function of greater international commerce. Activity in offshore markets grew as a percentage of total financial activity, taking market share away from traditional onshore financial markets, in a significant example of competition in laxity. This section describes this shift, illustrated in several figures, below.

Several broad phases can be distinguished in this series of competitions-in-laxity, as nonspecific assets relocated to jurisdictions with more liberal process regulations. In the first round of competitive laxity in the late 1950s and 1960s, London and the Bahamas drew assets into novel financial products which had not previously existed, and attracted assets that might otherwise have gone to Switzerland. In the second round by the late 1960s, assets that might have gone to London were shifted to the Bahamas and the Caymans. The third round in the late 1970s saw these assets drawn into other, newer offshore centers in the Caribbean, British centers in the Isle of Man and in the Channel Islands of Jersey and Guernsey, and other European centers.

In the fourth round in the early 1980s, some American assets that once might have gone to the Caribbean were retained 'onshore' in New York IBFs. In a fifth round, still newer offshore havens emerged in the late 1980s and 1990s, as did (in a sixth round) newer international banking facilities.

## 3.1 London is 'offshore': The birth of eurodollars and eurobonds

The euromarket and many other international financial transactions conducted in London's City are in effect 'offshore'. Finance in London, as in New York, is divided between a closely regulated domestic financial sector, and a much more lightly regulated international sector. There is a clear split in London between financial activities which serve the domestic British market, and those which serve international finance. As one longtime observer of international finance cogently observed, there was little regulation in London's eurocurrency markets:

> In contrast to national financial markets, where governmental supervision ordinarily ensures that at least minimal standards of good financial practice are adhered to, the Eurocurrency market was never subject to systematic guidance or regulation by monetary authorities. Eurocurrency banks traditionally were free to take whatever risks they felt were warranted by their own pursuit of profit: low reserve ratios, exceptionally narrow margins between deposit and loan rates, and lending on poor credit ratings. Eurocurrency loans were generally unsecured, and banks frequently lent through intermediaries without knowing anything at all about the end-use of their money. As the market expanded over the years, such questionable practices tended to increase steadily (Cohen 1977).

The international dealings of London's financial City are reasonably described as 'offshore.'

The City has a long history of antipathy toward formal regulations on international finance. Another scholar described the City of London's regulatory schema as follows:

> Foreign banks are attracted by the British method of regulation, one which provides sympathetic regulators and relatively lax rules. The institutions of regulation are such that the regulators themselves approve of and promote the further internationalization of the city. [. . .] [The Bank of England] is also seen as a sort of lobbyist for City interests. The Governors have, in recent years, openly supported the policy of maintaining regulations at a minimum, in effect keeping government out of the banking system. The three most recent heads of the Bank of England have all favored development of the Eurodollar market, the increase of foreign banks in Britain, and the removal of limits to competition. [. . .] [International banks] are attracted by the absence of rigid procedures—there is no battery of bank examiners or constant statements to be assembled (Kelly 1977: 58, 59).

Many financial dealings in London's City were in effect offshore, and remain so.

The use of London's City and various havens as a source of finance was so much taken for granted by the 1990s that finance was simply described as a global market. However, to understand the growth of island centers such as the Bahamas, the Caymans, Jersey and Guernsey, or Nauru, it is necessary to understand the birth and growth of euromarkets. The original 'eurodollars' referred to holdings of US dollars in banks outside of US borders which were not just accepted as deposits but were lent on as dollars, starting in 1957. 'Eurocurrencies' are any major currency holdings which were re-lent outside the issuing country. 'Eurobonds' were bonds denominated in one of these eurocurrencies, issued outside the jurisdiction of the borrower. They were introduced in 1963. 'Euro CDs' were certificates of deposit issued in a eurocurrency. Eurodollar CDs were introduced in 1966, euro-sterling CDs in 1967. Collectively, all these financial transactions are called euromarkets. Such holdings were minimal from 1914 to the 1950s, and were often illegal. Yet they became essential to the functioning of offshore centers and indeed for the globalization of finance, and they originated in London.

By 1957 the eurodollar market began to grow exponentially. (See Figure 3.1, early roots of euromarkets.) In 1958 foreign dollar deposits in UK banks nearly doubled to $US308 million; they doubled again in 1959, and yet again in 1960. By 1963 more than $US3 billion in eurodollars were deposited in British banks alone. On average, foreign dollar deposits in UK banks grew more than 30 per cent in each of the next fifteen years. By 1975 they topped $US100 billion, an increase of 7,000 per cent in eighteen years. The growth continued, topping $US1 trillion in 1979, $US2 trillion in 1982, nearly $US3 trillion in 1984, and $US4 trillion in 1986.

By 1994 the most heavily traded financial instrument worldwide was the eurodollar contract, which obliged buyer and seller to borrow and lend one million eurodollars in three months' time. Such contracts were typically bundled into loans from tens to hundreds or thousands of millions of dollars. More than 100 million such contracts changed hands that year.

## 3.2 From London and the Bahamas to the Caymans

Even with the most narrow definition of 'offshore' (which excludes London and New York 'International Banking Facilities' or IBFs), by the 1970s the overall relocation of finance through offshore island havens was striking. The offshore islands' proportion of deposit banks' total foreign assets had grown to 11 per cent in 1972. That offshore proportion then doubled over the next decade, to 22 per cent by 1982 (excluding London and New York).[6] New York IBFs were introduced in 1982, and attracted some Caribbean-based assets back to the US.

[6] Calculated by the author from US Federal Reserve data.

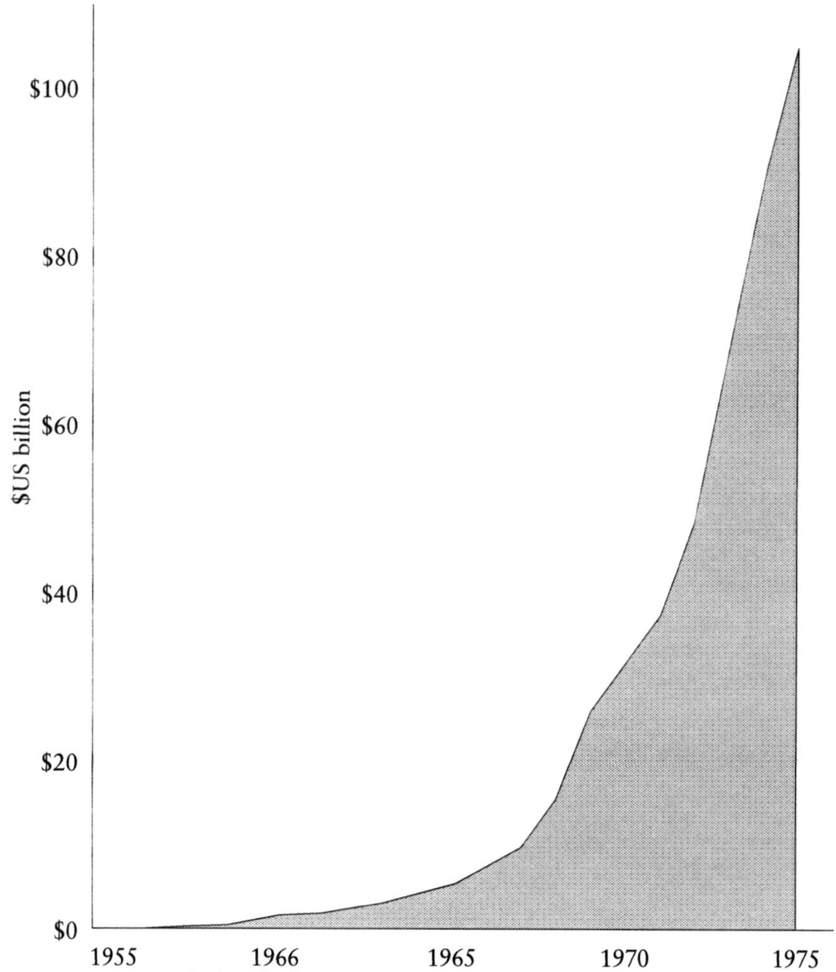


*Source*: Bank of England

*Figure 3.1*: The early roots of euromarkets; dollar-denominated external liabilities of UK banks, 1955–1975

The number of US bank branches overseas grew quickly from 1965 to 1975, and the share in offshore centers grew even faster than those onshore. Offshore branches grew to comprise a striking 41 per cent of total US overseas branches by 1975, up from 18 per cent in 1965. (See Figure 3.2, number of US bank branches in offshore and non-offshore centers, 1965–1975.) The growth in the Bahamian and Cayman Islands' share of US overseas branches is particularly striking from 1969 onwards. (See Figure 3.3, US banks' overseas branches, 1965–1975, % by region.) By 1973 one out of every five US overseas branches (many of them shell companies) were based in these two islands alone, skyrocketing from just 1 per cent in 1968. In these same four years London's share of US banks' overseas branches fell by one-fourth, from 10 per cent in 1966 to 7.5 per cent in 1975. In a clear case of regulatory competition, firms relocated their business through Nassau. When pressure was exerted in the Bahamas following the Nixon scandals of 1973, the Caymans picked up the slack. US bank branches in the Caymans jumped from three in 1973 to thirty the next year.

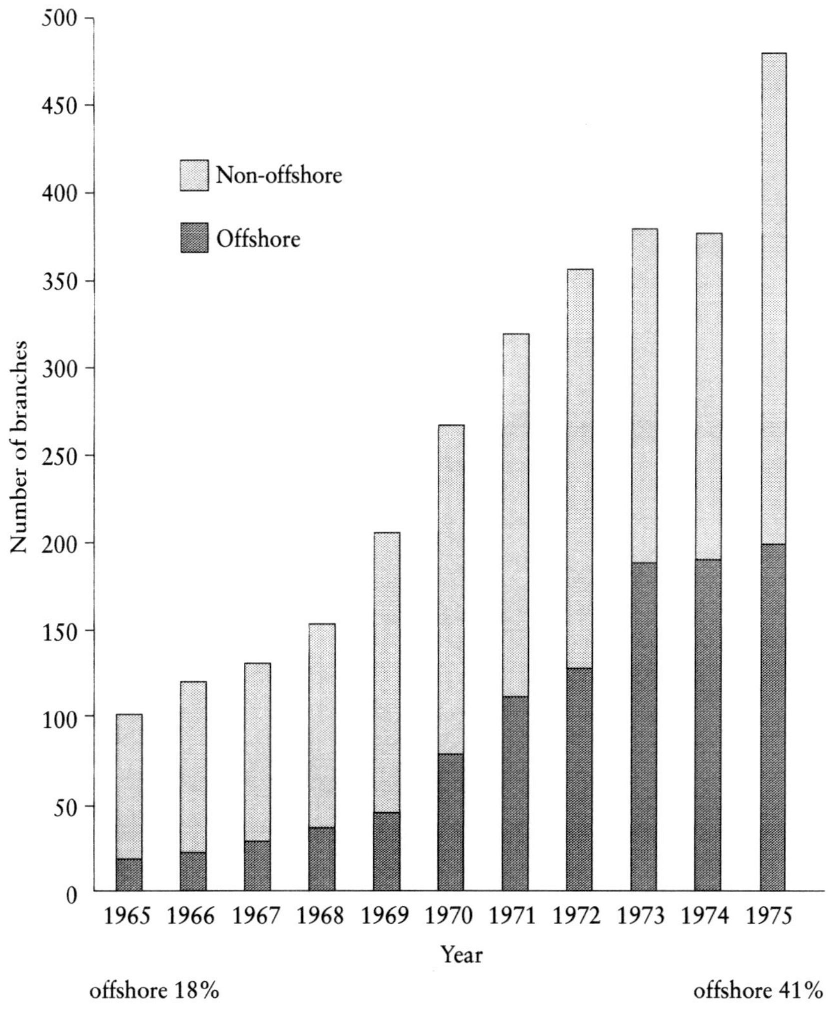


*Figure 3.2*: Number of US bank branches in offshore centers and non-offshore centers, 1965–1975

The value of assets held in these offshore branches also grew dramatically. In 1969, 67 per cent of the assets of US banks' foreign branches were in London alone, and only 7 per cent were in all of Latin America and the Caribbean. Four years later, in late 1973, assets of branches ostensibly based

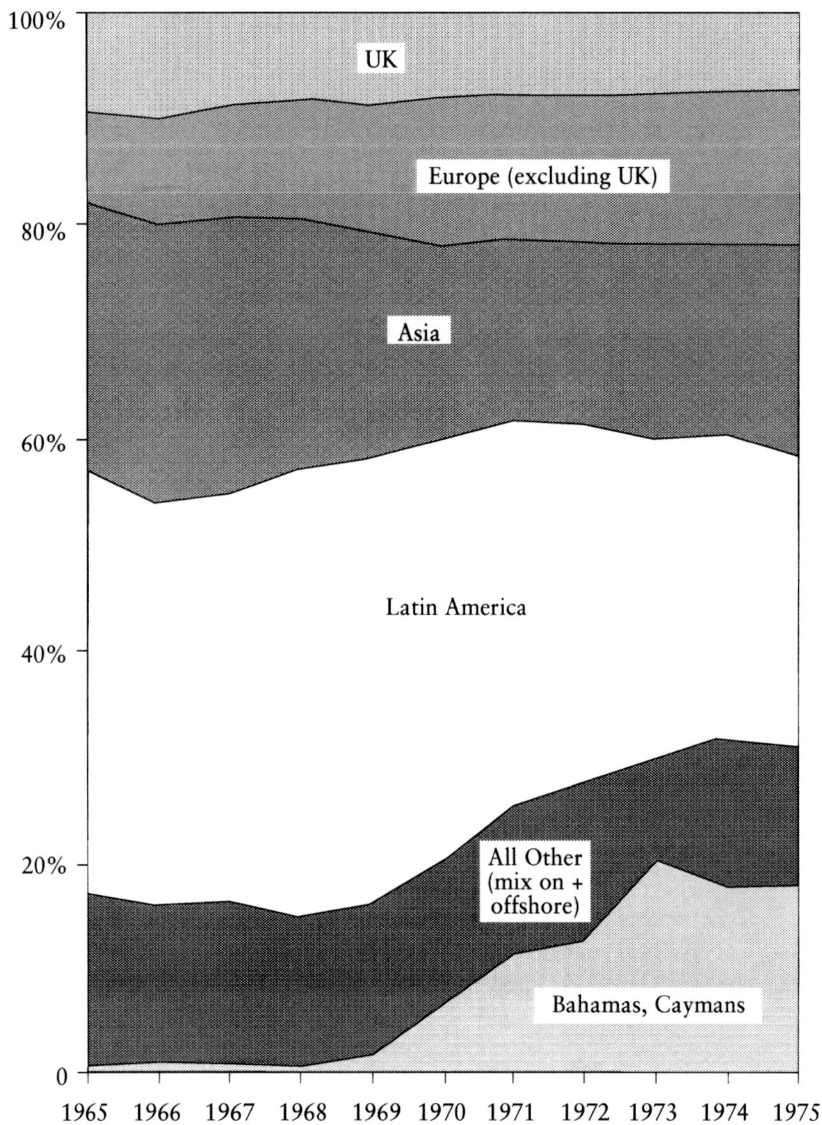


*Source*: author's calculations, US Federal Reserve

*Figure 3.3*: US banks' overseas branches, 1965–1975 (% share by region)

in Nassau and the Cayman Islands alone accounted for an astonishing 19 per cent of these banks' overseas assets. London's share fell from 67 per cent to 50 per cent.[7]

The value of offshore assets was increasing faster than international banking in general. In two years alone, from 1971 to 1973, resources in the Bahamas and Caymans shell companies more than tripled from $US6.2 billion to $21.1 billion. (There was no growth in Latin America outside of the Caribbean.) Resources in London also grew, but not as fast: from $US33 billion in 1971 to $US57 billion in 1973. Offshore assets rose from $US27 billion in 1972 to $US1,097 billion in 1988, by which time over half were in new offshore havens. See Figure 3.4 which shows the growth of assets in the Bahamas, Caymans, and other offshore centers outside London and New York.

The Cayman Islands became an offshore banking center *par excellence*. By 1991, 40 per cent of all cross-border loans to US firms (excluding US banks) originated in 'Cayman' banks. The dollar amount was more than $US110 billion, up from $US15 billion only eight years earlier in 1983. In contrast, less than 15 per cent of cross-border loans to US firms originated directly in the second largest supplier, the UK. More than 31,000 international companies were registered in the Caymans by 1994, including 534 banks and roughly 500 insurance companies, among a population of only 32,000 people. Bank deposits in Cayman financial institutions exceeded those of all Manhattan's banks.[8]

## 3.3 Emergence of new offshore centers 1960s onwards and relocation to them

Although London and the Bahamas were the first offshore centers, others emerged in the Caribbean from the 1960s onward, luring banks away from traditional locations and their rigid regulations. By 1975 most major international British and American banks had offshore activities in the Caribbean. The total Caribbean's share of US branches grew to 22.4 per cent in 1975, even as the Bahamas and Caymans share retrenched from a peak of 20 per cent in 1973 to 18 per cent. Between 1965 and 1975 Latin America's share outside the Caribbean fell from 40 per cent to 27 per cent as regional banking shifted to the Caribbean islands. Asia's share fell from 25 per cent to 20 per cent. The relocation from London to the Bahamas,

[7] Calculated from data in Andrew F. Brimmer, 'Prospects for Commercial Banks in International Monetary and Capital Markets' (paper delivered at *Financial Times* conference on World Banking, Jan. 1974). Brimmer was one of only two Federal Reserve Board members who opposed the rapid expansion of offshore banking.

[8] Robert N. McCauley and Rama Seth, 'Foreign Bank Credit to US Corporations: The Implications of Offshore Loans', *FRBNY Quarterly Review* (Spring 1992: 52–65). Thanks to Monica Rodriguez for this and other helpful materials and discussion. See also Arnold S. Goldstein, *Offshore Havens* (Garrett Publishing 1995).

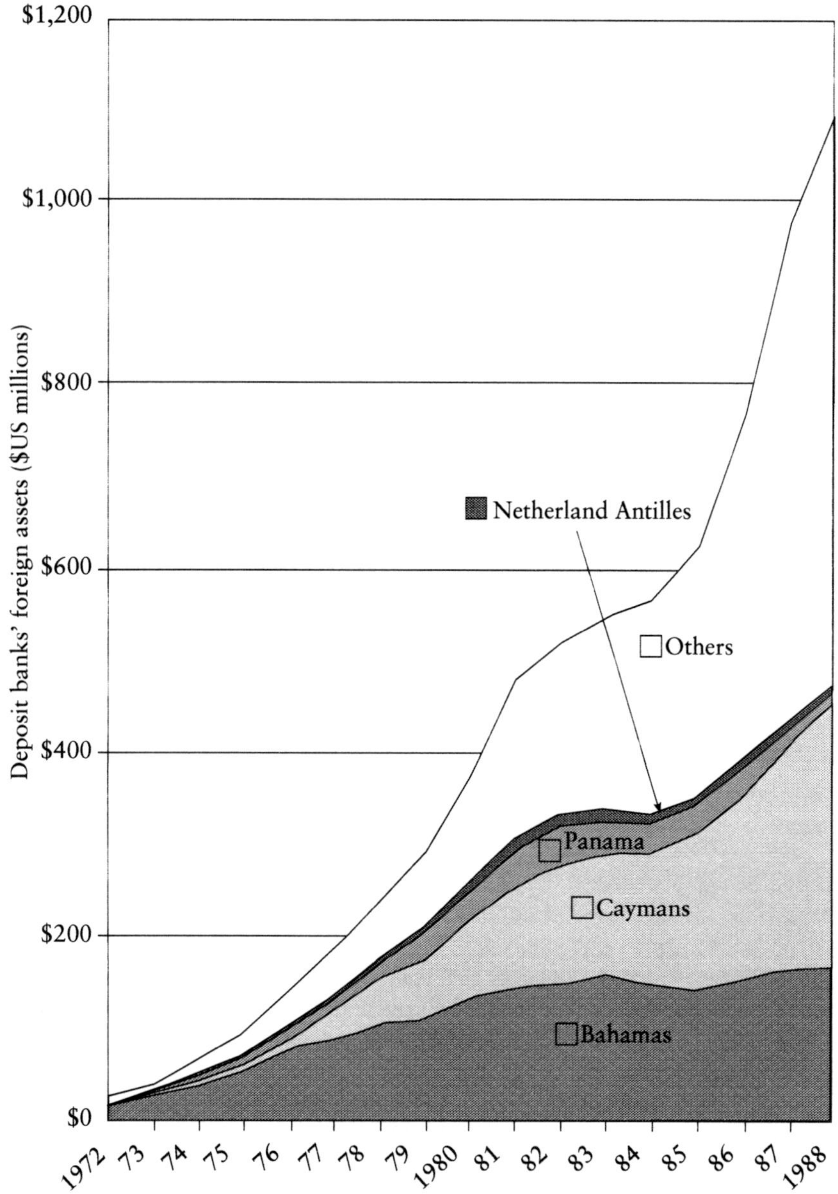


*Source*: US Federal Reserve

*Figure 3.4*: Competing offshore centers emerge, 1972–1988

from the Bahamas to the Caymans, and then to other Caribbean islands are further examples of competition-in-laxity, within the broader picture.

The top Caribbean centers expanded to include Trinidad and Tobago, the Netherlands Antilles, Dominica, and Panama. By 1974 major banks with branches in one or more of these six havens included BOLAM (Bank of London and Montreal), Barclays Bank, the Royal Bank of Canada, Citicorp, Chase Manhattan, Bank of America, J.P. Morgan, Manufacturers Hanover, Chemical Bank, First National Chicago, Banque Nationale de Paris, and the Algemene Bank of Nederlands. British investment banks there included Morgan Grenfell, Hambros, Kleinwort Benson, Schroder Wagg, Hill Samuel, and Guinness Mahon. Noticeably absent at this time were German and Japanese banks.

These centers were later joined by Anguilla, Antigua, Aruba, Barbados, Bermuda, the British Virgin Islands, Grenada, Montserrat, St Kitts and Nevis, St Lucia, St Vincent and the Grenadines, and the Turks and Caicos islands. In Europe, offshore centers were developed in the Channel Islands of Jersey and Guernsey, the Isle of Man, Andorra, Cyprus, Gibraltar, Ireland, the Madeira islands, and Malta. In Asia, Hong Kong, Singapore, and Macau served as offshore centers with varying degrees of regulation, later joined by the Cook Islands, Labuan (Malaysia), Marianas, the Marshall Islands, Nauru, Nieu, Vanuatu, Samoa, and by various underground banking systems. In the Middle East, Bahrain, Oman, and the United Arab Emirates emerged, along with informal but significant *hawala* systems. Historical financial centers such as Liechtenstein, Luxembourg, and Monaco also expanded.

## 3.4 Swiss roots, and seeds from 'Moscow on the Thames'

This Chapter focuses on the post-World War II offshore financial system. To backtrack, centuries-old traditions in Switzerland and its tiny neighbor Liechtenstein influenced this system, but did not create it. The historical origins of Swiss banking are well described by Fehrenbach (1966). The First World War bankrupted most European governments, and led them to adopt neo-mercantilist policies which took more than fifty years to unwind. Switzerland, by contrast, retained its pre-1914 traditions, never imposed restrictions on foreign exchange, and backed its franc with gold. To the extent the system within Switzerland is lax, it is a case of 'regulatory chill'. Bank secrecy was a longstanding Swiss practice, with roots in the ancient Roman *actio iniuriarum* and the Germanic *lex Visigothorum*. 'Critics who later claimed Swiss banks geared their policies to attract foreign money, simply never had any understanding of either Swiss banking history or the Swiss mind' (Fehrenbach 1966: 41). Stringent secrecy laws protect Swiss banks; unlike disclosure laws, they do not impose a cost on them. Swiss banks operated under stringent prudential banking laws and practice, with rigid liquidity and capital requirements. The movement within Switzerland, however slow, has been toward slightly more stringent disclosure requirements, albeit much less than within most OECD countries, since the early 1960s (UN ODCCP 1999: 9). Swiss financial markets had been open for centuries, and so they do not explain how and why eurodollars, eurobonds, and Caribbean offshore centers became such a prominent part of global finance from 1957 onward.

Some observers trace the start of the modern capitalist eurodollar system to seeds sown by the communist Soviet and Chinese governments. This story is partly apocryphal, as small foreign currency deposits long predated the Cold War. Also in mid-1955 the British Midland Bank had begun to innovate with dollar deposits (Schenk 1998). It is true that in 1949–1950 the revolutionary Maoist government placed its dollar balances with Soviet banks in Europe, to guard against American seizure. By 1957 the Soviet Union added its own dollar balances after a temporary US freeze on bank accounts of all countries involved in the October 1956 Suez Crisis. The Soviet government transferred its dollar balances to the state-owned *Banque Commerciale pour l'Europe du Nord* in Paris and Moscow Narodny Bank in London. These Soviet-owned banks financed East–West trade. Their bankers were not averse to making profits and so they lent out the dollar-denominated foreign currency deposits. However, these transactions were small and short-term.

The modern offshore system began in London in 1955–1957, and was followed in fits and starts by American banks, with the creation of other centers in the Caribbean and elsewhere. The historical roots in Switzerland, with the footnote of Moscow's banks, merely provided the backdrop.

## 4. Regulations in offshore financial centers are lax

The lack of regulation in offshore financial centers is well known and documented, hence this section is brief. A 1991 US State Department report noted that 'these banks and corporations were [. . .] established to serve [. . .] the armada of regional and international businesses who seek constant competitive economic advantage in an almost boundary-less financial world'.[9] In the competition to attract funds, some offshore havens may offer no taxes, no interest rate or currency exchange controls, no disclosure or reporting requirements (combined with stringent privacy and confidentiality laws), no audits, little diligence on international agreements, few licensing requirements or investigations, nonexistent or weakly enforced prudential regulations on capital or reserves, rapid processing without knowledge of the customer, informal procedures that bypass formal laws, and no immigration checks or extradition treaties for business people.

[9] US Department of State, 'International Narcotic Control Strategy Report', US GPO March 1991: 367.

Whereas in most advanced industrialized countries the laws governing financial transactions take up yards of shelf-space, in offshore centers the laws may be measured in pages. Securities issued in the Cayman Islands, for example, need not meet US SEC disclosure requirements. Offshore banks are less likely to be solvent than are onshore banks. They also have a lower ratio of capital to risk-weighted assets (Errico and Musalem 1999). The US IRS calculated that it lost $US75 billion in annual tax revenues to offshore centers in 2001. As mentioned, by 1985 tax havens accounted for a quarter of US MNCs' gross assets and nearly a third of their net income.

Obviously some offshore centers are more regulated and more responsible than others, and the exact nature of the regulations is important if one is evaluating the policy advantages or disadvantages of offshore finance. The purpose of this Chapter, however, is simply to establish and explain the origins of laxity. This is not to downplay the policy importance of systemic stability and regulations on money laundering, tax evasion, and other criminal activity; nor to cast doubt on the enormous efficiency gains made from liberalized capital markets.

The international activities in London and New York are more regulated than those in most offshore island havens, although the former make use of the latter extensively, but they are less heavily regulated than purely domestic financial activities. The development of 'international banking facilities' (IBFs) is discussed below.

Regulators' responses to the exit to offshore finance described above included two steps toward further liberalization. First, a variety of measures were adopted which allowed firms greater flexibility in financial operations overseas; these are discussed below. Second, regulators created what were essentially free-trade zones for offshore transactions. These included New York's IBFs, the Japanese Offshore Market, and Thailand's Bangkok International Banking Facilities (BIBFs). These fueled another round of competition-in-laxity. Following their debut in 1982, by mid-1997 IBFs accounted for roughly half of US banks' total cross-border assets, attracting some Caribbean-based assets back to the US Thailand's BIBFs, established in 1993, spurred short-term offshore borrowing and unhedged lending onshore. They grew 38 per cent annually, and accounted for two-thirds of Thailand's short-term inflows by 1995. (Arguably, they contributed to the 1997 Asian crisis which began in Thailand. See Errico and Musalem 1999; Haggard 2000.)

## 5. British bankers started the modern offshore system

The trends described above clearly show a relocation of finance to offshore centers. How and why did these trends occur? As with shipping, the twentieth-century offshore financial system was created by a confluence of private and national interests. Modern offshore finance first arose in London and the Bahamas: the former the center of world finance, the latter a British colony located conveniently near American dollars. The financial industry led the way in establishing these centers of laxity, and top British (and later US) regulators backed up these decisions. They shared the goals of mobilizing capital with a minimum of government interference, even as they struggled intensely at times with each other over the details of implementation or timing. Top bank regulators faced occasional battles for turf with other government agencies, but generally prevailed.

Many firms and thousands of individuals played a role in the creation of the modern offshore financial system. However, in the context of the study of regulations, to leave this creation in the mists of impersonal 'market forces' would imply a false fatalism. It was the Bank of London and South America (BOLSA) that really took the lead, beginning in 1957, though one can find earlier seeds of the modern system in Midland Bank in 1955, and the Bank of Nova Scotia and Moscow Narodny Bank in 1956. One cannot give an adequate account of the creation of offshore finance without giving credit to financial leaders such as George Bolton and 'Rowley' Baring. This emphasis does not denigrate the contributions of many others, nor does it deny the broader historical forces at play.[10] Rather, it is designed to illuminate the human agency involved in the creation of offshore markets. Apart from a few historians this history is not well known or published; hence this section focuses on the early period, 1957–1982, in some detail.

## 5.1 The Bank of London and South America (BOLSA)

In February 1957 George Bolton left his position as Executive Director at the Bank of England and took over as Chair and chief executive at the private sector Bank of London and South America (BOLSA). He held that position until March 1970. Simultaneously, he remained one of the twelve non-executive directors in the Bank of England's Court of Directors for a decade, until 1968. He semi-retired from BOLSA in 1970 but remained president until his death on 2 September 1982.[11] These details are important because under Bolton's leadership BOLSA became the first private sector bank to make extensive use of offshore US dollars.

By the mid-1930s Bolton had become one of Britain's top experts on foreign currency, especially dollars, and he was in charge of the Bank of England's (hence Britain's) foreign exchange operations during the

[10] Siegmund Warburg developed eurobonds in 1963, with some assistance from Bolton, some five years after BOLAM was founded.

[11] See Bolton's obituary in the Bank of England's quarterly in-house staff magazine, *The Old Lady*, March 1983. His obituary in the *Financial Times* on 3 September 1982 runs to a sparse 65 words.

Depression and World War II. He was part of the British delegation to Bretton Woods, was Britain's first representative to the new IMF/World Bank, was promoted to Executive Director at the Bank of England, and served as the UK director to the Bank for International Settlements. He worked at the Bank of England for twenty-five years before heading BOLSA. Bolton's footprints are found all over the construction sites of the modern financial architecture.

For several years in the early 1960s BOLSA was the largest eurodollar dealer. BOLSA was clearly in the purview of the Bank of England: even before Bolton took over, Governor Cameron Cobbold had talks in 1955 'about the future of BOLSA'.[12] Thus, while leading the private sector in the development of offshore dollars, George Bolton remained affiliated with Britain's top financial regulatory body as non-executive director. One of his first acts at BOLSA was to create a foreign exchange department, and he instructed his dealers to look for dollars. One dealer wrote: 'In September 1957, we started to canvas banking connections and other correspondents [banks] in continental Europe for dollar deposits and we very quickly began to collect funds.'[13] Arguably, this marks the beginning of euromarkets.

In less than a year, BOLSA forged a joint venture with the Bank of Montreal to be named the Bank of London and Montreal (or BOLAM). BOLAM's head office was created in Nassau, the Bahamas, and not in London, Montreal, or New York. The choice was not coincidental. The Bank of England had a seat on the currency boards of the Bahamas and the Cayman Islands, the Duke of Windsor was Governor of the Bahamas, and the protectorate followed British law, offering some protection to BOLAM's assets. The Bank of Nova Scotia had opened a branch there in 1956, as did Canadian Imperial Bank of Commerce in 1957. American banks would follow three years later. Beginning in October 1958, BOLAM expanded from the Bahamas into several other Caribbean and Central American centers, including Trinidad, Jamaica, Honduras, Panama, and Costa Rica.

Far from today's notion that 'globalization' would somehow diminish Britain's sovereignty or power, Bolton saw his work as furthering Britain's national interest. London's City had a competitive advantage in international finance, and he encouraged other firms to help build the offshore system. Bolton's goal was 'to see what could be done to prevent any further decline of British influence'. In a 1963 speech to the Imperial Defence College, Bolton concluded: 'the national interest cannot escape in the future being guided by economic interest.' Bolton was not committed to a

12 Governor's Note, 5 July 1955, C48/156, Bank of England Archives (Jones 1993). Cobbold was aware by June 1955 that Midland Bank was seeking dollar deposits unrelated to its commercial business. Note by JLH, 'Banks Liquidity', BE C43/111 (Schenk 1998).

13 Unnamed BOLSA dealer, quoted in Fry 1970: 32. Lloyds Bank created BOLSA in 1923, out of a merger of two of the oldest British banks in Latin America: the London and River Plate Bank, and the London and Brazilian Bank. For the early history of BOLSA, see Joslin 1963.

free-market ideology *per se*. He was committed to the City's interests, which he saw as consonant with Britain's interests.

Bolton semi-retired in 1970. He would be succeeded at BOLSA by none other than his successor at the Bank of England, and the second-in-command there: Deputy Governor Maurice Parsons. The pattern of 'gamekeeper turned poacher' continued, with bank-led preferences for lax offshore regulations supported by regulators.[14]

## 5.2 Baring Bros. Bank and George 'Rowley' Baring (Lord Cromer)

BOLSA and Bolton received supported from a banking dynasty. The Baring family bank had long been at the heart of London's traditional financial circles. Baring Brothers & Co. was founded in 1762 by two merchant brothers, Francis and John Baring. With early success in funding trade, the Barings became bankers to the Crown. Baring Bros. quietly maintained this role until its collapse on 25 February 1995.[15] A Baring family member has also served as a director (or higher) in the Bank of England for nearly half of the period from 1805 through 2003.[16] Besides running the family bank, helping govern the Bank of England, and managing the Crown's finances, the Barings were also tightly involved in the British colonial empire. The Bank founder Francis became a director of the British East India Company. His second son, Alexander (Lord Ashburton) was Ambassador to the US. His grandson Francis (Baron Northbrook) was Chancellor of the Exchequer, and Lord of the Admiralty. His great-grandson Thomas (Lord Northbrook) was Viceroy of India (and then also First Lord of the Admiralty). Evelyn (the first Lord Revelstoke, aka Lord 'Over' Baring) was the penultimate governor and virtual dictator of colonial-Egypt; his first son

[14] The good-natured 'gamekeeper turned poacher' metaphor has long been applied to the revolving door in London's City. *The Economist*, 28 October 1978, wrote: 'The Bank of England is supposed to act as the City's go-between with the government, but it is increasingly hard to be gamekeeper, poacher, and have its own butt.' When the Bank of England's Deputy Governor Kit McMahon became head of Midland Bank in 1996, David Lascelles of the *Financial Times* asked: 'And how does the gamekeeper turned poacher now view the banking authorities?'

[15] Its management had failed to detect $1 billion in losses by former 'boy wonder' turned 'rogue trader', 27-year-old Nicholas Leeson. With only a high school education, Leeson led his Singapore division to report the most 'profits' of any Baring Bros. division. But after three years the 'error account #88888' where he hid all his losses was uncovered. The losses amounted to more than twice Barings' capital. Leeson was sentenced to six and a half years in a Singapore prison. No charges were filed against any Barings management, auditors, or regulators, despite Singapore's allegations of inadequate supervision. What remained of Baring Bros, was bought out by ING, to create ING-Barings. See the British *Report of the Board of Banking Supervision Inquiry into the Circumstances of the Collapse of Barings*, London 1995. Also Singapore's *Report of the Inspectors of Barings Futures (Singapore) PTE LTD*, 19 October 1995.

[16] Baring's family directors in the Bank of England (and their terms) included: Alexander 1805–1817, Thomas 1848–1867, Edward 1879–1891, John 1898–1929, Rowley 1961–1966, and another John 1983–1991.

Evelyn Jr. (later Lord Howick) was the last colonial governor of Kenya, and a second son was Lord Chamberlain to the King; his grandson, George 'Rowley' Barings (the third Lord Cromer) is discussed below. It would be difficult to identify a firm and family which more seamlessly integrated the financial sector and the state.

George Rowland Stanley Baring (1918–1991, the third Earl of Cromer) banker and Bank of England Governor (1961–1966), lived in the pinnacle of the City's establishment. His career bridged the private sector and government service so frequently that the two are difficult to disentangle. His career also spanned the Atlantic, helping him build ties from London to New York and Washington. In business, 'Rowley' Baring kept a very low profile, unlike the flamboyant Bolton. It is clear, however, that Baring was aware and supportive of euromarkets, and under his direction Baring Bros. & Co. made use of offshore centers. Ultimately, in 1981 Rowley Baring himself retired for ten years to—of all places—the island of Jersey, a Channel Islands offshore center.

He began his career in 1946 with the family bank, founded by his great-great-grandfather. He spent a year working for J.P. Morgan in New York, then returned to London to become managing director of Baring Brothers & Co. investment bank at the age of 29. After eleven years there Baring returned to the US in 1959 on behalf of the British government. He served for two years as Economics Officer at the British Embassy and simultaneously UK Director of the IMF and World Bank. (Bolton had been the alternate UK director, from 1952 to 1957.) There, Baring acquired data and knowledge of euromarkets.[17]

In 1961 Baring was offered and accepted the role of Governor of the Bank of England (discussed below). The other two contenders were the chairmen of Lloyds Bank and Morgan Grenfell bank. Baring returned to London at the age of 43, the youngest Governor in 200 years. As Governor from 1961 to 1966, Baring was arguably the world's top banking regulator.

By 1962 he had advanced London's role as an international financial center by encouraging what he called an 'entrepot business in capital'.[18] Under Baring's governorship the Bank of England was fully aware of eurodollar developments. In its June 1964 *Quarterly Economic Bulletin*, the Bank wrote: 'Banks in London have been able to attract large sums in dollars [. . .] They are able to operate on a fairly small profit margin because the additional overhead expenses of conducting their Eurodollar activities are minimal.'

[17] Baring and his wife Esme also entertained many of the most important financial and political players in New York and Washington, DC at that time. Esme (née Harmsworth) Cromer, *From This Day Forward* (Stoke Abbot: Thomas Harmsworth, 1991). *Who's Who* lists Baring as the Managing Director of Baring Bros. & Co. through 1961. Thanks to Eton College for this reference.

[18] George 'Rowley' Baring (Lord Cromer), Governor of Bank of England, speech October 1962.

On leaving the Bank of England, he returned to Baring Brothers as the senior managing partner from 1966 to 1970. From 1967 to 1970 he also chaired the OECD high level committee on capital movements. Simultaneously he chaired the City's powerful Accepting Houses Committee, which determined which banks could provide specified services. Baring quietly lobbied on their behalf. In 1970 he became Chair of a consortium US-European bank, the London Multinational Bank, which was involved with eurocurrency deposits and eurobonds. Its partners included Chemical Bank, Credit Suisse, and Northern Trust of Chicago.

Baring returned to Washington as Britain's Ambassador to the US between 1970 and 1974, during the period of American suspension of gold-convertibility of the dollar and the end of Bretton Woods exchange measures. He then resumed his chairmanship of London Multinational Bank from 1974 to 1977. He also served on the boards of and advised various companies, including Morgan Guaranty Trust, Union Carbide, and IBM-UK.[19] He retired to Jersey in 1981, and died on 16 March 1991. His death was honored by then-President George H.W. Bush, and three former British Prime Ministers, among others.

In both the private and public sectors, Rowley Baring supported the free flow of capital, without regulatory barriers. In 1973 Baring wrote (in Pringle 1973: xi): 'the establishment of London as an international financial centre [. . .] has been largely due to freedom from detailed banking legislation.' The creation of offshore banking was not a case of government officials being overwhelmed by an anonymous market herd. Bolton blazed the way for offshore finance, with the knowledge and support of Governors Cobbold and Baring; they were joined by many others.

## 6. The Bank of England supported City banks

The two preceding portrayals should help rectify the myth that offshore finance was the result of an anonymous herd of renegade financiers. Although BOLSA and Baring were led by powerful bankers and regulators who took the lead in creating offshore eurodollar markets in London and in the Caribbean, they could not have succeeded if they had not been joined by many others in the private sector. They also received the approval of the Bank of England.

The Bank of England was the dominant British authority for the regulation of international banking, even though bureaucratic turf battles occasionally pitted it against the Treasury or other government ministries. The details of the Bank of England's relationship with the executive branch of

[19] Some sources say he also returned to the family bank; Stephen Fay reports 'Barings decided not to take him back'.

government are complex, but for starters they can be summarized neatly: the Bank ensured that London's financial system was strong, and the executive branch largely left it alone.[20] With various ups and downs, that autonomy lasted for centuries. It declined some during World War II and the Bank was nationalized in 1946, but the Bank retained control over most regulatory matters. The Bank of England exhibited complete authority on offshore finance, and had enormous influence on broader policies such as currency devaluation. In June 1998 the formal supervision of banking was turned over to the newly created non-governmental organization, the Financial Services Authority (FSA). Although occasionally portrayed as a shake-up of the way in which London regulates finance, the FSA is funded by the financial services industry and its Board includes the current Deputy Governor of the Bank of England and executives from Citigroup, ABN-Amro, and HSBC. The FSA's current chairman is Howard Davies, former Deputy Governor of the Bank of England.

For over 300 years London's preeminence as the world's greatest financial center has centered around the so-called 'Old Lady of Threadneedle Street'. Modern banking grew up around 'The City', which refers to the unity of the Bank of England and London's private bankers in the 'Square Mile' around the Bank. Since World War II, most of the Bank's Governors were or became prominent bankers. These include Lord Catto 1944–1949 (Morgan Grenfell bank), Rowley Baring 1961–1965 (Baring Bros.), Gordon Richardson 1973–1983 (Schroders bank), and Robin Leigh-Pemberton 1984–1996 (National Westminster bank). Throughout the period under review, the Bank of England remained supportive of offshore finance.

In Bolton's first three years at BOLSA, from 1957 to 1960, he was supported by Bank of England Governor Cobbold, with whom he had a close working relationship. The 'Cobbold–Bolton era of intermittent radicalism' was how one former Bank of England Executive Director and chronicler, John Fforde, referred to their time together. Bolton was disappointed to have been passed over as Governor himself. Four years older than Cobbold, he acted largely on his own authority and Cobbold supported him. In the following years (1961–1966), Bolton's decisions were supported by Governor Baring, discussed in detail above, and then by Baring's appointed successor, Governor Leslie O'Brien, 1966–1973.

In January 1963 Governor Cobbold drafted a letter to Charles Hambro of Hambros Bank, stating the Bank of England's clear support for the eurodollar business. It suggests his fear of capital flight (that is *de facto* relocation competition-in-laxity):

[20] Independent central banks pose a conceptual challenge for narrow Realist views of a unitary state actor embodied in the head of state. See Eugenia and Mark Toma (eds.), *Central Bankers, Bureaucratic Incentives, and Monetary Policy* (Kluwer Academic Publishers, Dordrecht 1986).

It is *par excellence* an example of the kind of business which London ought to be able to do both well and profitably. That is why we, at the Bank, have never seen any reason to place any obstacles in the way of London taking its full and increasing share. If we were to stop the business here, it would move to other countries with a consequent loss of earnings for London. [. . .] To drive the business from London would be wrong as it would continue in other places and the reputation of London as a monetary centre would suffer in the process.[21]

In short, Cobbold preferred laxity to the possibility of losing market-share.

The Bank of England deliberately encouraged this deregulated environment in London for decades. In the mid-1980s the Bank played a fundamental role behind the scenes in shaping the Parkinson–Goodison bill at the heart of the October 1986 Big Bang of deregulation. Big Bang very quickly drew to London up to half the turnover in large French and Italian shares and a quarter of large German shares. In 2001 Governor Eddie George offered a retrospective on 'the impact of tax and regulation on financial institutions and markets'. He noted that 'a large part of the reason why London became the centre of activity for the Euromarkets was that it was considered [. . .] "a very warm place for doing business". That much, I hope, has not changed over the subsequent decades, and I like to think that the Bank of England has played its part in making it so.'[22] Generally, the Bank of England stood ready to help, willing to accept the loss of national control over interest rates and flows of funds in exchange for the growth in the City's business and influence. But it was private bankers who led the way.

## 7. US BANKERS EXPANDED THE OFFSHORE SYSTEM

A similar pattern of bank initiatives and central bank support emerged in the US (despite the differences in banking culture with Britain). These are discussed below in turn, beginning with US bank activities in euromarkets, then the Caribbean.

### 7.1 US bankers in euromarkets

Although British banks and regulators blazed the way for offshore finance beginning in 1958, American banks and regulators were not far behind. They pursued offshore markets in London and in the Caribbean, accounted for 32 per cent of eurodollar deposits by year-end 1962, and were dominant in eurodollar markets by 1965 (Schenk 1998: 230).

American banks opened a presence in London in part to service US corporate clients who had begun to expand their foreign direct investments, and

[21] Letter from H.B. Mynors to Sir Charles J. Hambro. Drafted and vetted by Governor Cobbold, 29 January 1963. BE EID 10/22. Quoted in Schenk (1998: 236).

[22] George in Robert and Arnander 2001.

in part to participate in euromarkets. London's City was open to US and other international banks. When Bolton first moved to BOLSA in 1957 there were roughly eighty such banks in London. A decade later, in 1967, there were 114. This grew to over 150 in 1970, to over 240 by 1973, and to 447 in 1986. It was Chase Manhattan Bank's chair who said in 1985 that London's City is 'a very warm place for doing business'.[23]

US banks led developments in euromarkets with rapid innovations in finance, such as euro CDs and floating-rate notes. J.P. Morgan bank had long-standing ties to London, and its CEO Preston Lewis was instrumental in leading Morgan to trade in eurodollars early on. Citibank played a significant role as well. The *Wall Street Journal* opined on 6 May 1975: 'A cynic might say that the banks of the United States are divided into two classes. The first class is composed of First National City Bank of New York [Citibank] and the second is composed of all the others.' Walter Wriston of Citibank is credited with establishing negotiable certificates of deposit (CDs) in the early 1960s, to get around Regulation Q interest rate caps. Soon after, Wriston hired a young anthropologist, named Michael von Clemm, to work in London. Von Clemm made a name for himself by proposing that Citibank issue dollar-based euro CDs, in partnership with the European investment bank White Weld, Inc. The idea came from an official in Bernie Cornfield's Swiss-based Investors Overseas Service (IOS). 'IOS had $50 million to play with and wondered if Citibank issued certificates of deposit in Eurodollars.'[24] Citibank was also the first to ask for and receive Bank of England permission to issue sterling-based CDs. Euro CDs became the standard euromarket product. Von Clemm went on to become the chair of Credit Suisse/First Boston, then joined Merrill Lynch. Bernie Cornfield went on to help form the Fund of Funds in the Bahamas; later his IOS would later be taken over by Robert Vesco and both would be indicted.

## 7.2 US bankers in the Caribbean

American banks also greatly expanded the use of Caribbean offshore centers. American tax evaders had used the Bahamas during the 1930s, and alleged mobster Meyer Lansky moved his operations there in 1959 when Castro confiscated his Havana casinos. However, the legitimate Bahamian market for American banks was expanded, once again, by First National City Bank (Citibank) and by Chase Manhattan. They opened branches in Nassau in 1960, two years after BOLAM was headquartered there. Other banks and financial firms followed, large and small. These included John

[23] Quoted in John Plender and Paul Wallace, *The Square Mile: A Guide to the New City of London*, 1985: 32. Data on US branches in London from *The Banker*, various years.

[24] Michael Moffitt, *The World's Money*, 1983. See also Jones (1993: 325) and Collins (1988: 378).

Templeton's Fund of Funds (by 1962), and George Soros' Quantum Fund.[25]

Member banks of the US Federal Reserve greatly expanded the Caribbean offshore markets. In 1968 alone, twenty such banks applied to establish branches in Nassau, in order to participate in euromarkets. The number of American banks' branches in the Bahamas jumped from 1969 onward, surpassing their number of branches in London by 1971. Outstanding loans from US branches in the Bahamas doubled to $US6.9 billion from $US3.3 billion a year earlier. These Caribbean branches helped US firms gain market share over their rivals in London. Competition in London had decreased banks' spread from 0.75 per cent to 0.5 per cent in 1971, prompting G.A. Costanzo, Executive VP from First National City Bank to 'raise the question for some banks as to why they should be in the Eurodollar market at all'.[26] The Caribbean centers offered lower costs of doing business, enhanced by more lax process regulations. The regulatory impact was a movement toward a lower common denominator, among competing jurisdictions.

The impact on profits of US money-center banks from their overseas expansion in this period was dramatic. Annual reports show that from 1970 to 1974 the percentage of total earnings which came from overseas activities doubled or tripled for most of the seven money-center banks. Costanzo of Citibank exulted: 'In our wildest dreams we didn't think it would turn out as well as it has.' On average, overseas profits rose from 21 per cent of total profits in 1970 to 47 per cent in 1974.[27] This growth in profits is not necessarily because of the shell companies; part of the causality is the other way around: banks wanted a lax and low-tax regulatory environment through which to channel their profits, and they were granted it.

## 8. US GOVERNMENT SUPPORT OF OFFSHORE FINANCE

Regulation of banking in the US is shared between several branches and departments of government. For large banks in the US the top banking authority is the Federal Reserve. Smaller banks are regulated by the FDIC

[25] Thanks to Pierre Rinfret for calling John Templeton to the author's attention; personal communication, January 2002. Templeton moved to Lyford Cay, Nassau and became a British citizen in 1964; his managed funds grew to more than $US20 billion. Templeton was honored for his philanthropic support of religious studies, by various heads of state from the US, Britain, and other countries, throughout the 1990s.

[26] G.A. Costanzo, quoted in Stanley Penn, 'Your Bank's "Nassau Office" May Be Just a Desk and Chair—But Looks are Deceiving', *Wall Street Journal*, 5 July 1972, 26.

[27] G.A. Costanzo, quoted in Edward Foldessy, 'US Banks Find Money in Offices Abroad; Foreign Profit Gains Outpace Home Results', *Wall Street Journal*, 26 May 1972, 28. Bank profits earned overseas increased from 1970 to 1974 as follows: Citicorp from 40% to 62%, Bankers Trust from 16% to 52%, Chase Manhattan from 22% to 49%, Manufacturers Hanover 13% to 47%, J.P. Morgan from 25% to 45%, Bank of America from 19% to 39%, Chemical Bank NY from 10% to 33%.

and Office of the Comptroller of the Currency (OCC), located in the Treasury Department. The Internal Revenue Service (IRS, also in Treasury), Justice Department, and Congress have also weighed in on regulatory matters. US banks and bank associations have therefore had a broader range of points within the government to monitor and to influence. Despite occasional investigations and reviews, they generally received support for their offshore activities.

## 8.1 The Federal Reserve

The US Federal Reserve is the top regulator of US banks' foreign operations, under section 25 of the 1913 Federal Reserve Act, enacted by President Woodrow Wilson.[28] The US Federal Reserve revised Regulation K in 1957, the same year that George Bolton became head of BOLSA. Regulation K authorized the creation of overseas corporations under the 1917 Edge Act to hold equity positions in overseas banks and to own and finance non-banking foreign operations. US banks had initially moved overseas to service their corporate clients' foreign direct investments, but they began to compete with foreign banks overseas, and to use overseas markets as a source of funds for domestic US markets. At the behest of major US banks, the US government supported these overseas activities in a variety of ways.

In contrast to the McFadden Act, which prohibited domestic branching across state lines, these export-oriented Edge Act Corporations could be set up anywhere inside the USA, and could operate domestically or abroad. In contrast to Glass-Steagall laws, which from 1933 to 1999 separated commercial banks, investment banks, and other financial services, US banks abroad could underwrite securities and own investment banks and insurance companies. In contrast to the Sherman and Clayton Anti-Trust Acts (but consistent with the Webb-Pomerone Act) US firms operating overseas were exempt from antitrust provisions. In contrast to Regulation D, reserve requirements did not initially apply to deposits at foreign branches. Reserve requirements (in the absence of bank failures) would increase the cost of doing business, hence US banks could lend more cheaply in London. (The Bank of England also imposed no reserve requirements on non-sterling deposits, and it allowed securities to be issued in foreign currencies.) In short, the US had two sets of regulations, one for domestic companies and one for US subsidiaries operating overseas, designed to enhance their international competitiveness. These are arguably steps in competitive deregulation.

[28] Overall, 12 of the 19 US Federal Reserve Board members are effectively selected by commercial banks. The Board consists of 7 governors appointed for near-lifetime 14-year terms by the President, one of whom the US President designates Chair for a 4-year term, subject to Senate confirmation. They are joined by 12 regional Federal Reserve Bank presidents, who are chosen by regional committees. These regional committees consist of 6 directors chosen by the top commercial banks in each region (known as 'member banks' of the Federal Reserve System) and three directors chosen by the Board.

The Federal Reserve liberalized the activities of US banks operating abroad in 1963, when it revised Regulation M such that bank branches could now 'exercise powers (with certain exceptions) that are usual abroad'. These powers included setting up mutual funds, corporate underwriting, and offering client confidentiality, all activities prohibited to banks within the USA. The Federal Reserve again revised Regulation M in 1967 to permit direct ownership of foreign bank stock. Regulation Q had long limited the interest that banks in the USA could pay, but it did not apply to their overseas activities. The higher rates available outside the USA encouraged customers to deposit and borrow dollars abroad. By 1969 the Federal Reserve had authorized the growth of branches in the Bahamas and the Caymans.

The impact of these relaxed regulations governing overseas finance was significant. In 1958 there were only nine Edge Act subsidiaries. By 1973 there were 103, each of which could own other foreign subsidiaries. By 1996 there were 850 Edge Act bank subsidiaries. Many of these would be difficult to distinguish from their onshore owners, outside of their legal paper existence. Nearly 99 per cent of their assets were in the 378 'large' companies, each with more than $US50 million in assets. In fact, of these 378, the average value of assets per company was a sizable $US1.28 billion (Whalen, OCC 1998; Kelly 1977). Shell companies in the Caribbean were another vehicle by which large American firms joined and helped expand the London and eurocurrency markets.

US banking regulators were well aware of this growth, from the inception. A British observer described it as follows:

> Largely for tax reasons there has been a significant growth in shell branch activities in the Bahamas and Cayman Islands. In 1969 the Federal Reserve began to authorise the creation of these branches [. . .] Increasingly, however, the leading banks have begun to make use of the tax advantages offered by these locations. These operations are essentially an extension of activities in the London market, being primarily concerned with inter-bank activities.[29]

The overall growth of US branches and assets in the Caribbean was illustrated in Figures 3.3 and 3.4 above. The series of policy measures taken by the US Federal Reserve allowed that growth to occur.

The Federal Reserve Board (FRB) closely monitored the 1960s developments in the Bahamas. Two of the FRB's seven governors had some reservations about the rapid expansion of US banks there. James Robertson, Vice Chair of the Federal Reserve, felt banks should have the same privileges back in the USA: 'My primary objection is that they aren't branches in any sense of the word. They are simply desk drawers in somebody else's desk. Why

[29] Derek F. Channon, *British Banking Strategy and the International Challenge*, London: Macmillan (1977: 163). Channon offers no evidence for imputing the 'initial design' motive of the Fedederal Reserve.

make banks go through a sham proceeding to obtain certain privileges?'[30] Andrew Brimmer was concerned that the Nassau shell banks could hurt the US balance of payments, by attracting dollar deposits from Europe with a higher interest rate. Overall, Robertson and the five other governors approved of the offshore centers. The Federal Reserve noted that the Caribbean branches offered 'a means of avoiding the high cost of setting up branches in the Eurodollar market in London'.[31] The Federal Reserve deferred matters of criminal behavior to the Department of Justice and IRS. Overall, support from the highest regulator in the country was clear.

## 8.2 Other US government regulators

Although the Federal Reserve was the top regulator, other branches of government and other departments also influenced offshore finance. Rather than attempt an overview here of the complex US banking regulatory structure, a few policy examples and personal anecdotes illustrate their role. In general, they were responsive to bank lobbying.

A variety of broad-based US policies in the 1960s and 1970s helped create unintentional incentives for offshore finance. Most of these regulations applied only to domestic operations, they did not apply to overseas branches and subsidiaries of US banks. These developments are well known and include the impact of restrictions on financial products, reserve requirements, interest rate ceilings, capital controls, and financial disclosure requirements.[32] They also include the Interest Equalization Tax (IET 1963), the Foreign Credit and Exchange Act (FCEA 1965), and Foreign Direct Investment Restraint Program (FDIRP 1972). The IET made it more expensive for foreign borrowers to get dollar loans by penalizing the sale of foreign securities to US investors. The FCEA restricted US bank credit to foreigners and the FDIRP compelled US firms to finance their foreign investments using foreign markets. These effectively encouraged US multinationals to keep surplus offshore funds in the eurobond and eurodollar markets. The demand for dollar loans then switched to banks and branches outside the US, creating an incentive for US banks to establish branches abroad.

It is not clear how well the Kennedy and Johnson administrations anticipated the impact of these policies. Some bankers did. When the IET was enacted in July 1963, the head of Morgan Guaranty, Henry Alexander, reportedly gathered together his senior colleagues and forecasted: 'This is a day that you will remember forever. It will change the face of American

30 'Banks that Seek Branches in the Bahamas Run Into Delay', *New York Times*, 2 October 1968.

31 'Reserve Board Allows 14 US Banks to Open Branches in Bahamas', *Wall Street Journal*, 21 February 1969.

32 See James Hawley's laudable *Dollars and Borders: US Government Attempts to Restrict Capital Flows, 1960–1980.*

banking and force all the business to London. It will take years to get rid of this legislation' (Kynaston 2001: 280). The IET was, in fact, gotten rid of in 1974. Offshore finance remained.

The Secretary of Treasury himself has generally supported offshore finance, even if various divisions within the US Treasury Department (notably the IRS, and occasionally the OCC and Secret Service) expressed concerns about it. President Eisenhower's famous Secretary of Treasury, Robert Anderson, himself founded the World Banking Corporation in Nassau after leaving office in 1961. Anderson had also served as Deputy Secretary of Defense and Secretary of the Navy and Eisenhower once said he deserved to be President. His reputation drew customers.[33] (Anderson would later develop business ties with Vesco and Cornfield. In the mid-1980s he pled guilty to charges of illegally running an offshore bank and income tax evasion.) Other Secretaries and Under Secretaries at Treasury and State have also been supportive.

George Ball was appointed Under Secretary of State for Economic Affairs in January 1961, by President Kennedy. He had first met Siegmund Warburg, the father of eurobonds, in 1947. Ball was Warburg's 'close friend and main channel of influence in Washington, DC' who 'encouraged [Warburg] to create financial markets in dollars outside the United States' (Attali 1985: 246). After leaving office in 1968, Ball became chair of Lehman Bros. until 1982.

Assistant Treasury Secretary Paul Volcker (later Chairman of the Federal Reserve) sought comment from the head of Morgan Guaranty's international bank, Walter Page, when the Johnson administration considered limiting eurodollar holdings of US banks abroad. Page said it would be the death of US banking abroad. The proposed regulation was subsequently dropped (Chernow 1990).

Similarly, a bill aimed at stopping tax evasion and fraud via foreign secret bank accounts was scrapped in late 1969, after lobbying by top banks. The bill had been drafted by the Nixon administration's Justice and Treasury Departments, including the IRS, and sent to Congress on 17 December 1969. Within days, top representatives of the First National City Bank, Chase Manhattan Bank, Bank of America, Chemical Bank and the American Bankers Association met with two authors of the bill, Eugene Rossides, the Assistant Secretary of the Treasury, and IRS Commissioner Randolph Thrower. The bankers urged them not to endorse the legislation, arguing that the proposed bill would complicate record-keeping. As a result of bank lobbying, the IRS, Treasury and State Departments, and the Nixon White House reversed their position, claiming the bill would be too burden-

[33] *The Wall Street Journal* later highlighted his activities: 'Former Treasury Secretary's Reputation Gets Him Into Big Business Ventures' (3 April 1973: 44).

some on banks. The Nixon administration withdrew its support of the bill, claiming that 'it went too far'.[34]

Robert Morgenthau, the US Attorney for the Southern District of New York, testified in Congress that banks opposed the Bank Secrecy Act for simple profit motives. Morgenthau had initiated tax fraud investigations with the late 1960s Foreign Bank Account Project, including cases of campaign contributions. He was removed from office on 15 January 1970, just a month after the bill was introduced. Ralph Nader charged that he was removed 'to assure that the Wall Street banking establishments would be protected'.[35]

In later amendments to the bill, bankers would receive support from an unlikely group, in another example of a 'Baptist and Bootlegger' coalition: the American Civil Liberties Union (ACLU), which was concerned about the Bank Secrecy Act's impact on individual privacy. Ultimately, under bureaucratic pressure from the Justice Department, a weakened version of the Bank Secrecy Act was passed and signed into law (PL 91-508) on 26 October 1970. As Carl Desch, Senior VP at First National City Bank, said: 'It was a motherhood bill [. . .] a hard bill for bankers to oppose. Who doesn't want to get the tax dodger with the Swiss numbered account?'[36] Bankers did not get everything they wanted, but they had substantial success.

A number of colorful political figures also became involved in these offshore centers. Their role in developing offshore centers may be relatively small, but they signal high-level US government knowledge and support of the centers, even outside the Federal Reserve. A few examples are listed here.

The Nixon administration also condoned offshore havens for pecuniary reasons. Illegal campaign contributions to the Committee to Re-Elect the President coming from major corporations and individuals, including Robert Vesco, were allegedly funneled through the Bahamas by Commerce Secretary Maurice Stans and Attorney General John Mitchell. SEC Chair William Casey (later Reagan's CIA director) had begun an investigation into Vesco, unaware of his ties to Nixon. Casey was moved up and out to become Under Secretary of State for Economic Affairs in February 1973, and Nixon replaced him with 35-year-old Bradford Cook, a Republican Securities and Exchange Commission attorney. Also in 1973, Richard Allen

[34] 'Nixon Aides Bow On Foreign Banks', *New York Times*, 24 December 1969: 1.

[35] 'Big Cases Remain as Morgenthau Leaves', *New York Times* (*NYT*), 16 January 1970; 'Nader Sees Cabal To Protect Banks', *NYT*, 6 February 1970; 'Tangled Web', *Wall Street Journal*, 1 July 1974; 'Foreign Bank Accounts', Letters to the Editor, *NYT*, 11 March 1970; 'Panel Votes Curb on Swiss Accounts', *NYT*, 18 March 1970; 'House Votes Curb on Fraud in Using Swiss Accounts', *NYT*, 26 May 1970; 'Senators Clash on Banking Curb', *NYT*, 3 August 1970; 'Senate Votes Controls on Funds Hidden Away in Foreign Banks', *NYT*, 19 September 1970.

[36] 'Bankers, Civil Libertarians Unite to Fight US Law Making Bank Accounts Less Secret', Richard Leger, *WSJ*, 29 June 1972: 34. The amended bill limited IRS and other Treasury divisions' access to bank records, and did not restrict American citizens' purchases of US stocks abroad to evade taxes, among other changes.

(Nixon National Security Council member, later Reagan's NSC advisor) consulted to Vesco's attorney (Howard Cerny) 'to examine the prospects for establishment of an "off-shore" or unregulated financial center on one of the Azores, similar to those in the Bahamas and elsewhere'. Allen introduced Cerny to Casey.[37] The IRS had begun to investigate tax evasion in the Bahamas by the 1960s, in Operation Tradewinds and Operation Havens. IRS agent Richard Jaffe was accused of going too far in his investigations of prominent tax evaders, who allegedly included Nixon supporters. Nixon's IRS Commissioner, Donald Alexander, brought Jaffe under criminal investigation in 1975, and the investigations were suspended. (The charges were later dropped.[38])

The Office of the Comptroller of the Currency (OCC), which regulates smaller domestic banks, offered little resistance to offshore banking in general. The senior deputy for banking supervision, Paul Homan, defended the usefulness of establishing offshore branches in 1979, arguing that eurodollar markets made them more competitive with foreign banks. He acknowledged that the Bahamas and Cayman Islands did not permit access to OCC examiners.[39]

Again, these political appointees did not create the offshore system; but neither did they go out of their way to regulate it. Their main importance to the offshore finance story is that they reveal government support for offshore bankers at a crucial time of expansion.

Overall, US bankers' expansion into the Caribbean centers was supported by the top US regulators as a way to increase US banks' access to London and the international financial markets. These offshore centers are a reflection of the influence of firms and the power of the Federal Reserve over other US bureaucracies such as the Customs Service and IRS in the Treasury Department and the FBI and Drug Enforcement Agency in the Department of Justice.

Offshore centers reflect the priority given to mobilizing capital over other government goals, sometimes conflicting, such as systemic stability, providing transparent information to investors, raising taxes, catching offshore

[37] Peter Osnos, 'The Republicans in Detroit; Link Between Reagan Aide And Vesco Raises Concern', *Washington Post*, 15 July 1980, A12.

[38] Personal communication with Jaffe, March 1999. US Congress Committee on Government Operations, Subcommittee on Commerce, Consumer and Monetary Affairs, Oversight Hearings into the Operations of the IRS, October 1975. On allegations of who was on the list Jaffe was investigating, see testimony by witness TW-24, p. 79. See also: 'Corporate Bagmen are Probed', Jack Anderson and Les Whitten, *Washington Post*, 2 August 1976; *New York Times* (*NYT*) series by Marilyn Church and Martin Arnold, 26 March, 30 March, and 2 April 1974; 'IRS Chief Heard of Scofflaws', *NYT*, 7 October 1975; 'Alexander's IRS Job Imperiled by Fight Tied to Halting Tax-Evasion Inquiry', *NYT*, 8 October 1995; 'IRS Head's Old Firm in Bank Inquiry', *NYT*, 27 October 1975; 'Bahamas' Castle Bank Ceases Its Operations, Blames Probe by IRS', *WSJ*, 5 May 1977; 'Judge Asserts Casey, CIA Chief, Misled Stock Buyers in '68', *NYT*, 15 July 1981.

[39] US Congress, Ways and Means Committee, Subcommittee on Oversight, hearings on offshore tax havens, April 1979: 348.

tax-evaders and criminals, and stopping the flow of drugs and money laundering. Offshore centers are not necessarily a sign that recent 'globalization' has changed the power dynamic of business–state relations, nor changed the role of the state in the international system. US financial institutions' competitive position *vis-à-vis* their foreign competitors was strengthened, not weakened, by the Regulation K/Edge Act and authorization of shell companies. The US Federal Reserve acted to promote the interests of the dominant US banks and other financial institutions (and arguably the US and global financial system as well) just as the Bank of England had acted to promote the interests of London's City. The international outcome stems from the 'old wine' of domestic bureaucratic politics and political economy.

## 9. Supply: Who offers 'offshore banking' and why?

For the British and American governments, the goal of allowing offshore financial activity in the City and IBFs was to enhance the competitiveness of their financial sectors in London and New York, while keeping an eye on that activity.

For small island country governments, the benefits were substantial and straightforward. The conditions which allowed for the emergence of offshore financial centers, and the incentives for the offshore state, were similar to those for convenience-flag states. They benefitted in terms of employment, economic growth, and tax revenues. For example, by 1990 nearly 20 per cent of the Caymans' employment came from offshore companies, as it did in Britain's Channel Islands. The Cayman government earned $US20 million a year from registration and licence fees (about the same amount as Liberia earned from shipping registration fees). In Guernsey and Jersey, 55 per cent of GDP came from offshore companies; in Bermuda it was 30 per cent. In Jersey, 88 per cent of government revenue came from offshore activities. Roughly 100,000 companies were registered in the four Channel Islands by 1998. The pool of financial talent developed in an offshore center can also increase the country's access to global capital markets, improve a state's own financial system, and attract foreign direct investment (Palan and Abbott 1996: 177; Hampton 1994: 244–5).

Similar to the developments that occurred in the US state of Delaware, over time dominant offshore havens developed a variety of other attributes which attracted business. These attributes included network advantages of clusters of expertise and skilled services in law, accounting, and judicial treatment, reputation, and so on. The more dominant havens may favor some more stringent regulations.

## 10. 'Dogs that growled but didn't bite'

Offshore finance avoids a host of specific domestic regulations and many havens' existing regulations lack the 'bite' of enforcement. Despite occasional efforts by agencies such as the British Parliament, Inland Revenue, US Congress, IRS, DEA, and FBI to regulate offshore finance more stringently, bureaucratic control of the issue has been dominated by central bankers and top Treasury officials. Offshore finance grew as a result of decisions made by American and British bankers and regulators in the 1950s to encourage the re-liberalization of international financial markets, following the financial nationalism that had grown out of the two World Wars.

### 10.1 *Subcase*: Some movement upward

In select instances, some members of the financial community sought more stringent regulation when it was to their competitive advantage. For example, in 1975 US brokerage firms pressured the SEC to increase its regulatory supervision of foreign companies. The brokerages had long argued that foreign firms benefitted from a lax regulatory environment, thereby circumventing US securities regulations and gaining an unfair advantage in US markets. Securities and Exchange Commission Chairman Roderick Hills backed them up.[40] In 1998 a number of Western private sector banks suffered when Russian criminals laundered $US70 billion through the tiny Pacific island of Nauru. Citicorp and other leading banks had two main responses to policy proposals. First, any US-led initiatives had to be homogenous (multilateral). Second, the banks wanted to be told specifically which havens were bad actors. Within two years, these demands were met.

In February 2000 the US, the UK, and other major financial powers agreed, through the OECD's Financial Action Task Force (FATF), on a 'name and shame' strategy to blacklist fifteen jurisdictions which did not meet their criteria for co-operating in the fight against money laundering.[41] The list has been updated several times since. This listing and consultations with the FATF has improved money-laundering conditions in a number of these territories and countries. Notably, the offshore powerhouses of the Bahamas, the Caymans, Liechtenstein, and Panama appeared on the first list in 2000 but spruced up their oversight by 2001 and were removed from the blacklist. Israel, Lebanon, and St Kitts and Nevis were removed by 2002. Six new countries were added in 2001: Egypt, Grenada, Guatemala, Indonesia, Myanmar, and Nigeria, and—in 2002—Ukraine. Eight countries remained

[40] Roderick Hills' testimony, Oversight Hearings Before a Subcommittee of the Committee on Government Operations, US House of Representatives, 94th Congress, 2nd Session, June/July 1976.

[41] See www.oecd.org/fatf/ and www.fatf-gafi.org/, accessed February 2003.

on the list throughout: the Cook Islands, Dominica, Marshall Islands, Nauru, Nieu, the Philippines, Russia, and St Vincent and the Grenadines. Such a list could have been developed at any time, in principle, and could cover not just money laundering but any other regulation or policy objective agreed upon. Nonetheless, the list did have some impact, moving some financial flows away from such countries as Nauru, thus arguably raising standards from the very bottom of the barrel.

Likewise in the UK, the Financial Services Authority (FSA) was created on 20 May 1997 to manage banking supervision and investment services regulation. The FSA is financed by the financial services industry. In June 1998 formal responsibility for banking supervision was transferred to the FSA from the Bank of England but, as noted above, a former BoE Deputy Governor chairs the FSA and a current BoE Deputy Governor sits on the board, along with financial executives. The FSA has undertaken a variety of measures to combat money laundering. Its approach is more educational, identifying risks and best practices, than it is regulatory.[42] It is worthy of further study as a subcase, on reducing money laundering and terrorist funding operations while maintaining a 'warm environment for business'.

## 10.2 The continued laxity of offshore regulations

It would be a mistake, however, to deny that offshore finance generally is still anything but a case of competition-in-laxity.

The change of US administrations in January 2001 reversed the progress made by Larry Summers and Will Wechsler in the Clinton Treasury. In May 2001 Secretary Paul O'Neil said he 'had cause to re-evaluate the United States' participation' in the FATF. He went on to say:

> Although the OECD has accomplished many great things over the years, I share many of the serious concerns that have been expressed recently about the direction of the OECD initiative. [. . .] The United States simply has no interest in stifling the competition that forces governments [*sic*]—like businesses—to create efficiencies. [. . .] In its current form, the project is too broad and it is not in line with this Administration's tax and economic priorities.[43]

Council of Economic Advisers (CEA) head Larry Lindsey was equally critical of banking legislation. According to one former Treasury official: 'The Bush team originally did more than back off from pursuing them further, they originally sought to undermine what had already been accomplished.'[44] The Bush administration was poised to halt or reverse many of the regulations on offshore finance.

[42] UK Financial Services Authority, www.fsa.gov.uk/pubs/other/money_laundering.pdf, last visited 24 July 2003.

[43] US Treasury, Secretary O'Neill Statement on OECD Tax Havens, 10 May 2001, www.ustreas.gov/press/releases/po366.htm last visited 24 July 2003.

[44] Interview with the author, 21 March 2003.

The tragic events of 11 September 2001 had a twofold effect on the focus of OECD money-laundering regulations. Antiterrorism regulations were strengthened and enforced to crack down on Al Qaeda (and other predators caught in that net). Paradoxically, proposals for new regulations on offshore finance not related to terrorism were allowed to wither. Republicans on Capitol Hill and the Bush administration resisted until the very end the few anti-money laundering provisions that made it into the 'US Patriot Act'. The Justice Department did use section 319 of the Act to seize criminal funds from foreign banks' interbank correspondent accounts in the USA, but this did not apply to US banks. Treasury Secretary John Snow lamented (15 May 2003) that Saddam Hussein had hidden billions of dollars 'in the international financial system behind a maze of front companies and straw men'.

Amid the fervor after 9/11 some Congressmen proposed legislation to penalize 'unpatriotic' US firms (such as Black and Decker) who fled for tax havens, by making them ineligible for government contracts. Even before 9/11 various US Congressional bills in 2000 (sponsored by Congressman Jim Leach, Senator Charles Schumer, and others) would have authorized the US Treasury to quarantine any country which did not meet American banking standards. However, the preponderance of business lobbying squelched all of these proposals; too many powerful firms benefitted from offshore tax havens to be easily swayed.

Every detail of finance can be (and often has been) subjected to regulation. The late twentieth-century system of international finance was no more inevitable than was the creation and adaptation of the international financial institutions which maintain it, including private-sector interbank settlement institutions, the BIS, IMF, Bank of England, and Federal Reserve.

At one extreme, the US and British governments could have required their banks' foreign branches and subsidiaries to obey home country domestic regulations; or made it illegal for any home company to conduct business with an offshore financial center, seizing the assets of firms who violated the law; or barred any foreign (or domestic) firm which used an offshore center from doing business within their borders; or required banks to balance deposits and loans with the capital held by the bank within a given country; or imposed the same regulatory constraints on deposits of foreign currencies which they imposed on their own home currency; or imposed various liquidity ratios, reserve or capital requirements, and any number of other prudential or reporting requirements, for firms using offshore centers. By and large, they did not. One can argue that it is a good thing that none of these measures were broadly tried. They seem inconceivable today, and would cause widespread disruptions in financial markets and economies worldwide if implemented now. They would face enormous resistance from the business, policy, and academic spectrums (and would predictably lead to capital flight). However, at the dawn of the new global financial system, after World War II and into the 1970s, these policy measures were deliberated and decided on.

A host of other, less Draconian measures could still be adopted, and some are currently under consideration. Some proposed measures would more rigorously enforce greater accountability, transparency, reporting, or public disclosure of the funds which passed through every offshore center. Such measures would allow market mechanisms, such as Moody's or Standard & Poor's, to evaluate the financial risk these centers posed. (In 1994, for example, it was revealed that Nomura Securities had $US2.5 billion in losses hidden in a Cayman Islands subsidiary.) Other measures would increase the requirements on audit trails to identify the individuals liable for every transaction. Another measure is a variation on the proposed 'Tobin tax', a tax on transactions involving an offshore financial center and severe penalties for failure to disclose such transactions. Although never politically popular, 'taxes are what we pay for a civilized society', in Oliver Wendell Holmes, Jr.'s famous words. However, there is no international tax, and some argue that there is no international society.

That these and other measures were not undertaken, despite the conflicts with other policy goals such as financial stability and fighting crime, may be an example of regulatory chill.

The findings of this book suggest that the extent to which such measures are actually implemented will depend in large part upon the support of the major financial firms involved. The major banks' competitive advantage is not to compete with fly-by-night money launderers. One might expect them to support certain barriers to entry in the future, in the form of carefully crafted, stringent market-access regulations on offshore finance, to the extent that the added costs of regulation do not outweigh the gains of decreased competition.[45]

## 11. Offshore finance: Conclusion

This Chapter is by no means a complete account of offshore finance, but it does offer insights into the creation of that system—a system which accounted for over half of all international finance by the 1990s. Bankers generally favored lax process regulations: except in times of crisis, when they turned to governments for stability.

[45] As a caveat to future researchers, it takes considerable time and effort to unearth these details. Citicorp, panel report and internal interviews, 1990, 1999. See also the Basle Committee on Banking Regulations and Supervisory Practices, 'Statement on Prevention of Criminal Use of the Banking System for the Purpose of Money-Laundering' (December 1988); Gilmore 1992; and the OECD's Financial Action Task Force (FATF) 2000.

Bank crises include Baring's first failure in the 1880s, its last one in 1995, various Bank of England 'lifeboats' to bail out failed banks (e.g. 1973), the 1974 failures of Franklin Bank and Bankhaus Herstatt, the debt crisis sparked by Mexico in August 1982 and the US Treasury measures which helped resolve it around 1990, the BCCI collapse in July 1991, sterling's devaluation and Britain's withdrawal from the EC exchange rate mechanism in September 1992, Mexico's peso crisis in 1994, Daiwa Bank's $US1.1 billion losses in September 1995, the Asia–Russia–Brazil crises beginning in the Fall of 1997, and Long Term Capital Management failure in September 1998. In each of these cases governments were intimately involved in preserving market stability and reducing systemic risk. Financial markets are limited in their ability to achieve collective action solutions without leadership by central bank authorities. The specter of bankruptcy at that level is not played by the normal market rules. When prices, markets, or currencies collapse, a race to the exit is individually rational but collectively irrational, creating a potential downward spiral.

Normally, however, top regulators and especially central bankers have supported the move to liberalized markets. The mobility and liquidity of these non-specific assets facilitated this regulatory competition-in-laxity, in all four forms: relocation, market-share, *de jure*, and regulatory chill. The competition-in-laxity was facilitated: (1) *de facto* as banks relocated assets to offshore centers; (2) *de facto* as these less stringently regulated centers gained market share; (3) *de jure* as the US Federal Reserve changed its regulations governing overseas operations, as London underwent its Big Bang, and as the US, Japan, Thailand, and other centers created international banking facilities to bring banks back; and (4) arguably by 'regulatory chill' as prudential, transparency, and money-laundering regulations failed to make progress.[46]

The general trend toward fewer government controls should not be obscured by frequent clashes over the details of financial regulations and bureaucratic turf battles. If one were to believe that offshore finance emerged 'over the heads of regulators' or that it was 'inevitable' it would be hard to explain the early and important involvement of George Bolton, Rowley Baring, and other leading financiers and regulators. Conversely, governments did not pluck from the sky the idea of offshore finance, they followed the preferences of top bankers. It could have been equally 'inevitable', for instance, had New York simply taken over London's role (Kynaston 2001: 99). To the extent that liberalized financial markets are desirable, it is worth asking how the British and American governments 'got it right', and whether they could have moved any faster or made the global distribution of capital flows even more efficient, or equitable.

[46] The straw man outcome, that the entire world adopted the very lowest regulations of Nauru, did not occur.

The emergence of offshore banking centers parallels the shipping case, and predates by decades any discussion of 'globalization'. Some havens are both major offshore financial centers and FOCs, notably, Panama, Malta, and Cyprus. As with shipping, the wider case is one of competitive deregulation, alternating from heterogeneous laxity to a lower common denominator among competing states. The striking feature is the movement toward laxity. Competition led financial firms to seek jurisdictions with lax process regulations, to lower the cost of doing business. Offshore banking centers grew rapidly from the 1960s into the new century. They were encouraged by a wide variety of financial players, from the top bankers highlighted in this Chapter, to individual 'bootleggers', to the International Monetary Fund (IMF).[47]

A complete account would examine other centers, such as Liechtenstein and Luxembourg, Ireland, Hong Kong and Macau, Panama, Lebanon, Bahrain, the *hawala* system, and so on. It would also examine other reasons for the continued growth of offshore finance, including fixed exchange rates and their collapse, the OPEC boom of the 1970s, sovereign lending, new communication and computing technologies, globally linked financial markets, more details on regulatory asymmetries, increased cross-border trade (licit and illicit), balance of payments crises and dollars accumulated overseas by US trade deficits, capital controls, new financial products, greater confidence in international financial institutions, support from the International Monetary Fund and other institutions, higher domestic taxes and regulations, and the proliferation of new states, to name just a few. However, this book's three simple propositions explain a great deal of the offshore case, and are consistent across industries.

Overall, financial firms' search for favorable regulations led to a lower common denominator outcome, as regulations were *de facto* homogenized downward. By the late 1990s major onshore markets themselves had deregulated to such an extent that offshore centers were losing some of their attraction. 'Harmonization of tax regimes, financial liberalization under prudential oversight, and capital account liberalization have reduced the appeal of offshore banking for industrial economies, where the distinction between onshore and offshore banking has become progressively blurred' (Errico and Musalem 1999: 39).

[47] On regulatory asymmetries and the creation of offshore financial centers, see Richard Dale 1984 and 1992; the IMF 1984; Blum 1984; and BIS 1987. 'Regulation shopping' is not new. In the European Renaissance, Mediterranean bankers similarly escaped Catholic usury restrictions by using the Jewish diaspora and by lending abroad: Genoese bankers to Spain; Venetians to the Byzantine Empire; and Florentines to England and France. Fernand Braudel notes (1984: 157–169) that 'Genoa was the most extraordinary example of convergence and concentration the European world-economy had yet witnessed [. . .] Genoa's reign remained from beginning to end extremely discreet: comparable [. . .] with the Bank for International Settlements at Basle [today].'

It is important to remember that neither 'laxity' nor 'stringency' as used in this book implies a policy judgement. As in the shipping case, the creation of offshore finance has created enormous efficiencies in the allocation of capital worldwide. It may also have created problems for other policies, such as transparency, accountability, equity, and the enforcement of a wide variety of criminal laws. As the introductory quote from Ralph Winter suggests, weighing the merits and demerits of a lax or stringent legal system requires further empirical research, often on a case-by-case basis.

In short, state regulatory interests in shipping and banking were shaped by leading firms. Key decision-makers supported the relocation of these industries overseas, promoting a national interest defined in part by the leading private firms involved. These lax systems were not the result of 'escape' from a unified state, even though some less influential government agencies favored greater regulation. Ironically, this book's propositions suggest that it is the same large multinational corporations which are attacked by some critics whose support may be necessary to achieve the higher common regulations these critics seek.

Although this book begins with two significant cases of lower common denominator outcomes, it must be emphasized that LCD outcomes are by no means the necessary result of open economies, as the remainder of this book demonstrates. The symmetry of cases in this book elucidates the causes of each outcome and does not estimate their prevalence. Indeed, the evidence suggests that these cases are relatively rare, although important. The extreme ease and low cost of relocating ship registration, or moving funds to an offshore center, or incorporating a firm facilitated these competitions-in-laxity. By contrast, in more asset-specific investments, as in many if not most foreign direct investments, relocating would involve considerable cost. In fact, there is good reason to believe that open economies may move regulations 'up' (Vogel 1995). The next two Chapters analyze cases with higher common denominator outcomes; Chapters Six and Seven analyze cases of (higher) heterogenous outcomes.

## Appendix: Examples of other LCD cases

Delaware is both the sponsor and the victim of a system contributing to the deterioration of corporation standards. This unhappy state of affairs [stems] in great part from the movement toward the least common denominator.

William L. Cary, former Chair of the Securities and Exchange Commission (SEC), 1974

No one denies that Delaware's open bidding for corporate charters has led to a steady lessening of the restrictiveness of state corporation law. [. . .] The history of state corporation law is thus largely a history of drastic reduction of legal restrictions on management and of the legal rights of shareholders. This movement has not been at random but has rather occurred as corporations have sought charters in states with less restrictive codes. Other states have then adopted similar codes in response.

Ralph K. Winter, Jr. (1977)[48]

## Delaware incorporation

The incentives and pressures for a competition-in-laxity can occur domestically, as well as internationally. Within the USA, states compete to influence decisions by managers as to where to charter their corporations. US state laws have jurisdiction over major corporate issues such as fiduciary responsibilities owed to stockholders, the distribution of power between managers and stockholders, and mergers and dissolutions.

There is an unambiguous pattern of migration of charters to states with regulations favoring corporations, in particular to Delaware. More than 50 per cent of all publicly traded US corporations were chartered in Delaware by the 1970s. Approximately 80 to 90 per cent of those firms which reincorporated between 1925 and 1983 relocated to Delaware.[49]

Delaware eventually attracted corporations via favorable corporate laws (not lower taxes). The general trend was toward deregulation.[50] By 2000, 30 per cent of its total tax collection came from corporate franchise taxes, amounting to $US3,000/household. Further revenues were generated from the well-paid legal and accounting industry in the state.

A similar trend occurred in Pennsylvania, which lost eighteen firms between 1960 and 1968, then revised its code to reflect Delaware's more firm-friendly provisions. Pennsylvania then gained twelve firms. Similarly, several firms left Michigan for Delaware, then returned to Michigan after Michigan revised its code to resemble Delaware's. In another example, Microsoft moved its charter from Washington State to Delaware in 1986, out of concern over the liability limits of its directors. In order to bring back Microsoft's charter, Washington revised its business laws in 1993 to let

[48] Winter defended Delaware, arguing that shareholders' control over stock constrains degenerative competition. Legal and economic studies debate who benefits from state competition for charters.

[49] Romano 1985: 225–283; and 1987. See also Fischel 1982; Charny 1991; Bebchuk 1992; and 2002; Nader *et al.* 1976 cited by Winter; and citations to literature on law and economics in the first and last Chapters of this book.

[50] Delaware also led in a number of laws which offer protection to corporate officers against liability suits and hostile takeovers. These did not impose a differential cost to firms. See Choi, Kamma, and Weintrop 1989. Delaware's 'poison pill' statutes, designed to thwart hostile takeover attempts, could be adopted by firms without shareholders' approval. Most studies conclude that these statutes have negative wealth effects on shareholders. Delaware offered a credible commitment to maintain legal codes favorable to corporations: its human assets were invested in corporate law, its state constitution required a two-thirds majority to change incorporation codes, and it stood to lose a major source of revenues.

companies indemnify officers, and Microsoft returned.[51] Thus, the outcome is categorized here as 'common' among competing states.

## Other similar cases

This Chapter has focused on banks and the banking supply side of offshore finance, but one could equally look at bank clients and customers on the demand side, notably the large corporations whose financial needs were increasingly met through offshore finance, beginning in the early 1960s. Enron's 2,832 offshore subsidiaries may (or may not) be an extreme case but virtually all large multi-national companies (MNCs) use offshore finance as a matter of course. Whether Enron could have fooled stock analysts, accountants, and investors without its offshore companies is an open question. Some aspects of the Enron case reveal the limits of corporate power. Enron had a market capitalization of $US63 billion and (through the efforts of its CEO, Kenneth Lay) was one of George Bush, Jr.'s biggest single campaign contributors, yet the company still went bankrupt and fell under SEC indictment amid widespread critical news coverage. Political influence was not enough to maintain a failed business model and corrupt accounting practices. Enron's lobbying expenditures for electricity deregulation, which amounted to $US30 million/year by some estimates, did impact regulations in a variety of US states and in countries overseas.

Much has been written about the 'competition in laxity' among various bank regulators within the domestic US banking system. Federal Reserve Chairman Arthur Burns warned of such a possibility in 1974, and the debate has continued. A 1992 US Federal Reserve Bank article concluded:

> Much of the blame for high rates of bank failure throughout the 1920s was placed upon competition between state and federal authorities. Because banks could choose the less costly of federal and state charters—and the associated regulations—state and federal regulators were forced into a 'competition in laxity' if they were to sustain the realm of their bureaucratic influence (Flood 1992: 51),

This competition-in-laxity has a similar logic to that found in the shipping and offshore banking cases.

Digital technologies and the internet vastly reduce the transaction costs of firms and may facilitate new forms of competition-in-laxity. Business models based on invasions of personal privacy, insider-trading, gambling, intellectual property, spam, child pornography, and other regulated activities may thrive in offshore havens (Leebron in Bhagwati and Hudec 1996). For example, the companies which replaced Napster (Kazaa, which then

[51] With Microsoft, Lotus Development Corporation and Ashton-Tate relocated their incorporation to Delaware. These were the three largest software developers in the world. States which lost the largest number of incorporations included New York, Illinois, California, New Jersey, Michigan, and Texas.

broke into Sharman and Blastoise) are headquartered in Vanuatu and the Channel Islands to avoid US copyright laws. Sharman asked US courts to dismiss a lawsuit against it on the grounds it has no assets in the USA.

In six of the seven surveys Levinson (1996) cites, environmental regulations played a role in industrial relocation within the USA. Levinson concludes the evidence is lacking, even though surveys underestimate controversial intent.

Some production standards in Europe have coalesced around lower standards, in limits on air and water effluents, lead, and PCBs, etc. (Golub 2000).

Cases from the WTO include Australia's laws on salmonella, US restrictions on Venezuela gasoline imports, Japan's fumigation process for imported fruit, Canada's import restrictions on Ethyl Corp's fuel additive (MMT), and Canada's export restrictions on PCB-contaminated waste.

Critics argue that the spread of genetically modified foods (GMOs) reflects the spread of *laissez-faire* US regulations. These debates are highly contentious.

Regulations affecting global climate change do not show a movement downward, but they have not moved upward as fast as some policy advocates would wish. This may reflect the logic of 'regulatory chill', although the conceptual and empirical implications need to be analyzed carefully. To date no binding regulations have been implemented. The Kyoto Treaty and Rio Convention goals are just beginning. Most proposed regulations have been on the process side, emphasizing energy efficiency in manufacturing processes. The bulk of most countries' assets are in support of domestic transactions. This book's propositions suggest that owners of these assets would resist the change to higher process regulatory outcomes. Product market-access regulations, conversely, might lead to higher but divergent outcomes. Large, powerful firms with specific investments across borders would likely push for common product market-access regulations. One sees some differentiation among firms' strategies, for example in the split between BP and ExxonMobil. On global warming issues, too, private interests are likely to influence the timing and shape of regulations.[52]

The share of tropical timber harvested under lax environmental harvesting process regulations grew considerably for decades. (Higher product market-access regulations and consumer boycotts have shifted some market share into sustainable practices, as discussed in later Chapters below). It is arguably another example of a 'market share *de facto* competition-in-laxity'.

Fisheries worldwide have seen stocks of fish drop dramatically. In the past fifty years, according to Myers and Worm (2003), 90 per cent of all large

[52] Thanks to members of a 1995 World Economic Forum panel and to Darby Jack for discussion of climate change. The panel included Henry D. Jacoby (MIT), Ronald G. Prinn (MIT), Robert E. Wilhelm (Exxon), and Kurt E. Yeager (EPRI).

fish (tuna, marlin, swordfish, sharks, cod, and halibut) have been depleted. Regulation of mass-harvesting has been limited, and fishing boats often 'flag-hop' (see Chapters Two above and Six below) to avoid existing regulations. Panetta *et al.* (2003) call for fundamental reforms of ocean policies.

When California enacted occupational health standards on workplace air quality, an archetypical process regulation, a large number of California's furniture refinishing industry relocated to Mexico's *maquiladora* border.

# PART III
# HIGHER COMMON DENOMINATOR

# 4

# *Montreal Protocol on Chlorofluorocarbons (CFCs)*

The Montreal Protocol has been widely heralded as a victory of international cooperation and good sense over powerful corporate interests that sought to block regulation. However, the perception that producer interests obstructed an international agreement—and that they had to be subdued to secure whatever environmental benefits the Protocol may generate—is seriously misleading. [. . .] In fact, at critical junctures, American CFC producers *supported* the Montreal Protocol.

Daniel F. McInnis 1992

On 16 September 1987 delegates from twenty-four major countries to the Montreal Convention reached agreement on the Protocol on Substances that Deplete the Ozone Layer.[1] As revised, the Protocol phased out production of chlorofluorocarbons (CFCs) by 1995, and reduced production of halons, carbon tetrachloride, and methyl chloroform.[2] The sale and distribution of new CFCs would be foreclosed. Trade sanctions would be imposed against countries not complying with the Protocol. The effect of the Protocol was widespread: 70 per cent of the US food supply depends on refrigeration at some point, and CFCs were the best coolant available. The global market for CFCs in 1990 totaled nearly two billion dollars. However, far from fighting the restrictions tooth and nail, as one might expect if one assumed industry opposed all regulations, dominant producers ended up supporting the Protocol. Indeed, by 1994 DuPont was poised to phase out CFC production early; in an ironic twist, the EPA requested DuPont to continue production for another year.

[1] Members of the MIT Chlorine Seminar clarified the scientific issues of this case for the author, whose research in this area was funded by a grant from the V. Kann Rassmussen Foundation and the MIT Initiative on Environmental Leadership. For a valuable constructivist approach to this case see Litfin 1994. More generally see Benedick 1991; Weiner and Maxwell in Ehrenfeld 1993. On the coalition of the 'green and the greedy' see Oye and Maxwell 1993. On epistemic communities see Haas 1992; Solingen 1993.

[2] The Montreal Protocol was made increasingly stringent in Helsinki in 1989, London in 1990, Copenhagen in 1992, Montreal in 1997, and Beijing in 1999. Unless otherwise specified, the entire set of agreements is referred to here loosely as the 'Montreal Protocol'. The London revision also included a non-binding resolution to phase out hydrochlorofluorocarbons (HCFCs) by 2030. The UNEP website www.unep.org/ozone/index.shtml, last visited 24 July 2003, maintains related documents.

This Chapter first summarizes the industrial structure and asset specificity in the CFC industry, then reviews heterogenous regulations in the 1970s. It next discusses the steps leading toward the 1988 Protocol, and the intimate role of industry in achieving that higher common denominator outcome.

## 1. Industrial structure and asset specificity in the CFC industry

It is necessary to understand the role of dominant multinational producers in order to understand this movement toward homogenous, stringent market access restrictions. Just over a dozen firms worldwide produced CFCs. The three largest were E.I. Du Pont de Nemours Company (DuPont) in the US, Imperial Chemical Industries (ICI) in the UK, and Elf-Atochem in France. (Elf Atochem purchased Pennwalt in 1989; it also owned Racon.) Each had large multinational investments. DuPont accounted for 25 per cent of the world market. It had factories in the USA, Canada, the Netherlands, Japan, and Latin America. In the USA, DuPont controlled nearly 50 per cent of the market and Allied Signal held another 25 per cent (Morrisette 1990: 15).

However, the major producers' hold on the market was slipping. As CFCs became an undifferentiated commodity and new competitors entered the market, prices fell and alternative uses of industry assets became more valuable. Importantly, asset specificity for CFC transactions was declining. Even before the Montreal Protocol took effect, ICI and others sunk large specific investments into substitutes for CFCs (see below). The asset specificity of substitutes investments was high but without government intervention to restrict CFCs the demand for substitutes would be low. Unlike in the shipping case, ICI and DuPont could not simply move production offshore, as the existent supporting business infrastructure would be too expensive to replace and the cost of transporting CFCs too high. Without government intervention to restrict CFCs, the value of these investments would be very low. In effect, ICI and DuPont moved away from market contracting and instead contracted with governments to retire CFCs. The Montreal Protocol was a transaction-specific regime. It created a *de facto* cartel for CFC producers, giving them hope for windfall profits to fund continued investments in CFC substitutes.

## 2. CFCs 1974–1985: Heterogeneous regulations on aerosols

From their invention in the 1930s through their widespread use by the 1960s, CFCs were hailed as a wonder. They replaced the more dangerous ammonia, sulphur dioxide, and ether vapor used in industry and offered many new uses. Concern about their environmental impact arose in 1970. DuPont and twenty other international CFC producers created the Fluorocarbon Technical Panel (FTP). The FTP spent over one million US dollars per year on independent research.

Concern over CFCs initially centered on supersonic transport (SST) jets, nuclear testing, and nitrogen-based fertilizers. Then, in 1974 Mario Molina and Sherwood Rowland demonstrated that CFCs could percolate into the upper atmosphere, release chlorine through decomposition, and catalytically destroy ozone.[3] Popular debate in the USA shifted to the use of CFCs in consumer aerosol sprays. Personal vanity, it seemed, might be destroying the earth.

In this unilateral US phase, new products emerged with the potential to replace CFCs as aerosol agents. The new business interests' investments were domestically specific. They used the aerosol debate to their advantage, promoting stick deodorants, mechanical pumps that were less expensive than aerosols, and other propellants such as butane (Leone 1986: 33 ff). The US market leader in consumer products, Johnson Wax, saw a first-mover advantage and in 1975 announced that it would phase out use of CFC propellants. Sales of non-aerosol deodorants jumped 800 per cent from 1975 to 1976, and non-aerosol hair-sprays captured nearly 25 per cent of the market (compared to only 4 per cent in 1973). Amid rising concern and movement among state legislatures Oregon banned CFC propellants and soon the federal government stepped in (Dotto and Schiff 1978).

CFC-competing industries actively supported proposed CFC aerosol bans, catching the major CFC producers off-guard. In 1976 the US Congress passed the Toxic Substance Control Act (TSCA), which gave the EPA discretionary powers to regulate all non-pharmaceutical and pesticide chemicals. In March 1978 the EPA and FDA issued regulations under TSCA and the Federal Food, Drug, and Cosmetic Act, which prohibited virtually all use of CFCs as propellants. The ban took effect December 1978. It destroyed 55 per cent of the US domestic CFC market. DuPont, with 25 per cent of world CFC production, saw its US market plummet 50 per cent. It was left with low profits and a CFC surplus.[4]

[3] Molina and Rowland (1974) pursued their research despite industry-funded criticism. Congressional hearings were soon held. DuPont's R.L. McCarthy testified that the chlorine-ozone hypothesis was at that time speculative, but 'If creditable scientific data [. . .] show that any chlorofluorocarbons cannot be used without a threat to health, DuPont will stop production of these compounds'. US House of Representatives, Committee on Interstate and Foreign Commerce, 11–12 December 1974.

[4] Benedick 1991: 24; McInnis 1992: 137. Data on market demand from Weiner and Maxwell (1993). US demand for CFCs continued abated as a refrigerant, blowing agent, and semiconductor cleanser. Tracing the decision process at DuPont reveals that in the mid-1970s heterogenous regulations caught DuPont off-guard. DuPont learned from this and applied these lessons in the 1980s.

In Europe and elsewhere, although consumer awareness reduced demand for CFC aerosols, no regulations were imposed. The British government opposed bans, in part to preserve domestic demand for Britain's largest manufacturer, ICI. Eighty per cent of the UK's CFC consumption was for aerosols, and ICI was the world's second largest producer of CFCs (next to DuPont).

ICI's demand remained strong; DuPont's was cut in half. Between 1974 and 1985 the US market share of world CFC production plummetted from 46 per cent to 28 per cent. The twelve EEC countries' market share grew from 38 per cent to 45 per cent (Benedick 1991: 26). In this period, DuPont lobbied the US government to pressure European governments into banning aerosol sprays, with no success. The USA had delayed British and French landing rights for the Concorde, and Europe viewed US lobbying for CFC bans as 'environmental neocolonialism', motivated by economic interests (Morissette 1989: 803).

## 3. The ozone hole creates an opportunity: DuPont moves to support HCD regulations

The US CFC industry learned from its mistakes in the heterogenous US aerosol regulation. First, with DuPont's leadership it created a unified front: the Alliance for Responsible CFC Policy. The Alliance lobbied to ensure that future CFC regulations would include major overseas competitors. Unilateral regulations were to be avoided. An Alliance brochure stated that its goal was to ensure that regulation of CFCs 'be pursued on an international basis and be based on sound scientific facts' (McInnis 1992).

Second, industry increased funding for research on ozone and CFCs, to obtain more accurate evidence and to plan for long-term (twenty-year) investment decisions that involved billions of US dollars. One industry-sponsored project conducted by a National Oceanic and Atmospheric Administration (NOAA) laboratory led to a doubling of estimates on CFC-related ozone depletion. Another project led to the publication in May 1985 of research that identified what came to be called the Antarctic 'ozone hole'.[5]

Although scientific uncertainty remained (and in some circles continued through the 1990s) a consensus began to emerge that the ozone layer needed protection, based on some of the industry's own studies, and those

[5] Joseph Farman led the expedition. See J.C. Farman, B.G. Gardiner, and J.D. Shanklin, 'Large Losses of Total Ozone in Antarctica Reveal Seasonal $ClO_x/NO_x$ Interaction', *Nature* 315, May 1985: 207–210; Chemical Manufacturers Association, 'Searching the Stratosphere: Industry's Contribution to Scientific Understanding of the Ozone Depletion Issue' (Washington, DC: CMA, 1991: 8). On industry's Alliance for Responsible CFC Policy, see Hahn and McGartland 1989: 607 ff.

conducted by NOAA, NASA, the World Meteorological Organization (WMO), and the United Nations Environmental Program (UNEP). Pressures increased in the USA for the restriction of CFCs. International consideration of the issue was led by the UNEP, culminating in the Vienna Convention for the Protection of the Ozone Layer, in March 1985.[6] The Vienna Convention called for action, but implemented none.

Contrary to the view that business opposes all regulations, and contrary to a purely intergovernmental view, in early 1985 some US industry officials began to lobby the Reagan Administration to support the Vienna Convention. Allen Wallis, Under Secretary of State for Economic Affairs in the Reagan administration, had resisted the Vienna Convention negotiations in early 1985. Industry officials were alerted by frantic phone calls from the US negotiating team in Vienna. The industry officials in turn lobbied in favor of the agreement. Richard Benedick, the head negotiator for the US State Department, writes:

> Eleventh-hour *private-sector interventions* with the administration thus *enabled the United States to join* in signing the Vienna Convention. The incident curiously [*sic*] foreshadowed the more protracted attempt two years later by anti-regulatory forces within the Reagan administration to overturn the US position on the Montreal Protocol. *In both cases, American industry ultimately backed the international agreement.* [. . .] On four occasions during the ozone negotiations the US government either reversed or went close to reversing its position. It is noteworthy that on the three occasions since 1985, pragmatically oriented American industry forces intervened in *favour* of the international regulatory regime.[7]

US industry wanted to 'level the playing field' and shape global regulations to its competitive advantage. It did so, while publicly protesting that an immediate ban on all CFCs would be economically catastrophic. Consistent with Stigler's dictum, industry supported regulations which worked to its favor, even to the extent of lobbying against the deregulation policy of Republican President Reagan. This book's propositions reveal there is nothing 'curious' about this.

DuPont's preferences changed in this period. Initially, industry was united in calling for more scientific research before regulatory action was implemented. US industry strenuously and successfully resisted, as late as May 1986 when the Natural Resources Defense Council sued the EPA to enforce even more

[6] Many ideologues and industry studies disputed the alleged connection of CFCs, ozone destruction, and lethal changes in ultra-violet radiation reaching the earth. As late as 5 October 1997 the *Washington Times* scoffed at believers in this 'myth'.

[7] Benedick 1991: 46–47, 202 (emphases added). The Vienna Convention was a precursor to the Montreal Protocol. It called for 'harmonizing appropriate policies to control, limit, reduce, or prevent human activities [. . .] should it be found that these activities have or are likely to have adverse effects' (section II.2.b). The Vienna Convention entered into force in September 1988, one year after the Montreal Protocol was signed and four months before it was ratified.

stringent heterogenous US controls.[8] Four months later, and sixteen months after publication of the 'ozone hole' research, DuPont did an about-face.

*In September 1986 DuPont and the US manufacturers' Alliance for Responsible CFC Policy changed tactics, to support global restrictions on CFCs.* Although proof was lacking, DuPont concluded a new Position Statement release 'that it now would be prudent to limit worldwide emissions of CFCs while science continues to provide better guidance to policy makers'. DuPont would support 'a reasonable global limit on the future rate of growth of fully halogenated CFC production capacity'.[9] A cap on production indicated a willingness to shift capacity to alternatives. DuPont advocated government incentives to develop substitutes, and sought higher homogenous market access restrictions on CFC products.

*DuPont's change in tactics, to support higher standards worldwide, played a key role in bringing about the Montreal Protocol.* As Donella Meadows *et al.* remarked: 'Something happened, between March 1985 in Vienna when there was no real action, and October 1987 in Montreal, when the first international ozone-protection protocol was signed.'[10] That 'something' was the decision by DuPont.

## 4. Industry anticipated MAS in substitutes?

DuPont, ICI, and Atochem had begun multimillion dollar research programs on CFC substitutes (including HFC134a) in the 1970s. Substitutes were technically feasible, but not justified economically. Substitutes would cost over four times more than CFCs, and could not compete with them in an open (unregulated) market. Research fell to nothing by the early 1980s (before the ozone issue arose).[11]

News of the ozone hole prompted industry to reconsider substitutes. Existing CFC producers held patents on most CFC alternatives.[12] Additionally, the billions of dollars required in seeking substitutes would effectively act as a barrier to entry for smaller firms if CFCs were restricted.

[8] Richard Barnett before US Congress, Senate Committee on the Environment and Public Works, Subcommittees on Environmental Protection and Hazardous Wastes and Toxic Substances, 100th Congress 1st session 1987, *Ozone Depletion, the Greenhouse Effect, and Climate Change*. Firm-level decisions on how much to spend on legal proceedings, and when and how to engage in them, bear further research.

[9] In *Environmental Conservation* 13 Winter 1986: 363, 'DuPont Position Statement on the Chlorofluorocarbon-Ozone-Greenhouse Issues'; and McInnis (1992: 143).

[10] Meadows, Meadows, and Randers (1992). The authors downplay the impact of the Antarctic ozone hole, and credit the UNEP for the change. This offers no explanation as to why UNEP's role changed then, when it had been active on the issue for over a decade.

[11] Richard Hoppe, 'Ozone: Is Industry Getting Its Head Out of the Clouds?' *Business Week*, 13 October 1986: 110–111. Ironically, another reason to terminate the program was the cost of testing for adverse health effects from substitutes.

[12] A 1988 EPA review of patents concluded that existing CFC producers in the USA were also the most likely producers of alternatives: *Federal Register* 53, 12 August 1988: 30606.

ICI decided to reinvest in HFC-134a, calculating that first-mover advantages would give it a competitive edge. A team of eight scientists headed by James Steven began the secret effort. ICI ended up spending $US500 million on HFC-134a research.[13] Other producers followed suit. By mid-1987 ICI had set 1995 as a target for commercial production of substitutes. It beat that target by five years. Its largest production plant was located in Louisiana and it had other plants in Europe and Japan. Production was for both local markets and export, with capacity greatly exceeding demand in the UK alone. Given the high MAS of these investments, if a CFC ban were *not* enacted, ICI would have suffered.

Adding to the incentive to invest in substitutes was the rise of increased competition from new entrants in the CFC market. Production of CFCs had become relatively cheap and easy. CFCs had become an undifferentiated commodity, with competition based mainly on price (and added service). New production facilities were planned in the Soviet Union, China, and developing countries. Combined with the American ban on aerosols, the industry faced excess capacity. Asset specificity fell, as alternative investments became more profitable. Despite rising demand from 1982 through 1987, real prices fell for CFC-11, CFC-12, and CFC-22. (See Figure 4.1, CFC prices 1982–1986.)

Weiner and Maxwell (1993) conclude that profit motives spurred the drive for substitutes:

> By the mid-1980s, the production of CFC11 and 12 was no longer as profitable a business as it once was [. . .] International regulation mandating a switch to CFC substitutes offered major producers the possibility of new and more profitable markets in the long term [. . .] Much [national] attention was paid to ensure that neither DuPont nor ICI gained a competitive advantage against each other [. . .] Indeed, as the largest producers, they will be joint winners, with small producers, which are unable to compete in the new [capital-intensive] markets, being the primary losers (Weiner and Maxwell 1993: 49).

By the early 1980s DuPont's profit margins on CFCs were only 4 per cent, versus 6 per cent for other DuPont products.

The *Wall Street Journal* observed: 'If successful, the substitutes business stands to bring much higher profits. DuPont has referred to the current business as a "cash trap," the result of excess production and low prices.'[14] CFCs had become an undifferentiated commodity sold on world markets. ICI, DuPont, and Atochem hoped to create patentable, profitable, and

[13] *Wall Street Journal*, 13 August 1986: 25; *Business Week*, 17 May 1993. HFC-134a has its own risks: it may be a more potent source of 'global warming' than some CFCs: see Jorn Siljeholm, 'Ranking Chemical Risks' (forthcoming).

[14] 'Dupont Plans to Product Refrigerant Harmless to Ozone', *Wall Street Journal*, 30 September 1988, sec. 2, p. 32.

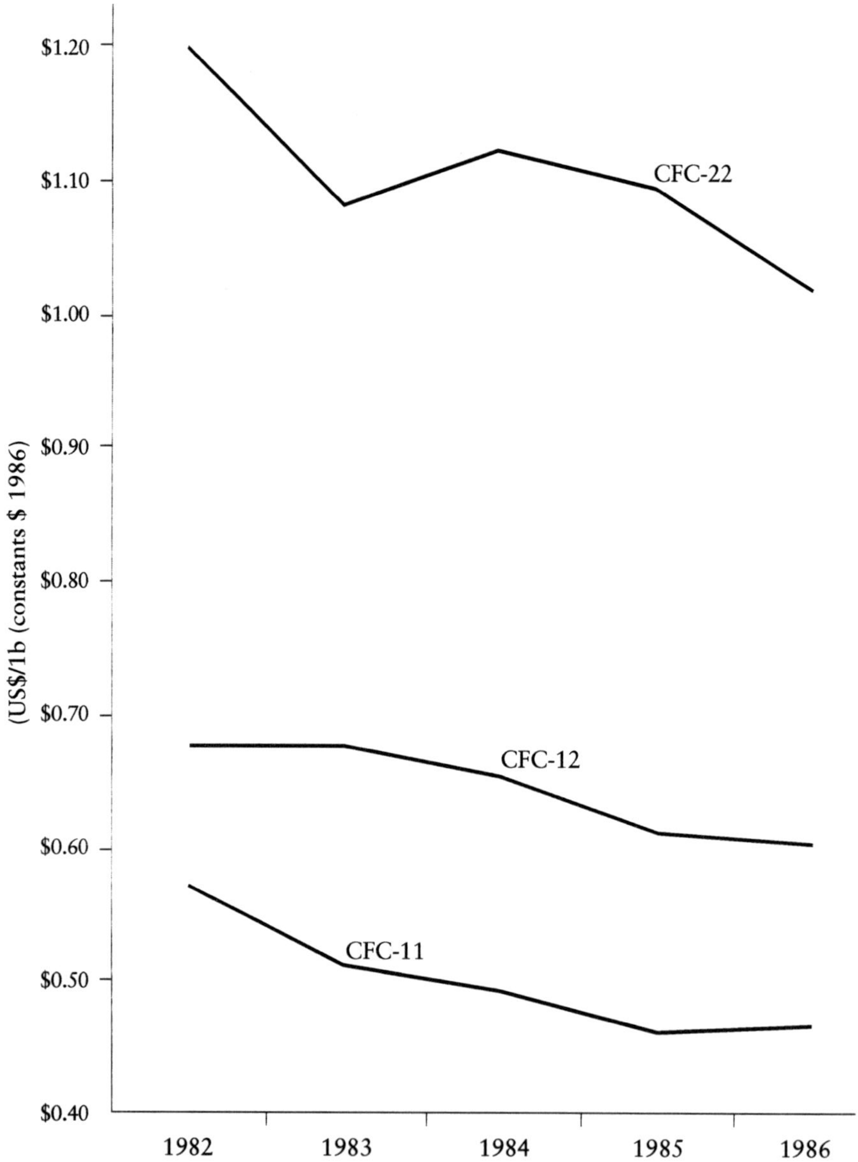


*Source*: US ITC, Weiner/Maxwell

*Figure 4.1*: CFC prices, 1982–1986

specialized substitutes.[15] Asset specificity in substitutes was only beginning, but industry may have acted strategically in anticipation of it.

## 5. 1986–1993: HCD, MARKET ACCESS REGULATIONS

Country's positions followed their industry's interests, including DuPont's in the USA. In October 1986 Congress introduced legislation that would limit foreign firms' access to the US market in the event international agreement was not reached. The first round of ozone protocol negotiations began in Geneva in December 1986, three months after DuPont announced its change in position. The USA supported a consumption phaseout on nonessential uses (aerosols). The UK, France, and Japan urged a production cap below current levels, following their industries' expressed desire for production phaseouts.[16] They feared heterogenous US action that would limit access to the US market for products containing CFCs.

DuPont initially favored controls on nonessential consumption (as opposed to production) in order to bring prices up, hold European competitors to American standards, and allow US surplus capacity to be exported overseas. ICI in Britain and Atochem in France initially favored a capacity freeze, in order to reach their full manufacturing potential (following new investments). Voluntary cutbacks in aerosol would be easily met in Europe, leaving open the possibility of exports to developing countries. Japanese semiconductor manufacturers supported the UK and France because they used CFC-113 as a cleaning agent.

Foreign fears of US market closure may have hastened agreement. The parties eventually compromised on a phaseout of production and on a somewhat unusual definition of consumption (production plus imports less exports). This ensured that industrialized countries would dominate exports to developing countries as long as production was permitted.[17] Both policies amount to a product market-access restriction, under this book's definition. The sale and distribution of CFCs would be curtailed.

[15] Not everything went according to plan. In 1990 Dr. Harry Rosin of the Dortmund Institute of Hygiene announced a non-patentable substitute coolant, blending propane and butane, using 1920s technology. East German producer FORON (née DKK) began production. In 1992 they sold over 100,000 of the 'Greenfreeze' or 'Clean Cooler' refrigerators in Germany alone. The CFC industry responded swiftly, labeling the refrigerators dangerous, inefficient, energy-consuming, and global-warming.

[16] Developing countries, including Argentina, Brazil, Egypt, Kenya, Mexico, Venezuela, and Yugoslavia demanded exemptions. South Korea and India boycotted the talks. Most were eventually brought in with promises of compensation. Article 5 allowed a country with consumption of less than 0.3 kg per capita per year at any time before 1999 to delay phaseout for 10 years.

[17] The Protocol made special provisions for developing countries. These are specific to this case, hence they are not pursued here.

The Montreal Protocol was signed in September 1987, over a year after ICI began to reinvest in substitutes and the year after the US Alliance changed tactics to support a phaseout. The Protocol called for a 50 per cent phaseout by 1998, with exceptions for CFC-113 in Japan.[18] The Protocol was to take effect in 1989, pending ratification. In response, ICI moved up its HFC-substitute deadline two years, to 1993. (In fact, ICI began UK commercial operation in 1990, and opened the world's largest plant in the USA in December 1992. Atochem also began 134a production in 1992.)

On 11 March 1988 the NASA/WMO Ozone Trends Panel released new evidence that CFCs were the cause of global (midlatitude) ozone depletion and the Antarctic ozone hole. Five days later, DuPont announced it would voluntarily phase out CFCs, and develop substitutes; ICI soon followed. In the following month the USA ratified the Montreal Protocol. Within eight months, twenty-four countries and the European Economic Community (EEC) had ratified the Protocol, bringing it into effect on 1 January 1989. Subsequent revisions to the Protocol (May 1989, June 1990, mid-1992, September 1997, and December 1999) hastened scheduled phaseout of CFCs, because by this time leading manufacturers had made their peace with substitutes.

French Prime Minister Pierre Beregovoy blocked a similar accelerated phaseout of hydrochlorofluorocarbons (HCFCs) and hydrofluorocarbons (HFCs). Elf Atochem, partly government-owned, was the world's largest HCFC producer at the time.

The production cap established a *de facto* cartel in CFCs for the US and European firms. The predictable result was to raise prices and profit margins. 'From an economic standpoint, these limits on production are no different from the production targets set by OPEC in trying to enforce its cartel. Just as limits on oil production raise prices, so do limits on CFC and halon production' (Hahn and McGartland 1989: 594, 601ff). Existing CFC producers were guaranteed their *status quo ante* market share under an EPA quota system which allocated production rights based on 1986 levels. New CFC competitors were not welcome.

It did not take long for CFC prices to rise. By April 1989 *Chemical Week* reported that 'Montreal Protocol provisions for CFCs have wrought a turnaround in the market. [. . .] CFC-11 and CFC-12 are in tight supply worldwide and prices are rising, up 30 per cent to 60 per cent over the past year in the US and around 15 per cent in Europe'.[19] Perfect substitutes were not available as existing equipment depended on CFCs.

[18] The Protocol text and revisions are in Benedick (1991). Originally, it combined staggered cuts in consumption of five CFCs and three halons (20% by 1994, 50% by 1999) with a 40% production cut (10% increase for LDCs). A 15% leeway in consumption was allowed to satisfy 'basic domestic needs [. . .] and for the purposes of industrial rationalization'. On ICI, see *Business Week*, 17 May 1993: 78 ff.

[19] David Hunter, 'CFC Prices Soar as Capacity is Cut', *Chemical Week*, 26 April 1989: 14.

Industrial consumers of CFCs were caught off-guard by DuPont's sudden change of position and were hurt by the higher prices. DuPont and the other producers benefitted. Their investments in substitutes were protected because the production phaseout guaranteed them a market. Higher prices funded the development of substitutes—for firms already in the CFC business. (In 1988 the EPA estimated that the phaseout mandated by the Montreal Protocol would create from $US1.8 to $US7.2 billion in 'windfall profits' for US industry by 2000.)[20]

In 1993 DuPont announced a voluntary CFC phaseout within a year: two years ahead of the revised Montreal Protocol schedule. ICI, DuPont, and ElfAtochem were producing HFC-134a in large quantities by May 1994. ICI led the way, with its first-mover advantages, with a total capacity of 50,000 metric tons/year at three plants.[21]

Ironically, in December 1993, the EPA asked DuPont to continue producing its full 1995 allowance of 38,000 tons of CFC-12. The EPA wanted the coolant to be available for CFC 'banks' for automotive air conditioning repairs after CFC production was due to halt in 1996. The EPA feared a consumer backlash: the cost of retrofitting automotive air conditioning was over $US300. By 2002 62 million vehicles in the US still used DuPont's Freon in their air conditioners.[22]

In 1994 Europe also faced a CFC shortage, as a result of its accelerated phaseout. When European Union officials tried to ease off that schedule by tripling import quotas for *used* CFCs, European industry protested angrily. The EU backed off, and tightened import controls on used CFCs (product market-access regulations). Satisfied, the environmental advisor to Elf Atochem (and the chairman of the European Chemical Industry Council's CFC sector group) predicted that 'only hundreds of tons of CFCs rather than thousands of tons will [now] be imported this year'.[23]

By 2002 the Montreal Protocol had been ratified by 183 countries. (The only exceptions were Equatorial Guinea, Eritrea, Guinea-Bissau, Afghanistan, Bhutan, Iraq, East Timor, Andorra, the Holy See, and San Marino.) The later amendments from London (1990), Copenhagen (1992), Montreal (1997), and Beijing (1999) were ratified by 163, 141, 80, and 34 countries, respectively, as of June 2002.

[20] *Federal Register* 53, 12 August 1988: 30604. With support from DuPont, Congress imposed a 'windfall profits' tax in 1990 of $US1.37 per pound of CFC production, rising to $US2.65 per pound in 1993–1994 and rising by $US0.45 in each successive year. An estimated $US450 million in revenues were raised in 1991 alone. By 2001 the excise tax on CFC imports was $US8.15 per pound (Gushee 1990: 7–8; Michael Levy).

[21] *Chemical Week*, 'ICI, ElfAtochem, DuPont, and Others Are Ready for HFC Growth', 4 May 1994: 14 (no 'other' companies are mentioned).

[22] *Washington Times*, 9 June 2001; 'DuPont Extends CFC Production After EPA Warns of Scarcity', *Chemical Week*, 5–12 January 1994.

[23] *Chemical Marketing Reporter*, 18 April 1994: 9.

### 6. Montreal Protocol case: Conclusion

This book's propositions fit this case well. Two dominant firms had high market concentration. Asset specificity in CFCs was declining; as profit margins fell investments in alternatives became more profitable. Initially, US heterogeneous product market-access regulations on use of CFCs in aerosols hurt DuPont and Allied Signal. These US producers objected to the heterogenous measures and seized the opportunity presented by scientific evidence to help achieve homogenous restrictions which covered competitors worldwide. They devoted assets to the development of substitutes, and supported the adoption of stringent product market-access regulations in common with all major producing countries. These regulations had a significant impact. HCFCs largely replaced CFCs and in September 1995 DuPont closed its last CFC-11 and -12 production facilities. By 2002 CFC emissions had declined dramatically and the depletion of the ozone layer had slowed (although it may take 100 years to recover). HCFCs themselves were being replaced by HFCs in a number of applications. Black-market smuggling occurred—US Customs Agents seized 2.5 million pounds of CFCs from 1996 to 2001, valued at up to $US25 per pound—but this is evidence of the stringency of the regulations, the curtailment in supply, and the resulting high price of bootlegged CFCs.

Industry had at first sought direct subsidy of research on substitutes. As CFC production was squeezed, industry benefitted from oligopoly profits.[24] Later, industry pushed to have those profits guaranteed to existing producers, through the EPA quota system. When the market for alternatives to CFCs seemed certain, CFCs themselves became the restricted 'substitute', in Stiglerian fashion.

A year before the Montreal Protocol was signed, DuPont changed its position and indicated its support for limits on worldwide emissions of CFCs. According to the chief US negotiator there, private sector interests backed the UNEP proposals, sometimes against the initial wishes of Reagan administration officials (Benedick 1991: 202; Rowlands 1995: 113). Sixty US embassies were instructed to lobby for the Protocol; Taiwan allegedly faced US trade-retaliation unless it complied (Braithwaite and Drahos 2000: 264).

Since 1987 the specific details of the protocol have been revised five times. In 2001 a close observer summarized that process:

> Letting regulations adapt to changing technical possibilities promoted an intense effort by private industry to reduce the use of ozone-depleting chemicals and develop substitutes for use in products like air conditioners and refrigerators. By participating, industries were better able to solve the technical problems they faced in meeting

[24] If industry had created such a cartel arrangement on its own, it might well have been charged with Stiglerian price-fixing.

existing and anticipated regulations, and they could spot commercial opportunities in the phasing out of the old chemicals. Since 1987 the use of ozone-depleting chemicals has declined 90 per cent worldwide at modest cost, an achievement that once seemed unthinkable.[25]

The coalition of environmental and business interests in this case were responsible for a dramatic improvement in the world's eco-system.

According to the Executive Director of UNEP, Mustafa Tolba, the Protocol had more to do with industry's competitive advantage than with the environment: 'The difficulties in negotiating the Montreal Protocol had nothing to do with whether the environment was damaged or not. It was all who was going to gain an edge over who; whether DuPont would have an advantage over the European companies or not.'[26] DuPont's role is consistent with this book's emphasis on producer preferences and its three propositions. A similar role for dominant firms is found in the next case study, on bank capital requirements.

[25] Edward A. Parsons, *New York Times*, 31 July 2001. Parsons was a consultant in the White House Science Office under Bill Clinton, and a professor at Harvard's Kenney School.

[26] Tolba quoted in Deborah MacKenzie, 'Now it Makes Business Sense to Save the Ozone Layer', *New Scientist*, 29 October 1988: 25.

# 5

# *Basle Accord on Capital Adequacy*

The one banking topic this decade that really matters: capital adequacy.

*Euromoney* (July 1988)

People of the same trade seldom meet together, even for merriment and diversion, but the conversation ends in a conspiracy against the public, or in some contrivance to raise prices.

Adam Smith, *The Wealth of Nations* (1776)

The Basle Accord was motivated by several factors. First, bank regulators were interested in enhancing banks' capital position, in order to enhance banks' ability to absorb losses due to LDC debt and other exposures. Second, they saw a need to forestall a possible competition in regulatory laxity in bank capital adequacy standards.

Joel Trachtman (1991)

In December 1987 central banks from the world's major industrial powers reached agreement to require private banks to raise capital (as a percentage of risk-weighted loans). Implementation of this Basle Accord showed some movement toward a higher common denominator outcome (hence its inclusion here) but also some continuing heterogeneity between countries.

This Chapter first provides an overview of the 'puzzle' posed by the Basle Accord.[1] As with the other case studies it then summarizes the industrial structure and asset specificity of international finance (including contracting structures on sovereign lending). The case study in section four examines heterogenous movements in the regulation of capital prior to the Basle Accord, and the impact of the 1980s debt crisis on them. Section five discusses the largely failed multilateral efforts toward regulatory homogeneity through the Cooke Committee. The sixth section on bilateral US–UK agreement denotes the point at which real movement toward the Basle Accord occurred. That movement was cemented when the USA persuaded Japan to join, as discussed in section seven. Section eight discusses the final negotia-

[1] The French spelling of Basle is used in this book for the period 1975–1994, following the convention of that time and to further differentiate the 1988 Basle Capital Accord from the 1989 Basel Convention on Hazardous Wastes. After 1994, the conventional usage changed to the German spelling, hence Basel II. The Capital Accord was not a formal treaty, but an expression of agreement among central bank governors.

tion and implementation of the Accord. The ninth section explains that considerable heterogeneity remained in the use of capital requirements worldwide and that new heterogenous measures were taken in the early 1990s. The final section reviews the case. (An appendix summarizes the basics of bank capital for lay readers.)

## 1. The puzzle: Common regulatory movement upward, counter to secular trends

On 15 July 1988 the Standing Committee on Banking Regulations and Supervisory Practices (the Cooke Committee) at the Bank for International Settlements (BIS) announced that its members had reached agreement on a proposal for 'international convergence of capital measurement and capital standards'. Ironically, a leading economics textbook (Krugman and Obstfeld) published that same year observed that 'cooperation, technically complex and politically difficult, is unlikely to occur in the near future. In particular, international agreement on reserve requirements and other financial regulations would be required.'[2] Lower capital ratios reduce the cost of lending for banks, *ceteris paribus*, making them more price-competitive. This creates incentives for a competition-in-laxity, which in fact occurred. The average capital ratio for major US banks dropped by half from 1960 to 1980 (Kane, Portes, and Swoboda 1987). Those incentives for laxity were enhanced by increased globalization of finance, new competitors (bank and nonbank), and new financial products, including off-balance sheet risk-management instruments, new technologies, and debt failures (BIS 1986; IMF 1994; Kapstein 1988). The question then is why did cooperation occur to the extent it did, when it did, after twelve years of weak efforts toward homogenous bank regulations and at a time of stagnation in the Uruguay GATT Round, worldwide secular trends toward banking *deregulation*, and Reagan administration tendencies toward unilateralism?

The timing and details of that agreement cannot be explained without reference to dominant private sector interests and government responses to them, unusual contracting arrangements among banks, the extensive multinational investments of global finance, and subtle US threats of market closure to banks which did not meet requirements approved by the USA.[3]

[2] Krugman and Obstfeld 1988: 636–646, quotation on p. 639. Reserve requirements and capital requirements are not identical but face similar co-ordination problems.

[3] The 'Basle Accord' was first circulated by the BIS' Committee on Banking Regulations and Supervisory Practices, in the Consultative Paper on Proposals for International Convergence of Capital Measurement and Capital Standards, December 1987. The revised final accord was entitled 'Report on International Convergence of Capital Measurement and Capital Standards', July 1988, commonly called the 'Basle Accord'. See Kapstein 1988, 1991, and 1992; and Tobin 1991. Thanks to several executives at Citicorp and BIS staff for discussions of these issues.

The Basle Accord had distributive aspects as well as the more widely touted 'public good' aspect of stabilizing the world banking system. To the extent that it averted a financial crash nearly everyone realized absolute benefits. Debtor countries benefitted in absolute terms to the extent that it averted a global financial crash that would have cut foreign investment even further and reduced demand for their exports. But other deals more favorable to debtor countries could also have averted a crash.[4] The relative distributive aspect of the Basle Accord is emphasized here. The relative winners were financial institutions in industrial countries, especially the USA, the UK, Germany, and Switzerland, who solidified their position in negotiations on LDC sovereign debt. (Within this group, well capitalized banks and non-bank financial service providers benefitted most.) The relative losers, arguably, were those developing country governments whose negotiating position was weakened by the strengthened capital position of lenders.

The impact of the 1988 Basle Accord on the entire LDC debt issue is difficult to evaluate in isolation, and is beyond the scope of this study. Fears of a systemic financial crisis eased by 1991. Bank critics argued that stabilizing the world financial system came at a considerable cost to developing countries. The global financial system remained intact but debt problems continued to plague many developing countries. Bad loans were made to corrupt and undemocratic regimes. The resulting debt overhang scared away future investors, forcing countries to raise money domestically at very high interest rates. Bankers countered that only private financial markets could provide the level of capital which developing countries needed to finance investments because governments and taxpayers in developed countries were not to shoulder that burden.

As the debt crisis eased in the early 1990s the differences between banks became more important and homogenous bank action became less important. By 1994 the Accord and subsequent heterogenous measures benefitted US and European banks against their Japanese competitors.

Thus, there are two phases in this case. The first phase involved the relationship between all lenders and their sovereign borrowers in the 1980s, and resulted in movement upward toward homogeneity. After the debt crisis had eased, the later and more nationalist phase involved the relationship between individual banks and their regulators in different countries. This latter phase showed lingering heterogeneity in capital standards, despite the Basle Accord. A chronology of key dates in the first phase is shown in Figure 5.1.

[4] See Bergsten, Cline, and Williamson 1985; Aggarwal 1985, 1987; Sachs 1989; Dornbusch, Makin, and Zlowe 1989; Fernandez 1990. NB: the Basle Accord was only one of many factors affecting developing country debt.

*Figure 5.1*: Chronology of events in 1988 Basle Accord case

| | |
|---|---|
| 1982: | Mexico announces it cannot meet its payments schedule. |
| 1983: | Revised Basle Concordat. US Congress passes ILSA. |
| 1984: | Japanese banks expanding in US and European markets. US banks protest lower capital standards in Japan. Volcker urges G-10 on capital ratios. |
| May: | Continental-Illinois bank bailout. |
| July: | US regulators propose heterogenous 5.5% primary capital ratio. All nine major US banks already above 5.0%, most above 5.5%. Proposal adopted in eight months. |
| 1985: | US tightens entry requirements for Japanese banks. Baker Plan on LDC debt. |
| July: | Federal Reserve working group on risk-based capital standards. OCC, FDIC join. |
| 1986: | January, FRB circulates proposal for bank review; they object to heterogeneity. |
| July: | Volcker contacts Leigh-Pemberton (BoE), about convergence of capital standards. |
| Sept: | Cooke Committee: 'It is not possible . . .' |
| Oct: | US–UK reach agreement on most capital standards issues. |
| Dec: | US informs Japan of US–UK discussions. |
| 1987: | January, US–UK agreement announced. |
| May: | Citicorp announces $US3 billion loan-loss reserve. |
| June: | IMC in Hamburg: leading bankers discuss capital standards (and Brazilian debt), with Volcker, Leigh-Pemberton, Pöhl, T. Ohta. |
| June: | Federal Reserve staff negotiates with Japanese MoF staff. |
| Aug: | Federal Reserve and Japan reach bilateral agreement, in NY, when Corrigan threatens to close market access to non-complying Japanese banks. |
| Sept: | US–UK–Japan trilateral agreement; presented to BIS as *fait accompli.* |
| Dec: | BIS releases draft proposal for bank review. |
| 1988: | June, IMC in Chicago: Cooke, Robinson: support Basle Accord. |
| July: | BIS publishes final capital agreement ('Basle Accord'). |
| 1992: | December, deadline for implementation. |

## 2. Industrial Structure and Governance of International Banking

Unlike other cases of movement toward stringent regulation (tuna-dolphin, infant formula advertising, CFCs) global banking is dominated by perhaps two dozen firms, not just a few.[5] Within every country a few banks do

[5] The number depends on the region under consideration. American banks are present worldwide (and particularly dominant in the Americas), Asian banks are more prevalent in Asia, French banks in former French West Africa, and so on.

dominate major transactions, and this was especially so in the case of sovereign lending. They acted as an oligopoly on certain large-scale domestic financial transactions. In the 1980s in the USA these were the nine money-center banks, later reduced to three.[6] In the UK it was the Big Four; in Japan the top eleven commercial banks; in Germany the big three. These banks exerted considerable sway with their domestic regulators in the establishment of supervisory practices. Worldwide, however, these banks faced collective problems in organizing to stabilize financial markets. The biggest source of financial instability in the 1980s and the biggest collective action problem facing banks was developing country debt (Cohen 1986). Thus, attention is called to several unusual governance structures.

However, the fragmented nature of the market structure in sovereign lending is somewhat illusory, for five reasons. First, most sovereign loans were syndicated among banks. Each major bank held 'pieces' of many loans jointly with other banks. This spread their risk and unified bank interests. Second, contractual cross-default arrangements forbade individual banks from renegotiating debt alone. This also gave banks a 'united face' and greatly increased their cohesion and negotiating power.[7] Third, banks joined together in Bank Advisory Committees (BACs), a governance structure which presented a unified negotiating position to each sovereign borrower. Citicorp chaired (or co-chaired) the BAC for seven of the Baker Fifteen countries, including three of the four largest debtors.[8] Fourth, the co-ordinating body of central bank regulators, the Bank for International Settlements (BIS), had an intimate relationship with the financial community. J.P. Morgan and other financiers had helped lead to the creation of the BIS itself, and for over fifty years Citibank served as the official US representative. Finally, top bankers achieved some collective action through their annual International Monetary Conference (IMC) meetings. Thus, a somewhat surprising outcome (high homogeneity with 'many' actors) turns out to involve a unique set of governance structures. This acts as further confirmation of the book's propositions on industrial structure.

[6] As of 2002 the three biggest were Citigroup, Bank of America, and J.P. Morgan-Chase, along with 'super-regional' banks such as Wells Fargo, Bank of New York, Bank One, and FleetBoston. The local US banking system is unusually fragmented, with 13,000 smaller banks in 1990; this number declined by several thousand over the next decade.

[7] The contracts involved *ex ante* transaction costs, in Williamson's terms, in drafting, negotiating, and safeguarding the initial contract. They also involved *ex post* contractual costs in the unifying governance structure of the Bank Advisory Committees, and effecting secure commitments.

[8] The BACs negotiated on behalf of all bank creditors simultaneously. They were dominated by the five largest US banks. US banks held the largest share of debt to the 'Baker-15' countries, with 25% of total medium- and long-term private bank claims. The top 25 holders of sovereign debt held, on average, 45% of each country's outstanding loans. Citicorp led all other banks in lending to developing countries. Compliance was achieved primarily through *ad hoc* bargaining. If that failed, lead banks might threaten to reduce the interest rate of unwilling bank participants, or to have it capitalized.

The key regulator in this case, the BIS, acts as a central bank for central banks. It offers short-term bridge loans to governments, collects data, publishes reports, and performs other measures to stabilize world financial markets. Its assets are almost as large as those of the International Monetary Fund (IMF) and it holds over 10 per cent of world monetary reserves. It was created in 1929 as part of the Young Plan, named after Owen D. Young, Chair of General Electric (with business ties to J.P. Morgan and a director of FRBNY). The committee which drafted BIS' statutes also included the heads of Citibank (then called First National Bank of the City of New York), First National Bank of Chicago, and representatives of J.P. Morgan. The US government refused to buy into the BIS in 1929. In its place, the three top US banks jointly purchased shares on behalf of the United States and in fact were the official US representatives at BIS for many decades. Japan similarly was represented by Japanese banks. Only in 1987 did Citibank formally transferred its proxy vote to BIS management, after years of approving BIS decisions.[9] Simmons (1993) argues that the impetus for BIS itself came from private and central bankers: 'Its impulse came from private and central bankers. Indeed, politicians were shocked at what these bankers proposed. Government officials ultimately bought into the BIS only because they needed the financiers' cooperation in reorganizing Germany's debt.' In the 1988 capital agreement, governments again needed financiers' co-operation to stabilize world financial markets. In the 1920s, as now, market access was the primary 'stick': '[BIS was] in a position to reward German compliance with favorable access to international trade, and to punish defection by coordinating economic sanctions' (Simmons, p. 22). As described below, a similar linkage of market access was used by England and the USA to gain Japanese support for capital standards; for all Basle Accord signatories to uphold the Accord; and for the USA, England, and others to raise capital requirements even further.

Internationally, major banks compete fiercely; but they share certain common interests. Financial markets are interdependent and bankers need to protect the stability of the international financial system. The annual International Monetary Conference, comprised of CEOs from the world's largest 100 banks, was one means by which they attempted to overcome collective action problems. It is akin to an international, financial version of the US Business Round Table. Speakers typically include the top figures in international finance, such as Alan Greenspan, Paul Volcker, Otto Pöhl, Alexandre Lamfalussy, Jacques de LaRosiere, Lloyd Bentsen, James Baker, Leon Brittan, and Toyoo Gyohten. The off-record Conference permits central bankers, government officials, and private bankers to engage in free-ranging discussion.

[9] Background interviews at Citibank, July 1990, and August 1999; and Simmons 1993, Table 2, 378. US representatives at BIS came from the Federal Reserve Board, Federal Reserve Bank of New York, OCC, and FDIC.

Thus we find five factors that contributed to a more unified governance structure than the number of banks involved might indicate, including a close working relationship with the top regulator, the BIS. Nonetheless, the final outcome of the case shows some lingering heterogeneity. This is arguably the result of dominant bank interests within major countries, which shaped domestic regulations to their advantage.

## 3. Asset specificity in international banking

Sovereign and corporate lending to developing countries were highly asset specific multinational investments.[10] Loans were dedicated to transactions with particular sovereign or corporate borrowers. As the debt crisis progressed after 1982 the secondary market resale value of those loans declined. This gave banks a further incentive to ensure that the transactions were not prematurely terminated. Sovereign lending also involved human assets dedicated to negotiating those loans. The reputation and identity of the negotiating parties in these relationships was significant. As the debt crisis deepened in the 1980s sovereign lending became even more human asset specific. Members of the Bank Advisory Committees negotiated intensively with their counterparts from debtor countries both to reschedule payments and to compel new lending. The high asset-specificity of sovereign lending created incentives for a more unified governance structure among contracting parties. That structure reflected dominant bank interests.

## 4. *Status quo ante*: Heterogeneity, debt crisis

Countries' accounting systems showed considerable heterogeneity in their definition and treatment of bank capital up through the mid-1980s. The Mexican and subsequent debt crises made financial markets jittery and increased scrutiny of banks' financial positions. This section describes the initial heterogeneity, the debt crisis, and responses to it that affected bank capital.

### 4.1 Heterogenous capital standards in the 1980s

Banks' capital-to-assets ratios declined from the early 1970s into the 1980s. This reflected competitive pressures for lower-cost lending. Foreign banks

[10] The asset specificity of banking services varies greatly by product area. (Bankers refer to financial services as 'products' and no distinction is implied here.) Many other financial products, by contrast, were lower in asset specificity than sovereign lending. These included retail credit-card operations (responsible for half of Citicorp's profits) and 'blind' euromoney transactions. Regulation of these latter financial products showed movement toward laxity, with the development of offshore finance (see Chapter Three above).

grew increasingly active in the US market, particularly Japanese banks. As the debt crisis emerged in the early 1980s, US banks and the Federal Reserve Board wanted to improve world financial stability and also to improve US banks' position *vis-à-vis* Japan and a unified Europe.[11]

There was considerable heterogeneity in the status of capital adequacy measures among countries. Differences included the definition and valuation of capital, the formulas used to measure capital adequacy, the weighing of risk, and the minimum amount of capital required. (See Figure 5.2, capital measures.) Numbers were often incompatible between countries. Japanese regulators had only recently begun to examine capital/asset ratios, relying on other means to evaluate bank safety. European countries relied on an *ad*

*Figure 5.2*: Capital measures: Heterogeneity in 1986 *vs*. 1988 Basle Accord

| | US | UK | Japan | Germany | France | Basle |
|---|---|---|---|---|---|---|
| **Capital**: equity, disclosed reserves | Yes | Yes | Yes | Yes | Yes | Tier 1 |
| preferred shares | Yes* | Yes | No | Yes | Yes | Tier 1 |
| undisclosed reserves | No | Yes | No | No | No | Tier 2 |
| undisclosed hidden values | No | No | Yes* | No | No | Tier 2 |
| revaluation reserves | No | Yes* | No | No | Yes | Tier 2 |
| perpetual debt | Yes | Yes* | No | Yes | Yes | Tier 2 |
| general loan-loss provisions | Yes* | Yes | Yes | No | Yes* | Tier 2 |
| term subord. debt | No | Yes | No | No | Yes | Tier 2 |
| other: minority holdings (US), pension and bad-loan reserves (Japan), *Genussscheine* (Germany), *titres participatifs, subordonnés* (France) | | | | | | |
| **Deductions**: | | | | | | |
| interbank holdings | No | Yes | No | No | Yes | No |
| goodwill | Yes | Yes | No | No | Yes | Yes |
| **Gearing ratio:** | Yes | Yes | Yes | No | No | No |
| **Denominator:** | assets | liability —capital | assets | n/a | n/a | risk-weight |

*Significant part of capital for given country.
*Source*: Tobin 1991: BIS 1987

[11] On Europe, see Dennis Weatherstone, 'An American View of Europe's Consolidation in 1992', remarks before the Swiss-American Chamber of Commerce (Zurich, 20 June 1988), reprinted in *American Banker*, 24 June 1988: 4.

*hoc* approach, with close working relationships between domestic banks and their central bankers. In 1979 France introduced a risk-related capital standard (quite different from that eventually agreed on by the BIS). In 1980 the UK unilaterally adopted an informal risk-weighted, capital-asset measure.

In the US from the 1950s to the 1970s, the 'Analysis of Bank Capital' (ABC) system was risk-weighted. Banks were required to hold capital equal to 0.4 per cent of face value on US Treasury bills and 10 per cent on business loans. With the rapid innovation of new financial instruments in the 1970s the system became more complex and difficult to administer. Large banks began to fall behind the capital supposedly required by regulations. By the mid-1970s the system was phased out and replaced with other regulatory measures (including reserve requirements). By 1980 the average level of capital for US money-centered banks was roughly 6.3 per cent of assets, half the amount of only two decades earlier (Tobin 1991: 271). After 1981 the US ended its 'case-by-case' approach, which remained common in European countries.

## 4.2 The 1980s debt crisis

In late August 1982 the Mexican government shocked the international financial community by announcing it could not meet its payments schedule to private banks.[12] This marked the beginning of the debt crisis of the 1980s. Brazil, Argentina, and other developing countries also faced payments problems. Bank failures in the US and Europe compounded the problem.[13]

Worldwide, financiers held their breath to see whether the world's financial system could withstand the shock. It did, at a cost to both borrowers and lenders. Fears of a systemic crisis led to a drastic reduction in new lending to developing countries and protracted negotiations with major banks. The debt crisis focused the attention of regulators on the adequacy of bank capital as a way to buffer G-10 countries against future worldwide shocks.

## 4.3 US response to the debt crisis: Banks oppose heterogeneity

By 1981 regulators in the US had begun to move toward more stringent capital standards on their own: 'In 1981, US authorities, alarmed by the slump in prudential ratios over the previous twenty years and the impact of the LDC debt crisis, decided that tougher capital requirements were needed

[12] Mexico did not 'default' on its loans nor was it in arrears on them. It rescheduled loans through negotiations with banks. To bankers, the difference is crucial.

[13] Italy's Banco Ambrosiano was taken into government control on 10 July 1982 to prevent collapse. The eighth largest US bank, Continental Illinois, required a massive injection of Federal Reserve funds in May 1984, after large depositors withdrew $US6 bn in less than 10 days. See Sprague 1986.

to reinforce the financial system and protect the federal deposit insurance fund'.[14] Regulators began by increasing standards for highly localized banks. The debt crisis spurred on those measures.

In 1983 the US Congress passed the International Lending Supervision Act (ILSA). ILSA called for the Federal Reserve Board to raise levels of capital across the US banking system, increase regulation, and improve co-ordination between agencies within the USA. ILSA also encouraged 'major banking countries to work toward [. . .] strengthening the capital bases of banking institutions involved in international lending' (quoted in Kapstein 1991: 13). Bankers objected to heterogenous measures which would undermine their global competitive position, by raising costs.

Federal Reserve Chairman Paul Volcker supported the banks and argued to Congress and bank supervisors that regulatory homogeneity should occur gradually, and should be multilateral or the 'functional equivalent' of it. In Volcker's view, competitive deregulation had already gone too far. Echoing American bankers' complaints about Japan, Volcker sought a 'level playing field' where one bank could not underprice another because it had less capital. Volcker first presented the US Congressional request to the BIS in March 1984; the central bankers there thought homogenous policy was too much to ask.

The failure of Continental Illinois Bank in May 1984 gave added urgency to calls for higher capital standards. Only two months later, in July 1984, the Federal Reserve, FDIC, and OCC proposed a heterogenous 5.5 per cent primary capital-to-assets minimum ratio. The proposal was not a big jump for US banks. At year-end 1983 five of the nine money-center banks already had capital ratios at or over 5.5 per cent and none were under 5.0 per cent. Even by December 1984 all nine money-center banks had raised their capital ratios to over 5.5 per cent. The proposal was adopted in March 1985.[15]

In July 1985 the Federal Reserve Board began to consider implementing risk-based capital standards. It was soon joined by the OCC and FDIC.[16] Six months later, in January 1986, the Federal Reserve Board circulated risk-weighted capital proposals for 'public review'.

US banks were not pleased with the heterogenous proposals which they argued would disadvantage them in terms of foreign competition. In May 1986 the American Bankers Association (ABA) in 'formal comments to the

[14] David Fairlamb, 'Beyond Capital', *Institutional Investor*, August 1994, 40 ff. The USA had encouraged more private sector lending to developing countries and reforms within them under the 1985 Baker Plan. The 1989 Brady Plan prompted renegotiations. The issue here, however, is capital standards.

[15] Harvard Business School, 'Citicorp': 1985: 23, written by William B. Allen, Jr. under the supervision of Associate Professor Scott P. Mason; from *Bankers' Magazine* September–October 1985.

[16] In 1986 the BIS published two widely cited studies: *Recent Innovations in International Banking*; and *The Management of Banks' Off-Balance Sheet Exposures*. Both emphasized the necessity of risk-weighted adequacy requirements.

[Federal Reserve] Board stated that the proposal would exacerbate the competitive inequities that existed between US commercial banks and their foreign peers and between commercial and investment banks' and would thereby undermine the ability of US banks to compete.[17]

Homogenous multilateral standards were a different issue. To restore capital levels, US banks 'supported the concept of risk-based capital and had encouraged the regulatory authorities to develop an agreement at the international level' (Tobin 1990: 45–46). The banks' reactions were analogous to that of DuPont on CFC restrictions: they were willing to go along with stringent capital regulations if they were homogenous worldwide, particularly including Japan. They did not like heterogenous restrictions that raised their cost of doing business. US banks went along with the Federal Reserve's earlier 5.5 per cent proposal for two reasons: concern over bank failures was real enough, and the proposal differentially hurt Japanese banks. At the same time, on other regulatory issues, banks launched major lobbying strategies for deregulation.[18]

## 4.4 Citicorp loan-loss reserves, May 1987

To jump ahead, on 19 May 1987 Citicorp Chairman John Reed announced an increase in Citicorp loan-loss reserves of three billion US dollars. Analysts were stunned. Reed and Citicorp's chief negotiator on sovereign debt, William Rhodes, were leading spokesmen on the issue. The announcement was widely interpreted as strengthening the bank's hand in negotiating sovereign lending. By setting aside three billion dollars Reed showed that Citicorp could handle the problem and indicated his resolve in continuing to push for repayment of those loans. Citicorp's stock rose following the announcement and other major banks soon followed suit.

The treatment of Citicorp's loan-loss reserves would become a central issue in the capital discussions. Citicorp's announcement came soon after completion of a confidential US–UK agreement on capital and in the middle of confidential US–Japan negotiations on capital. (These are discussed below.) The next month, June 1987, top bank CEOs met at the annual International Monetary Conference (IMC) in Hamburg, Germany. They discussed general principles for the forthcoming renegotiation of debt for

[17] American Bankers Association, Comments to the Federal Reserve Board, 23 May 1986: 339.

[18] Namely, market access overseas under the Uruguay Round, concern over Europe's Second Banking Directive, securities settlement issues in the G-30, and removal of the US McFadden and Glass-Steagall, which prohibited banks from operating across state lines and from investment banking and selling securities. Glass-Steagall was repealed by 2000. Regulatory officers at Citicorp noted that they did not take a formal, consistent position on the Basle Accord because they needed to 'pick and choose' which issues were most important: author's interviews at Citicorp, 23 and 27 March 1992.

Brazil, the country with the largest outstanding debt.[19] They also engaged in discussion with central bank governors about proposals to raise capital standards.

There was also debate within the US regulatory system on how to treat loan-loss reserves. The Federal Reserve Bank wanted them counted as part of capital, arguing that they were set aside to cover general losses. This was consistent with Federal Reserve support for the Baker Plan. The Office of the Comptroller of the Currency (OCC) argued that loan-loss reserves simply reflected the real market value of existing loans, and should not be counted as capital. England (and later Germany) supported the OCC. By 1987 Volcker and US banks won out. Volcker informed the June 1987 International Monetary Conference (IMC) that general loan-loss reserves would be counted as capital, albeit not pure (Tier 1) capital.

## 5. Failed multilateral efforts through BIS: 1983–1986

Much attention has been given to the role of the BIS Supervisory Committee in multilateral efforts to raise capital. While the Committee made progress in defining and measuring capital, ultimately it was not able to secure regulatory change. This section steps back in time and summarizes that multilateral effort.

### 5.1 The Cooke Committee

Multilateral efforts to homogenize bank regulations began as early as 1974 with the Group of Ten's Basle Standing Committee on Banking Regulations and Supervisory Practices (hereafter, the 'Cooke Committee') at the Bank for International Settlements (BIS). The Cooke Committee was commonly named after its longstanding chairman, W. Peter Cooke, who headed up banking supervision at the Bank of England. The Committee consisted of central bank representatives from Belgium, Canada, France, Germany, Italy, Japan, the Netherlands, Sweden, the United Kingdom, and the United States, plus Switzerland and Luxembourg. Each country had two representatives at the table. US representation was expanded to four, a sign of US influence and of its fragmented regulatory structure. Through protracted discussions, the Committee laid some technical groundwork for the Basle Accord in defining capital and risks, but did not reach agreement. Stephen Fay (1987) and David Kynaston (2000: 666) suggest that Peter Cooke was 'moved downwards and sideways' in September 1985, following the

[19] David Lascelles, 'Volcker Voices Doubt On Third World Debt Provisions', *Financial Times*, 25 June 1987, p. 35: S40; *American Banker; Frankfurter Zeitung* 25 June 1987.

collapse of Johnson Matthey Bank in October 1984 and supervisory failures of the Crocker National and Midland banks.

The Committee's first Basle Concordat (1975) had laid out general principles for host and parent countries' division of responsibilities and for home-country consolidation of regulation.[20] In June 1982 the Cooke Committee issued a paper 'calling for supervisors to resist any further erosion in capital ratios' and to raise capital levels. The 1983 Revised Basle Concordat refined the measurement and definitions of risks and capital adequacy. No specific proposals were agreed on.

In early 1984 Paul Volcker persuaded the Group of Ten central bank governors on the BIS Board to again discuss capital standards. Over some objections from the German and French delegates, the BIS Board instructed Peter Cooke to investigate co-operation on capital standards. By September 1984 Cooke had made recommendations for the creation of an 'Observation Ratio' framework, using six tiers of risk (BIS 1985: 9). No movement toward homogeneity of standards occurred.

## 5.2 Cooke Committee languished by 1986

Tobin (1991) concludes that despite the work of the Cooke Committee no regulatory homogeneity was seen or likely:

> It is likely that situation would have continued without the development of a separate negotiation. The truly multilateral effort in the Basle Committee had failed to reach convergence. [. . .] [C]onvergence did not occur gradually through a consensual process, because fundamental political [economy] issues were involved. [. . .] It is doubtful whether any concrete results would have emerged from the Basle Committee process (Tobin 1991: 210–211).

Although the Cooke Committee played an important role in clarifying the analytical issues involved, it was not responsible for agreement on the Basle Accord.

Indeed, as late as September 1986 the Cooke Committee itself circulated a paper to central bank supervisors worldwide which stated that it was not possible to recommend even a single definition of capital, let alone regulate it: 'It is not possible to recommend one single, generally-accepted definition of capital [. . .] Over time, it is hoped that the exercise will assist in determining the divergence between the capital position of different national banking systems.'[21] The paper merely expressed hope that the 'divergence' between heterogenous standards could be determined.

[20] The principles included: support by central bankers for private banks with liquidity problems within their borders; parent banks to be held responsible for the losses of their overseas branches or subsidiaries, supported by their central bank; consortium banks to be supported on a *pro rata* basis by the parent banks. Kapstein 1992: 329.

[21] This paper was circulated to bank supervisors worldwide. Quoted in Tobin 1991: 208.

## 6. US–UK bilateral agreement: Late 1986

Yet behind the scenes the USA and UK had already begun negotiating a bilateral agreement on capital standards. In four months the USA and UK were able to reach agreement. This bilateral agreement paved the way for the Basle Accord.

### 6.1 US–UK bilateral accord: 1986–1987

In February 1986 the Bank of England and the US Federal Reserve Bank began private bilateral talks on capital adequacy. To the USA, the talks 'required a fundamental rethinking of the appropriate definition of capital, since each country brought its own definition to the negotiations'.[22]

In July Volcker and Bank of England Governor Leigh-Pemberton met to discuss a common approach. That July meeting marked the beginning of real movement. Leigh-Pemberton advocated stronger international coordination among securities regulators. But there was no international consensus on capital standards. The EC was looking into the issue but had taken no action. Great Britain was dissatisfied with the EC approach, which reflected Germany's mandate on the definition of capital. '[C]ountries continued to defend their own capital standards. Germany, saw no need of standardization among G-10 countries, given its own rigorous capital requirements.'[23] Capital in Germany was defined by law; and regulators claimed they could not alter it. England was also dissatisfied with European movement toward a European Monetary System and was eager to sidestep the EC initiative.

Federal Reserve and Bank of England staff met in September and October of 1986. They quickly resolved major issues.[24] The meetings were kept confidential until final agreement was reached. On 8 January 1987 the Federal Reserve Board and the Bank of England announced agreement on common standards for bank capital adequacy. This was only four months after the pessimistic Cooke Committee paper had stated 'it is not possible to recommend one single, generally-accepted definition of capital'. The US–UK agreement would later provide the basis for the Basle Accord.[25]

[22] FRBNY *Quarterly Review*, Winter 1987–1988: 27. The UK had moved to its own use of capital requirements earlier.

[23] Kapstein 1999: 339. US, UK, and German banks were well capitalized; less so were Japanese, French, and Belgian banks: *Financial Times*, 11 December 1987.

[24] Tobin (1991) suggests the major issues were resolved by October. Also in late October 1986 the UK began its 'Big Bang' of financial deregulation.

[25] 'Agreed Proposal of the United States Federal Banking Supervisory Authorities and the Bank of England on Primary Capital and Capital Adequacy Assessment, reprinted in 3 *Fed. Banking L. Rep.* (CCH) P33,151 (27 February 1987); and 52 Fed. Reg. 5, 135, 5, 136 (1987). For a discussion, see Malloy 1988: 88–105; Kapstein 1999: 339; and Tobin 1990: 29. On bilateral bargaining leading to multilateral agreement, see Oye 1991.

The American Bankers Association expressed concern about several details of the bilateral agreement. In particular, it noted the unfair advantage of banks operating in countries where the more stringent standard did not apply. It also worried that the government would use it to allocate credit, rather than relying on private market decisions.[26]

## 6.2 US–UK agreement pre-empted European initiatives; Cooke Committee resuscitated

The US–UK bilateral accord pre-empted European negotiations, which might have created a different standard which the United States had no part in negotiating. The EC was taken by surprise: the Commission was 'outraged' when it was informed of the US–UK agreement just the day before it was made public. The EC suggested that Britain might be in violation of the Treaty of Rome. The US–UK agreement also shocked the Cooke Committee. One member described it as a 'bombshell'.[27]

Facing pressure from the EC, British authorities immediately revived the languishing Cooke Committee. The Basle Accord would ultimately be announced by the Cooke Committee as the result of multilateral efforts. While true in part, the driving force was the US–UK agreement (and subsequent US–Japan agreement, discussed next). All parties benefitted from presenting the agreement through the auspices of the Cooke Committee: the US and UK avoided alienating other members, the other members saved face, and the Cooke Committee avoided being left behind.

The Cooke Committee met in January, March, April, and June of 1987 to try to reconcile the US–UK agreement to the goals of other BIS member countries. It encountered resistance from the Japanese and German delegations on the definition of capital. In Brussels, preliminary agreement was reached on a formula using two tiers of capital. The first tier of 'pure' capital (Tier 1) was to consist primarily of shareholders' equity. The second tier (Tier 2) included elements such as hidden assets, loan reserves, and subordinated capital, to be regulated at the discretion of national regulators. Other difficulties remained. Despite the US–UK agreement and the Cooke Committee's efforts at negotiations, no multilateral agreement had yet occurred.

## 6.3 June 1987 International Monetary Conference

As mentioned above, the month after Citicorp's loan-loss reserve was announced top bank CEOs met in Hamburg, Germany at their annual

[26] *American Banker*, January 1987. Edward Yingling's comments to the Federal Reserve Board, 23 June 1987, mimeograph; cited in Tobin (1990).

[27] Tobin (May 1990: 34) and personal discussion.

International Monetary Conference (IMC). Citicorp's reserves and the US–UK capital adequacy proposal were discussed. Besides bankers, also present at the Conference were Paul Volcker, chairman of the Federal Reserve; Robin Leigh-Pemberton, Governor of the Bank of England; Karl Otto Pöhl, President of the Bundesbank; Takeshi Ohta, Deputy Governor of the Bank of Japan; and Jacques de Laroisiére, Governor of the Bank of France and former Director of the IMF.[28]

Volcker assured Citicorp that provisions against Third World loans would be allowed as Tier 2 capital. He accepted that these loan-loss reserves did not fit the definition of Tier 1 pure capital, on the ground that they were a cost of doing business, not a cushion against loss. John Reed said he was 'greatly encouraged' by Volcker's comments.[29] The final Basle Accord would allow loan-loss reserves to count up to 2 per cent of assets for Tier 2 capital, phased down over three years to 1.25 per cent.

## 7. US–Japan: Market Access, Pressured Bilateral Agreement 1987

The 1988 capital-adequacy accord, signed in Basle by regulators from a dozen rich countries, had two purposes: to make banks stronger and to undercut the competitive advantage enjoyed by Japanese banks.

*The Economist*, 26 October 1991

The US then used off-the-record threats of market closure against Japanese banking products to pressure Japan into joining the US–UK agreement. These threats constituted product market access restrictions: restrictions on the sale of services which did not meet risk-based capital standards. This section describes the use of market access by the USA to raise capital standards in Japan, partly to strengthen the world's financial system and partly to improve the competitive position of US banks. Success in bringing Japan into the US–UK agreement was ultimately what clinched agreement on the Basle Accord.

Earlier in the 1980s Japanese banks began to undercut US banks with low lending rates. Japanese banks profited from high domestic savings, a large capital account surplus, ceilings on deposit interest rates, and a mushrooming

[28] German protesters blocked traffic to demand the forgiveness of Third World debt; they were removed by police: 'Protesters Mar IMC Meeting', *American Banker*, 24 June 1987 152/122: 3.

[29] Previously, US banks had been allowed to count reserves as 'primary' capital. Bank regulators made a judgement between 'general provisions', which are available to meet any losses, and count as capital; and 'specific provisions', which cover an identified credit risk and do not count as capital: Reed quoted in *Financial Times* (London), 25 June 1987: 35. Tax relief on loan loss reserves was also affected.

Japanese stock market that inflated banks' unrealized gains. By 1989 nine of the world's ten largest banks were Japanese (ranked by assets).[30]

In 1985 the Federal Reserve Bank subtly began to tighten entry requirements for foreign banks, particularly Japanese banks. US banks had complained that Japanese regulations gave Japanese banks an unfair competitive advantage. The Federal Reserve indicated that because Japanese banks were perceived to be undercapitalized they might be prevented from buying out US banks or setting up new financial establishments in the USA (Tobin 1991: 237).

The US–Japanese informal discussions on capital adequacy began while the US–UK deal was being negotiated. When the US–UK agreement was announced the USA increased pressure on Japan. New York Federal Reserve Bank President Gerald Corrigan, meeting with Ministry of Finance officials in Tokyo, urged Japan to participate. Several Japanese banks had only recently filed applications with the Federal Reserve Bank for primary dealer status. Newspapers reported veiled protectionist threats of a 'zone of co-operation' that could restrict foreign bank activity unless the Japanese government adopted the new risk-based standard. The Bank of England's Brian Quinn remarked that 'If I were a Japanese bank or a Japanese supervisor, I would be a little worried'. The Japanese press reported in June 1987 that the US Congress was prepared to block further entry of Japanese banks into the American market.

Japanese regulators emphasized their 'hidden reserves' (then-undervalued real estate and corporate equities) and argued that US/UK weights were too high. Without the hidden reserves Japanese banks had lower capital/asset ratios than US banks. With the reserves included, Japanese ratios were higher than those of US banks. The difference is crucial. 'Fed officials [. . .] said the primary push for the standardization of regulations came from people [US bankers] complaining that the Japanese banks were operating at much lower capital levels than other world-class banks and thus had a competitive advantage.'[31]

Japanese banks held a far greater percentage of assets in equity securities than their American or European competitors. Although hidden, these were believed to be larger than all other forms of capital for Japanese banks. Japanese banks would sell securities to cover losses. Until then securities were unrealized gains. Japanese regulators identified these potential gains as a revaluation reserve, and counted 70 per cent of that reserve as capital. Other OECD countries refused to allow banks to mark equity portfolios to market value, because of the volatility of the equities markets.

[30] This also reflects currency valuations and the fact that US banks had moved into non-asset based financial products.

[31] *New York Times*, 12 July 1988. The context makes clear that US bankers are the 'people' referred to.

By May 1987 Paul Volcker had pushed the UK–US accord heavily at the BIS, in the USA, and in Japan. That month Gerald Corrigan, head of the Federal Reserve Bank of New York, again visited Tokyo where he was quoted by the Japanese press as saying that 'the most important reform' Japan could make would be 'a better alignment of Japanese capital requirements with those of other leading countries'. Ultimately, Japan agreed.[32]

Two months later, in August 1987, US Federal Reserve Bank and Japanese regulators met in New York to discuss their bilateral agreement. Tension was high at that meeting. Gerald Corrigan reportedly banged his fist on the table and demanded that the Japanese delegation sign the agreement by the next day or face restrictions on market access. The Japanese delegation reportedly stayed up all night on the telephone to Tokyo, and the next morning signed the agreement.[33]

## 8. Realization of the Basle Accord

With the three largest financial centers in the world near agreement on capital standards and at least one of them (the USA) willing to withhold access to its markets in order to achieve multilateral agreement, it was not long before the Basle Accord was signed. This section discusses the trilateral agreement between the USA, UK, and Japan; their presentation of a united front before the Cooke Committee; acceptance of the Basle Accord by private bankers; and the impact of the Accord in implementing higher common capital standards. (The penultimate section nine discusses lingering heterogeneity in those standards).

### 8.1 Trilateral (US–UK–Japan) agreement and presentation to BIS, 1987

Nine months after the US–UK bilateral agreement, US, UK, and Japanese regulators reached a trilateral agreement in London on 13 September 1987. They used the Brussels formula of two tiers of capital. A total capital-to-assets ratio of 8 per cent was required, of which at least half had to come from Tier 1 capital.[34] The UK wanted a three-year phase-in for the Accord, Japan wanted five years. Compromise was reached on five years with interim

[32] *American Banker*, 7 May 1987: 2; *Economist*, 30 May 1987.

[33] Anonymous sources familiar with the meeting, interviews October 1990. *Euromoney* later reported a different story (July 1988: 40), that the Japanese Ministry of Finance 'believes it got off lightly'. The Ministry was surprised that its proposal to include 45% of hidden assets in Tier 2 capital got through. Two compromise backup plans had been prepared in case it did not.

[34] 'Eight per cent was also the amount used in the final Basle Accord. The choice of eight per cent was "seat-of-the-pants stuff" ', admitted Peter Cooke later. 'Seven and a half per cent was what we felt comfortable with, and we added a half a per cent cushion for good measure and said eight': quoted in *Institutional Investor*, August 1994: 40.

goals. In addition, the three agreed that Japanese banks could count 45 per cent of unrealized capital gains as part of their Tier 2 capital. Japan had wanted 70 per cent; the USA and UK had sought less.

Four days after the US–UK–Japan agreement, Federal Reserve representative William Taylor presented the substance of the proposal to the Cooke Committee meeting in Basle. The trilateral agreement was not made public but at the conference table the British and Japanese representatives took the same position as the USA (the British more actively; the Japanese in acquiescence). The other G-10 representatives present at the meeting recognized the agreement as a *fait accompli* and accepted it to avoid being upstaged (Tobin 1990, 1991).

The trilateral agreement formed the basis for the Basle Accord, although the details for the multilateral accord took three months to work out. US and British regulators lobbied their counterparts in Japan, as well as France and Germany. Japanese regulators expressed concern over the valuation of hidden assets. French regulators argued there was no objective measure of 'enough capital'; they stated that bank safety depended rather on bank activities and the quality of management. The definition of supplementary capital was expanded for the French, to include unrealized gains on physical assets. German regulators wanted corporate equities treated as capital but German representatives were divided. The Bundesbank supported the agreement; the German government representative resisted the two-tier arrangement, preferring a more strict definition of core capital as mandated by German law. The final Accord recognized the hesitation of 'one participant' (Germany). German negotiators held out until the last minute but ultimately signed. (On German institutions and foreign policy see Banchoff 1999.)

The definition of capital and the risk-weights assigned to assets were at the core of the agreement. In both cases, the Basle Accord tended to allow national regulators greater discretion than in the US–UK agreement. (Capital measures are compared in Figure 5.2, above.) Tier 2 capital included virtually all capital definitions in use. Risk weights were lowered below the US–UK accord for virtually all asset categories, showing some movement toward LCD. Nonetheless, the agreement on Tier 1 capital did show some movement toward more stringent common standards.[35] It is for this reason classified as a higher common denominator outcome *writ large*.

Finally, on 10 December 1987 it was announced that Committee members had reached agreement on a draft proposal for 'international

[35] Other issues included: treatment of interest rate risk for holdings of government securities; treatment of credit risk exposure associated with interest rate and foreign exchange contracts; treatment of transfer/country risk distinctions; types of recognized collateral; treatment of loan commitments; the weighting system to permit some national discretion in assigning weights to asset categories: Tobin, May 1990: 37.

convergence of capital measurement and capital standards'.[36] The agreement was presented as the result of efforts by the Cooke Committee. After agreement was reached by the central bank governors the proposal was circulated to private bankers for comments.

## 8.2 Acceptance by private bankers, 1987–1988

The Basle Accord in part reflected the general interests of American and European banks, but their regulators were still concerned that private banks could obstruct the agreement by lobbying their domestic governments. By March 1988 regulators of G-10 countries were engaged in selling the accord to their banks (*Financial Times*, March 1988). That behavior is consistent with this book's propositions; it is not consistent with models in which governments thrust regulations onto the private sector.

At the June 1988 International Monetary Conference (IMC) in Chicago, Peter Cooke addressed bankers' concerns. Certain aspects of the new capital rules might need review, Cooke said, such as treatment of sovereign risk, core capital definitions, and treatment of mortgage-backed securities. However, the overall structure of the rules could not be changed without jeopardizing the whole initiative. Recognizing the danger of heterogeneous regulations, Cooke appealed to bankers and national regulators: 'Do not press so hard on the detail to justify the present *status quo* [*sic*] in your country that you compromise the wider goal.'[37] To allay concerns, Cooke stressed that the Basle rules were only intended to be a 'broad brush framework' for individual countries to implement.

The draft Basle Accord received strong support from American Express CEO, James D. Robinson, III, speaking at the June 1988 IMC:

> We have a collective interest in a stable and sound international monetary system [. . .] Internationally, both the competitive and the regulatory framework for financial services need to be enhanced. All of our institutions are affected by the health of the world financial and trading systems. [. . .] *On the regulatory front, greater convergence of regulations between countries is needed.* [. . .] Banking regulators and supervisors have increased their joint efforts over the past few years to improve their understanding of international banking markets, to share information, and to develop compatible standards and procedures. The Cooke Committee of the Bank for International Settlements has paved the way for several initiatives, *including the recent international agreement to increase bank capital adequacy requirements for*

[36] BIS Committee on Banking Regulations and Supervisory Practices, 'Proposals for International Convergence of Capital Measurement and Capital Standards', BIS, December 1987. The proposal includes several minority views (widely believed to be from Germany, Japan, and France).

[37] Cooke quoted in 'Proposed Capital Rules Need To Be Reviewed', *Financial Times* (London), 8 June 1988: 32/S40. David Lascelles, Banking Editor: Chicago. Cooke's title was listed as 'assistant director', Bank of England.

*the world's major financial countries* and to address the new areas of risk management. *That progress should continue.*[38]

American Express, as a nonbank not subject to the capital requirements, undoubtedly found them easier to support than banks did.

US banks nonetheless accepted the agreement with some revisions. One Senate staffer noted: 'It just never became an issue around here. [. . .] nor were there any banks calling up to get us to do anything' (quoted in Tobin 1991: 247). One exception was that US banks did protest classifying preferred stock in Tier 2. Congressional representatives voiced that concern. In the final Basle Accord, US bank demands were met and preferred stock was moved up to Tier 1 as the only dilution of the 'pure' capital Tier.

The final 1988 Accord reflected US bank interests in another way: it avoided distinguishing between foreign and domestic banks, and did not assign the former a higher risk-weighting. US banks had complained they would be disadvantaged by rules that allowed EC banks to treat other EC banks as domestic. Instead, the final July 1988 Accord distinguished between OECD countries (low-risk) and non-OECD countries (higher-risk).[39] Most bankers accepted the key elements of the draft Basle Accord. On 15 July 1988 the final Basle Accord was released.[40]

One must be clear here: there is no evidence that bankers worldwide lobbied strongly *for* increased capital standards, and in fact many were not enthusiastic about them. Some bankers expressed reservations to central bank regulators about the Accord. For example, Chemical Bank Chairman, Walter Shipley, said he 'broadly supports the Cooke initiative but is a harsh critic of the way the Basle Accord treats "goodwill" '.[41] Bankers were bothered that nonbanks (such as GE Capital or American Express) were not covered by the agreement. The nonbanks were more enthusiastic about the Accord. The inflexibility of the agreement obscured differences between banks, such as Citibank's greater geographic dispersion of risk. Also, regulators in different countries interpreted the regulations differently; e.g. French regulators were accused of not enforcing much of the agreement.[42]

However, bankers worked vehemently *against* other proposed strategies for managing developing country debt, such as non-voluntary debt resched-

[38] *American Banker*, 153/135 13 July 1988: 18 (emphases added). Robinson was head of the American Express Corporation, a nonbank; and also head of the Financial Services Council (a lobbying group of banks, securities firms, thrifts, insurance companies, and finance companies, spun off from the ABA).

[39] The only exception was Saudi Arabia, which protested its exclusion, and was ultimately included in the low-risk category.

[40] Later that year W. Peter Cooke retired after 33 years of service to the Bank of England, and joined a private sector firm.

[41] *Euromoney*, July 1988: 48. Under the regulations, goodwill is assigned no value; the goodwill in a cash acquisition is wiped off a bank's equity, a reversal of previous US practice. Shipley lamented it 'throws a road-block in the consolidation of America's fractionated banking system'. Shipley was known for his anti-regulatory stances.

[42] Interview with Citicorp executive committee members, March 1991.

uling. They saw capital standards as the lesser of two evils and had an interest in accepting it. Further, US banks lobbied strongly against heterogenous measures to increase capital requirements.[43]

European banks also generally accepted the agreement. Some complained about currency problems such as foreign exchange risk; others were reluctant to reveal previously secret details of their balance sheets.

Top bankers' support for homogenous regulations continued the following year at the June 1989 IMC meeting in Madrid. David Scholey, chairman of S.G. Warburg Group PLC, warned that capital and investment banking markets around the world could be threatened by 'competitive deregulation' between the various leading financial centers. Given that there was no centralized structure to co-ordinate the relaxation of barriers in capital markets, Scholey said, the leading central banks had created rules to ensure the stability of the commercial banking system. Scholey proudly noted that 'such a process in the securities markets [by contrast] is in its stumbling infancy'. By 1993 the BIS countries would add additional capital requirements on financial derivatives.[44]

## 8.3 Impact: Initial trends toward homogeneity, 1988–1999

The Basle Accord had a significant impact on banks, beginning with the agreement in 1988. Many banks shifted their asset bases and capital to comply with the new regulations. They divested subsidiaries, securitized and sold assets (loans), retained more earnings, lowered dividends, and cut operating costs. The 1988 Accord became an accepted world standard, with well over 100 countries applying the Basle framework to their banking system during the 1990s.[45]

The Accord forced Japanese banks to retreat. As *The Economist* noted, undercutting the competitive advantage enjoyed by Japanese banks was one of two goals of the Accord (the other was to strengthen all banks): 'The accord is working. [. . .] Japanese banks, once the scourge of better capitalised rivals, have retreated from international markets.'[46]

[43] Several years later, when the developing country debt crisis eased and credit was tight, bankers would become more vocal in their criticism of the Basle Accord. They complained about the artificial allocation of capital and risk. Continued heterogeneity in implementing the capital accord reflected their interests. *The Economist* Financial Survey, 9 September 1992, 'Nightmare in Basle'; and 'Who's Who on BIS', *International Economy*, September/October 1992.

[44] *American Banker*, 154/112: 5, 9 June 1989. IOSCO studied ways to homogenize capital standards for non-bank securities firms beginning in 1987 (IOSCO Report 10 August 1989). Banking products also changed significantly from the 1960s onward, as disintermediation from traditional banking continued, and derivatives and non-asset based products grew in importance. For an introduction see IMF, *International Capital Markets*, 1994, Chapter III: 'Derivatives and Supervisory Issues'.

[45] Most but not all offshore financial centers formally complied, but enforcement in many was lax. See Chapter Three above on offshore centers.

[46] *The Economist*, 'The Cross of Capital', 26 October 1991.

A joint US Treasury Department–Federal Reserve report on capital equivalency, mandated under the Foreign Bank Supervision Enhancement Act of 1991 (FBSEA), asserted that twenty of the twenty-two countries surveyed 'are implementing uniformly the Basle minimum capital ratios'. The twenty-two countries surveyed accounted for 97 per cent of the total US assets of foreign banks operating in the USA. However, the report conceded that some differences between countries remained:

> [N]ational discretion is provided regarding whether to allow banks to include certain of the components in tier 2 Capital and, to a lesser degree, in Tier 1 capital. The discretion exercised by national authorities with regard to the capital components results in definitions of qualifying capital that are equivalent, although not identical, among countries subscribing to the Accord.[47]

The Fed-Treasury report went on to argue unconvincingly: 'A fundamental premise of the Basle Accord is the acceptance of [differences in capital instruments and accounting practices in other countries] in order to advance the international convergence [*sic*] of capital standards.' The problem was, as the next decade demonstrated, that acceptance of differences does not advance convergence.

## 9. *Subcase*: Lingering heterogeneity, post-1991

Up to this point this case study has emphasized the movement toward a higher common denominator. That is only part of the story. The second part is lingering heterogeneity in implementing the Accord and heterogenous regulatory movements after it, followed by calls for reform in 1999. These are discussed in turn.

### 9.1 Definitions, data, and heterogeneity

Banks have considerable leeway in reporting their accounts. The timing of tax realizations, 'hidden values' of realizable amounts in excess of recorded asset values, and a variety of other recognized accounting techniques give banks financial flexibility in raising capital. Regulators also have considerable leeway in their calculation of capital adequacy. Tier 1 capital remained fairly rigid in definition, but tinkering with asset-risk weights and the definitions of Tier 2 and assets (such as nonperforming loans) continued to allow regulators considerable heterogeneity in implementing the Accord.

The lack of agreement on definitions and data confidentiality make it difficult to reach precise conclusions on the Accord's effect. Indeed, reliable comparative time series data were simply not publicly available on most

[47] Board of Governors of the Federal Reserve System and Secretary of the US Department of the Treasury, Report to *Congress on Capital Equivalency*, 19 June 1992.

banks' capital ratios. A member of the BIS Basle Committee on Banking Supervision secretariat wrote:

> Unfortunately, the BIS does not publish the data you are looking for, nor are 'official' statistics which compare capital ratios for banks from different countries available from any other institutions to my knowledge. Some time back [annually 1989–1991] the IMF [. . .] made an attempt to estimate capital ratios for a sample of banks from various countries. *Euromoney* and the *Institutional Investor* occasionally provide capital numbers for the largest world banks. One must be careful in interpreting that data, however, given different accounting and reporting conventions.[48]

These data incommensurabilities are an indication of continued heterogeneity in bank capital standards, despite the Basle Accord of the late 1980s.

It is clear that the Basle Accord had less impact on reducing cross-national heterogeneity than was first hoped. As one example, the *Institutional Investor* (referred to above by the BIS secretariat) noted critically that Japan's banks would be below the minimum 8 per cent level if not for their liberal interpretation of the Accord:

> The seemingly robust ratios shown in [Japan's] rankings [. . .] also have to be viewed skeptically. Japanese institutions actually have little regulatory capital left. If it weren't for Japan's liberal interpretation of the Basel rules, these banks would fall well below 8 per cent. [. . .] In fact, despite talk of capital 'standards,' the rules are not as easily applicable across national boundaries as supervisors first hoped. Different countries still have different rules for provisioning, marking to market, disclosure, and accountancy that distort the way that capital and risk are measured and ratios calculated. According to Japanese accounting standards, for instance, the non-performing loans of Japan's Mitsubishi Bank are 572 billion yen; according to US rules, 1.150 trillion yen (August 1994, 40 ff).

The article went on to emphasize the considerable heterogeneity in capital standards and the flexibility used by national regulators to bend interpretations of the rules to the advantage of their producers.

Care must be taken in comparing capital ratios between countries. Consider two sets of data published by the IMF (also referred to by the BIS secretariat). Early IMF data on capital/asset ratios, published from 1989–1991, are shown in Figure 5.3. The data are from 'official sources and Fund staff estimates'. Beginning in 1992, the IMF switched to OECD data for capital-asset ratios. These later data are shown in Figure 5.4. The later data show considerably lower estimates for Japan and France and higher estimates for Germany.

The IMF was cautious about heterogeneous definitions in both its early and later estimates: 'Owing to differences in national accounting practices, the figures must be interpreted with caution. In particular, provisioning

[48] Personal communication to the author, from a member of the Basle Committee on Banking Supervision secretariat, Bank for International Settlements, 5 December 1994. The Committee uses its own unpublished data to evaluate compliance with the Accord.

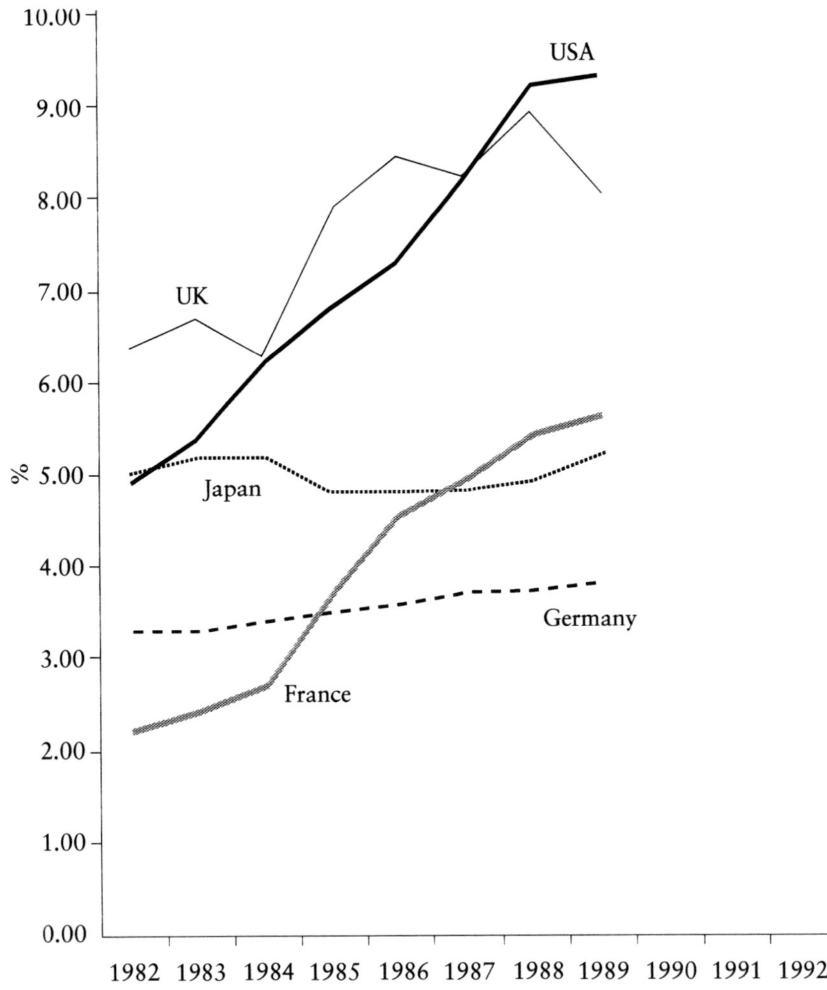


*Source*: IMF International Capital Markets (not BIS definition)

*Figure 5.3*: Capital/asset ratios 1982–1989; early IMF estimates, *c.* 1989–1991

practices vary considerably across countries, as do the definitions of capital.'[49]

Despite the problems in data commensurability, it is clear from the IMF data that capital ratios in the USA and UK were higher than in other countries. That these two countries were the major movers behind global capital

[49] IMF, *International Capital Markets*, various years 1989–1993, table entitled 'Capital/Asset Ratios of Banks in Selected Industrial Countries', sources are Bank of England and OECD. The Fund suggests that 'cross-country comparisons may be less appropriate than developments over time within a given country'.

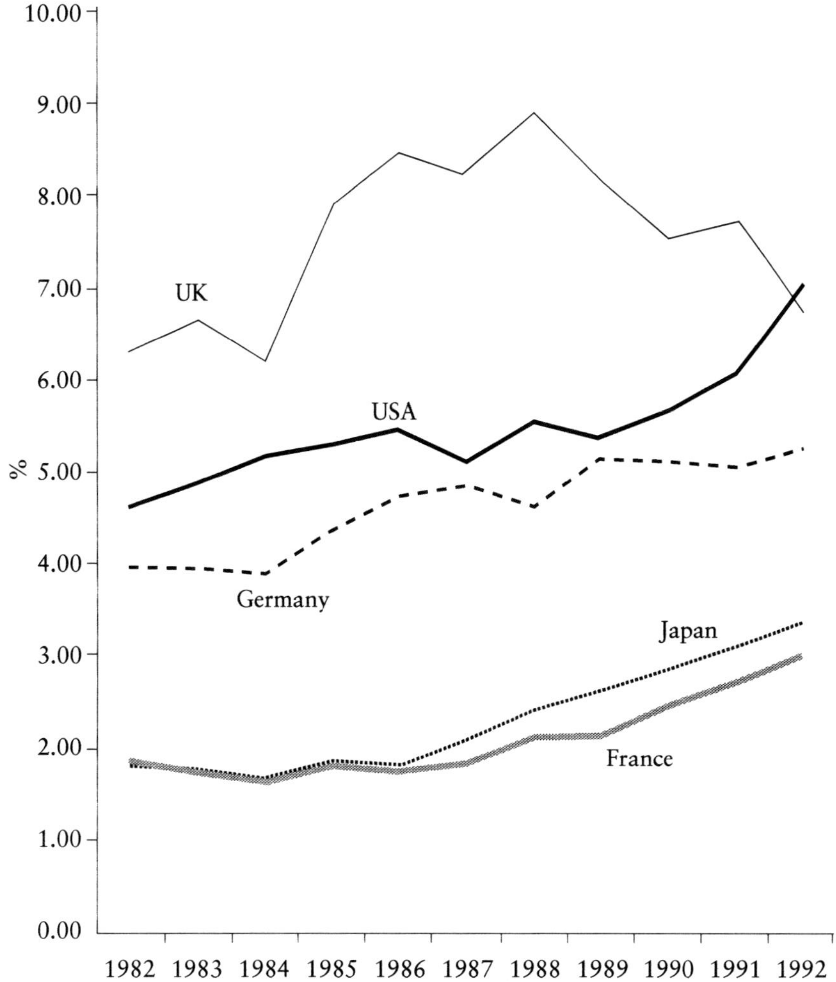


*Source*: IMF 1993 International Capital Markets (not BIS definition)

*Figure 5.4*: Capital/asset ratios 1982–1991; later IMF estimates, 1993

standards and are the two leading financial centers in the world is consistent with this book's emphasis that regulations reflect dominant producer preferences.

## 9.2 Heterogenous implementation

Fears of financial collapse from the LDC 'debt crisis' eased by 1990, when the first 'Brady Plan' was completed with Mexico to restructure its debt.[50] Concomitantly, it became clear that differences would remain between countries with respect to their treatment of capital.

Enforcement of the Basle Accord remained national, not international, and the regulators' main threat was a cease and desist order. This threat lacked credibility for domestic banks, since 'it is unlikely that a bank will be closed [by domestic regulators] solely because it is under the prescribed capital levels'.[51] A more credible threat was posed to foreign banks: restricted access to domestic markets by host-country regulators. Heterogenous protectionism had not disappeared.

Considerable national differences remained in the definition of Tier 1 and Tier 2 capital. For example, the USA, France, and others allowed loan-loss reserves to count as capital. Canada did not, although the Canadian Superintendent of Financial Institutions, Michael McKenzie, was quite revealing in his comment: 'We have some distance to go in resolving with the [financial] industry what our real position on this subject is.'[52] A 1996 amendment on trading risks allowed some banks for the first time to use their own systems to measure market risks. Differences in national accounting continued through 2002.

## 9.3 Impact and heterogenous response in Japan

Japanese banks were restricted by the crash in the Tokyo stock and real estate markets, which brought down their unrealized gains with it. The *Far Eastern Economic Review* observed in 1993 that Japanese banks were forced out of certain markets: 'Japanese banks are in a crisis, resulting in a withdrawal from European and US activities [. . .] Loans to the US have declined from 38% of the [Japanese] foreign loan total in 1989 to 27% of the total in 1992. Asset trimming has resulted from higher capital adequacy rules of the Bank for International Settlements.'[53] One effect of the Basle Accord was to reduce the inroads Japanese banks had made in the USA and Europe over the previous fifteen years. That is one sign that the Basle Accord did in fact have an impact. However, the Japanese government also responded to the interests of Japanese banks with more lenient interpretations of capital. By contrast, other countries imposed even more stringent restrictions on capital in the next few years.

## 9.4 Heterogenous measures to raise capital requirements, post-1991

[50] Officers from the lead US banks were in close contact with Secretary of Treasury Nicholas Brady and his aides on the plan, including David Mulford, by February 1989. Although the banks and Brady often clashed, they also worked closely together. The Brady Plan pressured banks to offer some concessions on principal and interest payments in addition to new lending (20-60-20, respectively); and backed them with zero-coupon US Treasury bonds. The details of the negotiations were left up to the private Bank Advisory Committees and debtor countries.

[51] On the credibility of regulators' threats, see Kapstein 1999: 346.

[52] *Financial Times*, 2 September 1989.

[53] Jonathan Friedland, 'Accent on Asia: Banks pull back from US and Europe' (Japanese Banking), *Far Eastern Economic Review*, 8 April 1993, 156/14: 74.

Thus, by 1991 a number of countries (including the UK, USA, Switzerland, and Singapore) unilaterally raised their capital requirements above the Basle Accord standards, in different ways. For example, the Bank of England varied the rule according to the individual bank and could demand ratios of 15 per cent or more.

As US bank capital levels rose, the USA led the way in implementing even more stringent heterogenous measures than called for in the Basle Accord. US actions followed the BCCI scandal and the savings and loan crisis. The US Federal Deposit Insurance Corporation Improvement Act of 1991 (FDICIA) established five levels of compliance with US regulations. The top level, 'well capitalized', required a Tier 1 ratio of at least 6 per cent and a Tiers 1+2 ratio of at least 10 per cent. (The next level, 'adequately capitalized', corresponded to the Basle Accord: 4 per cent and 8 per cent, respectively).[54] US regulators also examined leverage ratios and sought 'tangible common equity' levels of at least 4 per cent of assets.

Simultaneously, the US Foreign Bank Supervision Enhancement Act of 1991 (FBSEA, embedded within the FDICIA) moved supervision of foreign banks from the state level to the Federal Reserve Board. It imposed 'national treatment' on foreign banks. The FBSEA required Federal Reserve Board approval before a foreign bank can set up offices in the USA, established mandatory standards for entry, and allowed termination of a foreign bank's offices for 'unsound practices'. Most foreign banks operate their subsidiaries according to home-country guidelines. The Bank Acts imposed a long examination process on foreign banks, who in effect had to meet guidelines of two sets of regulators.

The FDICIA and FBSEA had the *de facto* effect of protectionist measures. (They were justified with the noblest of reasons, namely to prevent future BCCI crises, and with popular support for a 'level playing field'.) Analysts at Ernst and Young highlighted that heterogeneity:

> US guidelines requiring banks to have capital above the levels set by the Bank for International Settlements is making it more difficult for foreign banks to enter or expand in the United States. [. . .] 'The US first sought an international benchmark [the Basle Accord] and then turned around and added higher capital standards in the 1991 banking act.' [. . .] [R]egulators have in practice declined to approve an application from a foreign bank if it fails to meet US standards.[55]

The head of the Federal Reserve Bank of Atlanta, Robert P. Forrestal, conceded: 'I recognize that this new law may do more than protect the US banking system from unsafe banks'; but Forrestal expressed hope that, by using access to US markets as leverage: 'The effects of the new law will

[54] See also developments in Europe, notably the European Community's Capital Adequacy Directive (CAD) and Investment Services Directive (ISD). The CAD takes effect at the end of 1995.

[55] *American Banker*, 19 October 1993: 8.

probably spill over into other countries that may then be influenced toward supervising their own banks on a consolidated basis.'[56] The US Federal Reserve was again using market-access for (financial) products as a bargaining chip to affect regulations in foreign countries.

The new, more stringent US regulations became effective on 16 June 1992. Citicorp, even with its huge loan-loss reserves, was able to exceed the more stringent US guidelines, meeting the 'adequate' level in 1992, and the highest 'well capitalized' level by 1993. By 1994 the average total capital ratio for US banks was 13 per cent, fully 8 per cent of which was Tier 1 capital. (Japanese banks, by contrast, averaged a total of only 9.25 per cent by March 1993.[57])

The Basle Accord was not a pure public good. Unlike a true public good, dominant countries could in fact exclude other countries from benefitting by closing access to their markets.[58] Further, there were some advantages to banks of raising capital requirements as long as it was done gradually. Higher capital ratios are not always a competitive disadvantage, they can also build a comparative advantage by keeping competitors out and enhancing reputation. As the executive managing director of Standard and Poor's Ratings Group noted in 1994, 'The experience of the past five years shows that being well-capitalized is a tremendous competitive advantage'.[59] Well capitalized banks are rewarded by the market with higher credit ratings, cheaper funds, and larger business volumes. They are also rewarded by national regulators, who are more likely to approve acquisitions, new ventures, and other 'judgment calls' to well capitalized banks.

## 9.5 Toward a new (and more heterogenous) capital accord: Basel II

By 1999 a consensus on three substantive critiques of the accord emerged among banks and regulators. Large banks had developed *ad hoc* 'internal ratings based' (IRB) systems which, they argued, allowed for more sophisticated methods of calculating risk. A flat 8 per cent charge for claims on the private sector gave banks a perverse incentive to move high-quality assets off their balance sheets, thus reducing the average quality of bank loan portfolios. Also, the 1988 Accord did not recognize credit risk-mitigation techniques, such as collateral and guarantees.[60]

As a result, in June 1999 the Committee released a proposal to replace the

[56] Forrestal, cited in Bureau of National Affairs, Report For Executives, 10 June 1992, 'Fed Unlikely to End Foreign Bank Activity in US in Light of FDICIA, Official Says'.

[57] *Institutional Investor*, August 1994: 40 ff. *Financial Times*, 28 May 1993: 28. Japanese data are for the 11 major banks. Their capital ratios did grow, from an average 8.21% in September 1991: *Financial Times*, 27 November 1992: 27.

[58] Samuelson (1954) shows that the key elements of a public good are non-rivalry and non-excludibility in consumption.

[59] Clifford Griep, quoted in the *Institutional Investor*, August 1994.

1988 Accord with a more flexible and risk-sensitive framework. As of 2003 this proposal had not been adopted, let alone implemented. This book's emphasis is on *de facto* implemented standards, hence Basel II is mentioned here only in passing. The proposal placed more emphasis on banks' own internal control and management, the supervisory review process, and 'market discipline' involving disclosure. The new proposal offered more complex measurements of credit risk including internal ratings based approaches. It also added a new category, operational risk, and maintained the measurement of market risk.

The first 'consultative' proposals for the new accord were made available to banks, regulators, and others in June 1999. The second consultative package was made available in January 2001, with a May–June deadline for comments and a 2004 target for implementation. Over 250 such comments were received, the majority of them from banks and other financial firms. The comments were so critical that BIS postponed its anticipated date of implementation, several times. BIS acknowledged the role of firms:

> A widely-expressed comment from banks in particular was that the threshold for the use of the IRB [internal ratings based] approach should not be set so high as to prevent well-managed banks from using their internal ratings. Intensive work has taken place in the eighteen months since June 1999. Much of this has leveraged off work undertaken in parallel with industry representatives, whose cooperation has been greatly appreciated by the Basel Committee and its Secretariat.[61]

By May 2002 the target date was set back to 2005. In July 2002 the committee pushed back the deadline again, with the third 'consultative' package to be released in the second-quarter of 2003, and implementation delayed until 2006. Britain's FSA noted that Basel II 'will involve less change here than in most other countries'.[62] US regulators, and US banks, seemed equally satisfied with the outcome. With the 1980s debt crisis no longer posing a systemic risk or threat to solvency, and Japanese banks focused on inward difficulties, some retrenchment toward heterogeneity seemed likely.

[60] Quoted from 'The New Basel Capital Accord: An explanatory note', Bank for International Settlements, January 2001. The bankers' consensus on spelling changed from Basle to Basel in this period.

[61] 'The New Basel Capital Accord: an explanatory note', Bank for International Settlements, January 2001.

[62] UK Financial Services Authority, *Plan and Budget 2003/04*: 6.

## 10. Basle Accord: Summary and conclusion

The overall regulatory outcome of this case (HCD) is less clear than in the other case Chapters, but the historical details are consistent with this book's three propositions. Capital standards were raised, although not implemented uniformly, and banks which later raised their capital above levels set by the Basle Accord were rewarded by the market with higher credit ratings. Gradually increasing capital regulations may thus not have imposed as high a cost on banks as some feared. More important than the level of capital required at any given time may be the rate of change in capital requirements and their timing in regard to other competitive conditions.[63]

The 1988 Basle Accord case began with heterogenous definitions and requirements for bank capital in 1980. Following crises in sovereign lending and private banking, US regulators began to explore ways to reverse a perceived creeping competition-in-laxity in capital standards. Banks sought ways to stabilize financial markets without forgiving debt. American bankers voiced concern about the increased entry of Japanese banks into the US market and the lower capital standards in place in Tokyo. The Federal Reserve responded to US banks in two major ways. First, it tightened entry requirements for Japanese banks. Second, it refrained from imposing heterogenous risk-weighted requirements that would have hurt US banks.

Volcker approached Leigh-Pemberton and initiated a US–UK bilateral agreement. Even though the Cooke Committee reported in September 1986 that it was not possible to recommend one definition of capital, the Federal Reserve and Bank of England staff worked out just such an agreement three months later and announced it in January 1987. That bilateral agreement provided the basis for the Basle Accord. The US brought Japan into the US–UK agreement by quietly threatening to close market access further. The trilateral agreement was presented to the Cooke Committee as a *fait accompli*. Following some adjustments by national regulators and further adjustments in response to their banks, the Basle Accord was announced in July 1988 under the auspices of the BIS. It did raise Tier 1 capital standards worldwide. Nonetheless, as section nine above explained, considerable heterogeneity remained in world capital standards.

The Basle Accord case study can be evaluated with respect to this book's propositions on two levels: first and most broadly in terms of the relationship between all lenders and sovereign borrowers; second and more narrowly in terms of the choices made by individual banks and their national regulators.

[63] Regulators may protect domestic interests by the timing and rate of regulatory change. In addition, credit ratings inherently involve questions of perception. The Accord may have changed those perceptions.

On the broadest level dominant banks fought hard to strengthen their negotiating position with sovereign borrowers and to stabilize world financial markets. Higher capital standards were not the banks' first choice to that end, but they were much preferred to many other choices on the public agenda. Despite competition in the global financial market, banks co-operated through *ex ante* contractual arrangements on syndicated loans and through *ex post* governance structures in their Bank Advisory Committees. Banks and central bank regulators also worked together in this regard through the auspices of the Bank for International Settlements. The BIS was the brainchild of leading financiers in 1929 and for many years the US and Japanese shares in BIS were held and represented by the leading private banks in those countries. The working relationship between banks and regulators was close. BIS' original mandate under the Young Plan was to raise Germany's cost of defecting on reparations by reorganizing its official creditors (Simmons 1993: 382–383). Although catastrophic events in Germany blocked that mandate, to the extent that the BIS facilitated agreement on the Basle Accord it may have played a similar role in stabilizing financial markets and organizing private creditors in the 1980s.

The subcases of narrow choices made by banks and their national regulators also reveal the pressures and outcomes identified in this book's propositions. Pressures for competition-in-laxity led to lowering capital standards by 1981. Limited efforts were made by the Federal Reserve to raise standards to stabilize the domestic market, but US banks resisted more stringent heterogenous standards that would impede their competitive position. Ultimately, the Basle Accord was achieved through the threat of US market closure to foreign banks which did not meet the higher standards. Certain details of the Accord, such as the inclusion of preferred stock as Tier 1 capital at the behest of US banks, reflected the specific interests of money-center banks in different countries. Those diverse interests were also reflected in lingering heterogeneity. The US continued to raise capital standards above the Accord's level after 1991, at which time those standards differentially impeded the expansion of Japanese banks into US markets. US banks did not protest those later heterogenous measures nor their *de facto* protectionist effect. As the debt crisis eased in the early 1990s the differences between banks became more important than unified action among them. By 1999 the Basel Committee was adjusting its proposals for a new capital accord, in light of banks' preferences.

This case has lessons beyond capital requirements and the Basle Accord. US banks were hurt by the corporate malfeasance, negligence, and outright fraud which emerged in 2002, and which contributed to a decline in wealth that year of eight trillion US dollars. Major banks were both directly and indirectly implicated. Citigroup and Salomon Smith Barney were under investigation; JP Morgan Chase's stock price fell 60 per cent from November 2001 to November 2002. Advocates of financial self-regulation (see Bratton and McCahery 1995) faced new challenges and opportunities following these corporate financial scandals, discussed further in the book's conclusion below. Bebchuk (2002) describes the $US1.4 billion in fines imposed in 2003 as a 'slap on the wrist' and 'business as usual'. Overseas, the *Financial Times* noted that if 'the Japanese banks start to recover their market share in overseas lending, US and European banks may yet persuade the regulators to take a closer look at one aspect of their business—their treatment of bad debts'.[64] With Japan's economy suffering a decade-long recession, the Nikkei being down from 39,000 to below 8,000, unrealized losses straining their Basle I compliance, and Japan's financial system in dire need of reform, trade-generated conflicts over heterogenous domestic regulatory structures were not over.

The first Appendix to this Chapter explains capital adequacy for lay readers; the second briefly addresses two other cases of HCD outcomes: the highly specific case of regulations on phosphorus matches (phossy-jaw) and the broader case of European regional integration.

## Appendix (A): Explanation of capital adequacy

Capital adequacy regulations require banks to maintain capital equal to a certain percentage of their assets. Bank capital consists mainly of equity, reserves, and retained earnings. Traditional bank assets consist mainly of loans plus securities, fixed assets, and cash (less any specific loan-loss reserves). A bank may raise its capital-to-asset ratio by retaining profits, issuing debt or equity to investors, or selling off loans and restricting new loans. In a consolidated balance sheet assets are equal to liabilities plus capital, by definition. (Bank liabilities consist mainly of deposits, short-term borrowings, and long-term debt.)

Bank capital is one measure of banks' stability.[65] Raising capital relative to loans strengthens a bank's financial position (and can improve its credit ratings) but it also increases the cost of lending. Banks therefore need to balance their incentives to reduce capital, so as to reduce their cost of lending and underprice competitors, with their incentives for prudential lending and credit ratings.

The Basle Accord capital requirements divide capital into two categories. Tier 1 is core or 'pure' capital. It consists of resources such as common stock and retained earnings which are freely available to meet losses. Tier 2 is less

[64] *Financial Times*, 25 October 1994; citing David Marshall, IBCA (bank credit rating agency).

[65] Capital and reserve requirements are two mainstays of banking regulations. Reserve requirements are the percentage of customer deposits that banks must set aside in the form of reserves. Raising reserve requirements allows less lending, because the ratio determines the expansion of deposits that can be supported by each additional dollar of reserves.

available capital, including preferred stocks, undisclosed reserves, general loan loss reserves (up to 1.25 per cent of total capital), hybrid debt-capital instruments. Total capital adequacy must be over 8 per cent, of which first-tier capital must be at least 4 per cent.

The Basle Accord also divides assets into four categories of risk, with (somewhat arbitrary) assigned risk weights of zero per cent, 20 per cent, 50 per cent, and 100 per cent. The lower the risk weighting, the less capital required. Extremely secure assets such as OECD government bills carried a risk weight of zero per cent, meaning they do not need to be reserved against. This creates a regulatory incentive for banks to hold OECD government bills. Claims on other OECD banks (including multilateral development agencies such as the World Bank) carried a risk weight of 20 per cent. Collateralized home loans carried a risk weight of 50 per cent. All other private sector loans, including those to blue-chip corporations and non-OECD banks, carried a risk weight of 100 per cent, meaning the entire value of the asset must be reserved against.

With the growth of financial services and products including complex derivatives and options, along with more complex models for evaluating risk, traditional measures of capital adequacy have been challenged.

## Appendix (B): Examples of other HCD cases

### Phosphorus matches ('phossy-jaw')

A similar story of the interplay between corporate and public interests and government regulations is found in turn-of-the-century regulations on phosphorus matches.[66] The use of phosphorus in matches led to a disfiguring and sometimes fatal condition among workers called *phosphorus necrosis* or 'phossy-jaw'. The case has both international and US federal aspects.

Internationally, the French match monopoly led the way in discovering a substitute product (sesquisulphide) and ended phosphorus match production in 1897. Switzerland, the Netherlands, and Germany soon followed suit, followed by Luxembourg, Denmark, and Italy. In 1906 these countries signed an international treaty severely restricting phosphorus match production.[67]

[66] This section is drawn from Moss (mimeo 1993, published in Moss 1994). Thanks to Moss for an advance copy of this paper and discussion of it. An early critic of phosphorus match production was Karl Marx, who noted that a Vienna physician in 1845 discovered a form of 'lock-jaw' to be peculiar to 'lucifer-matchmakers' using phosphorus. Abridged in Tucker (1978: 367–368).

[67] Moss 1993: 7–10. The French monopoly was concerned over liability for its workers. Finland and Denmark prohibited the use of phosphorus matches twenty years earlier; that case has not been examined. It is not clear to what extent France, Denmark, and others who banned phosphorus matches domestically also imposed restrictions or tariffs on imports, either to protect domestic industry or as a market access 'club' to shape regulations abroad.

However, the USA, Britain, and other major exporters experienced a temporary regulatory chill.

> [They] continued to resist enacting such legislation for fear of damaging their match export trade. Unless virtually all nations agreed simultaneously to prohibit phosphorus match production and trade, those that refused would stand poised to dominate the remaining global market. Competition among nations thus posed a problem similar to that which competition among the various American states would later present (Moss 1993: 8).

Internationally, the fear of lost competitive advantage prevented movement toward stringent regulations among exporting countries, even though the hazard to workers was clear.

Likewise, within the USA, 'state legislators feared that if they prohibited phosphorus without the cooperation of their neighbors, match producers in their states would choose to leave rather than begin to produce non-poisonous sesquisulphide matches' (Moss 1993: 2). Domestically, the fear of industrial relocation within the USA initially prevented movement toward stringent US regulations.

The dominant match producer was the Diamond Match Company. With assets invested for distribution across the USA, Diamond 'regarded the prospect of uneven state regulation as highly unfavorable'. Diamond and other companies opposed heterogenous state legislation which would 'introduce chaotic conditions into the whole trade situation'. They argued that it would put match factories in states that banned phosphorus 'at a most serious disadvantage as compared with its competitors in other States having no such prohibition'.[68] Diamond was particularly opposed to heterogenous state laws (ibid. 16–17).

Diamond purchased the US patent on sesquisulphide matches, the substitute for phosphorus. The president of Diamond then offered to sell access to its patent in 1909 if the federal government banned the use of phosphorus in match production.

In another example of public and private interests coinciding, Diamond worked with the head of the American Association for Labor Legislation (AALL), John B. Andrews, in promoting anti-phosphorous regulation. Diamond convinced other manufacturers to purchase sesquisulphide licences and initially required them to pay a tax if they produced more than their existing market share.[69] (The parallel to DuPont working with environmental negotiators and establishing a production quota is intriguing.)

[68] Moss 1993: 3, quoting letters from match manufacturers to the House Ways and Means Committee dated 22 December 1910 and 11 January 1911. Coincidentally, the president of Diamond in 1911 was Edward R. Stettinius, Sr., the father of the man who founded Liberia's flag-of-convenience, discussed in Chapter Two above.

[69] Ibid. 18–19; 24. Diamond soon backed off from the tax, under pressure and later conceded even its patent.

Consistent with this book's model, the US House initially resisted regulations. 'Many members expressed either uncertainty or downright hostility toward the proposed legislation. [. . .] Other Committee members remained suspicious about what Diamond Match stood to gain from such legislation and whether Congress would be handing Diamond a monopoly on a silver platter.' Congressmen questioned the jurisdiction and role of federal labor regulations and the use of taxes to 'destroy an industry or to regulate sanitary measures that belong entirely to a State'. The Chairman of the Ways and Means Committee, among others, suspected that Diamond had a substitute product which it would unveil once phosphorus was banned, to undercut its competitors.[70]

The AALL sided with Diamond, arguing before the House that state legislation would lack the homogeneity necessary for competitive fairness; that collective action problems made achieving comparable laws among competing states perhaps impossible; and that local producers of phosphorus matches would find it profitable to sell matches within their own state even if prohibited from 'exporting' across state borders (ibid. 21–22). In short, statewide asset specificity would contribute to heterogenous regulations.

Diamond executives also testified in favor of a bill which prohibitively taxed the sale of phosphorus matches. Along with nine other major producers, Diamond also 'petitioned the President for special tariff consideration should the legislation go through'. A smaller producer, conversely, testified against the bill and accused Diamond of trying to force him out of business (ibid. 23).

With support from both labor and major industry, and graphic evidence of the health problems created by phosphorus match production, the House soon passed the bill. In the Senate, Southern Democrats opposed the bill as an invasion of states' rights, and drew analogies to turn-of-the-century regulations against Southern oleomargarine in favor of dairies (ibid. 30–31). But with support from Henry Cabot Lodge and others, the Senate also approved the bill, and President Taft signed it into law on 9 April 1912.

The bill banned the import of phosphorus matches within nine months and their export within twenty-one months. It imposed a domestic tax within fifteen months, which rendered the production of phosphorus matches unprofitable and effectively eliminated them (ibid. 33).

In this case, as in the others examined, it is clear that dominant corporations played a necessary and important role in securing the passage of regulations.[71] In both the international phossy-jaw case and even more clearly in

[70] Ibid. 1993: 21, 25. Representative John Dalzell (R-PA), House Committee on Ways and Means, 20 January 1911, quoted in ibid. 21.

[71] Consistent with Moss, this does not imply corporate *control* of the political process, nor that the 'Baptists' in this case (the AALL) were unwitting dupes. Moss is careful to distinguish his views from those of Weinstein (1968).

the domestic case, the actors, the coalitions, the positions they take, and the final outcome are remarkably consistent with this book's propositions.

### European integration?

The question mark is deliberate. Analyzing the broader case of European integration is beyond the scope of this book, and it involves many LCD, HCD, and HET subcases. However, there is evidence that the role of business in shaping the overall drive for homogenization of European regulations cannot be ignored. See, for example, Mennis and Sauvant (1976); and Milner (1988) on the politics of international free trade. Maria Green Cowles (1994 and 1995) argues that the dominant European manufacturers group, the European Round Table of Industrialists (ERT), was instrumental in the move toward the Single European Act and regulatory homogeneity:

> More than any other business group, the ERT has played an important role in shaping the larger regulatory framework of the Community. [. . .] [M]ore than any Member State, the ERT has influenced the underlying ideology of that regulatory framework. [. . .] [T]he CEOs sought to develop a political organization to relaunch Europe, to create the regulatory framework for a European market.[72]

The original members of the ERT, meeting in April 1983, included the leading officers of Volvo, Renault, ICI, Unilever, Olivetti, Thyssen AG, Siemens, Philips, Shell Oil, Fiat, Nestlé, and Ciba-Geigy.[73] Citicorp's Walter Wriston contended that 'The business community is dragging the EC even faster than the politicians' (PBS-TV Wall Street Week in Review, 25 September 1992).

Moravcsik expresses a contrary view (1998: ch. 5; 1999), arguing that 'immediately after the White Paper, the ERT actively discouraged the Commission from pursuing the "Europe 1992" agenda'. Moravcsik avows that only once momentum had gathered among member states did the ERT actively support it. He downplays the roles of Philip's CEO Wisse Dekker, Fiat's Umberto Agnelli, and Volvo's Pehr Gyllenhammer in creating the ERT, and the influence of the ERT on the 1987 Single European Act (SEA). However, he acknowledges that proposals such as Dekker's Europe 1990 plan were 'worked out in close informal collaboration with Council and Commission officials'. And while Moravcsik emphasizes Etienne Davignon's governmental role, Davignon moved in 1985 from the EC to join (and later chair) the largest private-sector holding company in Belgium: Société Générale de Belgique. Separating these two roles is not trivial.

[72] See also Mennis and Sauvant 1976; and Helen Milner (1988). Other sources downplay the role of business in European integration. *Inter alia*, see Moravcsik (1991) and Sandholtz and Zysman (1989).

[73] Shell and Unilever pulled out of the ERT early, in part because their investments were less European and more globally oriented.

Cowles' detailed process-tracing is compelling. In a June 1983 memo to EC Commissioner Davignon, the ERT declared that 'the creation of a unified European market is essential'. The ERT laid out a number of specific measures to realize that goal. These included 'integrating the European market by allowing for the development of common standards', and facilitating 'transnational industrial structures by eliminating fiscal impediments to mergers and restructuring, and simplifying the transactions between parent companies and their subsidiaries'.[74] If Cowles is correct, then powerful firms in concentrated industries with high multinational asset specificity were engines of regulatory homogenization, to reduce transactions costs, even at the complex level of European integration. This is consistent with the other cases here analyzed.

Domestic producers, conversely, tended to oppose standardization. They benefitted from the unique standards contained in 100,000s of pages of national standards. The Deutsches Institut für Normung (DIN), for example, had 5,000 employees and spent over $US40 million per year for standardization. Similar institutes elsewhere include the British Standards Institution (BSI) and the Association Française de Normalisation (AFNOR). Their standards range from guidelines for material testing in nuclear reactors to the size of fountain pen refill cartridges and the width of the line such a cartridge must be able to draw.[75]

The movement toward unification in the 1980s was the latest in a series of steps toward integration following World War II.[76] Analyzing this entire process is even further beyond this book's scope. However, it is not surprising that coal and steel were the first European industries to move toward a common regulatory framework after 1945: they also had high cross-border asset specificity (MAS) in the scope and location of their operations.

Williamson (1985) offers tantalizing support here: 'In particular, comprehensive integration [. . .] is widely believed to be the organizational means by which complex products and services are [. . .] efficiently brought to market. [. . .] The standard example is the integration of iron and steel making, where the realization of thermal economies is said to require integration.'[77]

[74] ERT, Memorandum to EC Commissioner Davignon, 'Foundations for the Future of European Industry', 10 June 1983, cited in Cowles (1994: 218–219). Internal corporate memos may reveal more than interviews with officials who have incentives for selective memories and perceptions.

[75] Dowling and Leidner (1990: 5); Walter Mossberg, 'As EC Markets Unite, US Exporters Face New Trade Barriers', *Wall Street Journal*, 19 January 1989: 1. Elsewhere, see discussions over 'Technical Barriers to Trade' in the Uruguay and Doha Rounds of GATT/WTO talks.

[76] The 1951 Treaty of Paris created the European Coal and Steel Community, a free trade area for coal and iron among Germany, France, Italy, and the Benelux countries. Jean Monnet (French visionary politician) and Robert Schumann (French foreign minister 1948–1953) led the effort. Their goals were to legitimate Adenauer but contain Germany; to reach Franco-German reconciliation; to create a vision of a united Europe; to stabilize Italy; and to achieve economic growth.

[77] Williamson (1985: 86–87), citing Bain (1958: 381).

The asset specificity of investments in the 'thermal economies' of coal and steel was high. Williamson is referring to vertical integration within a firm, but this book's argument is that the underlying logic has additional ramifications. Intriguingly, the precursor to the European Community and EU was the European Coal and Steel Community.

# PART IV
# HETEROGENEITY

# 6

# *Mexican Tuna-dolphin*

What was once a fitful, competitive struggle for the canned tuna market has burst into full transnational battle. Sales campaigns and marketing counteroffensives are being plotted by field generals with the same kind of care that strategists deploy in a hot war.

StarKist, *Annual Report* 1987

To the extent that market concentration and dedication of assets to multinational transactions increase, this book's propositions suggest a long-term trend toward HCD. However, regulations can also be imposed as a protectionist barrier to entry against foreign firms. Interdependence does not guarantee co-operation; it may even provoke conflict. Nationalist pressures rise as countries face economic downturns. Movement toward regulatory homogeneity is not a given, nor is continued economic integration, liberalization, or openness. Two cases of heterogeneity are examined next. The first case concerns US regulations banning imports of tuna from Mexico (and others). The second case concerns guidelines on advertising infant formula within the USA.

The US–Mexican dispute over tuna-dolphin is a well known but poorly understood case of heterogeneity. It served as a focal point for trade-and-the-environment disputes within the GATT/WTO system. This Chapter examines the imposition of a stringent market access restriction on the importation and sale of tuna caught with methods lethal to dolphins. In brief, the leading American tuna processor capitalized on consumer sympathy for dolphins to boost its market share, in an alliance with an environmental group. It was assisted by federal legislation which a GATT panel later ruled to be inconsistent with international law. The USA unilaterally flouted the GATT ruling for nearly a decade but Mexico chose not to pursue the matter for fear of upsetting other economic ties with the USA, notably implementation of the NAFTA.

As with the other case studies, this Chapter begins with a brief introduction and the industrial structure and asset specificity in the tuna industry. The role of private sector decisions by America's leading tuna canner in affecting the heterogenous outcome is discussed next. The fourth section discusses the impact of the US policy on the industry and ecology of the Eastern Tropical Pacific (ETP, near Mexico). The GATT ruling on that policy has become widely cited and is discussed in the fifth section. The sixth section summarizes the US legislative history of dolphin protection (with some evidence of lobbying interests) followed by a conclusion.

## 1. The international political economy of tuna

The USA embargoed foreign tuna imports on twenty-three occasions in the fifteen years between 1975 and 1990. The US tuna fleet repeatedly lobbied for protection and tuna was declared a sensitive product and excluded from the Uruguay Round fisheries initiatives. The USA banned Mexican yellowfin tuna imports from 1980 to 1986, in retaliation for the seizure of American tuna-boats fishing within Mexico's 200-mile coastline.[1] After that ban was lifted in 1986, Mexican tuna exports tripled in three years from 32,000 tons to 96,000 tons, despite a longstanding US tariff of 12.5 to 35 per cent.[2] Two-thirds of Mexico's tuna harvest was exported; the USA accounted for 15 per cent of those exports in 1990.

On 12 April 1990 StarKist Inc. announced a unilateral suspension of tuna purchases that were not dolphin-safe. It was quickly joined by the other two largest canners. Four months later, on 28 August 1990, a US federal judge again banned imports of Mexican tuna, this time on the ground that Mexican tuna purse-seiners did not meet US standards for protection against dolphin mortality in the Eastern Tropical Pacific (ETP).[3] The standards were based on the US Marine Mammal Protection Act (MMPA). ETP dolphins were never an endangered species, and by 1989 their population was growing.[4] Mexican tuna posed no human health threat.

Rather than reach a multilateral agreement on dolphin protection, or let consumer preferences determine the demand for 'dolphin-safe' tuna, the US

[1] Henceforth, 'tuna' here refers to yellowfin tuna caught in the Eastern Tropical Pacific (ETP), if not otherwise specified. The ETP lies off the coast of California, Mexico, Central America, Colombia, Ecuador, Peru, and Chile. Only 14% of the world's tuna was caught there.

[2] The tariff on unprocessed tuna was lower than on the more value-added canned tuna. Since 1972 the US tariff on imported tuna was 12.5% *ad valorem* on canned tuna packed in water and 35% on canned tuna packed in oil. A reduced rate of 6% on water-packed tuna was allowed, up to a quota of 20% of the domestic sales (International Trade Commission 1990: 5–20).

[3] The 28 August 1990 embargo against Mexico, Venezuela, Vanuatu, Panama, and Ecuador resulted from a preliminary court injunction; see *Earth Island Institute v. Mosbacher*, 929 F. 2d 1449 (9th Cir. 1991), aff'g 746 F.Supp.964 (1990). The embargo was temporarily lifted on 7 September for Mexico and Venezuela, reimposed 10 October for Mexico, stayed on appeal on 14 November, then took permanent effect on 22 February 1991. A further embargo was imposed by court order of 26 March 1991 on Mexico, Venezuela, and Vanuatu. On 15 March 1991 the National Marine Fisheries Service announced an embargo on intermediary nations.

[4] The National Research Council 1992: 70. Also, *Ocean Development and International Law*, 1994. Some dolphin 'stocks' were 'depleted'. A stock is a 'biological subdivision of a particular species that occupies a discrete range and is different genetically from other subspecies of the same species'. Depleted stocks were those that had fallen 40% below the estimated level prior to dolphin setting (Reinhardt, Vietor, and Duxbury 1994).

Congress and courts unilaterally and completely banned the sale of tuna that was not caught using dolphin-safe methods.[5] The legal moves and denial of market access followed shifts in consumer demand, a retail price war, and the voluntary end of dolphin-lethal tuna purchases by market-leader StarKist and the other two dominant firms. The regulations met with StarKist's enthusiastic support. As discussed below, on 25 January 1991 Mexico and others requested a dispute settlement panel of the GATT, which ruled in Mexico's favor.

## 2. Industrial structure and asset specificity of the tuna industry

### 2.1 Industrial structure

The US tuna processing industry was an oligopoly. Three large companies controlled 71 per cent of the US canned tuna market in 1989. Heinz (StarKist) had a 36 per cent market share, Van Camp (Chicken of the Sea) had 21 per cent, and Unicord (Bumble Bee) had 14 per cent. Other companies combined had 29 per cent. Of these, private label firms had 17 per cent (the largest, Pan Pacific, had roughly 5 per cent); Japanese firms had 6 per cent. The parent companies of the big three tuna labels were major producers of packaged foods: H.J. Heinz Inc., for example, had assets of $US4.9 billion, annual net sales of $US6.6 billion, and an annual gross profit of $US2.5 billion in 1991. Pan Pacific, by contrast, ultimately sold its tuna business for under $US10 million.[6]

The 'big three' were American-owned in 1988. Chicken of the Sea and Bumble Bee were sold to Indonesian and Thai interests but their transactions and assets remained domestic despite the change in ownership. They had even weaker ties to the ETP than StarKist. The sale of ownership had little impact on regulations within the USA, as the firms' assets, management, employees, branding, business strategy, and government ties remained multi-domestic and solidly American.[7]

[5] Labeling requirements were also imposed, under the 1990 Dolphin Protection Consumer Information Act. The National Research Council released a book-length study (1992) concluding that improved fishing techniques would allow for acceptable levels of dolphin mortality.

[6] Market and sales data from 'Market Reports' 1994; Heinz *Annual Report* 1992; Pan Pacific.

[7] In November 1988 P.T. Management Trust (Indonesia) purchased Van Camp from Ralston Purina, for $US260 million. A leveraged buyout separated Bumble Bee from Castle and Cooke in June 1985. StarKist was poised to buy Bumble Bee but terminated the agreement in July 1987 following Justice Department opposition to the sale on antitrust grounds. Pillsbury purchased Bumble Bee one year later (August 1988) for $243 million; but sold it the next year (1989) to Unicord of Thailand. Production was not integrated across borders, they were multi-domestic.

Only 14 per cent of the world's tuna catch came from the ETP. The largest fishery was the Asian (Western) Pacific Ocean with 50 per cent, followed by the Indian Ocean (17 per cent and growing), and the Atlantic Ocean (15 per cent). The ETP was of particular economic interest to Mexico and other Latin Pacific countries and to small US canners.[8] For reasons unknown to science, only in the ETP do dolphins school with tuna.

By contrast to the major canners, the fishing industry was fragmented, had tiny revenues, and little national political influence. Their regulatory preferences would be swamped by those of the much larger canners.

## 2.2 Asset specificity

Most of StarKist's tuna-related assets were deployed domestically in the USA (and US territories) for marketing and canning. Its brand-name investments were domestic specific. Its multinational asset specificity (MAS) by contrast was low. Most of its tuna sales were in the USA. StarKist's market share in the USA was over 35 per cent; overseas in the UK, for example, its market share was only 5 per cent.[9] Earlier, the major tuna canners owned fishing vessels, but StarKist and the others sold their fishing vessels in the early 1980s.

StarKist's assets devoted to the purchase of raw tuna were non-specific. It was able to redeploy those to spot markets in Asia. Until 1975 the harvesting and processing sectors were closely integrated. As many Asian and Latin American countries invested in their fishing sectors the US canning industry had dissolved its ties to the tuna fishing fleet by 1979.[10] California had been the principal processing center for the US industry for decades. By the late 1970s the major US processors moved operations to the US territories of American Samoa and Puerto Rico, taking advantage of special tax provisions there. After 1980 canners turned increasingly to the international spot market and imports. StarKist closed its last California cannery in 1984 'in response to high costs and the Government's failure to provide relief from low-priced canned tuna imports' (Heinz *Annual Report* 1985: 17). Not all its demand for government regulation of market access was met. StarKist boosted capacity in American Samoa and Puerto Rico to make them the

[8] Inter-American Tropical Tuna Commission, *Annual Report*, 1992: 165; cited in Reinhardt, Vietor, and Duxbury 1994.

[9] Key Notes Ltd, 1991. One analyst familiar with StarKist estimated that 75% of its tuna sales were domestic; Heinz would not confirm that figure. StarKist's parent company, Heinz, was active overseas with other bottled, canned, and frozen food products. Forty-three percent of Heinz's overall sales came from overseas.

[10] National Research Council (1992: 30). After the canners dissolved these ties, supplier conflicts arose in the USA. Tuna-boat owners sued Heinz (StarKist), Ralston-Purina (Chicken of the Sea), and Castle and Cooke Inc. (Bumble Bee) in a US District Court on price-fixing and other antitrust grounds in February 1985. StarKist Foods filed its own antitrust and state law counterclaims against the plaintiffs in November 1985. StarKist paid a settlement out of court.

largest two facilities in the world. By 1989 39 per cent of US tuna was processed in American Samoa, and 55 per cent in Puerto Rico.

Despite Chicken of the Sea's and Bumble Bee's transfer to Asian ownership in 1989, their tuna sales were also largely specific to the USA. Like StarKist, they relied on brand-name recognition to boost sales and retail prices ('Sorry Charlie', 'Ask any mermaid', and 'Yum yum Bumble Bee' were familiar advertizing refrains to most Americans). Like StarKist, their asset specificity to fishing in the Eastern Tropical Pacific was low. The cost of switching to raw tuna suppliers in the Asian Pacific was relatively small.

Although StarKist had few assets dedicated to harvesting from the Eastern Tropical Pacific, the cost of abandoning the ETP was even cheaper for StarKist's Asian competitors. Ironically, this encouraged StarKist to act first, to avoid being trumped and miss out on the first-mover advantage of increased brand recognition.

For the smaller private label canners, assets were more specifically invested in the ETP. They depended on low costs and narrow profit margins and relied on fishers and canneries near the ETP to reduce transportation costs. The price of canned tuna fell from 1987 to 1990 and costs increased. Competition from overseas drove down net income from 1987 to 1990 for the three major labels advertising in the USA. Overall, US tuna processors' net income dropped each year from a high of $US111 billion in 1986 to a net loss of −$US49 billion in 1990, the year the embargo was enforced.[11] (See Figure 6.1, US tuna industry: net income.) It rose in the following year, 1991, after the embargo.

## 3. Private sector decisions and results

Heinz's green marketing strategy and its impact are discussed next. The evidence is clear that Heinz turned to a dolphin-safe policy before the law required it, and Heinz's green strategy helped catalyze the US dolphin-safe policy.

### 3.1 Heinz's green marketing strategy

In earlier years tuna canners had opposed stringent restrictions on ETP tuna. By 1990 StarKist's owner, the H.J. Heinz Company, not only supported the US ban but voluntarily pre-empted it by four months (Vietor, Reinhardt, and Duxbury 1994). On 12 April 1990, one week before Earth Day (and two days before 'International Dolphin Week' began), Heinz announced a

[11] US ITC, August 1992, p. D-20. Raw tuna prices rose steadily as a percentage of the cost of goods sold from 1986 to 1990, from 60.8% in 1986 to 69.9% in 1990. Direct labor costs actually fell over that same period, despite complaints about cheap labor overseas, from 8.4% in 1986 to 6.4% in 1990; p. D-23.

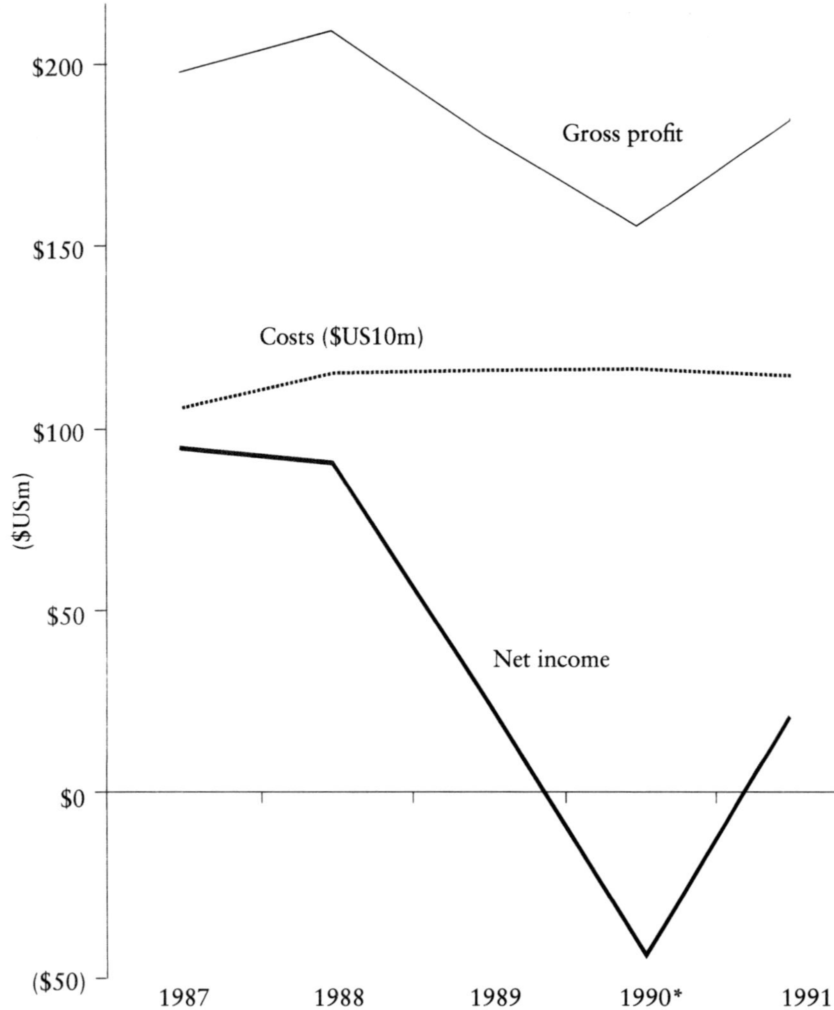


Source: US ITC, 1992. *1990 = US injunction against Mexican tuna

*Figure 6.1*: US tuna industry: net income 1987–1991

unilateral suspension of tuna purchases that were not dolphin-safe. Heinz's decision to buy 'dolphin-safe' tuna, and to support injunctions on 'dolphin-lethal' tuna is essential to understanding the outcome of this case.[12]

[12] Heinz had a history of support for public regulation; in 1906 founder Henry J. Heinz sent his son to Washington to lobby *in favor* of the Pure Food Act of 1906. Coincidental to this case study, the founder's grandson, H.J. (John) Heinz III, was a popular US Senator (R-PA) until his untimely death in an aeroplane crash in 1991.

Heinz deliberately adopted a strategy of green marketing. Its announcement came after years of attention to the dolphin problem and months of internal review and discussion. Since 1970 StarKist had funded training programs for skippers and given money for research on dolphin-safe fishing techniques. Well over half the tuna StarKist bought was already dolphin-safe by April 1990.[13] But changes in consumer preferences and media attention to the issue caught StarKist's attention.

In October 1989 (six months before Heinz's April announcement and nearly one year before US injunctions against Mexico) the president of Heinz, USA, J.W. Connolly, wrote to top management to encourage a dolphin-safe strategy: '[I] am interested in the possibility of seizing the environmental high ground by offering the only tuna guaranteed not caught off dolphins [. . .] I know about the potential cost impact on the procurement of raw tuna . . . However, [. . .] If I am right in this, and we can solve the procurement problems, we could have a very substantial volume opportunity.'[14] Connolly expected the other major producers to follow StarKist, but hoped it would take them a few months, thereby increasing StarKist's name-recognition as the leading 'green' tuna product.[15] If Connolly were correct, his plan would contrast sharply with the characterization by some activists that corporate greed is antithetical to protecting the environment.

A dolphin-safe policy involved significant costs, as Connolly noted. The average cost of raw tuna for the big three canners was $US905/ton in January 1990. Heinz estimated that a dolphin-safe policy would raise its fish costs by roughly 30 per cent, raising the big three average cost to $US1,153/ton.[16]

Market surveys showed consumer awareness of the issue growing: 63 per cent of consumers were aware of the issue in 1990, compared to only 50 per cent in 1988. Three-fourths of those surveyed said they would switch to a dolphin-safe brand. Eighty-six per cent of these said they would be willing to pay a higher price; 50 per cent said they would pay 21 cents or more.

[13] Keith A. Hauge, president of StarKist, suggested a figure as high as 90% dolphin-safe; the American Tuna Boat Association disputed that figure: *New York Times*, 16 April 1990.

[14] H.J. Heinz, internal company memo; cited in Reinhardt, Vietor, and Duxbury 1994: 11. This October 1989 memo came 2 months before a more glamorous meeting. That story begins with Sam LaBudde's clandestine video taken aboard a Panamanian ship (September 1987–February 1988), which he showed to a Hollywood crowd. Through a sequence of personal contacts from model Ani Moss to Jerry Moss (founder of A&M Records) to Bobby Shriver III to Eunice Kennedy Shriver to Robert Shriver Jr., Jerry Moss met Heinz's chairman Anthony O'Reilly in December 1989 and discussed the dolphin issue with him. Some observers credited that meeting (and another on 3 April 1990) with Heinz's decision. (See *NYT* 16 April 1990 and *San Francisco Chronicle*, 17 June 1990.) But Heinz had already begun their strategy months earlier.

[15] The strategic competitive elements of Heinz's move were recognized by August Felando, in 'Harmony Between Tuna Fishing and the Environment of the Eastern Pacific Ocean', paper presented to the World Conference of Tuna Fishing Countries, Tokyo, 3–6 December 1991: 34–35.

[16] Calculated from figures in Reinhardt, Vietor, and Duxbury 1994, provided by Heinz.

Industry-wide sales of tuna began to slip, as sales of the nearest substitute good, chicken, climbed.[17]

Environmental groups had protested about dolphin kills for many years. Marine biologist William Perrin first published an article about dolphin mortality in 1968. The Environmental Defense Fund filed suits beginning in 1972. The Humane Society had backed a tuna boycott since 1976, with little effect. Similarly, the Earth Island Institute's two-year boycott campaign did not hurt StarKist's sales, which actually grew during that period, as did consumption per capita.[18] Nonprofit groups' efforts did not yield implemented regulations for eighteen years, whereas four months after Heinz's decision, the USA implemented stringent product market access regulations.

Both Heinz and StarKist worked to make sure the announcement attracted attention. Heinz's chairman, Anthony O'Reilly, was media savvy. The *New York Times* described him as 'Ireland's leading press baron'.[19] Management met with lobbyists, public relations firms, and consultants. Heinz's Executive Committee approved the plan and appropriated $US9.2 million to implement it. Their public affairs departments arranged meetings with Members of Congress, Commerce Department officials, and environmental groups. At the press conference, O'Reilly was flanked by Senator Joseph Biden and David Phillips, head of the Earth Island Institute.[20] ABC News gave the story top billing, as well as a favorable spin:

> Peter Jennings: We begin tonight with the story that's going to be regarded as good news by people of all ages in America, from the corporate boardroom to the school lunchroom. The world's largest tuna canning company StarKist has said today it will no longer buy tuna caught in the kind of fishing nets which also trap and kill dolphins. It is another sign that environmental forces in America are having an effect on big business.[21]

An estimated 80 million television viewers saw StarKist's dolphin-safe tuna message. The ABC News broadcast featured clips of Heinz CEO Anthony O'Reilly's press conference; and briefly mentioned that Chicken of the Sea made a similar announcement and that Bumble Bee was expected to follow suit.

[17] Bruskin Research, for H.J. Heinz, 'Tuna and the Environment' fact sheet for retailers, April 1990, reprinted in Rienhardt, Vietor, and Duxbury, 1994. Major chicken producers, such as Tyson Foods, were active on their own regulatory fronts.

[18] *New York Times*, 21 May 1990; US ITC 1992: 3.10. The Earth Island Institute (EEI) was founded by David Brower after a falling out with Friends of the Earth (FOE), which he had founded in 1969. Former FOE staffer David Phillips became Director of EEI's Marine Mammal Project (and later Executive Director of EEI), and played an important role in this case.

[19] *New York Times*, 16 April 1990: O'Reilly is 'Ireland's leading press baron'. He controlled the newspaper *The Independent*.

[20] Phillips was reportedly a self-described 'no-holds-barred dolphin protection fanatic' (*US News & World Report*, 13 June 1994), who 'believed even a single [dolphin] mortality was too much'. (Reinhardt, Vietor, and Duxbury 1994; *idem* for marketing campaign expenditures.)

[21] *ABC World News Tonight* with Peter Jennings, 12 April 1990; transcript from Nexis-Lexis.

Two years earlier, network news shows had broadcast Sam LaBudde's gruesome video footage of dolphins being killed in tuna sets. LaBudde gained access to the Panamanian-registered tuna boat *Maria Luisa* by signing on as a crew member in September 1987, then clandestinely videotaped the sets over five months. He was quite conscious of his goal: 'I began to hope that we would make a dolphin set and that the animals would be killed, just so I could record it [. . .] I needed some to die so I could document it' (quoted in Brower 1989). He chose a good boat: its captain (Joseba) was Basque and had not skippered a tuna-boat in the ETP before. The *Maria Luisa*'s sets killed thousands of dolphin but only a very few tuna, sometimes only a dozen fish at a time when the average catch in the US fleet was over 18 *tons* of tuna per set. LaBudde's film received widespread attention and was screened before a Congressional committee on 13 April 1988.[22]

StarKist worked in advance to benefit from its decision in other ways beyond publicity. To gain a procurement advantage from its surprise announcement it stockpiled contracts on dolphin-safe tuna from the western Pacific. It devised a marketing campaign, launched on 12 April, featuring a bottle-nosed dolphin logo.[23] To gain brand loyalty it emphasized collaboration with environmental groups. Heinz Chairman Anthony O'Reilly did not disguise Heinz's business interests: 'This is one situation where virtue may have its own reward. We are hoping that this initiative has commercial impact.' In October 1990 Senator Biden lauded StarKist's efforts from the Senate floor:

> StarKist said we will not buy tuna caught on dolphin any longer and on our cans we are going to say 'dolphin safe.' But, Mr President, very quickly this standard began to be abused and weakened, not by StarKist but by others. That is why we need a standard for what 'dolphin safe' means and an enforcement mechanism so consumers can be sure [. . .] When StarKist made its announcement in April, some saw it as a way to take advantage of the upcoming Earth Day celebration, but is that not exactly what Earth Day is supposed to be about.[24]

As in the CFC case, 'virtue's reward' is necessary to understand the timing and shape of tuna regulations.[25]

## 3.2 Green strategy boosted Heinz's market share

The dolphin-safe policy was ultimately favorable to Heinz, although less so than some at StarKist had hoped. StarKist was able to boost its market by

[22] See Kenneth Brower, *The Atlantic*, 'The Destruction of Dolphins,' July 1989: 35 ff for a sympathetic account of LaBudde's story and a graphic description of dolphin-setting.

[23] Bottle-nosed dolphins, as shown in the 'Flipper' television series, do not live in the ETP. By 1994, 'Natural Sea' tuna (distributed to health-food stores by Natural Food Systems of Danville, CT) advertised on its cans: 'Flipper Seal of Approval', shown next to a smiling dolphin cartoon.

[24] Senator Joseph Biden (D-DE), 136 Cong Rec S 14953, S14973, 2 October 1990.

[25] Cited in the *Independent*, 'Dolphins Threaten US Tuna Fishermen', 29 April 1990.

6 per cent, from 36 per cent in 1989 to 40 per cent in 1990, to 42 per cent in 1992. Heinz annual reports succinctly trace those developments:

*1989*: StarKist Seafood's powerhouse, the 6.5-ounce can of tuna, continued its leadership in the market. Within this key segment, StarKist sales have been exceptional and market share has reached 36%. StarKist produced advertising *campaigns to stress its dolphin-safe* fishing policies [. . .]
*1990*: StarKist Seafood's *dolphin-safe tuna policy earned the brand an even more dominant market position*. The company's environmental leadership raised consumer approval of the StarKist label and helped its *market share exceed 40%, a historic high*.
*1992*: Tuna volume soared 13%. *StarKist market share hit 42%*, with total tuna product [including frozen foods, etc.] share near 50%.[26]

In just three years, StarKist's market share grew from 36 to 42 per cent.

The disappointment to Heinz was that prices continued to fall. As a low-cost commodity favored by lower-income consumers, canned tuna was poorly suited to a green marketing strategy. Heinz got the stringent regulations it supported, but these could only partially make up for market conditions. As ETP catches were unloaded raw tuna prices fell temporarily. Since StarKist had mistakenly stockpiled contracts in anticipation of higher prices it could not take advantage of the lower prices. Canned tuna sales in March 1993 were down by about 5 per cent over the previous year. Lamented J.W. Connolly, president of Heinz, USA:

Consumers wanted a dolphin-safe product, but they were not willing to pay more for it. If there was a dolphin safe can of tuna next to a regular can, people chose the cheaper product. Even if the difference was one penny. It was disappointing that the environmentalists were not able to come through for us at the cash register.[27]

Despite widespread awareness of the issue, consumers did not 'vote' for dolphin-safe tuna with their wallets. But the market access ban on dolphin-lethal tuna products precluded Connolly's disappointment from being translated into loss of market-share: consumers had no choice (unlike in Europe). Instead, that decision was made for them by the US government, with the enthusiastic support of the largest tuna canner.

[26] Heinz, *Annual Report*, 1987, 1989, 1990, 1993 (emphases added). *Ocean Realm* magazine reported (*c*. November 1990) that only StarKist met dolphin-safe standards and that mislabeling would be prosecutable if H.R. 2926 passed.

[27] Quoted in Reinhardt, Vietor, and Duxbury 1994, B3. *Forbes* magazine opined on 9 December 1991: 'Many business people are just as bad [hypocrites]. The US tuna fishing industry, for example, helped persuade Washington to block imports of Mexican-caught tuna, on the grounds that Mexicans were not as careful as US tuna fishers to avoid snaring dolphins in their nets. As soon as Mexican tuna was embargoed in February, US tuna fishers moved to hike their prices 10%.'

### 3.3 Heinz supported dolphin-safe legislation by 1990

The record suggests that, rather than fighting dolphin-safe legislation, by 1990 Heinz actively supported it. StarKist's CEO, Richard Wamhoff, wrote to Senator John Kerry on 8 October 1992 to indicate StarKist's past and ongoing support:

> Dear Senator Kerry:
>
> This letter is on behalf of StarKist Seafood Company and its parent, H.J. Heinz Company. [. . .] *StarKist enthusiastically supported the enactment* of the Dolphin Protection Consumer Information Act *in 1990 and*, despite considerable economic costs, *continues its firm commitment to its dolphin safe policy*. With respect to the International Dolphin Conservation Act [1992], we would like to make clear that StarKist generally supports the Bill and the policy set forth in the Bill [. . .] We have one concern regarding a provision of the Bill [. . .] [Namely, that the Inter-American Tropical Tuna Commission should be consulted in the determination of risks *outside* the ETP.] The above concern has been raised with many of the interested parties and *suggested language to address this has been shared with appropriate staff. Again, we want to make clear that StarKist and Heinz support the aims of the International Dolphin Conservation Act* and remain firmly committed to a dolphin-safe policy [. . .]
>
> *We stand ready to assist you and members of your staff to address in detail means to provide solid legislation* which meets the cause of marine mammal protection.
>
> Very truly yours,
> Richard H. Wamhoff,
> President and Chief Operating Officer, StarKist[28]

StarKist supported the 1992 legislation and registered concern only about restrictions outside the ETP.

In response, Senator Kerry stated his support for StarKist's concerns:

> [. . .] I would like to assure Mr Wamhoff that it is my expectation that the Secretary of Commerce will only exercise his or her authority [. . .] *after consulting with the appropriate segments of the tuna industry*, with scientific and regional fishery management organizations, and with conservation or environmental organizations.[29]

The record here suggests co-operation between industry and politicians, both sensitive (but not beholden) to consumer preferences.

Congress was aware that a heterogenous US *process* regulation alone would have created pressures for laxity. As Congressman Pete Stark (CA) stated: 'Recognizing that the United States fishing industry would be at a disadvantage relative to foreign competitors if tuna caught by foreign competitors using cheaper methods could be imported, Congress imposed an import ban on tuna from countries such as Mexico that did not enact

[28] Letter to Senator John Kerry, 8 October 1992, *Congressional Register* (emphases added).

[29] Senator Kerry's reply, 8 October 1992, *Congressional Register* (emphasis added).

similar protections for dolphins.'[30] The stringent product market access restrictions that the US imposed obviated any potential comparative disadvantage that heterogenous process restrictions would have posed.

## 4. Differential impact of the dolphin-safe policy

Heinz gained from its dolphin-safe policy. Others lost out, including small canners, fishers in the ETP, and non-dolphin marine life. These are next discussed in turn.

### 4.1 Small (private label) canners

The dolphin-safe policy hurt smaller, private label canners more than it did the big three, who could absorb the costs. Even one of the largest private-label canners, Pan Pacific, suffered heavy losses and was ultimately sold at a loss.[31] The annual reports of Pan Pacific's parent (Marifarm) company summarize the impact very clearly:

> The effect of the 'dolphin-safe' policy was to substantially reduce the harvesting of large yellowfin tuna from the [ETP] [. . .] Many of Pan Pacific's suppliers moved their vessels out of the fishing areas nearest Pan Pacific's California cannery, making it more costly for Pan Pacific to obtain tuna [. . .] As a result, a portion of the price advantage that Pan Pacific enjoyed due to its geographic proximity to the ETP has been diminished. The effect of substituting such smaller tuna for the larger, more mature yellowfin tuna is a lower case yield per ton of round fish and higher labor cost per case. Moreover, the greater distance to the Western Pacific fishing grounds increases transportation costs for fish deliveries to Pan Pacific and the likelihood that the vessels will deliver fish to canners in the Western Pacific. *The 'dolphin-safe' policy caused a disruption of the United States tuna industry and had an adverse effect upon the operations of the Company.*
>
> As a result, in 1990, Pan Pacific experienced a substantial decrease in its earnings from 1989 levels and provided a restructuring charge totaling $15,286,000 reflecting a reduction in value due to an economic impairment of its tuna business assets. The restructuring charge included a write-down of goodwill, a write-down of the long-term productive assets to their estimated net realizable value and a provision for certain obligations which Pan Pacific substantially incurred in connection with the reorganization of its tuna procurement and production processes. In addition, the tuna business has been experiencing significant competition from foreign canneries which are frequently able to sell their products in the United States market at prices lower than those charged by Pan Pacific [. . .]

[30] *Congressional Record*, 23 October 1991, 102nd Cong. 1st Sess., 'Environmental Protections Threatened by GATT'.

[31] Pan Pacific held almost one-third of the private-label market, prior to the dolphin-safe policy. In the private-label market, competitive pricing is the most significant factor. By avoiding the additional expense associated with brand-name promotion, Pan Pacific had been able to keep prices low.

> *Net sales decreased 11.8%* to \$73 million in 1990 from \$83 million in the prior year. This reflected a decrease in net sales in the tuna operations which was *primarily due to the April 1990 adoption by the domestic tuna industry of the 'dolphin-safe' tuna policy* and the Company's decision to sell its inventory then on hand at a substantial discount to previous market prices [. . .] Gross margins as a percentage of sales [. . .] in the tuna business were negative approximately 1.9% in 1990 as compared to positive margins of approximately 8.8% in 1989 [. . .] During 1990 and 1991, the changing supply patterns caused by the 'dolphin-safe' tuna policy and the labor cost advantage enjoyed by certain foreign producers created considerable uncertainty as to whether the processing and canning of tuna in the United States could remain a viable business (Marifarms' annual reports, emphases added).

The company's annual reports are clear that the dolphin-safe policy eliminated Pan Pacific's price advantage. Pan Pacific was also getting squeezed by lower-priced imports, but with fewer resources it was unable to take advantage of spot-market purchases in Asia as StarKist did. Ultimately, Marifarms decided tuna canning was not a viable business. It sold Pan Pacific on 18 December 1992 for \$8.3 million (less than Heinz budgeted for its dolphin-safe policy alone), recording a loss of \$9.6 million.

### 4.2 ETP fishers

Both the Mexican and the few US tuna boat owners and crews still fishing in the ETP bitterly opposed StarKist's decision and the follow-up government regulations. However, they lacked the power to oppose the big three tuna canners. The US fishing industry brought its dolphin mortality down to well under the level prescribed by the Marine Mammal Protection Act: 12,600 dolphins were killed by US boats in 1989; 20,500 was the level set under the MMPA. By 1993 total ETP dolphin mortality was down to 4,000 for all countries, including those that allowed dolphin-setting. It continued to fall, to 2,547 in 1996, and 1,636 in 2000. (See Figure 6.2, number of dolphins killed.) Nonetheless, the US embargo continued and the ETP fishing industry was devastated.

Teresa Platt, a San Diego boat owner, reflected on Heinz's decision: 'It was a bleak day for most of us [. . .] [T]o keep us from fishing responsibly [. . .] is crazy.'[32] By 1991 the US tuna fishing fleet had reduced its dolphin mortality rate down to 0.2% of the total dolphin population. Like many others, Platt sold her tuna boat. Others relocated, either by registering their boats under another flag (see flags-of-convenience case study) or by spending the million or so US dollars required to retrofit for fishing elsewhere. Over two-thirds of the US fleet had left the ETP by 1990.[33] To owners who

[32] Quoted in Reinhardt, Vietor, and Duxbury 1994: B1.

[33] In 1979, 98 large US tuna seiners worked the ETP; by 1989 only 30 did. According to Mexico, only 4 US vessels regularly fished in the ETP by 1991 (GATT Panel Report, 1991). According to Cong. Randy Cunningham of California, the economic impact to the USA of this

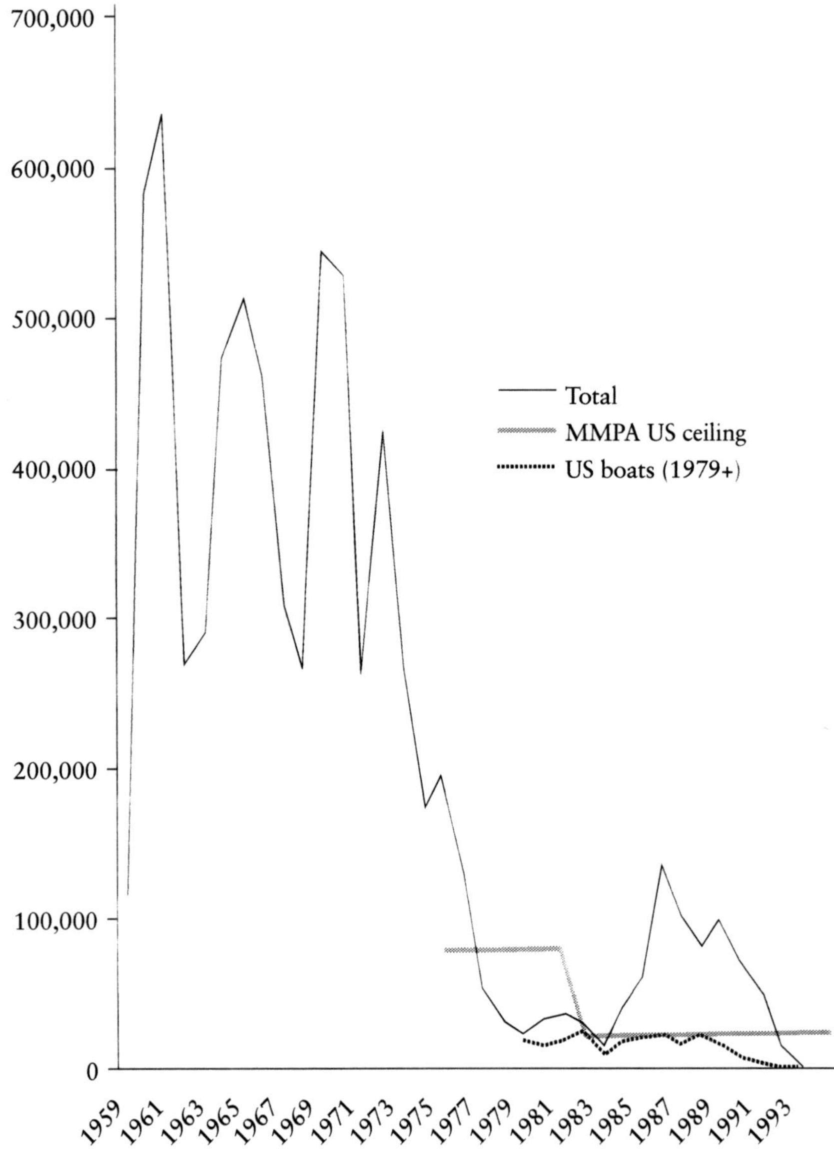


*Source*: National Research Council 1992, 1994

*Figure 6.2*: Dolphins killed in ETP tuna fishing, 1959–1993 (1990 total population = 9.5 million)

relocation between 1980 and 1984 included a loss of 12,500 jobs, $US294 million in household income, and $US1.32 billion in United States sales. The federal government lost $US58.8 million in income tax, and the state of California lost $US7.37 million in taxes (*Congressional Record*, 12 June 1991).

retrofitted, of course, the embargo on ETP purse-seined tuna was advantageous because it effectively reduced the supply of raw tuna competing on the market and protected their investment.[34]

The Mexican fishing industry was hurt even worse. They lost access to both the US market, and to markets in 'intermediary' countries that exported tuna to the USA. ETP yellowfin tuna was banned in France, Italy, and Costa Rica from 25 June 1991. Those countries feared losing access to the US market if they bought Mexican tuna. Felipe Charat, a Mexican boat owner, called the announcement by Heinz and the Earth Island Institute 'a Faustian alliance with the devil'.[35] The economist Jagdish Bhagwati succinctly characterized this view: 'Americans put dolphins ahead of Mexicans.' Reports estimated that over 15,000 Mexican fishing-related jobs were threatened as a result of the compromise, with a cost to Mexico of over $US200 million.[36]

## 4.3 Marine life in the ETP

For as yet unknown reasons, yellowfin tuna and dolphins school together only in the ETP. They do not school together in the western Pacific, Indian, or Atlantic Oceans. By the 1940s fishers began to use the surface-breathing dolphins as beacons for tuna. US boats developed purse-seining in the 1960s, encircling schools of dolphins and the tuna who congregated below them with 'seal bombs' and a mile-long wall of weighted drop nets, then winching together the bottom of the net and hauling it onboard. These techniques gave US boats a comparative advantage for a decade, before other nations' fleets began to do the same. Hundreds of thousands of dolphins were killed annually in the process, most initially by US vessels.[37] (See Figure 6.2, number of dolphins killed, above.) The US Humane Society took note, but the issue did not capture the public agenda. Concern from marine biologists and fishers alike (who relied on the dolphin to find tuna) eventually led to techniques less lethal to dolphins, including back-dropping and fine-webbed nets.

[34] Mexico argued before the GATT panel that 'Only after the United States fleet moved to other waters were more restrictive requirements imposed in 1988 for the protection of dolphin in the ETP—but not for the new fishing grounds of the United States fleet.'; a fact which the USA contested: paras. 3.14–15; 3.22.

[35] Reinhardt, Vietor, and Duxbury 1994: B2.

[36] Bhagwati and Hudec 1996: 180, 182. Bhagwati expressed a rather idealistic view of political change: 'Most important, if your values are good [. . .] they will spread because of their intrinsic appeal [. . .] [T]he pope has no troops.' Job estimates from William Lash III, *Society*, May 1994. Lash suggests 30,000 jobs were threatened but he offers no source or methodology. Diego Cevallos, 'Mexico Dissatisfied with End of US Tuna Embargo', *Inter Press Service* 31 July 1997.

[37] William Perry (Sea Frontiers, 1968) was among the first to call public attention to the issue.

The total dolphin population in the ETP was estimated at 9.5 million in 1989. Some species, such as the northeastern spotted dolphin, had been reduced to 33 per cent of their natural population. There was concern over them, although no species was ever threatened with extinction. By 1989 dolphin populations were growing at between 2 and 6 per cent per year.[38]

Ironically, the 'dolphin-safe' policies led to 'shark and swordfish hell'. Dolphin-safe fishing is not necessarily environmentally sound. The main alternative was 'log-setting' in which nets were set around floating logs. A report from the Inter-American Tropical Tuna Commission, seconded by Greenpeace, suggested that the tradeoff from saving twenty-nine dolphins would be to kill over 2,000 sharks, 38–75 billfish (such as swordfish), and five sea turtles, and greatly to increase mortality among juvenile tuna (thereby threatening long-term tuna stocks). (See Figure 6.3, environmental tradeoffs.) Even Greenpeace conceded that 'dolphin safe labels resulted in spilling the negative impact of commercial tuna fishing into waters outside the ETP, onto species other than dolphins'.[39] These findings led to a bitter split between environmental groups. Removing US purse-seiners from the ETP also left the fishery open to foreign vessels, which might not face the same consumer pressures to use more responsible fishing practices.

Critics and at least one former observer accused fishing crews of intimidating the dolphin-observers and preventing them from accurately reporting

*Figure 6.3*: Environmental tradeoffs in ETP fishing practices

For every 1,000 tons of adult tuna caught, the 'incidental catch' per method:

| | Dolphin-setting | Log-setting |
|---|---|---|
| juvenile tuna (tons): | 406 | 754,464 |
| sharks (#) | 2 | 2,980 |
| swordfish | 5 | 38 |
| sea turtles | <1 | 6 |
| dolphins | 29 | <1 |

*Source*: Inter-American Tropical Tuna Commission, 1994

[38] National Research Council 1992: 70. None of the dolphin species in the ETP are listed by the Convention on International Trade in Endangered Species (CITES) as being in danger of extinction. According to CITES, the only dolphins in such danger were *Platanista gangetica*, *Platanista minor*, *Lipotes vexillifer*, *Sousa chimensis*, *Sousa teuszii*, and *Sotalia fluviatilis*. These endangered species were not protected by specific US legislation, even though purse-seining was carried out near them in other waters. The main species in the MMPA are *Delphinus delphis* (common dolphin), *Stenella attenuata* (spotted dolphin), and *Stenella longirostris* (spinner dolphin).

[39] Greenpeace mimeo, 'Dolphins Are Not the Only Sacrifice: The Impacts of Commercial Tuna Fishing on Oceans, Marine Life, and Human Communities', 1993: 19.

dolphin deaths. The intimidation included physical threats, nearby detonation of 'seal bombs', distractions, and other hindrances.[40]

## 5. GATT's product–process distinction

The GATT Panel hearings and rulings support this book's distinction between market-access and process regulations.[41] Mexico protested to the GATT Panel that 'a measure regulating a product could not legally discriminate between domestic and imported products based solely on the production process; to do so would violate Article III'.[42] Mexico argued, *inter alia*, that the MMPA was discriminatory, noting that it was only imposed after most of the US fleet had left the ETP, and that 'off the Alaskan coast [i.e. in US waters] more than 15,000 dolphins were killed each year with drift-nets in squid fishing, with no special provisions to protect them [. . .] remotely [. . .] [like] those on which the embargo to Mexico was based' (para. 3.38). Indonesia suggested that 'The MMPA had been used as a means to [. . .] shield United States producers from import competition by exploiting public sympathy for dolphins'.[43] The GATT Panel did not impute protectionist motives to the USA, but it noted that was the *de facto* result.

On 3 September 1991 the GATT dispute settlement Panel ruled in Mexico's favor on both the direct and intermediary embargoes, concluding that they were contrary to the General Agreement.[44] The USA appealed the first Panel decision. A second GATT Panel report (June 1994) confirmed the findings of the first.

The key findings of the Panel were that US actions were inconsistent with the general prohibition of quantitative restrictions under Article XI, violated and/or were not covered by the 'like product' and 'national treatment' provisions of Article III; and that they were an inappropriate heterogenous (unilateral) approach to trade and the environment, that discriminated against foreign nations, imposed arbitrary, retroactive, and unpredictable restrictions on foreign firms; they went beyond US jurisdiction and violated foreign sovereignty.

[40] 'Where Have All the Dolphins Gone', EEI, mimeo *c.*1995.

[41] Comprehensive legal studies of this question are found in Trachtman 1993, Dorothy J. Black, 'International Trade *v.* Environmental Protection: The case of the US embargo on Mexican Tuna', *Law and Policy in International Business* v 4 n 1 (22 September 1992: 23 ff); and Don Mayer and David Hoch, 'International Environmental Protection and the GATT: The tuna/dolphin controversy', 'Special Issue on Legal Issues Affecting International Business', *American Business Law Journal* v 1/2: 87 ff (September 1993).

[42] GATT Tuna Panel Report I, para. 3.16. Indeed, to Mexico, the embargo under the MMPA was not even a tuna PPM regulation; rather it was an environmental policy instrument.

[43] First GATT Panel report, para. 4.15.

[44] 'United States—Restrictions on Imports of Tuna', Report of the Panel, GATT Doc. DS21/R (3 September 1991). Hereinafter 'first GATT Panel report'. The panel was headed by Andras Szepesi of Hungary, and included Rudolf Ramsauer and Elbio Rosselli.

In its analysis, the Panel recognized the protectionist risks of heterogenous import restrictions. The first GATT tuna Panel concluded:

> The text of Article III:1 refers to the application to imported or domestic *products* of 'laws, regulations and requirements affecting the internal sale [. . .] of *products*' [. . .]; it sets forth the principle that such regulations on *products* not be applied so as to afford protection to domestic production. Article III:4 refers solely to laws, regulations and requirements affecting the internal sale, etc. of *products*. This suggests that Article III covers only measures affecting products as such. [. . .] [E]ven if the provisions [. . .] enforcing the tuna harvesting regulations [. . .] were regarded as regulating the sale of tuna as a product, the United States import prohibition would not meet the requirements of Article III [. . .] Article III:4 calls for a comparison of the treatment of imported tuna *as a product* with that of domestic tuna *as a product*. Regulations governing the taking of dolphins incidental to the taking of tuna could not possibly affect tuna as a product (paras. 5.11, 5.15, emphases in the original).

In effect, the Panel recognized that heterogenous market-access regulations are protectionist. The US International Dolphin Conservation Act prohibited the importation of dolphin-lethal tuna to the USA, but a US fisher could have used dolphin-setting and sold that tuna catch overseas. As defined in this book, the US regulations were about market access, not process.[45]

As discussed in Chapter One above, the GATT's legal definition of 'product regulations' is more complex than the *market access* definition used in this book; this is a result of GATT's efforts to halt protectionism. Given that the motivation for the US embargo was to change Mexican production techniques, and given that no health threat was posed by Mexican tuna, and that the impact discriminated against Mexican tuna fishers (regardless of whether this was intentional or not), the GATT Panel interpreted the embargo as a process regulation: impermissible under the General Agreement. Mexico noted that under the GATT's legal definition 'It was not clear that there was in every case a meaningful distinction between regulations affecting the sale and purchase of a product and those affecting the production of the product' (Report I, para. 3.18).

Exceptions to GATT's general principles are provided in Article XX.[46] The Panel noted that the burden of justification was on the party invoking Article XX, as established in earlier precedents. The Panel ruled that the

[45] The MMPA of 1972 is PL 92-522, 86 Stat. 1027 (1972); amended PL 100-7111, 102 Stat. 4755 (1988); codified in part at 16 USC 1361–1407 (1988 and Supp. IV 1992). The Dolphin Protection Consumer Information Act of 1990 is in PL 101–627 § 901 at 104 Stat. 4436, 4465–4467 (1990); codified as amended at 16 USC § 1385 (Supp. IV 1992). The International Dolphin Conservation Act of 1992 is PL 102–523, 106 Stat. 3425; codified in sections of 16 USC (Supp. IV 1992).

[46] Article XX: 'Subject to the requirement that such measures are not applied in a manner which would constitute a means of arbitrary or unjustifiable discrimination between countries [. . .] or a disguised restriction on international trade, nothing in this Agreement shall be construed to prevent [. . .] measures [. . .] (b) necessary to protect human, animal or plant life or health', or '(g) relating to the conservation of exhaustible natural resources' (General Agreement).

USA had failed to do so. Even ignoring questions of sovereign jurisdiction, the Panel held:

> that if the broad interpretation of Article XX(b) suggested by the United States were accepted, each contracting party could unilaterally determine the [environmental] policies from which other contracting parties could not deviate without jeopardizing their rights under the General Agreement. The General Agreement would then no longer constitute a multilateral framework for trade among all contracting parties. [. . .] [Furthermore, the USA had not] exhausted all options reasonably available to it [. . .], in particular through the negotiation of international cooperative arrangements, which would seem to be desirable [. . .] [Moreover, because kill-ceilings depended on US performance,] the Mexican authorities could not know whether, at a given point of time, their policies conformed to the United States' dolphin protection standards [. . .] [S]uch unpredictable conditions could not be regarded as necessary to protect the health or life of dolphins (Panel report, paras. 5.22, 15.27–28).

The Panel concluded that the US embargo could not be justified under Article XX.

In favor of the USA, the GATT Panel affirmed labeling requirements as an acceptable trade practice: 'Any advantage which might possibly result from access to this label depends on the free choice by consumers to give preference to tuna carrying the "Dolphin Safe" label' (para. 5.42). These advantages were not conditional on government-conferred privilege.

The result of its deliberations was that 'The Panel recommends that the contracting parties request the United States to bring the above measures into conformity with its obligations under the General Agreement'. The USA appealed the first Panel decision. A second Panel report (June 1994) confirmed the findings of the first.

## 6. US LEGISLATION AND DOLPHIN PROTECTION

Two phases can be seen in this case: lax enforcement of process standards prior to Heinz's shift to a dolphin-safe policy, and stringent enforcement of product market access standards thereafter. A brief synopsis of the legislative role follows.

### 6.1 The Marine Mammal Protection Act (MMPA) of 1972

The Marine Mammal Protection Act (MMPA) was passed in 1972, following protests by animal rights activists over the clubbing of baby seals and killing of whales and dolphins. The MMPA was not limited to species facing extinction, unlike the Endangered Species Act passed the following year. The MMPA called for a phase-out on the taking of *all* marine mammals. In particular:

[the] immediate goal [is] that the incidental kill of marine mammals permitted in the course of commercial fishing operations be reduced to *insignificant levels approaching zero mortality; provided that* this goal shall be satisfied by a continuation of the application of *the best* marine mammal safety techniques and equipment that are *economically and technologically practicable.*[47]

The ambiguity of the wording 'best economically practicable' created much debate in the scientific community, bureaucracy, and courts. Commerce Department regulations to implement the MMPA came out in 1975. They set a ceiling of 78,000 dolphins killed per year by US-flagged vessels. The quotas commenced in 1976, to give industry time to develop new gear and techniques and to give the National Marine Fisheries Services (NMSF) time to implement an observer program to monitor ships. The US fleet easily met the MMPA ceiling. (See Figure 6.2 on dolphin mortality, above. US heterogenous process standards in this period were always well within reach of industry performance, if not actually less stringent.) Of importance to the GATT ruling, the MMPA set restrictions on other countries based on the results of the US fleet, not based on scientific or absolute standards.[48]

## 6.2 The GATT Panel and congressional lobbying

The GATT ruling became an issue in the US Congress. Piecemeal evidence of campaign contributions suggest that the pressures identified in theories of endogenous trade policy played a role in this case. These sums of money are not large and are not likely to have changed Congressional votes, but given their timing and their geographic and party variance, one can assume they had a purpose beyond individual support. No wrongdoing is imputed to these perfectly legal and on-the-record contributions; they are simply evidence of economic pressures.

Mexico requested a dispute settlement Panel under Article XXIII (2) of the GATT on 25 January 1991. The issue arose in the US Congress in the context of debates over the impact of NAFTA and the GATT on trade and the environment. It was not clear how strongly the US Trade Representative (USTR) would defend the US position before the GATT. The GATT Panel findings were released on 3 September 1991, eight months after Mexico's request.

In the meantime, lobbying of Congress picked up as indicated by a trail of campaign contributions. In March 1991 Senator John Breaux (D-LA) of Louisiana received $US16,000 in individual campaign contributions from sixteen individuals with economic interests in the tuna debate. These included several employees of StarKist. Joseph Bogdanovich of StarKist contributed $US1,000 to Breaux in March 1991, as did Martin Bogdanovich

[47] Emphases added, highlighting key terms in future litigation.

[48] The MMPA ordered the ban 'of commercial fish or products from fish which have been caught with commercial fishing technology which results in the incidental kill or incidental serious injury of ocean mammals in excess of United States standards': section 101(a)(2), MMPA.

(also of StarKist), Geraldine Bogdanovich ('tuna boat owner'), David Lawson (of StarKist, and US Tuna Foundation), and David Burney (US Tuna Foundation).[49] At various other times from 1989 to 1991 Joseph Bogdanovich contributed $US1,000 to others in Congress, including to: Senator Robert J. Dole (R-KS) and Representatives Don Young (R-AK), Peter Wilson (R-CA), John Barbieri (R-CA), Eni Faleomavaega (D-Am. Samoa), and William Lowery (R-CA). Geraldine and Martin Bogdanovich also contributed $US1,000 to Senator Fritz Hollings (D-SC), who introduced tuna-dolphin legislation in January 1992. Rep. Gerry Studds (D-MA) and Senator John Kerry (D-MA), who sponsored the 1992 Dolphin Protection Act, received contributions from Northeast Atlantic tuna fishers. (Kerry was the Senator to whom StarKist President Wamhoff wrote offering continued assistance 'to address in detail means to provide solid legislation which meets the cause of marine mammal protection'.[50]) The American Tunaboat Association (ATA) also contributed to Senator Breaux in March 1991. Eleven tuna boat owners residing in California contributed $US1,000 each to Senator Breaux. Breaux later introduced a bill to provide for the transfer of US-flagged tuna vessels to foreign registry (S1721—103rd Cong 1st Session).[51]

The Congressional legislation was not the only proposal on the public agenda to save dolphins. A US National Academy of Sciences study concluded that a ban on dolphin-lethal fishing was not necessary. Other countries proposed international co-operation on the setting of scientific standards as opposed to heterogenous US action. Senator Breaux initially sponsored bills that would set quotas on dolphin mortality or impose labeling requirements. Later, Breaux supported the 1992 Dolphin Conservation Act. (Press releases from StarKist quote approval for StarKist's policy from Senators Breaux and Joseph Biden, along with Greenpeace and the Earth Island Institute.[52])

Labeling requirements which left the environmental choice up to individual consumers were opposed by some in Congress, including Jim Bates (D-CA), who argued: 'With labeling [alone], we can assume every consumer [could] pay more for a "dolphin safe" product and less for a "dolphin-unsafe" product. Regardless of their choice, without a US fleet leading the industry in dolphin-safe methods and developing promising new equipment, many will choose to save money and more dolphins will die.'[53] The US embargo took that decision out of individual consumers' hands.

[49] Campaign contributions in this section are drawn from the Campaign Finance file, Lexis.

[50] Wamhoff to Kerry, letter in *Congressional Register*, 8 October 1992; quoted at length above. Thanks to Diane Coates for Congressional research here.

[51] It is not known whether or not these owners had already retrofitted their boats for operation outside the ETP.

[52] 'StarKist Dolphin Safe', brochure from StarKist, Inc., received December 1994.

[53] *Congressional Record*, 8 May 1990, 101st Cong. 2nd Sess, in discussion of The Dolphin Preservation Act of 1990.

As with the CFC and other cases, no Stiglerian normative judgement is implied here. Many would argue that StarKist should have undertaken this step many years earlier for normative and aesthetic reasons; others argue it should have pushed for a homogenous international agreement rather than a heterogenous US policy. (These are not mutually exclusive.)

The USA stood by its heterogenous market access ban even after the GATT ruled against it twice. Nearly a decade later—only after consumer preferences had changed to support the major companies in their 'dolphin-safe' campaign, only after consumers had re-established strong brand-loyalty to the three big US producers, only after dolphin-deaths had fallen by 97 per cent to less than 2,000/year from 150,000/year a decade earlier (and from over 500,000/year when US cannery-boats pioneered dolphin-setting in the 1960s), only after producers were no longer threatened by low-cost imports, and only after the US environmental community had split and Greenpeace recognized that dolphin-setting was less ecologically disruptive than the alternative of log-setting—only then did the USA technically legalize the importation of dolphin-set tuna, provided that scientific studies determined the imports were ecologically safe. Even then, the USA retained the right to block tuna imports any time it deemed they had an 'adverse effect' on dolphins. Further, NGOs had created a 'Flipper Safe' label, which a tuna canner could use only if it did not use dolphin-set tuna at all (and, incidentally, only if it paid an annual licensing fee to the 'Flipper Safe' program). By 2003, even with the vastly improved safety record, little if any Mexican dolphin-set tuna had entered the US market. In short, the GATT/WTO did not overturn US environmental law. In fact, to the extent Mexican (and other ETP countries) fishing practices were improved to protect dolphins, there was something of a movement toward a higher common denominator, as Mexico moved closer to US practices (Vogel and Kagan 2002). The US use of market-access (or threats to close it) may help explain why the worst fears of some environmental activists have not been borne out and one finds HCD in a number of regulations.[54]

## 7. Tuna-dolphin: Conclusion

The unintended killing of dolphins which school with tuna off the Mexican coast had been documented since the 1960s, when US boats were killing hundreds of thousands of dolphin every year. The Humane Society had filed lawsuits against the US tuna industry beginning in 1972, and supported a boycott on tuna since 1976. But that boycott did not change consumer preferences. (The number of dolphin killed was reduced as fishing techniques

[54] See Vogel 1995; Robert Kagan and Lee Axelrad, *Regulatory Encounters* (Univ. Cal. Berkeley Press, 2000).

improved.) Even when presented with graphic evidence of the killings in Sam Labudde's video in 1988, a renewed boycott campaign led by the Earth Island Institute had little effect on tuna sales. By that time, the US tuna canning industry had severed its ties to the ETP and dolphin deaths had dropped considerably as US fishers (and increasingly others) improved their techniques. By 1990, however, both StarKist and several members of Congress sensed they could capitalize on changing consumer preferences.

The importance of the market access *versus* process distinction is evident in the tuna-dolphin case. Congress considered but did not impose heterogenous process restrictions on the US industry. The initial MMPA process restrictions on the US tuna fleet were fairly lax, never cutting below the existing US kill-rate, and loosely enforced by the courts through 1988.[55] Even by 1990, Congress legislated only on labeling requirements. However, when a product market access ban was supported by the leading tuna canner, US laws were enforced severely. Mexican exports of tuna were not only barred from the USA but also restricted in France, Italy, and Costa Rica because of the US-imposed 'intermediary boycott'. As exporters of tuna to the USA themselves, those countries feared losing access to the US market if they bought Mexican tuna.

The heterogenous outcome in this period is explained by the interests and strategy of the leading tuna canner. StarKist's market dominance and investments specific to the US market gave it the wherewithal and incentives to support heterogenous regulations. Heinz-StarKist correctly determined by October 1989 that consumers and politicians alike would support such a move. StarKist began to develop a 'green-marketing' strategy to offer 'dolphin-safe' tuna. It was a first-mover when it launched the policy in April 1990, with the support of the Earth Island Institute and Senator Biden. A cartel was effectively created when the two other largest tuna producers joined StarKist. Jointly, they controlled over 70 per cent of the market. Government enforcement for that cartel came in August 1990, nearly a year after StarKist began to develop its dolphin-safe strategy. The Earth Island Institute won an injunction in Federal Court against the importation of yellowfin tuna from Mexico.

When the MMPA, supporting legislation, and court order were applied to foreign *products* entering the USA, they were rigorously implemented and had a significant impact. The dominant producer benefitted from stringent product market access regulations. These product market access regulations limited access to the US market by those foreign and smaller firms which relied on the ETP. That denial of market access pressured Mexico and others to improve their production methods, but it did not stop them from

[55] A Commerce Department inspector general investigated the NMFS Tuna Porpoise Management Branch in San Diego, which placed observers on tuna-boats. He concluded: 'Since passage of the MMPA in 1972, enforcement appears to have been lenient. Prosecution has been selective, settlements have been characterized by protracted negotiations to accommodate the tuna industry . . .', *The Atlantic*, July 1989.

dolphin-setting in the ETP. The US embargo was ruled contrary to the GATT. However, given the size of the US market, Mexico and others did not risk broadening the trade battle into a war.

The ecological impact was less clear. While between 4,000 and 20,000 dolphin were saved per year, the commercially viable alternatives to dolphin-setting depleted younger stocks of tuna and killed billfish, sharks, and sea turtles. US swordfish boats continued to kill dolphin with no special restrictions as did US squid-boats in Alaska, despite occasional environmental protests.[56]

The validity of this book's model is reinforced by the findings in this tuna case. Different values of the same explanatory variables identified in the cases of lower and higher common denominator outcomes led here to a case of heterogeneity. The next and last case also has a heterogenous outcome.

## Appendix: Chronology of events in the tuna-dolphin case

Late 1950s: US fleet pioneered dolphin-setting, millions of dolphins killed.

1972: MMPA goals not stringently enforced.

1975–1976: Commerce Department sets dolphin mortality quota of 78,000/year. US fleet easily meets quota with improved techniques. Legal battles ensue. Environmental Defense Fund sues; Federal District Court voids Commerce rulings. Fishing industry sues, Federal appeals court orders National Fisheries Service not to enforce fishing ban. Industry lowers its dolphin kill, amendments to MMPA reduce dolphin mortality quota to 20,500.

Late 1970s: US canners sever links with vessels (ending ownership and/or long-term contracts). Growth of Latin and Asian fleets. Catch increases. Prices drop in world spot-market purchases. Canner's position strengthens *vis-à-vis* harvesters. Fleets adopt more dolphin-friendly techniques; mortality drops.

1980–1986: 'Tuna war': US bans imports of Mexican tuna partly in retaliation for seizure and fine of US boats caught fishing in Mexican waters. Similar measures against Ecuador, Peru, and Costa Rica.

1981: US fleet meets quota; some relocate (flagged in Vanuatu, Panama,

[56] Audobon Society, 'The Bycatch Problem', www.audubon.org/campaign/lo/ow/iss.html, accessed 27 March 2002.

Mexico). San Diego fleet loses competitiveness. MMPA reauthorized. US dolphin mortality quota kept at 20,500.

1984: MMPA amended to extend indefinitely the US annual kill quota of 20,500. Enforcement relaxed.

1986 Aug.: Reagan lifts ban on Mexican tuna at summit with De la Madrid. Mexico offers tuna VERs. Mexican tuna exports surge, tripling by 1989. Mexican tuna fleet is second only to that of the USA. US tuna packing plants open in Samoa, Thailand, Puerto Rico; close in USA. From 1980 to 1984 US industry tuna employment drops by half, losing 12,500 jobs. Highest international dolphin mortality figures in over a decade: 133,000.

1987–1988: Sam LaBudde video of dolphins killed by Panamanian boat (Sept. to Feb.)

1988: MMPA reauthorized. Foreign fleets must reduce their dolphin mortalities to rates no more than twice that of the US fleet, or else face tuna embargo. US boats in the ETP required to carry an independent observer. Restrictions placed to save dolphins species that were 'depleted' (<40% of population) with 1989 deadline. Brief embargoes imposed under MMPA on tuna from Spain, Venezeula, Vanuatu, Panama, and Ecuador. By 1989, ETP dolphin populations grew by 2–6%/year.

1989: July, Rep. Boxer (D-CA) introduces the tuna labeling act, HR2926.

1989 4 October: Heinz pursues dolphin-safe policy as green marketing strategy. Hearings, Rep. Studds (D-MA): 'We do have the right to bar our markets to any nation that does not share our concern for [. . .] conservation.'

1989 December: Jeremy Ross meets with Heinz's O'Reilly, on behalf of pro-dolphin activists. Rep. Boxer and Sens. Biden and D'Amato introduce Dolphin Protection Consumer Information Act bills (DPCIA) to require a label stating whether or not the tuna was caught with dolphins.

1990 April: Heinz (StarKist) voluntarily ends dolphin-lethal tuna purchases; Chicken of the Sea and Bumble Bee follow.

1990 June: StarKist 'enthusiastically supports' labeling requirements. US Congress passes DPCIA. ETP tuna cannot be labeled 'Dolphin-Safe'.

28 August: 9th Circuit Court, *Earth Island Institute (EEI) v. Commerce Secretary Mosbacher*. Temporary injunction against Mosbacher enjoining the importation of yellowfin tuna from Mexico and all other countries fish-

ing in the ETP based on MMPA. Briefly lifted in September.

19 October: Federal court Judge Thelton Henderson rules that Mexico exceeds US standards for dolphin mortality; imposes injunction (primary embargo). Order for Preliminary Injunction, *EEI v. Mosbacher*, DC NCalif, No. C 88 1380 THE, 10/19/90. 14 Nov. Ninth Circuit Court of Appeals orders temporary stay on tuna embargo. 20 Feb. 1991 stay lifted, embargo resumes, *EEI v. Mosbacher*, CA 9, No. 90-16581.

1991 25 January: Mexico requests dispute settlement Panel under Article XXIII(2) of the GATT.

1991: European Parliament passed a nonbinding resolution to restrict tuna caught with means lethal to dolphins.

1991 3 September: GATT Panel Report, findings favor Mexico: USA bans an illegal trade barrier. USA appeals; continued embargo. Mexico tabled the issue temporarily.

1991 September: US District Court for Northern California, *EEI v. Mosbacher*: injunction to enforce the MMPA's secondary embargo. EEI won in January 1992.

1992 January/February: US District Court for Northern California, 785 F. Supp. 826; Judge Thelton Henderson. Secondary embargo on countries which import dolphin-lethal tuna (France, Italy, Costa Rica, Venezuela, etc.)

1992 March: President Bush proposed to lift the ban on imported Mexican and Venezualan tuna, in exchange for continued reductions in dolphin kills by their tuna fleets, and a five-year moratorium on purse-seine nets. Departments of State and Commerce and the USTR all support lifting the ban.

1992 June: IATTC member governments sign Agreement to take effect January 1993, aimed at progressively reducing dolphin mortality in the ETP. 19,500 for 1993, falling to >5,000 in 1999. (Colombia, Costa Rica, Ecuador, Mexico, Nicaragua, Panama, the USA, Vanuatu, and Venezuela.)

1993 September/October: StarKist supports International Dolphin Conservation Act (IDCA), provided IATTC is involved in assessment of areas beyond the ETP. Kerry assures. US House votes 389 to 15 to ban the sale or purchase of tuna caught in nets that kill dolphins (HR5419 Boxer/Studds), Senate passes similar bill (S1784 Kerry). Sen. Breaux (D-LA) proposes bill that allows some dolphin kills; it fails.

1993: IATTC international accord. New mortality quota by vessel for boats still operating in the ETP.

1994 May/June: Dolphin deaths in the ETP reduced to 10% of 1986 levels. 99.5% of netted dolphins are released unharmed. Dr Perrin: not a question of conservation. Second GATT council report. Confirms findings of first Panel report.

# 7

# *Infant Formula Marketing in the USA*

The overseas Nestlé infant formula case has been well studied.[1] According to conventional wisdom the World Health Organization (WHO) and UNICEF 'code of conduct', led by nongovernmental organizations (NGOs) and medical science, brought to heel a multinational corporation. At first glance the US infant formula case seemed to defy this book's proposed model. It is examined in detail precisely for that reason, to test the propositions in a 'least likely' case. Developments in the USA reveal a picture marked by special interests and more compatible with this book's propositions, if not a perfect fit. A revised interpretation is that Nestlé only agreed to abide by the WHO/UNICEF marketing code in 1984, more than a year after the two dominant US producers began a strategy to ban advertising as a barrier to Nestlé's growing entry into the US infant formula market. The US firms lobbied against the broader international WHO/UNICEF code at the same time as they opposed advertizing in the USA. Advertising restrictions limit the sale or distribution of products, post-manufacturing, hence they are a product market-access restriction. Therefore the *US* industry restrictions are categorized as a heterogenous case of product market-access restrictions.[2]

The US advertising 'code' was not a formal law. Neither was the WHO code in most countries. Both codes fit a broader definition of regulation: direction from a competent authority, guiding action or conduct. As will be seen, this lack of a formal law in the USA led to cracks in the industry code against advertising. Nonetheless, advertising 'restrictions' in the USA were widely known and respected. They were supported by the American Academy of Pediatrics (AAP). The clout for enforcement came from the professional opinion of the AAP, support by US industry itself, NGOs, and the media.

[1] A nuanced discussion of the WHO/UNICEF–Nestlé agreement is Sikkink 1986. This book's analysis of the US case complements and draws on hers, it does not replace it.

[2] Further investigations might examine in more detail the international case of Nestlé and the WHO/UNICEF code. The US case ended in an out-of-court settlement; the reader is again reminded that no evaluation is made here as to whether the behavior observed was morally good or bad. For the record, *ceteris paribus* the author supports breast-feeding and opposes the killing of dolphins.

## 1. Concentrated industrial structure and domestic human asset specificity

In the USA Abbott Laboratories (Ross Products) and Bristol-Myers Squibb (Mead-Johnson) controlled 80 per cent of the highly concentrated market with their Similac and Enfamil products. American Home Products (Wyeth Nutritionals) held another 10 per cent share in the USA and a bigger share overseas. (By 1996 Wyeth had sold its US interests to PBM Products.) By contrast, less than 10 per cent of Abbott's and Bristol-Myers' sales were in developing countries. Seventy per cent of Abbott's physical assets were in the USA.

Overseas, Nestlé dominated developing country markets with a 50 per cent market share outside the USA. One-fourth of its 303 factories were located in developing countries, and they contributed 20 per cent of Nestlé's total production. From 1978 Nestlé sought to enter the US infant formula market, without success: by 1993 Nestlé was able to gain only 6 per cent of that market, growing to 9 per cent by 2002.

Abbott and Bristol-Myers controlled the US market with their name-brand recognition, long-standing exclusive contracts with doctors and hospitals, loans and grants to medical students and pediatricians, conference subsidies, and free samples to parents of newborns. Those transactions were highly relation-specific. Brand loyalty among consumers was high, because parents tend to stick with whatever brand they receive from the hospital. The two dominant US firms did not need to advertise and their relationships with doctors and hospitals were hard for late-comers like Nestlé to duplicate. Infant formulas sold in the USA are very similar to each other, with twenty-nine basic ingredients mandated by the 1980 Infant Formula Act, hence product differentiation is difficult. The US firms' human asset specificity was high in marketing relationships specific to domestic US transactions; but their MAS was low.[3]

## 2. Background: Nestlé–WHO/UNICEF code

Higher morbidity rates among bottle-fed than among breast-fed infants were documented by health workers in developing countries by 1972. Infant formula marketing practices (including advertising, free samples in clinics, saleswomen dressed in nurse's uniforms, and misleading literature) discouraged mothers from breast-feeding their infants. The result was higher

[3] Thomas M. Burton reported the case in 'Methods of Marketing Infant Formula Land Abbott in Hot Water', *WSJ*, 25 May 1993. On overseas market share, see *NYT*, 22 May 1981. On identifiable US assets see Abbott Laboratories *Annual Report*, 1991. On the need for barriers to entry to sustain a cartel, see Aggarwal, Keohane, and Yoffie (1987) and citations to Chamberlain 1962; Itoh and Ono 1981; Kierzkowski 1984; and Scherer 1980.

morbidity from contaminated water used to mix formula and from unsanitary containers, lowered infant immunity (immunity is transmitted through breast-milk), higher birth rates (breast-feeding decreases fertility), and weakening of the mother–infant bond. Scientific articles pre-dated publicity by NGOs.[4] A UN advisory group and the World Health Assembly passed resolutions in 1974 urging appropriate regulation of advertisements. No such regulation occurred for ten years, until Nestlé agreed to it.

Activist NGOs picked up the issue. The UK's 'War on Want' publicized it widely in 1974.[5] A Minnesota-based NGO, the Infant Formula Action Committee (INFACT), was formed in 1977 and helped organize a consumer boycott of Nestlé in the USA and nine other industrial countries, joined by eighty-six other NGOs under the umbrella of the International Nestlé Boycott Committee (INBC). In 1975 international industry formed the International Council of the Infant Food Industry (ICIFI). Its members included Nestlé, England's Cow and Gate, five Dutch firms, four Japanese firms, US Wyeth, and one Danish and one French firm. Abbott-Ross never joined ICIFI, on the ground that it had higher internal standards. Industry's ICIFI was headed by a former WHO official, Stanislaus Flache. Contrary to the view that business always opposes regulations, ICIFI helped establish industry codes in several developing countries, including Peru, Kenya, Nigeria, Malaysia, and South Africa.[6] Nonetheless, protests continued. In 1978 Senator Edward Kennedy held hearings on the issue, and chaired a meeting with industry representatives. Joint WHO/UNICEF meetings in 1979 were attended by industry, government, doctors, and activists.

WHO completed a suggested code of conduct on infant formula marketing in 1981. It was adopted in May 1981, with 118 nations voting in favor (including the Swiss), three abstaining, and the USA opposed. Initially, ICIFI opposed the 1981 WHO code, and its implementation remained voluntary and sporadic. US industry, meanwhile, met by August 1983 to discuss a 'voluntary' code against advertising, to exclude Nestlé from the US market. In 1984 Nestlé changed its strategy, and stated its commitment to see an International Code of Marketing for Breast-milk Substitutes implemented by governments. Boycott activists in fifteen countries confirmed a significant change in Nestlé's marketing practices.[7] INFACT and the INBC called off their boycott. Implementation of the code was left up to individual

[4] See Jellife 1972; Kananneh 1972; and Plank and Milanesi 1973; cited in Sikkink 1986.

[5] Muller, March 1974. Muller's pamphlet 'The Baby Killer' was translated by a Swiss group into German and the title changed to 'Nestlé Kills Babies'. Nestlé sued the Swiss group for defamation and libel. See case materials prepared by Professor James E. Post of Boston University, 'Nestlé Boycott (A)', Graduate School of Business, Stanford University, 1981, cited in Sikkink 1986: 821.

[6] *Christian Science Monitor*, 18 May 1991.

[7] Sikkink 1986: 816, 835; 'Joint Agreement, International Nestlé Boycott Committee and Nestlé', 25 January 1984, signed by Carl Angst, executive vice president of Nestlé S.A. and William L. Thompson, clerk of the United Presbyterian Church, representing the International Nestlé Boycott Committee; 'Minutes of Press Conference, 4 October 1984.

countries.

Reliable data on the gross cost of the boycott to Nestlé is not available. One source estimated it to be as high as $US40 million.[8] In the meantime, annual developing country purchases of infant formula jumped from $US600 million in 1978 to $US2 billion in 1983. In 1988 the boycott against Nestlé was started again for a while and some NGOs have maintained it since then. Critics argued that Nestlé routinely violated several provisions of the WHO codes. Nestlé denied the charges.[9]

## 3. US INDUSTRY OPPOSED WHO CODE OVERSEAS AND SUPPORTED ADVERTISING RESTRICTIONS AT HOME

Over State Department protests, the top three US firms successfully lobbied the Reagan administration to oppose the WHO code on the grounds that it restricted free speech and was not warranted by scientific evidence. Yet the same firms supported a different marketing code in the USA, one that helped secure their domestic market share. Not only did they not oppose a US code against advertising; they actively sought it. Their first movements toward a self-imposed advertising ban were scared away in the face of a possible Justice Department antitrust inquiry. Soon afterwards they gained support from a prominent medical association, the American Academy of Pediatrics. Their industry group (the Infant Formula Council) co-ordinated a strategy to condemn consumer advertising. They simultaneously raised prices, supported by William Smart, Abbott-Ross' president in the early 1980s. A subsequent president of Abbott-Ross, Jack W. Schuler, opposed the price hikes, arguing 'You're going to get caught'. Schuler was fired by then-Chairman Robert A. Schoellhorn.[10]

Extensive negotiations ensued among the big three US producers. The first industry meeting took place in New York, the second at Chicago's O'Hare Hilton Hotel. The meetings continued for eighteen months, going through seven draft codes. By 16 August 1983 (one year before Nestlé settled with INBC) Lael F. Johnson, Abbott's general counsel and senior vice president, urged other members of the Council to adopt the US no-advertising clause. Johnson sought wording that did 'not present intolerable antitrust problems'. If federal antitrust enforcers objected, Johnson proposed, companies 'would then unilaterally address these areas in unilaterally adopting their

[8] Sikkink 1986, citing Post, 'Assessing the Nestlé Boycott'.

[9] 'Monitoring Report: Infant Foods Industry', INFACT, July–August 1984; Sikkink 1986: 833. The campaign was also a success for INFACT as an organization; it developed a permanent staff and went on to mount boycott campaigns against General Electric (nuclear weapons) and tobacco companies: *Infact Update*, Summer 1993.

[10] Details are from depositions in the Florida litigation, cited by Thomas M. Burton, *WSJ*, 25 May 1993.

own code'. At the same time industry raised prices and increased funding to the American Academy of Pediatrics (AAP), which opposed formula advertising.[11] Nestlé had told the head of the AAP, Dr M. Harry Jennison, that they 'were coming in to the US market' and he routinely reported this to the AAP board, which informed Abbott and Bristol-Myers.[12]

## 4. Support to and from the American Academy of Pediatrics (AAP)

The AAP received a total of $US1 million annually from the top three US formula makers for almost a decade. The formula industry's direct donations to the AAP accounted for 3 per cent of the medical group's $US35 million annual budget, much of that in foundation supports and grants, which were not part of the academy's operating budget. Fund-raising for the AAP's new building was in full swing by 1982, and continued through 1985. Manufacturers also spent millions designing hospital pediatric clinics.[13]

The AAP had long issued proclamations opposing formula advertising. Not all physicians' associations did.[14] The AAP was aware of industry support, and its relation to infant formula advertising. An internal AAP executive committee memo from 1986 states: '[T]here is a need to make this statement reaffirming the AAP's position on marketing, breast milk, lay advertising, etc. If there is a marketing war, there may be a shift in industry's distribution of funds and the AAP may have to cut back on anticipated income from industry.'[15] This is strong evidence that the AAP was aware of the connection between its position on marketing and its receipt of funds from industry. The AAP formally opposed hospital giveaways without a physician's approval, but critics contend that the group did little, if anything, to enforce that position. Giveaways were not banned by the US Council code yet a McGill University study concluded that they discourage

[11] Thomas M. Burton quoting FTC attorney Steven M. Kowal, *WSJ*, 25 May 1993; *American Lawyer*, January 1994.

[12] Author's interview with Jennison, 15 June 2002.

[13] See Gabrielle Palmer, *The Politics of Breastfeeding*, 1998; Naomi Baumslag, Dia L. Michels, and Richard Jolly, *Milk, Money, and Madness*, 1995; *Los Angeles Times*, 16 August 1993. The AAP noted that for several years it was in litigation in California and could not publicly discuss the case on the advice of its counsel. Court records were not available. The contributions were for a variety of small projects, not a lump-sum donation. See also Barry Meier, *NYT*, 15 June 1993.

[14] The American Medical Association (AMA) also opposed advertising. But the 75,000-member American Academy of Family Physicians refused to adopt a stance against formula advertizing. It argued in a 1991 report: 'A prohibition against any advertising of infant formula—a food and nonprescription product—might easily be seen by critics and patients as onerously paternalistic and perhaps self-serving': *NYT*, 4 November 1984.

[15] Cited in *NYT*, 15 June 1993. 'The AAP and like-minded organizations have no hard evidence to support the claim that direct marketing will reduce breast-feeding', the AAP conceded in a 1989 report, in part because no formula had been advertised in the USA.

breast-feeding. In the USA breast-feeding sank to only one-quarter of the population by 1970, though it rebounded to 62 per cent by 1982 following publicity over the Nestlé controversy.

The AAP director from 1979 to 1986, Dr Harry Jennison, acknowledged the influence of industry funding:

> The academy got caught up in greed. Manufacturers started giving money and it was so easy that people's eyes got big. The main thought was 'How can we get more?' . . . I think it's pretty clear now that we were used. [. . .] I did not realize at the time how much we were being bought off. Now that I know the formula companies were trying to manipulate the academy, I feel absolutely duped.[16]

The AAP had long opposed advertising; there is no suggestion that industry support altered the AAP's research findings or principles. Rather, it appears that industry effectively used the AAP to further its commercial goals.[17]

The impact a hospital can have on new mothers' practices is dramatic. In one example, Dr Barbara Philipp was able to increase Boston inner-city mothers' breast-feeding rate from 6 per cent in 1995 to 33 per cent in 2000. To qualify for the UN/WHO designation of 'Baby Friendly', a hospital must agree to pay for its own infant formula rather than accepting free formula from manufacturers, as most hospitals do. That requirement is one reason why just twenty-seven US hospitals were Baby Friendly in 2000, out of 14,800 hospitals worldwide.[18]

In a possible parallel to the US case, in 1980 Nestlé gave large grants to the president of India's Academy of Pediatricians while he was on India's committee to draft a domestic code on infant formula advertising. Publicity scuttled the proposal and India went on to develop even more stringent restrictions than were called for in the WHO code; its domestic industry also acquired a significant market share.

## 5. US INDUSTRY DESIGNS ITS OWN CODE

US industry executives reached agreement to restrict public advertising in January 1985, three months after Nestlé agreed to implement the WHO code. The US industry Infant Formula Council approved and implemented the anti-advertising code in February. The US code did not ban hospital giveaways nor did it ban subsidies to hospitals and pediatricians. Those marketing practices played to US industry's competitive strengths. 'The rela-

[16] Quoted by Barry Meier in *NYT*, 15 June 1993, and by Burton, *WSJ*, 25 May 1993.

[17] In a 1994 interview with the author, the subsequent AAP Director, James E. Strain, denied any conflict of interest with industry. He noted that the AAP forced Bristol-Myers to drop an infant formula advertising campaign in baby care magazines in the 1970s and that it stopped taking money from Bristol-Myers in June 1989 when Bristol-Myers produced a product advertised by Gerber under Gerber's name.

[18] *Boston Globe*, 10 September 2000.

tionship between the physician and the sales representative is critical to Mead Johnson's marketing strategy', noted Richard D. McWilliams, the company's director of formula marketing. Every parent wants to give their infants the best nutrition possible, so industry adopts a strategy of high profit margins which fund quality-based marketing to lock in brand loyalty. That loyalty can extend from one generation to the next. As of June 2002, the retail price consumers paid for Similac and Enfamil was roughly 75 per cent higher than for similar non-branded formulas such as those made by PBM Products (which purchased Wyeth's domestic operations in 1996).[19]

The US industry's self-imposed ban on advertising remained effective from 1985 through 1989 and beyond. Previously, US industry had advertised domestically. Bristol-Myers, for example, had advertised in the 1970s, before Nestlé threatened to enter the US market. Internal documents unearthed in subsequent lawsuits are refreshingly candid. A 1988 Bristol-Myers memo clearly states: '[It] is probably in our best interests to forestall any form of consumer advertising. The inability to advertise presents a significant entry barrier to new competitors.'[20] US industry consciously and explicitly used opposition to domestic advertising as a barrier to entry.

## 6. Entry barrier permitted price collusion

According to federal prosecutors, Abbott-Ross Laboratories and Bristol-Myers (Mead Johnson), engaged in 'facilitating devices' or signals leading to price collusion, bid rigging, and conspiracy to prevent advertising. Abbott-Ross and Bristol-Myers denied the charges.[21] From 1980 to 1993 Abbott raised its Similac prices (eighteen times in thirteen years) by 207 per cent, roughly six times the increase in the consumer price of milk, and three times the overall inflation rate. By 1987 it had sold over one billion US dollars' worth of formula, accounting for 25 per cent of its earnings. Bristol-Myers and American Home Products, then the second and third largest US manufacturers, allegedly engaged in lock-step pricing. Industry officials were aware of a need for confidentiality. Prosecutors alleged that internal memos on these issues included phrases such as: 'Be sensitive to what you put in writing', 'protect confidential information', 'get rid of unnecessary records', 'clean out your files before year end', 'clean files reflect a clean operation', and 'if only Mr Nixon had paid attention'.[22] Despite these efforts, the three

[19] *Richmond Times-Dispatch*, 20 May 2001; Thomas M. Burton, *WSJ*, 25 May 1993. An earlier US Industry Council code had been picked up by the Canadian Pediatrics' Society, and brought back to the USA by the AAP.

[20] Cited in the *NYT*, 15 June 1993.

[21] Neither Abbott-Ross nor Bristol-Myers responded to requests for information or commented on drafts of this case study. Their press releases state that they produce 25 varieties of infant formula each, some tailored to babies with special nutritional needs. No figures were supplied on the cost of these varieties.

firms' concern with confidentiality ultimately failed.

Among the consumers hit hardest by the high prices were the poor in the federal government's Special Supplemental Food Program for Women, Infants, and Children (WIC), according to prosecutors. WIC accounted for 40 per cent of the US infant formula market in 1991 (serving 4.4 million babies a month, over one-fourth of all babies born in the USA). Higher prices cut into WIC funds. A lack of funds prevented the WIC program from serving half of the eligible mothers in some areas. When WIC programs in Oregon, Tennessee, and Texas turned to competitive bidding, over the adamant objections of the US formula industry, the price they paid per can of formula dropped by 80 per cent.[23]

## 7. Cracks in the US advertising ban

The absence of a legal ban on advertising led to inroads by Nestlé. Nestlé was the world's largest food conglomerate by the 1970s. It introduced Carnation infant formula by 1985 and used that brand name to finally make inroads into the US formula market in 1988. Facing increased competition from Nestlé-Carnation, Bristol-Myers stretched the industry code in June 1989, with limited advertising initially under the Gerber brand name. In the late 1990s Similac and Enfamil began to be advertised in parenting magazines. Continued collusion between Abbott and Bristol-Myers was allegedly one reason why Nestlé held only a 9 per cent market share by 2002. The two big US firms still controlled 90 per cent.[24]

Even more significant, the 'voluntary' code led to federal charges of collusion and price-fixing. Ironically, if Abbott-Ross and Bristol-Myers had supported the WHO code earlier, they might have accomplished some of their goals without facing legal charges. They opposed that code in the hope of gaining overseas market-share. The double-edged sword of their strategy turned against them.

[22] Cited in Burton, *WSJ*, 25 May 1993. According to Florida Attorney General Robert Butterworth and Jerome W. Hoffman, chief of the Florida attorney general's antitrust section, 'There had been a longstanding agreement between all three companies to fix prices and to restrict advertising'. Quoted in the *Sacramento Bee*, 19 August 1993. Sen. Howard Metzenbaum (D-Ohio) was an early critic of formula pricing; see *Washington Post*, 13 January 1991.

[23] *Christian Science Monitor*, 26 August 1996; *Sacramento Bee*, 19 August 1993; *NYT*, 31 December 1990; and *Chicago Tribune*, 5 June 1988. Mike Hudson, executive director of Texas Children's Defense Fund, called Abbott-Ross's effort to prevent competitive bidding 'one of the most intense lobbying campaigns I've ever seen'.

[24] *Richmond Times-Dispatch*, 20 May 2001; Information Resources, 25 April 1993. Note that the AAP refused funding from Bristol-Myers after 1989, consistent with its principles. Nestlé agreed not to advertise its new-born formula, but began direct consumer advertising for its older-baby formula. Facing protests, Nestlé quickly dropped its advertisements in early 1989, but resumed some in 1991 as the FTC began its investigation of Abbott.

## 8. Federal litigation: Industry settles for $US230 million

The FTC announced its investigation of Abbott and others in 1991. Soon the big three US makers faced over thirty law suits from across the country. In May the industry settled consolidated federal antitrust litigation in Tallahassee, Florida, by agreeing to pay a total of more than $US230 million to drugstores, supermarkets, and the state of Florida.[25] It was one of the largest antitrust settlements to date. In early September 1993 Abbott settled charges of collusion by agreeing not to exchange marketing information with other baby-formula companies or to lobby them in efforts to prohibit consumer advertising. Abbott faced additional antitrust litigation, including charges of price-fixing on bids to provide formula to a federal nutrition program for poor families in Puerto Rico. A 1998 GAO report found that the wholesale prices of infant formula were still high in relation to the cost of production. An Italian court found similar price-fixing arrangements in 1999.

The US industry and the AAP suggested that the federal investigation was spurred by Nestlé. Nestlé in turn sued Abbott, Bristol-Myers, and the AAP in May 1993 for allegedly 'conspiring to keep Nestlé out of the baby-formula market by preventing consumer advertising of formula'.[26] This latest turn marks an attempt to reduce *de facto* protectionism. Nestlé's suit had some effect as by the late 1990s some advertising began to appear in the USA.

## 9. US infant formula: Conclusion

The US infant formula case has parallels to the tuna-dolphin case. They fit this book's propositions of higher heterogenous restrictions resulting from product market access restrictions, high market concentration, and domestic asset specificity. The duopoly of US infant formula makers kept out Nestlé by using advertising restrictions as a barrier to entry against a foreign competitor. In response to the duopoly's lobbying, the USA was the only government to vote against the WHO code against advertising.[27] Those overseas codes were only implemented when Nestlé agreed to them, in 1984. Even as US industry failed to prevent stringent marketing codes in overseas markets dominated by Nestlé, it succeeded in erecting marketing guidelines

[25] *WSJ*, staff reporter, 3 September 1993. The companies did not admit any wrongdoing.

[26] *WSJ*, 3 September 1993.

[27] The US government was not willing to push the issue further against these odds abroad nor was it willing to buck domestic opposition (including the Department of State). Therefore, in this case it did not threaten to close US markets to Nestlé.

as a barrier to entry in the USA. The US industry drew support from a respectable professional association, in a 'Baptist and bootlegger' coalition that excluded competition and raised prices.

However, that barrier to entry was vulnerable, because US industry did not seek (nor find) a formal US regulation against advertising; instead it relied on a voluntary code. By contrast, in the CFC case DuPont effectively used government regulation as a contracting mechanism.[28]

Other aspects of the case confirm the role of particular private sector interests in regulating economic behavior. The US industry supported protectionist codes that advanced its differentiated private interests, while defending them in terms of the public interest.

An interesting juxtaposition to the infant formula case is the case of tobacco advertising in Asia. That case is briefly summarized below followed by mention of other similar heterogenous examples (including some in Europe that run against integration there).

## Appendix: Examples of other HET cases

### Tobacco advertising in Asia

US tobacco companies' marketing investments in the USA declined in value in the 1980s as demand decreased. They sought markets overseas, particularly in Asia. Asian cigarette markets were typically dominated by national brands, often monopolies protected by restrictions on advertising. Those restrictions were supported by medical groups; and also supported by the local industry (as this book's propositions predicts). US tobacco companies, as powerful newcomers, sought to penetrate those markets via lower restrictions on advertising. They found partial success. Product market-access regulations supported by Asian firms with domestic asset specific investments were partly overwhelmed by leading American tobacco firms with increasing multinational asset specificity.

The US tobacco firms launched a lobbying campaign through the US Trade Representative (USTR) to lower advertising restrictions overseas. Sesser (1993) asserts that the Tobacco Heritage Committee (composed of seven American tobacco manufacturers) paid $US1.4 million to redecorate the elegant Treaty Room in the US Department of State in 1986 (with a tobacco-leaf *motif*) while tobacco negotiations were underway with Asian countries. R.J. Reynolds hired President Reagan's former National Security

[28] Braithwaite and Drahos (2000: 492) emphasize private sector standards: 'A deep mistake is to see standard-setting at an international organization as the decisive moment [. . .] [When] the majority of the hundred largest economies in the world were corporations rather than states, it is foolish to see harmonization of state standards as invariably more consequential than harmonization of private corporate standards. This is a different world from that of Max Weber.'

Adviser, Richard Allen, to lobby on its behalf; Philip Morris paid Reagan's former aide Michael Deaver $US250,000 in 1987, to help open South Korea's tobacco market. Sesser alleges that Philip Morris also hired former British Prime Minister Margaret Thatcher for one million US dollars per year to help open China's market.[29]

US tobacco companies argued that they faced unfair trade practices in Asian countries, where they competed against national monopolies which controlled markets through name-brand recognition and advertising bans. (Note the mirror-image parallels to the US tuna-dolphin and infant formula cases.) The USTR heeded these arguments. The USTR pushed even for advertising *minutiae*, such as limiting health warnings on cigarette packages in Taiwan to small print on the side of the pack (instead of large print on the front, as Taiwanese officials had preferred).

In the late 1980s the US pressured China, Taiwan, Japan, South Korea, and Malaysia to permit cigarette advertising. Press reports suggested that section 301 trade sanctions might be used to force market access. Those sanctions could include 100 per cent countervailing duties on exports to the USA from countries which did not meet US demands. Initially, Taiwan, South Korea, Japan, Malaysia, and China all conceded to US firms in various ways. The lobbying and threats of market closure had mixed success. By the 1990s the USTR faced a united front of 'bootlegger' Asian tobacco firms and 'Baptist' health experts in Asia and the USA (including a smoke-free White House), all opposed to lax regulations on tobacco. The USTR backed off from enforcing the 1986 agreements, and eased up in its opposition to countries' restrictions on tobacco advertising.[30] Thailand resisted US pressures by appealing to the GATT. The GATT ruled that Thailand could keep in place nondiscriminatory advertising restrictions, although it had to open its market to foreign cigarettes. US companies quickly gained significant market shares elsewhere (and the incidence of smoking rose) but in Thailand their market share remained small.[31]

### European 'Green protection'

In the EC, despite overall trends toward homogeneity, one finds protectionist 'cracks' supporting particular interests and justified as public goods. Green protectionism is the use of environmental regulations to support a particular domestic industry. A leading observer concludes:

[29] Stan Sesser, 'Opium War Redux', *New Yorker*, 13 September 1993. Sesser imputes no illegality, but implies a chummy relationship between government and industry.

[30] The tobacco issue was taken up by various public interest groups. See the Council on Scientific Affairs, 'The Worldwide Smoking Epidemic: Tobacco Trade, Use and Control', 263 *Journal of the American Medical Association* 3312 (27 June 1990). Also reports by the Advocacy Institute and INFACT: see *Infact Update* (Summer 1993).

[31] GATT, 'Dispute Settlement Panel Report: Thailand—Restrictions on Importation of and Internal Taxes on Cigarettes' (Geneva: GATT Secretariat, 7 November 1990).

If [EC] nations were allowed to adopt their own product standards [. . .] nations with stricter environmental standards would then likely attempt to 'protect' both their citizens and their industries by excluding goods produced in member states with weaker regulatory requirements. In the case of [process] standards, nations that had adopted more stringent pollution controls than other member states would find the goods produced by their industries placed at a competitive disadvantage.[32]

In short, nations would face a choice between protection, economic hardship, or laxity.

Specific examples include the following:

(i) German recyclers: Germany recycles 53 per cent of its glass; Britain recycles only 17 per cent. In April 1991 Germany approved laws that ultimately required companies to retrieve and recycle all product packaging, and many durable goods. The response exceeded even Germany's extensive recycling capacity: 80 million tons of recycled material were collected the first year of German legislation, and 400 million tons were expected in 1994. Foreign firms protested on a variety of grounds, e.g. that the mandatory take-back policy discouraged retailers from carrying imported goods, and created hurdles for small foreign firms.[33]

(ii) Danish bottlers: Danish consumption of beer per capita is the highest in Europe (after Germany) but Denmark imports very little beer. Danish regulations protect that bottling industry. A 1984 Danish law imposed recycling restrictions on imported beverage containers. The European Court of Justice upheld most of the law, ruling that it was not in restraint of trade but served a legitimate purpose under the Treaty of Rome.[34]

(iii) Canadian beer: Ontario, Canada imposed a 10 per cent tax on beer cans but not beer bottles (or other cans). Most beer imports from the USA were in cans.

[32] Vogel 1992: 5. See citations to Ludwig Kramer, 'The Single European Act and Environmental Protection: Reflections on Several New Provisions in Community Law', *Common Market Law Review*, vol. 24, 1987; Dirk Vandermeersch, 'The Single European Act [SEA] and the Environmental Policy of the European Community', *European Law Review*, vol. 12, December 1987. SEA Articles 100A and 130T (as with Treaty of Rome Articles 30 and 36) grant states the right to hold stricter environmental standards providing they are not a hidden barrier to trade. That judgement is left to the European Court of Justice. Directives based on Article 100A can be approved by a qualified majority.

[33] World Economic Forum Summit 1993, 'Extended Producers' Responsibility Laws: An Approaching Tidal Wave of New Recycling Regulation?', panel chaired by David H. Marks, with John R. Ehrenfeld, Gordon E. Forward, Gunnar Larsson, and Juan Rada. Also, Vogel 1992: 56 ff.

[34] 'Environmental Protection and Free Movement of Goods: the Danish Bottles Case', *Journal of Environmental Law*, 2:1, 1990; and Vogel 1992: 48 ff. Vogel cites other EC cases in chemical safety, hazardous waste disposal, and eco-labeling. On the earlier *Cassis de Dijon* case, see Karen Alter and Sophie Meunier (1992).

(iv) Many long-standing national regulations in Europe benefitted local producers. France restricted artificial sweeteners to protect the domestic sugar-beet industry; Germany regulated the contents of beer; Italy regulated pasta.[35]

[35] Vogel 1993. German beer laws date from the Renaissance; in part, they ensured that feudal rulers would receive taxes on locally produced ingredients.

# PART V
# CONCLUSION

# 8

# *Evidence and Implications*

Economic regulation is as much a tool of statecraft as military defenses ever were. Hence, insofar as external repercussions are considered, the logic of state regulation is in part the logic of conflict.

Edward Luttwak, *National Interest*, 1990

Edward Luttwak's words may exaggerate the role of conflict in international economic regulations but they are useful reminders of this potential. Nearly every economic activity in modern society is subject to regulations and is therefore affected by competitive pressures from interstate trade and investments when no central authority has resolved costly regulatory differences.

This book set out to answer a puzzle. It began by observing that initial cross-border variations in national regulations may lead to any of the following three basic trajectories for a given issue:

(i) convergence toward a lower common denominator (LCD);
(ii) convergence toward a higher common denominator (HCD); or
(iii) persistence of national differences (HET).

Examples of these trends exist concurrently. These trajectories constitute the book's dependent variable. The goal was to find a common thread of explanation across diverse cases (without attempting a complete explanation of any one case).

This conclusion first summarizes how well the book's answer to the puzzle holds up in light of the detailed case study Chapters. Next, it touches on some variability which the propositions cannot explain, including human leadership. It then examines the broader significance of these findings for scholarly debates in contemporary international studies. Finally, it summarizes the implications for policy-makers and business executives.

The book began with three related propositions to explain the pattern in international regulatory trajectories. Each proposition emphasized the incentives and options facing private sector interests, and government responses to them. The regulatory outcomes are viewed as the result of producer preferences, building on George Stigler's and Oliver Williamson's approach to law and economics. These propositions were explained in length in section two of Chapter One, above.

*Veritas* is in the details. As revealed in the case studies, these propositions stand up well. Rather than summarize the implications of each case study separately, these first three sections examine each proposition in turn, drawing on just some of the details from across all of the cases which support (or counter) it. These details greatly expand the number of observations beyond six cases. This is followed by a discussion of unexplained variance among the cases.

## 1. Process *versus* market access distinction

The first proposition emphasized the importance of the locus of regulations: on production processes or on the market access, sale, and distribution of products and services. These pointed to market size as an important corollary.

### 1.1 Process regulations: Laxity

Firms generally supported greater laxity in process regulations (or opposed greater stringency) and were often successful. Consider the following summary evidence from the case studies.

(i) The registration of ships to flags-of-convenience (FOC) countries clearly demonstrated the potential of process restrictions to lead to a competition-in-laxity. Following World War II shipowners increasingly registered their ships in Panama and Liberia to avoid taxes and labor, environmental, safety, and navigational process regulations. Registration was cheap and easy. Similar FOCs emerged in Cyprus, Malta, and so on, in a classic competition-in-laxity (both *de facto* and *de jure*). By 1994 more of the world's shipping flew a flag-of-convenience than a flag from the seven largest OECD fleets combined. Those FOC fleets were less expensive to operate but more prone to labor-abuses, pollution, and inspection violations. They were also three times more likely to sink.

(ii) A similar pattern of competition-in-laxity was found in the case of offshore finance. Several broad phases of regulatory competition were distinguished in this case study. First, London and the Bahamas drew assets into previously prohibited transactions in the 1950s–1960s, assets that might have otherwise gone to Switzerland. Likewise, the US Federal Reserve revised various regulations to allow US financial firms operating overseas to avoid the McFadden, Glass-Steagall, Sherman, and Clayton Acts. Second, by the late 1960s the Cayman Islands (and Bahamas) increasingly attracted assets that might have gone to London. Third, in the 1970s these assets were drawn into other, newer offshore centers in the Caribbean, British Channel Islands, and other European centers.

Fourth, American assets that once might have gone to the Caribbean were brought back 'onshore' when New York offered less strictly regulated International Banking Facilities (IBFs) beginning in 1982. Fifth, in the late 1980s and 1990s still newer offshore havens emerged, as did newer international banking facilities (in Thailand, Japan, and elsewhere). By the 1990s over half of all international finance was conducted offshore. Banks and other financial firms *de facto* relocated business to jurisdictions with more lax process regulations, these jurisdictions gained in *de facto* market share, home-country governments responded with *de jure* lax process regulations of their own, and a regulatory chill prevailed over various proposals to regulate offshore banking.

(iii) Nearly half a million dolphins per year were killed as by-catch in the 1960s when major US canners owned tuna-boat fleets. Enforcement of *process* provisions in the 1974 Marine Mammal Protection Act (MMPA) was lax through 1989, by which time the US canning industry had long severed its ties with fishing boats. The MMPA ceilings were above the actual levels achieved by the fishing industry as it improved techniques safer for dolphin such as net-backing. Enforcement of process regulations aboard US ships with observers was lax, to the frustration of the observers and environmental groups alike.[1] (It was not until the US banned the importation of Mexican products that the regulations were effectively raised.)

(iv) Emissions from smokestacks and drainpipes, habitat preservation, and other on-the-spot evidence are the most compelling measures of the stringency of environmental process regulations. One of the few (and leading) environmental economists who conducted empirical research on this problem was David Kolstad, president of the Association of Environmental and Resource Economists. A study by Xing and Kolstad (2002) finds a positive association between the amount of sulfur emissions in a host country (as a measure of lax environmental regulations) and inflows of US FDI in the chemical industry. They conclude: 'the statistical results show that the laxity of environmental regulations in a host country is a significant determinant of FDI from the US for heavily polluting industries.'[2] Even some who dismiss races-to-the-bottom as 'wrong' and a 'myth' concede that 'it is difficult to quantify compliance and enforcement in developing economies' and they credit watchdog groups for scrutinizing enforcement (Drezner 2000). Compliance is the relevant variable.

(v) Tax havens are a major aspect of international business and their primary function is to offer lower taxes on profits and more lax

[1] *Atlantic*, July 1989 263/1: 35.

[2] Though Xing cautions: 'we wouldn't bet the farm on this.'

disclosure requirements. Both are process regulations. Some suggest tax havens accounted for 31 per cent of US multinational firms' profits and 26 per cent of their assets, despite holding only 1.2 per cent of world population and 3 per cent of world GDP (Hines and Rice 1994; Hines 1996, 1997). Their emergence paralleled that of offshore banking.

(vi) Studies report conflicting results on the overall impact of profit taxes on corporate relocation (e.g. compare Hines, above, to Quinn 1997 and Swank 2002). Many market factors are involved in foreign direct investment (FDI) location decisions. Most FDI occurs between OECD countries. Bénassy-Quéré *et al.* conclude (2000) that high tax rates (both nominal and effective) do reduce a country's attractiveness to FDI. Within Europe, for example, Ireland attracted FDI at a faster rate than elsewhere after its corporate tax rate was reduced.

(vii) Firms routinely negotiate tax holidays and various regulatory perks not reflected in macro-level data or tax rates. FDI into Germany tripled between 1998 and 2000, despite Germany's high cost of labor, largely because Germany lowered its capital gains tax: a competitive deregulation to attract investment. Further, most macro-level FDI data focus on ownership and not on country of registration. The latter variable is the relevant one when analyzing the role of havens. For example, US-owned Ingersoll-Rand is legally headquartered in the Bahamas for tax purposes, although most of its operations are located in the USA. If Ingersoll-Rand bought a factory in Brazil, most data sources would understandably list this as outward-FDI from the US to Brazil. For the purpose of analyzing the impact of tax regulations, however, the Bahamas are the relevant jurisdiction. Corporate income tax rates in the Caribbean were typically less than 3 per cent compared to 36 per cent in the USA and 52 per cent in the UK and Canada.[3]

(viii) Similar patterns of process laxity were noted within the US federal system in the relocation of incorporation to the state of Delaware (Winter 1977). Sixty per cent of major US corporations and 40 per cent of all firms listed on the New York Stock Exchange are incorporated in Delaware. Eighty-two per cent of firms who reincorporate switch to Delaware.[4] With 783,000 residents, Delaware holds only 0.29 per cent of the US population.

(ix) In many of these cases, when one country or state offered lax process restrictions, firms in competing states also pushed for and

[3] Swank (1998) notes that governments may also reduce marginal corporate tax rates but close loopholes.

[4] Scholarship on Delaware incorporation is bifurcated and a veritable industry unto itself. See citations in Chapter One above.

achieved *de jure* deregulation: e.g. international ship registries in Europe, deregulation of certain banking products worldwide, convergence toward Delaware's code within the USA, and tax reductions in various countries.

Some free-trade votaries define away competitive deregulation by using a narrow or strawperson definition of races to the bottom. Rhetorically, this is a popular fallacy, but it is analytically indefensible. 'Races to the middle' may equally evince a competition-in-laxity. For example, if certain less stringently regulated Internet commerce activities take market share away from traditional commerce as a result of lower taxes or other regulations (music copyrights, gambling, pornography, unsolicited bulk email or 'spam') this is evidence of competition-in-laxity (*de facto* market-share form) even if regulations on Internet commerce eventually increase, but not up to the level of traditional commerce. Similarly, if labor standards in export-processing zones are lower than in OECD countries, market-share growth by these zones would be evidence of some competition-in-laxity (*ceteris paribus*) even if standards in the export zones are higher than in the rest of the host country (and even if both increase over time). Once again, laxity is not necessarily undesirable (Winter 1977; Swire 1996). This market-share growth may be justified normatively because poor workers in poor countries (living on the equivalent of two US dollars a day) may vastly prefer work conditions in an MNC factory job over any realistic alternative (especially if they are allowed genuine collective bargaining rights). There can be worse fates than a little competition-in-laxity, including the status quo of widespread underemployment, disease, starvation, and morbidity endemic in poor countries.

No serious scholar actually asserts that global regulations will fall to the absolute lowest enforced level of any country. No one expects Haiti to hollow out New Jersey's economy anytime soon with a 'giant sucking sound' (*per* Ross Perot 1993) no matter how lax are Haiti's regulations. This argument is a 'straw herring'—half strawperson and half red herring—and is not worth pursuing.

More meaningfully, competition-in-laxity comes in four forms: lowering of implemented standards, relocation of firms, increases in market share by less strictly regulated countries, and failure to increase regulations when they are warranted or expected. Implementation is the key, rather than the letter of the law. In some cases a more useful statistical parallel may be crime statistics rather than aggregate investment trends. In certain cases competition-in-laxity occurs, sometimes with significant policy implications. The case studies reveal that process regulations facilitated this outcome.

### 1.2 Market-access regulations: Stringency

Market-access regulations on products and services, on the other hand, are associated with movement toward greater stringency. The greater the dependence on a foreign market (as a percentage of export earnings in total or for a given product) the greater the importance of market access. Consider the following summary evidence from the case studies.

(i) Only when market-access restrictions on dolphin-lethal tuna *products* were imposed, by the US Congress and courts, were more stringent regulations enacted. These restrictions depended on industry support, not merely scientific or policy arguments. Mexico challenged this heterogenous US move and alleged in its GATT panel hearing that US squid-boats continued to kill dolphins, with no special restrictions and despite environmental protests. The GATT ruled in favor of Mexico. Despite many protesters' misconception, however, the USA continued to restrict Mexican tuna imports until Greenpeace and others convinced it otherwise, and dolphin-setting in the Eastern Tropical Pacific ocean (ETP) continued to decline. Mexico never retaliated despite the GATT ruling. Although some non-US producers still continued to dolphin-set there contrary to heterogenous US regulations, their catch was not permitted inside US borders.

(ii) Under the Montreal Protocol most countries in the world began to restrict the production of ozone-depleting CFCs by year-end 1988, foreclosing the sale and distribution of new CFCs. Major producers such as DuPont and ICI were able to patent substitute goods such as HFCs and benefitted further from this regulatory strategy. Smaller commodity CFC producers, including those in developing countries, were consigned to niche or grey markets. The USA allegedly threatened Taiwan with trade restrictions if it did not go along with the Montreal Protocol.

(iii) US infant formula makers acted together with medical authorities to restrict the market access of infant formula in the USA to certain channels.

(iv) Local tobacco firms in Asia acted together with medical authorities to restrict the market access of cigarettes to certain channels. (They were challenged, with mixed success, by powerful foreign [US] firms.)

(v) Similar effects were seen in the sub-sector oil-tanker shipping industry (where certain safety and construction standards were enforced) and the Basle Accord. Threats of tightened market access facilitated these agreements. In the Basle Accord, Japan was pressured into signing onto the US–UK accord at the risk of pressure from US banking regulators. (Moody's and Standard and Poor's later adopted these standards as prudential rules of thumb; the government regulations became a self-reinforcing market norm.)

(vi) A similar logic was seen in Danish bottle laws, German recycling laws, and Italian laws on pasta (Vogel 1992), and in US market-access restrictions on shrimp. In the shrimp-turtle case, those countries least-dependent on access to the US market (Suriname, French Guyana, Trinidad, and Tobago) were most likely to resist the regulations sought by the USA (DeSombre 2000).

(vii) Movement toward more stringent regulation of phosphorus matches occurred among major exporters only when a substitute product (sesquisulphide) was found and the leading producer could profit from a market-access ban on phosphorus match products.

In all these cases, movement toward stringent market-access standards reflected a strategic private sector interest as well as public interest concerns. Common standards may create network economies for all participants but they also often reward the standard-setter. The focal point of these coordination games is typically set by a leading firm (such as DuPont's HFCs, or Microsoft's DOS/Windows).

As noted in Chapter One above, market access helps explain an occasional exception to the process-laxity connection: dominant firms may support certain more stringent process restrictions (in a bleeding game) if those restrictions differentially improve their market position against competitors. Such was the case in the sub-sector of shipping devoted to large tankers. Here Shell Oil, Exxon, and other multinational corporations in the Federation of American Controlled Shipping supported certain more stringent regulations (albeit not as stringent as many labor unions and environmentalists wanted). Similarly, US firms encouraged the US Export-Import Bank to push for certain higher common denominator environmental regulations among the OECD export-promotion banks in those areas which benefitted US firms.[5] Both these cases were backed up with market-access regulations. Nike, Adidas, Reebok, Levi's, and Gap had their overseas labor-practices in the critical spotlight for nearly a decade and faced consumer boycotts (which changed consumer demand for their products). They moved toward higher labor-standards than did their low-cost competitors who supplied Wal-Mart and other discount chains in the US. The branded names turned to government intervention for higher common denominator standards which the non-branded firms resisted.[6] Likewise, it was large US-based chemical firms who 'exported' a stronger environmental ideology to large chemical firms in Mexico and Brazil (Garcia-Johnson 2000) partly to pre-empt more stringent regulations and partly for competitive reasons. The regulations became a source of competitive advantage, not a cost. These exceptions prove the rule. In the absence of rare competitive interests, firms favor lax process regulations and selected stringent market-access regulations.

[5] Author's interview with Export-Import Bank official, 10 September 2001.

[6] Thanks to a colleague for this example. On the spotlight effect in human rights, see Debora Spar, 'The Spotlight and the Bottom Line', *Foreign Affairs*, March 1998.

### 1.3 Market size

Market closure is the ultimate product market-access restriction; the threat of closure can be used to achieve other product regulations. Large national markets provide substantial leverage to influence market-access regulations. This was identified in earlier research (Murphy 1993, Murphy and Oye 1995). More recent findings confirm this was true in tariff-lowering successes often attributed to the GATT and WTO:

> The fact is, virtually *every tariff that has ever been lowered* by a government as a result of a GATT/WTO negotiation [. . .] *has been lowered because some exporters* somewhere in the world *valued the resulting market access*, and as a result their governments were willing to offer something of value in return (i.e., export access to their own markets through a reciprocal tariff concession of their own). In other words, despite two centuries of economic arguments extolling the virtues of free trade, the consumer gain that comes from freer trade is not the liberalizing force that has been harnessed by the WTO. Instead, much as labor and environmental interests claim, the *WTO is driven by exporter interests*. [. . .] *Those who seek lower tariffs and those who fear* race-to-the-bottom/*regulatory-chill problems share common ground that is delineated by the issue of market access* (Bagwell and Staiger 2001: 2, emphases added).

This book supports Bagwell and Staiger's insight that there is often common ground between those who fear a 'race to the bottom' and those who seek freer trade. The importance of market size was evident in the Basle Accord, tuna-dolphin, and other cases.

Market closure effectively bars the sale of a product. The threat of market-restricting product standards can be used to force compliance among competing states. This has two conditions. First, powerful firms must benefit differentially from the regulation. Second, their government must have enough market power to make a credible threat. These threats are not invincible even for powerful states. The USA could not, for example, enforce uniformity in the definition of capital (where estimates varied widely on the amount of capital held by Japanese banks in particular). In general, however, the USA and other large-market states were more likely to achieve regulatory success than were weak states.

## 2. Industrial structure: Degree of regulatory change

The second proposition concerns industrial structure and affects the degree to which process and product market-access restrictions took effect. Powerful firms in concentrated industries were able to exert more influence on the regulatory process. Consider the following summary evidence from the case studies.

(i) The world's two largest producers of CFCs, DuPont and ICI, were intimately involved in the restrictions on CFCs. In the early 1980s they slowed down heterogenous regulatory movements. Later in that decade, when support for homogenous regulations grew, they invested in substitutes and supported more stringent regulations. They even lobbied to support the Vienna Convention and Montreal Protocol against the predilections of the Reagan administration, and later moved faster than the EPA wanted to phase out CFCs completely. France, with the largest HCFC producer, Elf Atochem, was particularly effective in opposing restrictions on HCFCs or HFCs until the industry had a good substitute. The Executive Director of the UN Environmental Program, Mustafa Tolba, confirmed that the negotiations were more about differential gains between DuPont and its competitors than about the environment.

(ii) The largest US tuna canner, Heinz, supported stringent enforcement of a ban on dolphin-lethal tuna. It announced its own dolphin-safe policy four months before required to do so by law; the other two leading canners immediately followed suit, thereby squeezing out smaller players. These three held 75 per cent of the US market. Rather than wait for multilateral agreement on dolphin protection or let consumers decide whether or not to buy tuna with a dolphin-safe label, Heinz supported government intervention. It was at the behest of the major US tuna canners as well as environmental groups that the US government defended its heterogenous tuna-dolphin policy before the GATT in January 1991.

(iii) The two largest US manufacturers of infant formula had a combined 80 per cent market share. They co-operated to keep Nestlé out of the US market by restricting infant formula marketing in the USA, limiting it to the medical channels which they dominated.

(iv) The flag-of-convenience system was created by firms whose top executives also served at high levels in government. There was no oligopoly in shipping, but these men had unparalleled access to top government officials. The prominent businessmen (and later political appointees) W. Averell Harriman and John Foster Dulles created the Panamanian registry. The former Secretary of State (and former Chairman of US Steel) Edward Stettinius, Jr. founded the Liberian registry. Stettinius jointly owned several ships with Admiral William Halsey. In creating the Liberian registry he also received personal support from the Secretaries of the Army, Air Force, and other officials.

(v) Similarly, the offshore banking system was created by firms led by top British and American financiers, some of whom also served at high levels in central banks or Treasury departments. For example, by the late 1950s the Bank of London and South America (BOLSA) was led by one of the six highest-ranking executives in the Bank of England and its top expert on foreign exchange. George Bolton served simultaneously as a Bank of England director and the chief executive of BOLSA for over a decade, while BOLSA pioneered the growth of offshore banking in London's euromarkets, the Bahamas, the Caymans, and Panama, beginning in 1957. Bank of England Governor George Rowley Baring (Lord Cromer), the scion of England's Baring Brothers and Co. bank dynasty, approved of these developments. Baring conducted business in the British Channel Isles and retired there himself in 1981.

(vi) On the American side, Citibank, Chase Manhattan, and other major banks helped expand the offshore finance system both in London's euromarkets and the Caribbean by the early 1960s. A number of high-level American officials supported American banks, including former Treasury Secretary Robert Anderson, George Ball, Paul Volcker, and Richard Allen, in both their private-sector and governmental roles. Most offshore bank shell companies were large. By 1996 99 per cent of all such Edge Act company assets were held by firms with an average asset value of $US1.3 billion.

(vii) Despite the relatively large number of players in global finance, the Basle Accord raised capital standards worldwide. Here one finds unusual contracting arrangements between banks to overcome collective action problems in resolving the 1980s debt crisis and other policy issues. These contracting mechanisms included syndication of loans, cross-default clauses, and joint Bank Advisory Committees. One also finds close ties with a co-ordinating institution, the Bank for International Settlements (BIS), that helped unify bank interests. The BIS itself was created at the instigation of J.P. Morgan and other financiers from the USA, Europe, and Japan; the official US representative for more than fifty years was Citibank. The USA and the UK initiated the push for implementation of a higher capital standard; their banks had among the higher capital ratios worldwide. A transaction cost perspective explains these unusual governance structures well.

(viii) Dominant multinational corporations and the larger independent shipowners in the oil-tanker sub-sector pushed for more stringent regulatory action than did smaller independent owners.

(ix) In the US phossy-jaw case (discussed in the Appendix to Chapter Five above), regulations came about at the insistence of the oligopolist Diamond Match Company, which held a US patent on the substitute good, sesquisulphide.

(x) Historically, integration of the US economy into a single market was also led by powerful firms. Writing about the US Interstate Commerce Act and other measures which limited heterogeneity among the US states, Buxbaum and Hopt (1988) conclude: '[It] was corporate participation in the irresistibly developing national market that provided the motive force behind those judicial developments [in the late 1800s].'

(xi) During debates over NAFTA in 1993, Bhagwati proposed that US firms be required to live up to US environmental process regulations when they directly invested abroad.[7] He concluded later that his proposal was defeated by US firms. 'It did not take off [. . .] largely because US businesses [. . .] were reportedly unhappy at the thought that they would be subjected to any restrictions on their freedom to work with whatever local environmental and labor standards Mexico required' (Bhagwati and Hudec 1996 v 1: 33–34). This regulatory chill outcome is consistent with this book's propositions.

(xii) Many other scholars support these findings. Braithwaite and Drahos (2000: 27), for example, conclude: 'The most recurrently effective actors in enrolling the power of states and the power of the most potent international organizations (e.g. the WTO and IMF) are large US corporations.'

Alfred Dupont Chandler (1990) noted that the logic of *laissez-faire* capitalism may lead to the continued growth of large corporations which seek to capture economies of scale and scope.[8] To the extent that Chandler's conclusions and this book's propositions are true, one can expect regulations increasingly to reflect large corporate interests. 'Economies of scale and scope heighten the advantages of vertical integration for asset specific investments' (Williamson 1985: 92–95). Scale and scope may also increasingly reflect asset specificity, discussed next.

## 3. Asset specificity

The third proposition concerns variations in the asset specificity of firm-level investments (low or high, multinational or domestic). It, too, was also shown to be a useful explanatory variable. Summary evidence on these is next presented in turn.

### 3.1 Low asset specificity: Competition-in-laxity

Transactions involving investments with low asset specificity allowed firms to search for less restrictive (market governance) regulatory environments,

[7] Jagdish Bhagwati, 'American Rules, Mexican Jobs', Op-Ed Page, *NYT*, 24 March 1993. He repeated the proposal in 1996, to address political concerns 'however unfounded and illogical': Bhagwati and Hudec, v 1, 178–9.

[8] In the USA, for example, assets of the largest 500 manufacturing firms grew from 27% of GDP in 1955 to 47% in 2003. A contrary vision is expressed by Piore and Sabel: 1984.

or to flee the sector. Low asset specificity increased the exit option of firms, thereby reducing the corresponding options of governments. It facilitated a competition-in-laxity of process regulations as governments sought to attract (or maintain) these firms. Although these cases may be rare, it is worth considering the following summary evidence from the case studies.

(i) Ship-flagging presented an extreme case of low asset specificity, in which shipowners could shop among registries with ease. In response, convenience flag states maintained lax domestic process regulations and weak enforcement of international agreements.
(ii) Competitive deregulation occurred even in European countries in order to bring their shipping fleets back under their national flags (they removed manning requirements and lowered taxes).
(iii) As Liberian regulations were strengthened with the support of multinational oil corporations, other owners exited from Liberia to Cyprus and Malta.
(iv) As global capital became increasingly mobile from the late 1950s through the 1970s, a creeping indirect competition-in-laxity occurred in the regulation of bank capital. Offshore banking centers acquired an ever-larger share of the world financial markets.
(v) The ease of relocation of firms within the USA stalled efforts toward higher common denominator regulation of phosphorus matches (Moss 1994).
(vi) Certain parallels are evident in the cases of offshore banking centers and incorporation in Delaware, in which firms' relocation decisions are based on the comparative regulatory advantage offered by states.

These findings are consistent with those predicted. They are of considerable interest for digital-related commerce because of the latter's role in lowering the specificity of assets. If the Internet, for example, reduces certain transaction costs and facilitates market governance, it may also encourage havens which circumvent taxes and laws on insider trading, privacy, unsolicited bulk emails, gambling, child pornography, and the like.

### 3.2 Multinational asset specificity (MAS): Homogeneity

Transactions involving investments with high multinational asset specificity (MAS) led firms to search for a common set of rules under which to operate (unified governance) within their market area. Exit options were considerably more expensive to these firms. Consider the following summary evidence from the case studies.

(i) DuPont, as a global supplier of CFCs with asset-specific production facilities and marketing channels throughout the world, voiced support for common standards on CFCs, anticipated high MAS in substitutes, and strongly opposed heterogenous US standards.

(ii) With the growth of sovereign lending in the late 1970s bank asset specificity increased. The debt crisis gave leading banks worldwide an incentive to strengthen capital ratios in order to strengthen their hand against sovereign borrowers. Particularly in comparison with other proposals to resolve the debt issue, banks supported a higher 'level playing field' in capital standards worldwide. They, too, opposed heterogenous standards.

(iii) In the federal phossy-jaw case, competition-in-laxity among the American states was overcome only with the leadership of a firm with cross-border asset-specific investments and sales.

(iv) Within the ship registration subcase it was noted that oil supertankers are considerably more asset-specific than are cargo vessels. Further, oil-tanker construction and operation involve transactions more specific than the 'hit and run' transaction of flagging. Here one sees some movement toward higher common standards as supported by the large oil firms. (The standards were not as high as environmentalists hoped, although studies suggest that oil spills are not the most pressing environmental concern from shipping. Those other concerns were not addressed.) These oil firms maintained similar standards for their vessels no matter where they were flagged.

(v) Whereas the 1954 and 1962 conventions on pollution at sea failed to yield enforceable discharge and operational standards, Shell and other oil firms were able to establish load-on-top (LOT) as the legal standard worldwide. In so doing they explicitly violated earlier Conventions and presented their system as a near *fait accompli*. Governments responded by supporting the LOT system.

(vi) Other cases, not examined in detail here, lend *prima facie* support to these findings. In a modern example of 'Baptists and bootleggers' and in keeping with this book's propositions, in 1982 the US alcoholic beverage industry still favored federal regulations on alcohol. When President Reagan tried to deregulate it, he discovered to his surprise that industry wanted federal regulation, instead of fifty sets of state regulations. A spokesman for the National Beer Wholesalers' Association said that prior to regulation the industry was rife with monopolies, criminals, and unethical promotions. 'The industry has grown up with the [Federal Bureau of Alcohol, Tobacco and Firearms] and feels very comfortable with it.'[9] Similar homogenous federal regulations were sought by the US tobacco industry. Strong brand recognition nationwide meant high

[9] Spokesman for the National Beer Wholesalers' Association, quoted in *NYT*, 27 August 1982. Incidentally, Baptist and bootlegger coalitions may support lax regulations at times, not just stringent ones. For example in the offshore finance Chapter, it was noted that the ACLU joined with Wall Street bankers to lobby for a weaker 1970 Bank Secrecy Act.

multi-state asset specificity (MAS) in the domestic federal US context and firms sought homogenous regulations within that arena.

(vii) Adopting the metric system was favored by those members of the British Confederation of British Industry (CBI) with strong business ties to Europe. Other members with stronger business ties to the USA favored continuation of the imperial system of weights (as did import-competing firms). Both parties sought to operate under one set of standards in their given market. European exporters pressured Britain, leading to a 1989 EC Directive which mandated metrication by 2000. It has yet to be fully achieved.

(viii) A variety of international business associations have sought standardization of regulations affecting their members, often at the behest of those member firms with the largest global presence. These associations include the Business RoundTable (BRT), National Association of Manufacturers (NAM), International Chamber of Commerce, International Association for the Protection of Intellectual Property, International Association of Classification Societies (for shipping FOCs), Business Software Alliance, the Committee for Proprietary Medicinal Products, European Committee for Interoperable Systems, US-Trade, Liberalization of Trade in Services (LOTIS), International Automobile Federation (FIA), International Association of Insurance Supervisors, International Air Transport Association, International Federation of Pharmaceutical Manufacturers' Associations, International Organization of Employers (IOE), and so on (Braithwaite and Drahos 2000: 488–494).

(ix) The UN Center on Transnational Corporations concluded (1990: 61, 69–72):

> parent company policies and standards [. . .] were generally superior to standards contained in local environmental regulations. Standards of TNCs in pollution-intensive industries have exceeded local standards as indicated by all the country studies [. . .] [Eighty-three per cent of all parent companies] directed subsidiaries to operate within the standards adopted in the home country of the parent company.

Likewise, the USTR concluded: 'Most American multinational companies adopt worldwide environmental standards at their facilities regardless of where they are located [. . .] It is simply more efficient to use the same environmental standards in Mexico as in the United States.'[10] More recent findings corroborate these earlier studies (e.g. Vogel and Kagan 2002).

(x) European integration itself was arguably shaped by the preferences of dominant producers. Those with significant asset-specific invest-

[10] USTR interagency task force study, 15 October 1991.

ments across regional borders favored integration. (See the Appendix to Chapter Five above.) The members of the European Round Table of Industrialists (ERT) played an important coordinating role by April 1983. The ERT's 1984 report, entitled 'Europe 1990: An Agenda for Action', is remarkably similar to the EC's 1985 White Paper entitled 'Completion of the Internal Market' and the final 1986 Single European Act (Cowles 1994, 1995, and forthcoming). Britain's Lord Cockfield, who drafted the 1985 White Paper acknowledged that it was influenced by the ERT's report, and Jacques Delors recognized the 'continuing pressure' of the ERT, noting it was 'one of the main driving forces behind the single market'.[11] Williamson notes the 'thermal economies' in the coal and steel industries, which created the basis of the European Community.

### 3.3 Domestic asset specificity: Heterogeneity

Transactions involving investments with domestic asset specificity led firms to search for particular domestic regulations that reflected their interests. When domestic asset specificity was high, exit options became reduced and voice options became relatively more attractive. Governments were more likely to listen to their own producers than to foreign firms, even when not threatened by an exodus of firms. (When domestic asset specificity was low, firms could relocate overseas.) Consider the following summary evidence from the case studies.

(i) The three leading US tuna canners invested heavily in marketing within the USA. They relied on domestic brand-name recognition to charge price premiums and most of their assets were in the USA.[12] Heinz-StarKist began its dolphin-safe strategy one year before a US court injunction required it and announced the policy four months before the injunction. The favorable court injunction aided StarKist, Bumble Bee, and Chicken of the Sea to eliminate smaller and foreign low-cost competitors who had been cutting into their brand-name price premiums. Environmentalist groups had protested against the killing of dolphins for twenty years, since 1972, but US policy did not change until after Heinz's internal decision.

(ii) Mexico challenged the US heterogenous ban on ETP tuna and took the matter to a GATT dispute panel in January 1991. US canners

[11] ERT Brochure, September 1993; and Cowles, *The Politics of Big Business in the European Union* (forthcoming). See also Balanya *et al.* (2000); Apeldoorn and Holman (1994); Doherty and Hoedeman (1994).

[12] Although two canners were sold to foreign owners their assets remained located within the USA. They were operated as 'multi-domestic' firms without integration of production across borders.

successfully lobbied their government and the USA kept its heterogenous ban even after the GATT twice ruled against it. Dolphin deaths were brought down to less than 2,000/year (from several hundred thousand/year by US boats in the 1960s). Only after a number of changes which preserved StarKist's dominant position did the USA relax its formal regulation, and still little Mexican tuna entered the US market. After ten years consumers had re-established strong brand loyalty to the three big US producers and grocery chains stopped stocking Mexican tuna. NGOs created a 'Flipper-Safe' label for tuna caught without dolphin-sets. Furthermore, any time the USA deemed that Mexican fishers had an 'adverse effect' on dolphins it could embargo tuna imports. Mexican tuna remained limited in its access to the US market.

(iii) The top two US infant formula makers, Abbott-Ross and Bristol-Myers, controlled 80 per cent of the US infant formula market through these asset-specific relations with medical personnel. They dominated US marketing channels via hospitals and reaped premium prices for their brand names. They also funded medical authorities who spoke out against commercial advertizing. They co-operated to keep Nestlé, their Swiss competitor, out of the US market. Heterogenous restrictions on infant formula marketing were an effective and explicit barrier to entry. The US firms were able to raise prices sixfold above inflation.

(iv) At the same time as they opposed domestic advertising, the two US infant formula firms sought to advertise in overseas markets dominated by Nestlé. At the behest of the top US firms, the USA's was the only government which opposed the WHO/UNICEF code. At the same time it allowed domestic advertising restrictions.

(v) Lingering heterogeneity in the implementation of the Basle Accord and heterogenous measures after 1991 (to raise capital above the levels in the Accord) are in part the result of banks having enough domestic assets to merit voicing their concerns to domestic regulators. In the USA, this included concerns over competition from Japanese banks. As concerns over developing country debt waned, the domestic interests of banks re-emerged.

(vi) Domestic Asian tobacco monopolies were import-competitors. They supported heterogenous advertising restrictions because this acted as a barrier-to-entry to foreign competitors.

(vii) The British Federation of Small Businesses, representing small firms with domestic assets, opposed adoption of the metric system. Metrication would increase competition from continental European imports.

Asset specificity created incentives and constraints for firms and governments, but it was not fully deterministic. Over the long term, asset specificity may change as firms change their investment strategies, or as demand for products (and substitutes) changes. These firm-level decisions and others were noted in the case studies above. In general, however, low or non-specific assets facilitated a competition-in-laxity across borders. Similarly, highly specific multinational investments facilitated homogenous regulations among countries. Domestic assets facilitated heterogenous regulations, diverging among countries.

These propositions emphasize the importance of industries in influencing state choices. The findings on asset specificity are consistent with other research findings. Hiscox (2001) argues that the mobility of factors of production (land, labor, capital) can usefully explain trade policy. With mobile factors, the income effects of trade will be split along factor lines, e.g. labor *versus* firm owners. Conversely, if the factors are immobile, policy is better explained along industry lines, e.g. steel *versus* wheat. The micro-foundation findings of this book lend support to the conclusions of Frieden (1991), Alt *et al.* (1994), and Hiscox, and further explain why capital factor mobility strengthens class-based electoral parties: because the threat of competition-in-laxity and industry relocation is much greater than with immobile investments, thereby threatening domestic jobs. Alt *et al.* (1996) discuss the theoretical literature of endogenous trade theory and institutional economics, increasing returns to scale, and the variation in specificity at an industry level (e.g. textiles *versus* autos or steel). Alt *et al.* (1999) devise quantitative estimates of physical asset specificity on the industry level, based on research and development expenditures as a percentage of value added. They estimate human asset specificity in manufacturing industries, based on the percentage turnover in jobs. Their unstated emphasis is on domestically specific assets, not MAS. They conclude that these variables significantly predict the propensity of management and labor to lobby. This book further refines the Ricardo-Viner models of trade policy coalitions, building on theories of industrial organization and new institutional economics.

## 3.4 MAS and the resurgence in international commerce 1950–2000

A resurgence in international commerce followed the nationalism of the first half of the twentieth century. By the dawning of the twenty-first century most large firms had integrated their production on an international basis. They sourced raw materials, semi-finished goods, human capital, and financial resources from those localities with a comparative advantage, and from those firms with a competitive advantage. They invested in assembly overseas, sometimes to achieve lower unit-labor costs (thereby providing jobs for poor workers), but more often within wealthy countries (such as the USA and Europe) in order to integrate complex production processes with suppliers and buyers, to better understand and meet local consumer preferences, to meet domestic rules-of-origin requirements, to establish long-term distribution and marketing channels, to squeeze out competitors, to appease business-political considerations, and to achieve tax breaks, among other reasons.[13] World trade more than doubled from 1980 to 2000, and foreign direct investments (FDI) grew even faster than trade (Sauvant *et al.* 2000). For the reasons explained above, asset-specific FDI is thus often associated with increasingly homogenous regulations, and not the competition-in-laxity that some zealots fear. Major firms are more likely than local firms to implement similar factory standards wherever they invest worldwide.[14]

However, if prolonged economic recession, war, nationalism, 'clashes of civilizations', or other broad societal factors should lead to a decline in the quantity or specificity of cross-border assets, firms would face declining incentives to push for regulatory homogeneity. Growth in heterogenous regulations would then be expected.

Simple exporting need not always involve highly specific assets across borders, or MAS. Many small firms produce domestically and outsource exporting functions and foreign market penetration to any number of trading companies. Other firms outsource production and concentrate on the branding, marketing, and retailing links of the value-added chain. Still others operate as multi-domestic firms. For most large producers, however, integrated export production is likely to involve specific investments across borders.

Most large businesses are affected by regulations subject to international competition. Shambaugh (2000) effectively argues that globalization has expanded the range and domain of cases on which governments act, sometimes to influence the activities of firms in other jurisdictions. In these cases the ultimate policy instrument is governments' ability to restrict market access to products made by non-complying firms. (By contrast, if a foreign firm has little presence in the US market, for example, the US government has less ability to influence it through stringent market-access regulations. One example was France's Elf, which sold off its US subsidiary prior to expanding ties with Iran, against US policy wishes.)

The supporting data above are highlights from the case studies, and they offer considerable support for the three propositions with which this book began. The case study details offer further support, revealing not just six data-points, but many. It is striking that these propositions fit so well across such a diverse set of cases, in different economic sectors, geographic areas,

[13] See various works by Dunning, Doz, Kogut, Lizondo, Moran, Vernon, Wells, Almeida, Andreasen, Bergsten, Cantwell, Caves, Czinkota, Graham, Kobrin, Krugman, M. Porter, Mayo, Nollen, Romenelli, Ronkainen, Yoffie, and others, for explanations of why firms engage in integrated international production.

[14] Of course, institutional arrangements may also favor HCD. The EC's White Paper on 'Completing the Internal Market' declared that 'nations should not compete over standards that might adversely affect the public's health and safety or environmental quality' (quoted in Kahler 1996).

and regulatory issues. Further research on other cases will help determine the proposition's causal validity.

## 4. Future research directions

In 2001 a series of US corporate financial scandals came to light which will provide grist for a new generation of scholarship on corporate governance and the role of the Delaware system. These scandals included the collapse of the fifth largest capitalized firm in America (Enron) and of its blue-chip accountant (Arthur Andersen), the largest bankruptcy in US history (WorldCom), and investigations, settlements, or convictions of twenty-four other major firms. Suggestively, of these twenty-seven firms, 85 per cent were incorporated in either Delaware (20), Bermuda (2), or Switzerland (1), well above the national average.[15] Only 15 per cent were not 'haven' chartered: two in Michigan, one in New Jersey, and one in New York. The Delaware-based firms retained only 22 per cent of their market value whereas the non-haven firms retained 27 per cent. Future research can address whether and to what extent these scandals were enabled by a regulatory chill in the US system and whether self-regulation (as advocated by Bratton and McCahery in 1995) would improve or worsen governance, financial disclosure, and transparency.

There are a variety of other complementary tasks for scholarship by the next generation. Some narrow law-and-economics research ignores inconvenient questions such as power (both market power and political power, in legal, extra-juridical, and illegal forms), chronic asymmetries of information, negative externalities (environmental, labor, systemic), barriers to entry and exit, factor immobility, switching costs, stickiness, human capital, repercussions for unrelated contracts or contracting parties, working conditions, democratic theory, international society, identities beyond atomistic individuals, and—as this book has stressed—transaction costs. The assumptions which underlie these narrow law-and-economics models are downplayed to the detriment of research and policy alike. Also downplayed is the variation in firms' preferences for public policies. Relocation and lobbying decisions are not random. They occur at a certain point in time, in a certain jurisdiction, and by some firms but not others. Better research, such as Esty and Geradin (2001), Bebchuk (2002), and Sitkoff (2002) account for these factors. This research broadens the domain under which law-and-economics models can be applied.

[15] Arthur Andersen's spin-off consulting firm, Accenture, is also based in Bermuda. These findings are preliminary. They corroborate Bebchuk *et al.* (2002) who conclude that data since 1996 shows a reduction in Delaware shareholders' value. Earlier studies (Daines 2001) with data prior to 1997 showed an increase of 1.28%.

Outlier cases provide fertile ground for understanding the role of individual leadership, among other theories, as well as changing consumer demands. Other factors, such as institutional arrangements not examined in detail here, might moderate these findings or corroborate them. Future research may help identify when that is the case. For example, some US firms complained that the 1974 Foreign Corrupt Practices Act put them at a competitive disadvantage internationally, even though the first conviction did not take place for a decade and resulted in only a minor fine. Led by General Electric, these same groups have since the 1990s supported the multilateral adoption of US anti-corruption rules through Transparency International.[16] More research on variations over time and geography in the perceived harmony of interests would be valuable.

The broad set of cases of co-ordinated action toward lower common tariffs such as those achieved through the GATT have received extensive attention elsewhere.[17] It is precisely because of the pressures identified here that trade liberalization may require co-ordinated action on a broad set of issues. This study began with the assumption of open economies as a criterion for case selection; future work may benefit from re-examining the sources of those co-ordinated agreements (and resistance to them) in light of the three propositions.

More detailed non-US case studies would be helpful. The USA is the dominant economic power in the world, hence it formed the basis for many of the case studies examined in detail here. Research by Braithwaite and Drahos (2000: 476) justifies this US focus, inasmuch as the US played a major regulatory role in every one of the thirteen major economic sectors they examine. But national styles of regulation, of capitalism, and of government vary considerably (Vogel 1984). Additional research from outside the USA would help ensure that these propositions are not US-centric in their firm-level emphasis.

As noted above, the cases examined here are largely centered in industrial democracies in times of peace, from 1945 on. It would be helpful to examine cases involving agricultural societies, non-democracies, more non-Western societies, and times of war or crisis, to understand whether similar patterns existed in those conditions.

As one example, before the 11 September 2001 attacks on the World Trade Center and the Pentagon, most US airlines opposed requirements to

[16] The 1974 Foreign Corrupt Practices Act was adopted at the peak of other shake-ups in Washington, DC power circles, and other 'Sunshine Laws'. These historical anomalies may explain the Act's adoption. The first major conviction was not until 1985, when US-based Crawford Enterprises was fined $US3.5 million for having bribed officials of Mexico's PemEx with a total of $US10 million.

[17] See *inter alia*: Milner 1988; Yoffie and Milner 1987: 988; Goldstein 1993; Hudec 1993; Oye 1992; Bhagwati 1991; Magee, Brock, and Young 1989. On European integration, see literature cited in Chapter Two above. On NAFTA, see Grinspun and Cameron (eds.) 1993; Eden 1992.

fortify cockpit cabins. According to Larry Johnson, former head of aviation counter-terrorism for the US State Department, the airlines had opposed efforts to buttress the cockpit because the added weight would result in higher fuel consumption and hence higher costs.[18] Thus, they opposed stringent process regulations. The terrorist attacks created a national emergency which galvanized collective action pressures to provide safer transport, supported by the government and consumers alike. The US government quickly offered $US15 billion in subsidies and the airline industry began to improve its safety measures, amid accusations by European airlines of an unfair heterogenous bailout. As of 10 April 2003 the FAA required airlines to outfit their fleet with secure cockpits, for which Congress gave US airlines $US300 million. Predictably, foreign fleets operating in the USA will also have to meet this safety measure although they will not receive the Congressional subsidy. The requirement is likely to become homogenous worldwide, among all major airlines. Likewise, shipping containers coming into US ports are an Achilles heel of American homeland security. The logic of this book suggests that dominant international shipping firms will be crucial actors in determining the nature and timing of port security standards and procedures and that they will make use of those regulations to further their competitive position. So, too, with security measures on supply-chain management:

> The policy response [to 9/11] will necessarily put a greater premium on cooperation among [. . .] those corporations that have a proven capacity to enforce internal security measures through supply chain management and other practices. The result is likely to be a *'slow-lane' bias against transactions involving poorer countries and smaller, less internationalised companies* that are unwilling or lack the requisite resources or governance capacity to enforce enhanced security measures. In short, the response to September 11th *is likely to create even higher entry barriers* to the members' club of countries able to take advantage of the upside of globalization—at a moment when lowering the entry barriers for the poor and disenchanted is more important than ever (Brainard 2002: 237, emphases added).

The 2003 Container Security Initiative (CSI) prompted concerns among exporters to the USA that it would become a nontariff barrier. Likewise, US firms complained that the new European satellite navigation system, Galileo, used standards that were incompatible with the US GPS. On that evidence, even in the case of security crises, this book's propositions appear to hold true.

[18] Larry Johnson, 15 September 2001: 'Airlines are looking at it from a business standpoint. They operate in an industry with low margins. They don't have a huge profit margin. They're trying to save money, and find ways to cut corners.'

## 5. Implications for next-generation research: Self-interest and power explanations

The preceding sections of this Chapter summarized the specific theoretical conclusions of this research and the evidence for them. The next sections are broader and more exploratory. They discuss how the book's findings inform broader international and legal studies. The modern adage that 'money makes the world go round', and the classical Roman adage to find explanation in those 'who benefit' (*cui bono*) agree: material self-interest is a primary explanation of human behavior. Explanations based on self-interest and power are discussed here first, followed by non-material explanations.

As Richard Cooper (1968, 1972) identified decades ago, growth in cross-border commerce inevitably creates potential conflicts between governments as they seek to regulate economic activity within their borders (and beyond). Trends of complex interdependence have continued along the lines described by Keohane and Nye (1977/2000). Multilateral negotiations and institutions such as the World Trade Organization have successfully managed many conflicts but the potential number of conflicts exceeds current institutional capacities (Lawrence 1996; Sampson 2000; Gilpin 2002; Ikenberry 2002; Kupchan 2002). Despite fifty years of movement toward trade liberalization, open cross-border commerce is not a given. Pressures will always exist for heterogenous regulations which favor domestic firms over foreign firms, even as other regulations are homogenized upward or downward. Global interdependence is not federalism, and even federalism harbors regulatory competition.

This book further develops the approach of Stigler and more recent scholars in the economic theory of regulation or regulatory capture school.[19] However, whereas Stigler asserted firms' preference for stringent regulations as barriers to entry, this research differentiates the areas in which certain firms may seek deregulation (process regulations) or reregulation (product market-access regulations). It further differentiates firms' preferences based on their investment profile. It uses these distinctions to explain outcomes of inter-jurisdictional regulatory competition in the international arena. Unlike Stigler's somewhat libertarian view of regulatory capture, this book is agnostic on policy prescriptions. It recognizes that broad public interests may be served by coalitions with private interests. These public interests, such as a protected ozone layer, extend beyond short-term expressions of producer or consumer interests.

Steven Vogel (1996) offers a salient critique of private interest-based approaches, following Noll. Vogel offers a compelling explanation of the factors which influence policy-makers' supply of regulations, whereas this

[19] For example McCheson 2001; Peltzman 1991; Weingast 1981.

book has focused on firms' demand for them. All regulations affect some firms more than others; just because a firm benefitted from a change in regulations does not mean it caused the change. In order to avoid the *post hoc ergo propter hoc* fallacy common in some studies of regulatory capture one must trace the process by which the firm(s) influenced outcomes (see Noll 1989; Hertog 2000). Case study details exhume the timing and advocacy role of the principal firms.

## 5.1 Power and co-operation

National power, especially market size, has a major impact on which set or sets of domestic regulations are adopted internationally, in a given issue. The Triad of the USA and Europe, with Japan running a distant third, obviously dominate the international economic system, its institutions, and global trading rules. Business power is central to our understanding of a country's power in the international arena. The WTO's ultimate remedy for regulatory disputes—authorized market restrictions—has asymmetrical effects on states with different market sizes (Reinhardt and Busch 2001). WTO settlements offer a rhetorical high ground for winners, which is an important source of 'soft power' (Nye 2003), but in practice states with small markets may not benefit much from WTO-authorized sanctions. In the tuna-dolphin case, for example, Mexico would have had little impact on a large US exporter by imposing punitive tariffs because Mexico's market is relatively small. Worse, it would have been a Pyrrhic victory. Mexico would have suffered economic losses both from the higher costs of US goods under tariff and from the likely US linkage, reciprocity, and retribution on other issues. Conversely, if the US kept out a Mexican product with WTO authorization the Mexican exporter might well be crippled.

These findings are consistent with various incarnations of realism, hegemonic stability theory, commercial liberalism, and neo-dependency, but do not depend on them. (See Keohane (ed.) 1986; Moravcsik 1997; Mearsheimer 2001.) US and European hegemonic power is, in fact, more fungible—more easily divided and applied to narrow issues—than early theorists of interdependence recognized. This book tells the story from the perspective of powerful producers and states. These are the regulation makers. Weak producers or weak countries are regulation takers. Their story is largely one of suffering as they must, but the three propositions also offer strategic insight into how they may predict and maneuver around coalitions. Thucydides' broad dictum grants the weak the opportunity to bandwagon with or balance against stronger competitors, to shape or redefine interests and preferences, to link issues, and to inspire principles and hold accountable those who adopt them.

Oye *et al.* (1986) identified three predictors of international cooperation: the time horizon (and iterations), the number of players, and the payoff matrix. The findings of this book corroborate those predictors. Firms' high asset-specific investments across borders (high MAS) are likely to lead to a longer-term time horizon (or 'shadow of the future') as they surmount the 'obsolescing bargain' (Moran 1974; Vernon 1972). This longer horizon has been shown to facilitate co-operation. Iterations are typically recurrent among interdependent countries, especially for those economies comprising firms with high multinational asset specificity (MAS). Recurrent iterations also facilitate cooperation. A high MAS may also be associated with a smaller number of players, because it frequently acts as a barrier to entry. Mergers and acquisitions across borders—which accounted for more than 80 per cent of foreign direct investment in the late 1990s—further reduce the number of players in a given industry.[20] Again, having fewer players facilitates co-operation. Payoff matrices, on the other hand, are more varied. Thus, this book and other recent work on economic interdependence suggest that payoff matrices are the most significant variable in predicting variation in co-operation.

International regulations create one such form of payoff matrix. This book situates trade sanctions, including both heterogenous ones such as US 301 measures, and multilateral ones such as those authorized under the 1995 WTO agreements, in a broader pattern of higher product market-access regulations. Threats of market closure (or offers of market opening) greatly shape cooperation on these regulatory issues. The study of strategic interaction has also taken up this issue of payoff matrices (Lake and Powell 1999: 3).

This research contributes to the study of strategic interactions by avoiding the fallacy of revealed preferences. The theoretical propositions and six detailed empirical case studies differentiate firms' preferences *ex ante* and link these to observed outcomes and states' preferences. Transaction-cost economics helps explain producers' preference formation, which is a precursor to strategic interaction studies of negotiation. This allows scholars to analyze co-operative outcomes, independent of states' behavior (Frieden 1999: 40).

## 5.2 Defining the national interest

Next-generation scholarship must continue to define the national interest, before it can be defended. By bringing firms back in, this book has plunged into the details and micro-foundations of what drives state interests in a

[20] See research on the role of mergers and acquisitions in FDI, and the implications for competition policy, in the path-breaking UNCTAD *World Investment Report*, 2001, led by Karl Sauvant. For a sectoral example, see Kenneth P. Thomas (1998). Thomas examines how liberalization of capital flows has affected the relocation of automobile production. The number of non-state actors worldwide has increased in some issues, but is tempered by Triad power and the concentration of industries within them; further the number of players may not vary enough by issue to explain variation in outcomes.

variety of issues, thereby making state preferences endogenous to international relations theory.[21] These state-society findings are consistent with (neo)realist notions that interests drive politics, but instead of taking state interests as a given this book explains from where they are derived.

In cases of detailed economic regulation, leading producers played a significant role in defining those interests. Government representatives are still the key negotiators on most international regulatory issues. Business interests are occasionally at the intergovernmental negotiating table itself, as in the Trans-Atlantic Business Dialogue (TABD) but are more often in nearby representative offices or hotel suites while their interests are being represented. Increasingly, one sees direct firm–firm diplomacy, for example within international strategic alliances or within the TABD (Strange 1992, 1996; Evans 1993). In any case, this book suggests in which ways the national interest on these regulatory issues is influenced by powerful producers. Offshore finance pioneer George Bolton put it succinctly, addressing the Imperial Defence College in 1964: 'The national interest cannot escape in the future being guided by economic interest and by the reward of profits and capital development'. Understanding firms' different preferences, as laid out in this book, helps to disaggregate the national interest.[22]

Stephen Krasner's *Defending the National Interest* (1987) was sometimes mistakenly identified as a narrow *Realpolitik* perspective which discounts the influence of non-state actors.[23] However, he in fact depicts the USA (from the 1930s to 1975) as a weak state country in which corporate interests are successful much of the time. He wrote:

> Perhaps more than any other societal actor, large corporations are able to appeal to public institutions through all three forms of representation present in the American government: geographic, functional, and national. Because they often employ large numbers of people in geographically specific areas, they are important to particular Congressmen. Because they dominate large areas of the economy, they are important to the functional agencies of the executive branch. Because at least some of them are vital for the economy as a whole, they are important to the White House (Krasner 1987: 73).

[21] See earlier studies on the power of multinational firms *v.* state governments, e.g. Kindleberger 1969; Vernon 1971; Moran 1974; Gilpin 1975; Lindblom 1977; Bergsten *et al.* 1978; Krasner 1978; Katzenstein 1985. This book builds on their shoulders, by differentiating firms' preferences and linking them to states' preferences in the context of inter-jurisdictional conflicts.

[22] In times of economic or military crisis the state executive is more nearly a unitary actor, while it puts out political 'fires' and the polity rallies around the flag against foreign enemies, as in the US after the 9/11/01 attack on the World Trade Center. See also Nordlinger (1981) on the strategies by which states can increase their autonomy *vis-à-vis* interest groups (summarized at pp. 92–94, 111–112, 130–132).

[23] Krasner (1987) explicitly selects cases in which certain producers' influence was overridden (e.g. policies on oil in the Middle East which benefitted the entire US economy, and not just certain oil producers) and uses these relatively rare cases to identify a White House policy interest independent of those producers.

Building on Krasner, this book differentiates producer preferences in defining the national interest on a variety of detailed economic regulations. It is a further step in the theoretical specification of interest groups.[24]

The ranges of firms which political officials determined were vital for the economy as a whole may have expanded from 1980 onward, and their influence in shaping international regulations may have grown, for a variety of reasons. The reasons include: growth in firm size, both *sui generis* and through mergers and acquisitions; strategic alliances among firms; more homogenous consumer demand across countries; more resources devoted to lobbying and new strategies of influence (e.g. US 'soft money' campaign contributions were small until 1988); greater integration of world markets as trade and foreign direct investments have increased; and firms' adoption of more integrated production strategies. Further, free-market ideologies discredited many traditional government roles from the mid-1970s onward. With the end of the Cold War, economic concerns rose to the forefront of foreign policy in the 1990s. Conflicts between state interests and producer preferences declined (such as control over exports of militarily sensitive technology). Thus, firms' capabilities and incentives to affect regulations may both have increased.

In the cases examined here, major firms or industry associations often persuaded top officials of a harmony between the special interests of the firm(s) and the economy as a whole, or at least the official's own interests. They used a variety of means to do so, both hard power (e.g. campaign contributions, threats of capital flight) and soft power. The latter included alliances with 'Baptist' public interest groups, appeals to economic well-being, redefining issues to better suit their interests, putting items on the public agenda or keeping them off, mobilizing voters via print or television stories, providing chosen legislators with selective information or expertise which firms alone may have access to, drafting policy measures for overworked politicians, implementing regulations in ways that reflected their interests, and invoking the rhetoric of externalities or public goods. If perceived harmony varies over time or geography, such variations are a worthy subject for next-generation research in both international and domestic politics. Changing corporate strategy is one source of these changes in harmony.

The executive branch of government may well be able to implement preferences independent of private interests in these relatively rare and broad policy measures which affect the economy as a whole, such as the Bretton

[24] Milner (1997: 63, 37) focuses on governmental preferences but recognizes the role of societal interest groups which include firms and trade associations. 'Each interest group is rational; it tries to maximize its members' income—for example, wages, profits, and so on.' In broad policy changes a large number of business interests are affected, which gives government officials more room to play off one industry group against another. Still, US business was responsible for scuttling the 1948 International Trade Organization (ibid., pp. 147, 238–241). See also M. Smith 2000; Caves 1976; Milner 1988; McKeown 1983; Rogowski 1989; Magee, Brock, and Young 1989; Frieden 1991; Grossman and Helpman 1994; 1995.

Woods accords or their collapse, or in times of crisis or war (Milner 1997; M. Smith 2000). But for the daily preponderance of regulatory outcomes, identifiable private interests play a clear and present role in defining the national interest. In the relatively rare cases of grand policy change, idiosyncratic forces such as path dependency or charismatic leadership make it difficult to apply the ontology of positivist research, which seeks generalizations across large numbers of similar cases.[25]

Consistent with Nye's notion of soft power, Strange (1966) noted that market power includes the ability to give priority to certain social values over others. Strange's perspective that politics and diplomacy are common activity for firms and are not confined to politicians is very much in keeping with this book.

This book draws on Strange's work, but it does not support the end-of-the-state literature of the 1990s. Just because firms influence state preferences domestically does not mean that states have less influence internationally. To the contrary, states are the institution through which firms mediate many international conflicts. As Shambaugh (2000) concludes, globalization has not disarmed the state. Firms influence state decisions but they are still clearly subject to state authority, and rely on states to express their interests in the international arena.

Despite trends towards greater interdependence, one can still distinguish national identities in most firms, even in many cases of mergers or strategic alliances. The once-cited archetype of a truly bi-national firm, DaimlerChrysler, turned out to be a German firm (Daimler) with an American subsidiary (Chrysler). Daimler's chairman, Jurgen Schrempp, admitted as much in a candid interview:

> The structure we have now where Chrysler is a division, like Mercedes cars or like Mercedes trucks, was always the structure I wanted. We had to go a little bit in a round-about way, but that has to do with negotiations and with psychology and things like that. [. . .] When we sat in New York [in merger talks] we said you know, I mean for psychological reasons we need as many Americans as Germans on the board of management. [. . .] With Chrysler and the former Daimler-Benz, at that time if I had gone out and said look, eventually Chrysler will be a division of the DaimlerChrysler group, everybody [on their side] would have said 'no way we will do a deal like that'.[26]

In short, Daimler deliberately deluded Chrysler shareholders into thinking it was a merger of equals, when it was in fact a takeover. When Schremp's

[25] Positive methods for this are explored in 'Explaining Rare Events in International Relations', Gary King and Langche Zeng, *International Organization* 55/3: 693–715 (2001).

[26] Interview with Jurgen Schrempp, *Financial Times*, 1 December 2000. See also Bill Vlasic and Bradley A. Stertz, *Taken for a Ride: How Daimler-Benz Drove Off With Chrysler* (HarperBusiness 2001). The automobile industry exhibits greater cross-ownership of firms in different countries than many other industries. Pauly and Reich (1997) likewise conclude that the national character of corporations has endured.

strategy was revealed Chrysler's largest shareholder, Kirk Kerkorian, sued—in an American court. Ford and General Motors removed Chrysler from their American Automobile Manufacturers' Association. National identities remained clear, even in the DaimlerChrysler merger. Although international strategic alliances have become ubiquitous, with many policy and strategic implications, the average life-span of such alliances is six years. These can be effective for specific goals, but have not transformed the national basis of firms' identity. Home governments generally support their firms in international fora, whereas foreign governments are a harder sell. Most large firms now sell in or source from foreign markets, so they might be expected to 'resist protectionism' (Milner 1987) across the board. This book's propositions refine earlier models, in deriving firms' demand for regulations.

## 6. Implications for next-generation research: Non-material explanations

Theories that are based purely on material self-interest, power, methodological individualism, and instrumental or rational egoism have long been criticized in the social sciences. In Hayward Alker, Jr.'s priceless phrase, those who assume rational egoism risk becoming 'prisoners of their own dilemmas'.[27] One ambitious research step is to explain the social construction of the very identities and interests used to analyze the cases, and used by the actors within them. (Wendt 1999; Litfin 1994 very usefully analyzes the CFC case from this perspective.) Chapter Three above, which 'problematized the reified structure' of offshore finance, is a project in applied constructivism. Three other fruitful research avenues are institutions, agents, and ideas.

### 6.1 Institutions

The core definitions of institutions and regulations overlap: 'constraints on behavior' and 'direction from a competent authority', respectively. This book contributes to the next-generation study of institutions by focusing on regulations as the dependent variable, asking how they come about, by whom, and under what circumstances.[28] Although academic literature often treats institutions as a non-material explanation (hence their inclusion in

[27] Personal communication with Alker, *c.*1987. Some economists have suggested, partly tongue-in-cheek, that there is empirical evidence that 'studying economics inhibits cooperation'. Frank, Gilovich, and Regan 1993, 1996. See also Gilligan 1982; Mansbridge 1990; and Burlando and Hey 1997. On norms, see Kratochwil 1989; Finnemore 1993: 565–597; Ruggie 1998; Wendt 1999; Risse, Ropp, and Sikkink (eds.) 1999. More broadly, on the importance of culture in politics, even in the national security realm, see Katzenstein 1996 and T. Berger 1998.

[28] See general citations to Cyert, March, Olson, D. North, O. Williamson, Keohane, Ostrom, Buck and Ostrom, Young, Gibson *et al.*, Simmons and Martin.

this section) North (1991: 109) notes that institutions change as the result of the incentive structures facing private sector actors. This book's three propositions use the firm as an explanatory variable, thereby offering a succinct and palpable understanding of inter-jurisdictional regulatory competition. Explaining the genesis of institutions opens the door to more effective policy measures. By disaggregating the national interest and delineating some of its domestic sources, this book also avoids the causal circularity of an 'endogeneity trap' (Keohane and Martin 1999) common in some studies of institutions. More than with any other social actor or group, the basis of firms' preferences is clear.

## 6.2 Activists as agents

Abstract theories may lose the agency of politics. A political 'agent' has self-awareness of its situation and is capable of formulating alternatives. In the full story of politics, people push for conflicting goals so that outcomes are not (fully) determinate. In the search for generalizable theory, social science downplayed leadership and the role of individuals and norms.

More recently, fruitful research has been done on the role of activists in international relations.[29] That research complements this book well: if theirs focuses on Baptists, this book focuses on bootleggers.

Activists do not seek robust theories and it is a waste of scholarly time to treat their slogans as such. Rather, they seek to redefine issues and then to place those redefined issues on the agenda of public officials. These two steps, of issue definition and agenda setting, are recognized as the foundation of public policy.[30] Activists may deliberately seek to politicize issues, and to use moral leverage, to the consternation of those in power. For better and/or worse, anti-plutocracy activists did affect, at least marginally, the agenda within the World Bank, WTO, and trade offices throughout the OECD (Braithwaite and Drahos 2000: 31). Environmental, labor, and other social issues rose on the OECD agenda, partly in response to protests. A prominent firm discovered to be competing in laxity in environmental or fundamental labor standards runs the risk of critical media coverage and consumer boycotts. The latter might effectively act as 'nonprofit market-access regulations'. The problem is that in using 'globalization' as a symbol, activists may have been 'fighting the wrong enemy' (Graham 2000).

Activists may also be one source of change in consumer preferences, in effect using firms as a vehicle to transmit regulatory preferences (Litfin 1994; Keck and Sikkink 1998; Garcia-Johnson 2000). The certification of tropical hardwoods as sustainable or the certification of diamonds as 'war-free', for

[29] Haas 1992; Haas, Keohane and Levy 1993; Risse-Kappen 1995; Keck and Sikkink 1998; Finnemore and Sikkink 1998; Risse, Ropp, and Sikkink 1999.

[30] On issue definition and agenda-setting, see Bachrach and Baratz 1962; Edelman 1964; Gaventa 1982; Cobb and Elder 1983; Kingdon 1995; Riker 1996.

example, are unlikely to have occurred were it not for grass-roots activists who began the process. In this book, activists were seen to play a role in creating a climate which allowed Heinz, DuPont, Abbott-Ross, and Bristol-Myers to change their tuna-dolphin, CFC, and infant-formula regulatory strategies (respectively).[31] In a number of cases involving environmental or labor policy, credit has been given to the 'spotlight effect' in which activists generate media attention which causes MNCs to change their policies. If this effect is good for policy it poses a challenge to orthodox economic assumptions in which activists and the media's effects are exogenous. Indeed, some people dismiss street activists as irrational even while crediting their behavior for shaping policy outcomes through the spotlight effect.

## 6.3 Ideas and norms

A number of critiques of material explanations emphasize the role of ideas and norms, and the case studies in the Chapters above reveal several implications in this regard. First, ideas do matter, even within the material emphasis adopted in this book. All goods and services are the product of social interactions. Ideas shape these interactions, in the creation of new products, the identification of new market segments or marketing opportunities, new sourcing or distribution mechanisms, new business alliances, new production technologies, new financing tools, and new business strategies. None of these are predetermined, although they exist within material, financial, market, institutional, and political constraints. Business strategy is inherently ideational and agency-driven. Corporate executives anticipate consumer demand for products and services and must make large multi-year investment decisions accordingly, with limited information about the present and high uncertainty about the future. Producers will seek to fulfil norm-driven consumer demand (e.g. for green-labeled products) to the extent they perceive it as a viable market. Similarly, governments may highlight selected private sector interests in order to legitimize or gain support for a policy, as President Clinton did on climate change issues. Although this book emphasizes the material basis of interests, it also points the way toward novel next-generation constructivist research on business strategy: the mutual constitution of producer and consumer preferences.

Second, by definition, norms 'should' matter. Understanding the public implications of large firms' investments is a necessary and significant part of

[31] See Sikkink (1986) and Keck and Sikkink (1997) on the role of activists in the developing country infant-formula case. The impact of activists can be controversial. For example, the 'Buy American' and 'No Sweat' product labels were promoted by a united coalition of labor unions and various nonprofit groups in rich countries. These labels protected American textile workers, but arguably at the expense of poor workers in developing countries. Moran (2002) and Fung, Sabel, and O'Rourke (2000) suggests a number of creative solutions to the sweatshop problem. For most of the world's poor, the problem is not too much globalization, but not enough of it, or not in the right form.

any complete analysis of international regulations, one which has often been neglected in the positivist social sciences. Business executives, lawyers, academics, and policy-makers must have values and beliefs which help them anticipate and react to these interests, or else they will be 'hobbled by a crude psychology of material self-interest' (Keohane 2001: 4). Similarly, Hirschman (1986) warned against nihilistic 'reactionary rhetoric' which generalizes from selected policy failures. The economic interests of an individual firm or industry may not always coincide with the overall interests of a society. Firms may have incentives to pollute, to evade taxes or worker-safety regulations, to operate imprudently, to collude, to restrain competition, to kill dolphins as by-catch, as well as to create value and employment. The demand for regulations is almost always expressed using public-interest vocabulary such as the ever-popular terms level playing field, fair trade, the provision of public goods, avoidance of negative externalities, and other market failures. But many significant policy goals lack the driving force of a powerful industry.[32]

Norms alone are not enough to explain most regulatory outcomes. In many instances norms do not catch on. For example, NGOs tried for years to achieve a dolphin-safe tuna norm. After two decades of resisting, Heinz would ultimately join them, but consumers were not willing to pay more for dolphin-safe tuna in the supermarket. Thus, Heinz switched to a regulatory strategy which left consumers no choice. Tropical hardwood campaigns have also had mixed success. The greatest success came via product market-access restrictions in wealthy countries, supported by their domestic wood-products industries (Keck and Sikkink, 158–160). The outcome of these cases of inter-jurisdictional competition cannot be fully explained without this book's focus on producers' demand for regulation.

Three of the above Chapters' case studies are particularly important, if not critical, in that the received wisdom suggests their outcomes were determined by environmental or social norms and NGOs: the Montreal Protocol on CFCs, the ban on dolphin-lethal tuna imports, and restrictions on infant formula advertising. While norms and NGOs played an important role in these cases, it was clear from the case details that corporate interests were critical. Even these cases cannot be fully told without understanding the aspect of material self-interest. This is all the more true in the financial cases and others which attract no moral outcry, although they may impact on the welfare of millions or even billions of people. To unearth these material aspects takes considerable perseverance, as they are often deliberately concealed. The excavation is not a warm and fuzzy process leading to the sublime and godliness, but a rather mundane process leading to morally equivocal purgatory.

32 For example, the market has not yet provided bootlegger incentives for providing a social net for Africa, nor for treating Agent Orange dioxins in Vietnam.

Despite these conclusions—and because of them—individuals may well choose to work against the patterns and trends observed herein. Indeed, moral leadership is perhaps most needed on those issues for which a clear producer preference has not emerged, or has emerged in a way which does not benefit the public good (however defined). Moral obligations may require fighting, in the face of threats or established patterns, for a more just outcome. The structural and interest-based approach adopted in this book delineates the major earthworks of the policy battlefield, and the coalitions and strategies that policy-makers, business executives, and activists are likely to encounter.

## 7. Leadership and decision-making within constraints

The exact (proximate) timing and shape of individual decisions rests in the hands of decision-makers, not in the logic of abstract theories. The art of management and statecraft are part of the more complete picture. Within the constraints of this book's three propositions one finds firm-level and government-level decisions that offer individual managers and politicians leeway to succeed or fail in shaping enduring regulations and to succeed or fail in the marketplace. This section departs from the robust constraints of the propositions, using the case studies to illustrate these individual choices and to remind the reader of idiosyncratic forces exogenous to the model.

### 7.1 Leadership amid structural constraints

Key elements of choice that emerges in the case studies above are the decisions by business strategists and policy entrepreneurs to lead or to lag in inducing regulatory change. Firms' timing of investments in substitutes, lobbying, legal action or inaction, marketing campaigns, and public affairs led sometimes to first-mover advantages, but other times to first-mover failures. Successful first-mover firms worked closely with regulators and were able to judge when they might achieve regulations to their advantage. They also monitored product life cycles and as low-cost competitors gained market share (CFCs, tuna, banking) they strategically used regulations as a barrier to entry. The choices made by clever firms (or NGOs) might enable them to achieve desirable regulatory outcomes even in the face of better financed policy competitors. Politicians and regulators had to balance these pressures from competing firms, gauge the shape and timing of regulatory changes, and assess the legitimacy and legitimation of possible changes.[33]

[33] On governmental 'supranational entrepreneurs', see Moravcsik 1999.

Successful firms were able to develop technologies early and gain patents on them, such as those for CFC substitutes or sesquisulphide. They built economies of scope, such as the HFC-134a plant built by ICI, which scooped even DuPont. They built on their reputation as market leaders, such as Heinz-StarKist's dolphin-safe tuna policy. They chose new marketing channels and suppliers, such as non-ETP tuna for StarKist. They gained loyalty from buyers, such as Bristol-Meyers and Abbott-Ross with infant formula, or Johnson-Wax's heterogenous move on aerosols in 1975. They adapted to broader changes in the international system, such as BOLSA and Barings Bank. Latecomer firms were unable to achieve these investments in production, distribution, and management, and remained behind on the learning curve (e.g. HFC latecomers, Pan-Pacific tuna cannery).[34]

First-movers choose when and how to oppose regulations and when and how to support them. The DuPont case illustrates this brilliantly. DuPont learned a lesson in the 1970s when it was caught off-guard by a heterogenous US ban on CFCs in aerosols that Johnson Wax had supported. In response, DuPont formed a united front of American CFC producers to prevent further heterogenous action. When the CFC-ozone link first surfaced DuPont opposed CFC restrictions. It successfully defended itself against heterogenous restrictions on CFCs through 1986, including a suit filed by the National Resources Defense Council. DuPont changed its position, to the dismay of smaller firms in the industry alliance which DuPont had created, when scientific evidence confirmed the link to CFCs. The Montreal Protocol was not signed until one year after DuPont had announced support for limits on CFCs and invested in substitutes. Despite its earlier statements that a rapid phase-out was not possible and would cause economic damage, DuPont announced a more rapid voluntary phase-out one month before US ratification of the Montreal Protocol. It beat even that accelerated deadline by a year, until the US EPA requested it to maintain production. Prices of CFCs had skyrocketed; DuPont again cleverly led regulations, and worked with Senate staffers to support a windfall profits tax.

Heinz-StarKist equally successfully took *no* legal action against heterogenous injunctions on dolphin-lethal tuna imports (when it might have). Indeed, outside the courtroom Heinz sided with the Earth Island Institute plaintiff against the US Commerce Department and spent millions of dollars promoting its dolphin-safe product. It succeeded in placing its policy in the opening story of ABC News. These decisions were not completely determined by the variables identified in this book but they were facilitated by them. Less capable business executives might have failed to make these decisions.

[34] On first-mover business strategies, see *inter alia* Porter 1980: 186–191; Chandler 1990. Additional research on first–mover failures would be helpful.

Even successful first-movers experienced setbacks. For example, StarKist stockpiled non-ETP tuna contracts prior to cutting ties with the ETP, because it wrongly anticipated that prices would rise. Instead, prices fell as ETP tuna was unloaded on the market and StarKist was stuck with higher-priced contracts.

Regulations are clearly not the only determinant of most firms' success. Competitive advantage comes through understanding a firm's market niche and a panoply of business strategies. As Susan Strange noted (1996: 177), 'What governments do, in the way of erecting barriers, quantitative or *ad valorem*, to these [international] transactions is relatively marginal when managers of firms define global corporate strategies.' Even when regulations are costly, individual firms can continue to compete through innovations in financing, sourcing, production, distributing, marketing, and so on. For example, even though many shipowners fled to convenience-flag states to lower costs, many others remained to compete under national flags and more stringent regulations. Even though Pan Pacific failed to survive the dolphin-safe policy, a few small canners remained. Even though powerful US tobacco firms were marketing aggressively in Asia, the Thai industry was able to survive under nondiscriminatory restrictions. In cases such as these it will be helpful to understand the strategies firms used to compete successfully despite regulatory constraints.[35]

## 7.2 *Fortuna*: Unexplained variance

Despite the significance of their roles, neither powerful states nor firms are either omniscient or omnipotent. This research emphasizes the extent to which regulations reflect producer interests, but this obviously does not mean every firm can write its own legal code. To the contrary, firms compete with each other and other groups in the regulatory arena as well as in the market. The broader the regulation or policy and the more firms that are affected, the less ability any given firm will have to influence that policy. Regulatory strategies carry a significant cost to firms. Small firms simply cannot afford to play this game, or may do so only as one member of a trade association that seeks to overcome collective action problems for its members. Even powerful firms willing to devote resources to regulatory strategies cannot dictate the terms of regulations. Firms are a necessary part of those outcomes but they cannot create regulations just as they please.

[35] See Piore and Sabel (1984), Richard Locke (1993), and others building on their research. Piore and Sabel (ibid., pp. 205–220 and 265–267) examine how makers of specialty steel and mini-mill products, non-commodified chemicals, textiles in Italy, special-purpose machine tools in West Germany, and flexible-purpose machine tools in Japan were all able to survive against the 'bleak backdrop' of exiting production in advanced industrial economies. The authors argue that successes came with the re-emergence of a craft-floor paradigm of industrial relations which emphasizes well educated craftspeople, profit sharing, sophisticated flexible production technologies, rapid changes in product design, networks between small firms that act as a barrier to entry, and labor–management co-operation.

'Fate' (that is, factors beyond this book's focus) plays a significant role in every case.[36] A complete study would examine many factors unique to a given case. Some idiosyncratic factors (and examples of them) include moral values and beliefs (which motivated nonprofit groups in the infant formula, tuna-dolphin, and CFC cases, and arguably in passage of the Bank Secrecy Act, but which are absent in the Basle Accord and many other cases), science (e.g. the ozone hole, or research on the environmental and health effects of chlorinated compounds), epistemic communities (e.g. scientists in the CFC and infant formula cases), technology (improved dioxin detection or information technology in offshore banking), economic crises (developing country debt), international conflict (alliances in Europe), ideas, institutions (throughout the cases), labor unions, media coverage (Sam LaBudde's dolphin slaughter video, the *Torrey Canyon* oil spill, Lewis Powell's manifesto), domestic politics (contrast the access of different firms under the Thatcher/Major *versus* the Blair administrations, or the Reagan/Bush Sr. *versus* Clinton administrations), bureaucracies, class structures, and exogenous changes in consumer preferences (from any number of factors such as changes in norms, disposable income, demographic shifts, new information, media campaigns, or shifts in the *Zeitgeist*).[37] Acting under these conditions of uncertainty and complexity it is not surprising that business and government officials make mistakes or are unable to achieve all of their regulatory desires. However, it is rare to see an industrialized country's government support a regulation which substantially hurts home-country firms relative to foreign firms, at least without compensating them.

These findings may be less true in poor countries whose governments are more vulnerable to the influence and inducements of foreign negotiators and firms. Impoverished governments might sign onto such regulatory agreements for a variety of reasons, including side-payments, both legal and for personal gain. Even trade negotiators are not immune to market incentives and calculations of career alternatives. The average salary of government workers in Africa, for example, is under one thousand US dollars a year whereas the revenues from the two US auto manufacturers, GM and Ford, are greater than the GDP of all the sub-Saharan African countries combined.

In short, outcomes are shaped by the three propositions, but they are not fully determined by them. The book paints a general backdrop against which individual decisions are made. Historians are best equipped to offer a full account of each case. Nonetheless, it is striking that across such a diverse set of cases one finds a pattern of behavior that can be reasonably well explained by a few simple propositions. Despite the host of other variables

[36] *Fortuna* is Niccolò dei Machiavelli's term for fate in history: see *The Prince* (University of Chicago Press, 1532/[1985]); also Sebastian de Grazia, *Machiavelli in Hell* (Princeton University Press 1989).

[37] See Krieger 1986 on the broader social and political factors in the swing to conservatism in the 1980s.

which contribute to our understanding of regulations, the case studies above support the broad thesis of this book: that producers' varied preferences heavily influence regulations and are powerful predictors for regulatory outcomes in the context of global competition.

## 8. Practical Implications for Business and Policy Leaders

> Any theoretical argument concerning variables that could be policy-relevant must have real-world applications; otherwise, it becomes meaningless [. . .] The Ivory Tower exists for a good reason: we expect university-based intellectuals to reflect on the world at some distance, and not simply to do the work of policy commentators or journalists at a slower pace. But in our view, the separation from the world of decisions and consequences has gone too far in international relations.
>
> Lepgold and Nincic (2001)

Regulations are not born of scientific parents in sterile legislatures, nor nurtured in public bureaucracies insulated from the commercial world, nor thrust with equal effect on unwitting industries. For the non-academic reader, this book suggests several policy and strategic implications for firms, governments, and policy activists alike. These are summarized here.

Firms use regulations as a barrier against competitors and to create credible commitments to each other and to their governments. Regulations that affect interstate trade will naturally reflect the interests of powerful firms and those interests must be taken into account to design enduring policies.

Producers are likely to support stringent regulations on the sale or distribution of products to the extent that the regulations improve the firm's competitive position. Regulations may serve as a barrier to entry to competitors, protect firms' investments, restrict or promote investments in substitutes, raise prices, or enhance first-mover opportunities. Climate change regulations, for example, may receive powerful support from certain firms or industry groups if the regulations exclude competing products from the marketplace.[38]

Producers are likely to support deregulation on manufacturing process regulations to reduce their production costs. If the cost of regulation is high and the cost of relocation is low they may relocate, or threaten to do so. Market access offers a possible exception. If a major economic power seeks higher homogenous process regulations it may use access to its market as a lever to force those standards abroad. There is a general upward trend in environmental regulations in OECD countries and a potential benefit for regulatory first-mover firms and countries.[39]

38 Moore and Miller 1994; Prakash 2000.

39 Vogel and Kagan 2002; Garcia-Johnson 2000; M. Porter 1995; Cairncross 1991.

The implications of the mobility and asset specificity of firms' investments have been well covered above. For those who seek homogenous regulations (in common among competing states) firms with large asset-specific investments across borders will be important allies. The influential US National Foreign Trade Council, for example, has encouraged harmonization of antidumping laws. Firms are likely to seek favorable regulations as a credible commitment to protect their investments.

Although trade barriers have fallen over the last fifty years, the pressures that led to their erection in the first place have not disappeared. Adam Smith wrote that an invisible hand promotes domestically made goods over imports (Smith 1776: I:4:2). During economic downturns protectionist pressures are likely to increase. Heterogenous regulations can also create markets for substitute goods and force technological change. Firms investing in those substitutes early may reap first-mover rewards. They have strong incentives to support regulatory change. The head of fuel-cell maker Ballard Power Systems, for example, openly acknowledged that his firm owes its existence to government regulations.

Although large firms exert the most influence, small and medium-sized enterprises (SMEs) should also be aware of this book's conclusions as they are impacted by international commerce. SMEs provide the majority of employment, the bulk of taxes paid, and the preponderance of national income in most countries. But they are not united by a single trade association or representative in government. They are regulation takers, not regulation makers: the regulatory scheme enacted by others may constrain them or offer them market opportunities. Large firms support government regulations when it suits their corporate interests; they do not oppose government regulation across the board. Not paying attention to the regulatory agenda of major firms may subject SMEs to abrupt disruptions in their competitive position or supply chain. Barriers to entry may be erased or erected, intra-industry competition may stiffen, buyers or suppliers may be eliminated or empowered, substitute goods may become cost-competitive, all as a result of regulatory action sought by large firms. A clear example is in trade wars, in which retaliatory tariffs are imposed on foreign imports which are unrelated to the initial conflict. Large firms have better access to the policy process both to initiate the trade conflict and to shape the details of its implementation. Small firms who depend on the affected imports (or export markets) are left in the lurch.[40]

One can derive certain predictions from this book's propositions. To the extent that industrial concentration increases and these investments are dedicated to cross-border transactions, one can expect increased homogeneity of regulations across borders. Conversely, more heterogenous regulations

[40] See e.g. the effects of the US retaliatory tariffs on European imports in the US–EU WTO bananas case; many small US firms were hurt: *Time Magazine*, 1 November 1999.

would result if the global trading system were to suffer a deep and sustained economic recession that resulted in the reduction of firms' asset-specific investments across borders.

Coalitions between Baptists and bootleggers offer a powerful source of regulatory change by expanding the base of support and increasing credible threats of action. For example, large shipowners supported certain load-on-top oil-pollution regulations, alongside environmentalists. The ACLU appeared before Congress in 1970 to join Wall Street bankers in opposing the Bank Secrecy Act. DuPont's voice joined that of NGOs concerned about CFCs once atmospheric science on ozone depletion became clear. US infant formula makers funded the American Academy of Pediatrics, and both opposed the advertising of infant formula in the USA. Diamond Match Company worked in conjunction with a worker-safety union to ban phosphorus matches. The CEO of Heinz appeared on stage with the head of the Earth Island Institute to announce StarKist's dolphin-safe policy. When there is no other shelter, misery acquaints firms with strange regulatory bedfellows. By the late 1990s most large firms had created an executive position for 'corporate social responsibility' (CSR) and among American MBA students one of the largest campus clubs was Net Impact which focuses on CSR issues.

Environmental green seals of approval or 'eco-labels', for example the US label 'Flipper-Safe' tuna or London's Marine Stewardship Council label on sustainable fish harvests, have grown in popularity. Environmental groups may work jointly with domestic producers and governments to create eco-labels that testify to the environmental soundness of the product and its production. The precise details of labeling laws have a big impact, as evidenced by disputes over mandatory labeling of genetically modified organisms, bovine growth hormone, irradiation of food, tobacco, etc. To the extent that consumers recognize, trust, and value such a label it can act as a barrier-to-entry to firms (including foreign exporters) who do not comply. The labeling group would become the competent authority on that issue.

Opposing Baptist and bootlegger coalitions exist in the policy debates over trade and the environment. These clashing coalitions partly explain the rhetoric and heat over 'globalization' debates in the OECD countries (Kahler 1996: 27). Domestic US industry which seeks deregulation and internationally oriented environmental groups who seek HCD may both exaggerate the potential for competition-in-laxity. Both groups emphasize the potential cost savings to producers who flee to a lax regulatory environment, including total compliance costs of lobbying, public relations, implementation, and monitoring. Conversely, firms with high MAS and environmental groups who seek more stringent domestic regulations may downplay the extent to which regulations affect the location of new investments. These groups emphasize the relative insignificance of environmental costs in the overall cost of production. Similar clashes exist in the debates over trade and labor, where domestic industry and unions in rich countries may hold conflicting views from those held by multinational firms and workers in developing countries.

There is no unified corporate interest in many detailed regulatory issues. This fact allows policy activists to identify those firms which would benefit from a change in regulations and it allows select firms to focus their lobbying efforts. Both groups can deliberately create Baptist and bootlegger coalitions, splitting some firms off from their competitors. Thus Nike and Levi's ultimately supported higher labor regulations in opposition to non-branded firms (Sabel, O'Rourke, Fung 2001). Likewise, some firms such as IBM and Dell favored restrictions on campaign contributions (see www.CED.org). Restrictions on carbon-emitting activities are another example. These would affect a wide swathe of the economy, giving regulators the power to support 'green industry' against 'brown industry'. Because so many domestic-based sectors would be affected, however, governments face pressure to erect heterogenous climate-change regulations.

*Mutual Recognition Agreements* (*MRAs*) are a middle ground between movements toward laxity and stringency, and between commonality and heterogeneity.[41] In MRAs, products 'approved once' in any member county are 'accepted everywhere' for the purpose of trade. MRAs offer one convenient way to avoid protracted trade disputes over regulations. Europe led the way, e.g. with its 1970 Directive 70/220/EEC, which required mutual recognition of automobile emission regulations within Europe as a deliberate way of avoiding protectionist nontariff barriers. MRAs also helped greatly to facilitate integration of the single European market. More recently, since 1995 MRAs have been major goals of the Trans-Atlantic Business Dialogue (TABD).

As a less distinct dependent variable, MRAs are less useful analytically for theory building, but they are important from a policy perspective. Consistent with this book's emphasis, the clear drivers for MRAs have been major producers' preferences, with governments supporting their respective firms. The TABD consists of major corporations from the USA and Europe, paired with their government officials. Xerox Corporation and Goldman Sachs began preparations for the first TABD meeting in Seville in November 1995. European and US firms have rotated co-chairmanship since then, including BASF and Ford, Phillips and Tenneco, DaimlerChrysler and Warner-Lambert, Suez Lyonnais and Xerox (again), Lafarge and United Technologies, and Electrolux and PricewaterhouseCoopers. The host firms pay for the TABD Director's office, staff, and travel budget. US and EU governments are fully supportive of this effort. As US Under Secretary of

[41] MRAs do not obviate the utility of the three analytical trajectories used here (LCD, HCD, and heterogenous) just as warm water does not obviate the distinction between cold and hot. They do, however, raise an interesting new question as to what conditions lead to their implementation.

Commerce Timothy J. Hauser noted in Congressional testimony about the TABD, 'We should put the business "horse" before the government "cart"'.[42] TABD Director Jeff Werner notes that because US and EU standards are often quite high to begin with, it is 'less frequent that the TABD would look to raise them', with exceptions such as intellectual property.[43]

MRAs may not permanently resolve disputes. As one example from Europe, evidence of acid rain from automobile emissions led to heterogenous German laws, despite the EU's 1970 MRA Directive. By 1988 seven German *Länder* had imposed stringent product regulations which banned cars from the road on smoggy days unless they had catalytic converters and met US–German standards. (Germany was a major exporter of cars to the USA and so BMW, Mercedes-Benz, and Volkswagen had all met US standards.) The German regulations were challenged by the French government, which owned the Peugeot and Citroen car manufacturers. Ultimately, in 1989 an even higher common standard was agreed on by all, obviating the 1970 MRA Directive.

NGOs have played only a minor role in this process. The Trans-Atlantic Environmental Dialogue has died on the vine. Its website noted acerbically that 'TAED suspends its activities due to the failure of US government to stick to its commitments' (www.taed.org, accessed 14 March 2003). And the Trans-Atlantic Consumer Dialogue (www.tacd.org, last visited on 27 July 2003) has had only limited success. Other consumer groups are more critical of MRAs.[44] Policy activists complain that MRAs typically put downward pressure on health and safety regulations ('regulatory chill') because domestic producers face a competitive disadvantage from less strictly regulated imports. Further specification of these issues and evidence for them is needed.

## 9. The complexity of regulatory interdependence

These conclusions cast light on three implications of an increasingly interdependent world. First, inter-jurisdictional regulatory competition, the subject of this book, is likely to increase. Virtually all economic activity is regulated, with wide variation among countries' regulatory schemes. Increased trade, and the increasing roles of non-state actors, are likely to put more and more regulatory issues on the agenda. Further, as the tradeable

[42] US Under Secretary of Commerce Timothy J. Hauser, acting Under Secretary of Commerce for International Trade, in testimony before the Subcommittee on Trade of the House Committee on Ways and Means, Hearing on New Transatlantic Agenda, 23 July 1997, 105th Congress, first session.

[43] Jeff Werner, TABD Director, interview December 2001. See www.TABD.com, last visited on 27 July 2003. On broader trans-Atlantic trends of deregulation, protectionism, and integration see Canzoneri *et al.* 1996.

[44] For example, www.publiccitizen.org/trade/harmonization/MRA, December 2002.

sector grows in importance, market access abroad (and at home) becomes increasingly important. As seen in this book, this access plays a key role in the adoption of product market-access regulations as firms lobby their governments to keep competition out or to seek mutual recognition in foreign markets.

Second, higher common denominator (HCD) outcomes are more likely for several reasons. With increasing scale and scope, dominant producers are able to shape the nature and timing of regulations, take advantage of changes in social norms and public opinion, and use these regulations to their competitive advantage against low-cost producers who compete on price alone. The rapid increase in foreign direct investment (FDI) typically leads to greater multinational asset-specific (MAS) transactions, expanding the geographic area in which firms would like one set of rules. Similarly, international agreements on property laws, including intellectual property, copyright, patents, and trademarks, creates incentives for firms to seek common regulations. If homogeneity of consumer demand continues across borders and asset-specific FDI grows, it is likely to be followed by homogenous product market-access regulations. Trends in the nonprofit sector including networks of activists and the rapid sharing of information via digital technologies (email, cell phones, pagers, fax, video, Internet) may also contribute to HCD outcomes.

Third, however: other broad trends in globalization are conducive to heterogenous (HET) or lower common denominator outcomes (LCD). One sees increasing competition in many world markets, with profit margins falling for many branded goods. Market competition pressures firms to lower their costs of production, which may cause them to seek more lax process regulations. Furthermore, as barriers to capital mobility fall, firms are more able to seek the regulatory schemes they prefer and to pit government against government in credible threats of relocation. Governments have increasingly enacted policies to attract foreign capital. Tax holidays and other incentives to attract industry are one example.[45] Virtually all large firms negotiate for tax breaks prior to making an investment and they typically play off one location against others.[46] Other changes, such as the flexibility offered by computer-assisted production and other digital technologies, may also decrease the specificity of investments, thereby facilitating races to less stringently regulated environments. As globalization grows, so does the backlash against it. This creates opportunities for protectionist

[45] The effects of these policies can be mixed. For example, the tax incentives offered by Alabama to Mercedes-Benz or by South Carolina to BMW effectively redistributed state revenues to auto-plant workers, in a jobs program that would have been politically unlikely otherwise. Europe led the way on these debates. See citations in Bhagwati (1996: 30) to Redaway 1958; Johnson, Wonnacott, and Shibata 1968; and Tinbergen and Ohlin 1965.

[46] Germany's top industries, including DeutscheBank, Dresdner Bank, Allianz, BMW, and Daimler-Benz all threatened to move assets abroad in the late 1990s to compete with Ireland and other low-tax countries if the government did not meet their demands for lowered taxes. A reduction in Germany's capital gain tax soon followed.

or heterogenous regulations, encouraged by coalitions of domestic Baptists and bootleggers.

These findings do not predict a single trajectory of LCD, HCD, or HET. Instead, there are fundamental tensions between the trends. The outcomes may benefit some firms and societal groups more than others. It is precisely this differential among firms that drives the dynamic of international regulatory competition and co-operation, and drives the normative concerns of policy advocates.

Although producer preferences can be forecast, these forecasts are not completely determinate. Preferences involve business strategy and human choice. The conclusion of this book is not one of nihilistic acceptance that narrow material interests are the sole driver of outcomes. There is still room for leadership and creativity in both business and politics. The creation of new coalitions, new alliances, new business and political strategies, and so on, all depend on human agency. Governments are likely to have greater autonomy in devising policy solutions when a split in policy preference occurs between evenly matched producers or industries, or in times of crisis. Policy managers and activists can take advantage of this by deliberately identifying and assisting those firms or business associations whose policy preferences align with their own. Identifying the implications of large firms' asset-specific investments is as useful for a nonprofit group as it is for a corporation.

Only painstaking empirical research informed by theory allows an accurate portrayal of who the key actors are, their preferences, and their impact. Woe unto the researcher who assumed, for example, that firms oppose (all) environmental regulations, or assumed that the details of a state's interests can be fully deduced from its role in the international system, or that the rise of offshore finance is a sign of weakened state power, or that deregulation discredits theories of regulatory capture. These findings require significant investigation, sometimes years of it, in part because firms and government officials have incentives to downplay their mutual dependence publicly and to justify policies in terms of the public interest. (Firms are in a rhetorical bind which may laminate the truth: they often object to increasingly stringent regulations but they would poison public relations at home and abroad if they admitted to relocating for those regulatory reasons; see Levinson 1996.) This research approach avoids perennial academic debates and works toward a new understanding of 'who gets what, when and how' (Lasswell 1936/1956).

Academic theories provide a basis for distinguishing 'news from truth', for organizing oceans of information, for shaping questions, and for understanding causal relations. The main theoretical contribution of this book is the three detailed propositions and their relation to future academic debates. To the extent that these propositions continue to be borne out, they will contribute to the broader understanding of international law and political economy in a number of ways. Six general implications are summarized here.

First, private sector incentive structures are fundamental for the creation of economic regulations as institutions (North 1991). Second, there is a pattern in the variation of firms' preferences based on the specificity of their investments and the locus of regulations. There is evidence for some competition-in-laxity, properly understood, in major industries including banking and shipping. These cases raise significant policy concerns. The policy response cannot be a rollback of globalization but rather a better managed form of it. Large firms may push for and achieve higher regulatory standards. Third and related, this book elucidates the links between domestic political economy and international relations and opens up the black box of regulatory preferences.

Fourth, this book overcomes three research selection biases: (a) it avoids selecting only grand policies as a dependent variable. In grand policies, which affect many sectors, competing firms' or sectors' preferences are likely to be pitted against each other, creating unique levels of state autonomy. (b) It avoids selecting only formal laws, which can reflect legislator grandstanding, and instead focuses on implemented outcomes. High-level bureaucratic threats, nods, and leadership (as with Corrigan in the Basle Accord case, or Bolton and Barings in the offshore finance case) may equally shape who gets what, when, and how, but would be missed by an overly legalistic model. And (c) it avoids selecting institutions as an independent variable only, *deus ex machina*.

Fifth, although conflicts over regulatory preferences can be found between sectors, most detailed regulations are industry-specific or even product-specific. Citibank did not involve itself in the tuna-dolphin dispute; Heinz-StarKist did not join the Alliance on CFCs; DuPont did not involve itself in ship-flagging disputes; and shipowners did not get involved with bank capital requirements. Most regulations do not pit one industry against a regulatory rival of equal political influence. Only detailed case studies reveal firms' preferences and their impact.

Sixth and last, law and economics research on transaction costs may have suffered from too much success in analyzing monopolies/oligopolies, antitrust, and monopoly regulations. This success has led economists to pay less attention to the much broader array of regulations found in competitive markets. These include social, financial, environmental, labor, and international trade regulations, to which transaction cost concepts can also be fruitfully applied. This book illustrates the political significance of asset specificity in a variety of sectors and policy areas.

The thrust of this book is in one sense modest: understanding different business investments and interests is a necessary though not sufficient step toward understanding international regulatory outcomes. The three specific propositions delineated toward that end do not attempt a complete explanation of any one case under study. In another sense, however, the conclusion is more ambitious: the three propositions *are* necessary to understand all regulations which involve the potential for inter-jurisdictional competition. This encompasses a wide variety of geographic and issue areas. To the extent that the argument is successful, all future sufficient explanations must include them.

The essence of politics is strategic interaction between players. This will always involve the art of judgement as well as the science of understanding. Knowing when to push or pull whom, for what, cannot be read from a formula. For individual managers, politicians, or policy advocates this book's propositions must be seen as a framework for understanding the large-scale pressures within which they must work or attempt to surmount. Understanding these pressures is necessary to devise effective strategies for both private and public interests.

## Epilogue: Scholarship and the study of firms

Researchers with an interest in policy outcomes must study and differentiate between firms because their varied preferences are a necessary element of policy outcomes. Political science most broadly includes the study of who gets what, when, and how, but many social science and legal scholars have neglected the study of individual firms which profoundly influence societal outcomes. Vague references to market pressures or generic private sector interests are not enough as these do not capture differences between firms nor their impact.

The divide between business studies and international studies is an artificial moat. There are six good reasons for scholars of international studies to study and differentiate firms, and for business executives to learn from international studies, for purposes of theory, policy, and strategy. First, because firms play a major role in determining who gets what, when, and how. This is especially so in international issues, where a relatively small number of large firms account for the majority of trade and investments.

Second, because even in the traditional study of government one must first define the national interest before one can study its defense, and firms play an enormous role in shaping state preferences. Traditional studies of 'government' which exclude firms will not elucidate this causal source of policy unless they deliberately look for it. The questions one asks determine the answers one will find. Firms do not often publish their regulatory strategies on their web-sites or in their annual reports and are usually close-mouthed about them. Considerable perseverance is required to unearth firms' preferences and their impacts.

Third, because the field of international studies offers rich analytical concepts and theoretical literature with which to analyze power (market power and otherwise), strategic alliances and coalitions, complex interdependence, leadership, negotiations, decision-making, and firms as institutions with 'persistent and connected sets of rules and practices that prescribe behavioral roles, constrain activity, and shape expectations' (Haas, Keohane, and Levy 1993: 4–5). Likewise, business research offers analytical concepts useful to legal scholars, economists, and political scientists, including studies of strategic interaction, organizational behavior, and negotiations. Business strategists have moved away from a zero-sum view of competition (implicit in early works on strategy, such as Porter 1980) and toward a more networked view in which competition exists, but so also do alliances, close co-operation with suppliers, and feedback from buyers. They expand the palette of strategic options beyond a black-or-white dichotomy of competition and co-operation.[47]

[47] See Vernon 1971; Wells 1972; M. Porter 1980 esp. ch. 10; Chandler 1990; and Oster 1994 esp. ch. 17 on firm regulatory strategies; Locke 1998; Sabel and Piore 1984; Lake and Powell 1999.

Fourth, because firms' foreign direct investments (FDI) are the largest and most stable source of capital for many developing countries. FDI into developing countries dwarfed all governmental aid and official capital flows combined, in the 1990s, by a factor of ten to one. (Eighty per cent of such flows went to just ten developing countries, such as China, Brazil, and Mexico.)

Fifth, foreign firms may also push, for their own reasons, for the institutions essential to free markets and elections, such as an independent judiciary to adjudicate disputes and enforce contracts and a police force capable of upholding the law. To impoverished workers in poor countries, foreign firms are hardly the unidimensional embodiments of evil that some critics make them out to be. MNCs can be a major source of jobs, tax revenue, investment, education, and progress in both the economic and political spheres.

Sixth, however: because firms have such influence, their political role in a democratic society is worthy of serious and ongoing study by political theorists, legal scholars, and other social scientists (e.g. M. Smith).

Insofar as scholars depend on private-sector funding for research, or seek government office or business consulting opportunities, their work may become subject to the soft-power influence of their benefactors, for better or worse. These issues become increasingly salient as private-sector funding of education increases relative to other sources and as firms become increasingly involved in the regulatory process. If social scientists themselves do not explicitly address these possible biases, as is routinely done in medical research, it is not clear who will. Marcia Angell, MD, as editor-in-chief of the *New England Journal of Medicine* (*NEJM*), sought an independent editorial writer but found that most had financial ties to pharmaceutical firms:

> We found very few who did not have financial ties to drug companies. [. . .] What is at issue is [. . .] that close and remunerative collaboration with a company naturally creates goodwill on the part of researchers and the hope that the largesse will continue. This attitude can subtly influence scientific judgment in ways that may be difficult to discern. Can we really believe that clinical researchers are more immune to self-interest than other people?[48]

Likewise, the Deputy Editor of the *Journal of the American Medical Association* (JAMA), Drummond Rennie, concludes that 'academic-industry ties are common, and evidence exists that financial considerations bias the research record' (Cho, Rennie, *et al.* 2000). See also the editorial jointly published 13 September 2001 by *NEJM*, *JAMA*, and ten other top US and European medical journals. They opine:

> The academic enterprise has been a critical part of the [objective] process [. . .] but

[48] Angell, 'Is Academic Medicine for Sale?', 2000: 1518. T. Bodenheimer (same issue of *NEJM*) details some of the widespread biases which review studies have unearthed. See also Lewis Powell's 1971 manifesto.

> as economic pressures mount, this may be a thing of the past. [. . .] Corporate sponsors have been able to dictate the terms of participation in the trial—terms that are not always in the best interests of [. . .] the advancement of science generally. [. . .] These terms are draconian for self-respecting scientists, but many have accepted them because they know that if they do not, the sponsor will find someone else who will. Such issues are not theoretical.

The law-and-economics literature might similarly turn its analytic gaze inward and examine if the source of scholars' funding correlates with the questions they asked and avoided. These research questions follow from the logic, models, assumptions, and scientific methods we use; they are neither *ad hominem* nor conspiratorial.

Whether one loves large firms, admires them, hates them, leads them, just works for or studies them, multi-divisional corporations were among the most politically important and enduring social units of the twentieth century. They have evolved in the form of integrated international production, strategic alliances, mergers and acquisitions, outsourcing, cross-ownership, new business strategies, political risk management, creative forms of finance (mezzanine, project, securitization, various complex financial derivatives), the use of free agents, 'intrapreneurship', business-to-business online marketplaces, codes of conduct, corporate social responsibility initiatives, community outreach, and so on. But they have not been eclipsed. The modern form of corporate organization—large, publicly traded, and multi-divisional—did not emerge until after World War I (see Alfred Dupont Chandler 1962). In the grand sweep of history this is recent, but by the twenty-first century one hopes that the important social and political role of firms will be acknowledged. All four of the first multi-divisional firms on which Chandler based his seminal research still exist today: DuPont, General Motors, Sears, and Standard Oil of New Jersey (a.k.a. Exxon).[49] They have played a major role in shaping a wide variety of public policies. Unlike many social institutions commonly studied in introductory law and political science courses, including governmental bureaucracies, regimes, ideologies, and even countries, these firms have survived the Great Depression, two major World Wars, the Cold War, the gold standard and its demise, decolonization, and two waves of democracy and reversals. Surely they have earned a place in scholars' vocabulary and analysis.[50]

This does not mean that scholars must take for granted the self-portrayal

[49] Standard Oil of New Jersey was renamed Esso after its initials (SO), then renamed Exxon. In 1998 it remarried its sister firm, Standard Oil Company of New York—better known in recent decades as Mobil. This reunited ExxonMobil entered the 21st century as the Standard Oil Trust had entered the last century: the largest petroleum firm in the world with the most profits. Mergers do not diminish firms' power: they build it, even with a change of name. The basic business units, most employees, products, buyer and supplier relations, and so on remain recognizably intact.

[50] This is recognized by the growing contributions of political scientists employed in business schools and MNCs, e.g. Vogel, Yoffie, Goodman, Spar, Quinn, Levy, and McDermott.

of corporate press releases, nor journalism which relies on public relations output to determine the questions asked and the 'story'. No less a corporate spokesman than Peter Vanderwicken, the former head of corporate communications at J.P. Morgan, warned against this. In an outlet as pro-business as the *Harvard Business Review*, he wrote an article in 1995 titled 'Why the News is Not the Truth' in which he concludes: 'Most of what appears in the press as business news is corporate propaganda.' Vanderwicken is no loose cannon or populist ideologue; and his statement cannot be dismissed as exaggerated watchdog whistle-blowing. Yet he goes on:

> When I was an executive at a large public-relations agency, I was often amused to observe how many of the stories in the *Wall Street Journal* and the business section of the *New York Times* were essentially news releases [my] agency had issued the previous day. On some days, most of the stories were clearly identifiable as coming—some nearly word for word—from announcements by corporations or government agencies (Vanderwicken 1995: 146).

This is particularly striking as the two newspapers he mentions are among the more objective and independent news sources in the world. An earlier study by the *Columbia Journalism Review* (March/April 1980) similarly concluded that half of the *Wall Street Journal*'s news stories 'were based solely on press releases', often reprinted 'almost verbatim or in paraphrase, despite the byline "by a *Wall Street Journal* reporter".' Scholars must take the trouble to identify the underlying source of news stories in these and other less reputable media.[51] *Caveat lector*—and, one hopes, *caveat* scholars, who might unthinkingly rely on the press to frame the questions they ask, as well as the answers they propose. Social scientists should write about firms, but not necessarily as the firms—nor their critics—would like. There is no substitute for painstaking empirical research, based on a theoretical foundation.

[51] See also Weaver 1994. No disrespect is meant to this author's overworked friends and colleagues in the news industry who successfully conduct remarkably good journalism against all odds. Their task is Herculean, given the sum of public affairs resources pitted against them, the constant pressure of deadlines, and the remarkably limited financial resources at their disposal. *Time Magazine*, for example, has only a dozen full-time bureau reporters for the entire world outside the USA. Others struggle with strongly ideological publishers and editors.

# *Bibliography*


Ackerman, Bruce A. and William T. Hassler *Clean Coal/Dirty Air* (New Haven, CT: Yale Univ Pr, 1981)

Aggarwal, Vinod K. *International Debt Threat* (Berkeley, CA: Institute of International Studies 1987)

—— *Liberal Protectionism* (Berkeley, CA: Univ of California Berkeley Pr, 1985)

Aggarwal, Vinod, Robert O. Keohane, and David Yoffie 'The Dynamics of Negotiated Protectionism', *American Political Science Review* 81/2: 346–366 (June 1987)

Alker, Hayward R., Jr. 'The Dialectical Logic of Thucydides, Melian Dialogue', *American Political Science Review* 82/3: 805–821 (1988)

—— 'The Presumption of Anarchy in International Relations' (mimeo *c.*1985)

Alker, Hayward R., Jr., Lincoln P. Bloomfield, and Nazli Choucri *Analyzing Global Interdependence* (4 volumes), MIT Center for International Studies (1974)

Alker, Hayward R., Jr., and Thomas Biersteker 'Dialectics of World Order: Notes for Future Archeologists of International Savoir-Faire', *International Studies Quarterly* 28/June: 121–142 (1984)

Alt, James E., Fredrik Carlsen, Per Heum, and Kare Johansen 'Asset Specificity and the Political Behavior of Firms: Lobbying for Subsidies in Norway', *International Organization* 53: 1, 99–116 (1999)

Alt, James E. and Michael J. Gilligan 'The Political Economy of Trading States', *Journal of Political Philosophy*, 2: 165–192 (1994)

Alt, James E., Jeffry Frieden, Michael J. Gilligan, Dani Rodrik, and Ronald Rogowski 'The Political Economy of International Trade', *Comparative Political Studies* 29/6: 689–717 (1996)

Alter, Karen J. and Sophie Meunier-Aitsahalia 'Judicial Politics in the European Community', *Comparative Political Studies*, 26/4: 535–561 (January 1994)

Anderson, Jeffery 'The State of the (European) Union: From the Single Market to Maastricht, From Singular Events to General Theories', *World Politics* 47: 441–465 (April 1995)

Anderson, Leigh C. and Robert Kagan 'Adversarial Legalism and Transaction Costs', *International Review of Law and Economics* 20: 1–19 (2000)

Andrews, David M. 'Capital Mobility and State Autonomy', *International Studies Quarterly* 38/2 (June 1994)

Angell, Marcia 'Is Academic Medicine for Sale?', *New England Journal of Medicine*, 342: 1516–1518 (18 May 2000)

Ansiaux, Hubert J.N. *Dossier Pour l'Histoire de l'Europe Monetaire, 1958–1973* (Brussels: Vander, *c.*1975)

Aristotle *The Politics*, trans. Carnes Lord (Chicago: Univ of Chicago Pr, 1984)

Armijo, Leslie E. (ed.) *Debating the Global Financial Architecture* (Albany, NY: State Univ of New York Pr, 2002)

Attali, Jacques *A Man of Influence: S.G. Warburg* (Bethesda, MD: Adler & Adler, *c.* 1985)

Auboin, Roger *The Bank for International Settlements, 1930–1955*, Essays in International Finance #22, Princeton Univ Department of Economics, International Finance Section (1955)

Axelrod, Robert M. *The Evolution of Co-Operation* (London; New York: Penguin Books, 1990)

Bachrach, Peter and Morton S. Baratz 'Decisions and Nondecisions', *American Political Science Review* 57/3: 632–642 (September 1963)

Bachrach, Peter, and Morton S. Baratz *Power and Poverty* (Oxford, UK: Oxford Univ Pr, 1970)

Bagwell, Kyle and Robert W. Staiger 'The WTO as a Mechanism for Securing Market Access Property Rights: Implications for Global Labor and Environmental Issues' (mimeo May 2001)

Bain, Joe S. *Barriers to New Competition* (Cambridge, MA: Harvard Univ Pr, 1956)

Balaam, David N. 'The International Politics of Agricultural Trade', *Canadian Journal of Political Science* 23/4: 793–795 (December 1990)

Balanya, Belen, *et al. Europe Inc.* (London: Pluto Pr, January 2000)

Baldwin, David A. *Paradoxes of Power* (Oxford, UK: Basil Blackwell, 1989)

Baldwin, Robert E. *The Political Economy of US Import Policy* (Cambridge, MA: MIT Pr, 1985)

Banchoff, Thomas *The German Problem Transformed* (Ann Arbor, MI: University of Michigan Press, 1999)

Bank for International Settlements (BIS), Committee on Banking Regulations and Supervisory Practices (BCBS) 'Revised Approach,' www.bis.org/publ/bcbsca.htm (December 2001)

——'The New Basel Capital Accord: Consultative Document', www.bis.org/publ/bcbsca03.pdf (May 2001)

——'Statement on Prevention of Criminal Use of the Banking System for the Purpose of Money-Laundering' (Basle: BIS, December 1988)

——'Report on International Convergence of Capital Measurement and Capital Standards' (Basle: BIS, July 1988)

——'Consultative Paper on Proposals for International Convergence of Capital Measurement and Capital Standards' (Basle: BIS, December 1987)

Bank for International Settlements (BIS) *Recent Innovations in International Banking* (Basle: BIS, 1986)

——*Report on International Developments* (Basle: BIS, April 1985a)

——*The Management of Banks' Off-Balance Sheet Exposures* (Basle: BIS *c.*1985b)

Banks, Jeffrey S. and Barry R. Weingast 'The Political Control of Bureaucracies Under Asymmetric Information', *American Journal of Political Science* 36/2: 509–525 (May 1992)

Barback, Ronald Henry 'The Political Economy of Fisheries; from Nationalism to Internationalism' (England: Univ of Hull, 1966)

Barnett, Richard, testimony before US Congress, Senate Committee on the Environment and Public Works, Subcommittees on Environmental Protection and Hazardous Wastes and Toxic Substances, 100th Congress 1st session 1987 *Ozone Depletion, the Greenhouse Effect, and Climate Change*

Baron, David P. 'Majoritarian incentives, pork barrel programs, and procedural control', *American Journal of Political Science* 35/1: 57–91 (February 1991)

Baron, David P. and John A. Ferejohn 'Bargaining in legislatures', *American Political Science Review* 83/4: 1181–1207 (December 1989)

*Bartholomew v. Universe Tank Ships, Inc.* 263 F.2d 437, 442 (2d Cir.), cert. denied, 359 US 1000 (1959)

Bartley, Brennan 'Current Developments Surrounding the Business Judgment Rule: A "Race to the Bottom" Theory of Corporate Law Revived', *Whittier Law Review* 1991

Bayard, Thomas O. and Kimberly A. Elliott *Reciprocity and Retaliation in US Trade Policy* (Washington, DC: Institute for International Economics, 1994)

Bebchuk, Lucian A. 'Federalism and the Corporation: The Desirable Limits on State Competition in Corporate Law', *Harvard Law Review* 105/7: 1482–1509 (May 1992)

Bebchuk, Lucian A., and Assaf Hamdani 'Vigorous Race or Leisurely Walk: Reconsidering the competition over corporate charters', *Yale Law Journal* 112: 553–615 (2002)

Bebchuk, Lucian A., Alma Cohen, and Allen Ferrell 'Does the Evidence Favor State Competition in Corporate Law?', *California Law Review*, 90/6: 1775–1821 (2002)

Beitz, Charles *Political Theory and International Relations* (Princeton, NJ: Princeton Univ Pr, 1979)

Bénassy-Quéré, Agnès, Lionel Fontagné, and Amina Lahrèche-Révil 'Foreign Direct Investment and the Prospects for Tax Harmonisation in Europe' (CEPII Document de travail v 2000–06, April 2000)

Benedick, Richard *Ozone Diplomacy* (Cambridge, MA: Harvard Univ Pr, 1991)

Bennett, Colin J. 'Review Article: What is Policy Convergence and What Causes It?', *British Journal of Political Science* 21/2: 215–234 (April 1991)

Benson, William S. *The New Merchant Marine* (New York: Macmillan, 1923)

Benston, George J. *The Separation of Commercial and Investment Banking: The Glass-Steagall Act Revisited and Reconsidered* (Oxford, UK: Oxford Univ Pr, 1990)

Berger, Suzanne and Ronald Dore (eds.) *Convergence or Diversity?* (Ithaca, NY: Cornell Univ Pr, 1996)

Berger, Thomas *Cultures of Antimilitarism* (Baltimore, MD: Johns Hopkins Univ Pr, 1998)

Bergsten, C. Fred *'Reforming the International Financial Architecture'*, testimony before the Committee on Banking and Financial Services, US House of Representatives (23 March 2000)

Bergsten, C. Fred, William Cline, and John Williamson *Bank Lending to Developing Countries: The Policy Alternatives*, 1985

Bergsten, C. Fred, Thomas Horst, Theodore H. Moran *American Multinationals and American Interests* (DC: Brookings, *c.*1978)

Bermann, George A., Matthias Herdegen, Peter Lindseth (eds.) *Transatlantic Regulatory Co-Operation* (Oxford, UK: Oxford Univ Pr, 2001)

Bernauer, Thomas 'Between Cost-Sharing, Side-Payments, and Polluter Pays: Protecting the River Rhine Against Chloride Pollution', paper presented at the Harvard/ MIT Research Seminar on International Environmental Affairs (7 April 1993)

Bhagwati, Jagdish and Robert E. Hudec (eds.) *Fair Trade and Harmonization*, 2 volumes, incl. chapters cited here by Bhagwati, Alessandra Casella, Alan V. Deardorff, Daniel Farber, Robert Hudec, Alvin K. Klevorick, David Leebron, Arik

Levinson, Mitsuo Matsushita, Andre Sapir, and John Douglas Wilson (Cambridge, MA: MIT Pr, 1996)

Bhagwati, Jagdish 'Fair Trade, Reciprocity and Harmonization' in Alan Deardorff and Robert Stern (eds.) *Analytical and Negotiating Issues in the Global Trading System* (Ann Arbor: Michigan Univ Pr, 1994)

——*Political Economy and International Economics* (Cambridge, MA: MIT Pr, 1991)

——*Protectionism* (Cambridge, MA: MIT Pr, 1988)

Birdsall, Nancy, 'Asymmetric Globalization', *Brookings Review* 21/2: 22–27 (Spring 2003)

Black, Bernard S. 'Is Corporate Law Trivial?', *Northwestern Univ Law Review* 84/2: 542–597 (1990)

Black, Dorothy J. 'International Trade *v.* Environmental Protection: The case of the US embargo on Mexican Tuna', *Law and Policy in International Business* 4/1: 23 (22 September 1992)

Blankart, Charles B. 'Strategies of Regulatory Reform: An Economic Analysis with some Remarks on Germany' in Majone (1990)

Blatherwick, David E.S. 'The International Politics of Telecommunications' (Research Series #68, UC Berkeley, Institute of International Studies, *c.*1987)

Boczek, Adam *Flags of Convenience: An International Legal Study* (Cambridge, MA: Harvard Univ Pr, 1962)

Borkin, Joseph, *The Crime and Punishment of I.G. Farben* (NY: Free Press 1978)

Boster, Ronald S. 'Not On My Watch: Analyzing the Principal Causes of the Savings and Loan Crisis', *PS: Political Science & Politics* 24/3: 433–436 (September 1991)

Bradley, A. Jane 'Intellectual Property Rights, Investment, and Trade in Services in the Uruguay Round', *Stanford Journal of International Law*, 23/1: 57 (1987)

Brainard, Lael 'A Turning Point for Globalisation?', *Cambridge Review of International Affairs*, 15/2: 233–244 (2002)

Brainard, Lael, and Thierry Verdier 'Lobbying and Adjustment in Declining Industries', *European Economic Review*, 38/3–4: 586–596 (April 1994)

Braithwaite, John and Peter Drahos *Global Business Regulation* (Cambridge, UK: Cambridge Univ Pr, 2000)

Brandeis, Louis D., dissenting opinion in *Liggett Co. v. Lee* (1933)

Bratton, William W. and Joseph A. McCahery 'Regulatory Competition, Regulatory Capture, and Corporate Self-Regulation', *North Carolina Law Review*, 73: 1861–1948 (1995)

Bratton, William W., Joseph McCahery, Sol Picciotto, and Colin Scott (eds.) *International Regulatory Competition and Co-Ordination* (Oxford, UK: Oxford Univ Pr, 1997)

Braudel, Fernand *The Perspective of the World*, trans. Sian Reynolds (New York: Harper & Row, 1984)

Bredahl, Maury E. and Kenneth W. Forsythe 'Harmonizing Phyto-Sanitary and Sanitary Regulations', *World Economy* 12/2: 189–206 (June 1989)

Brewer, Anthony *Marxist Theories of Imperialism* (London: Routledge, 1990)

Breyer, Stephen *Regulation and its Reform* (Cambridge, MA: Harvard Univ Pr, 1982)

Brickman, Ronald, Shelia Jasanoff and Thomas Ilgen *Controlling Chemicals: The Politics of Regulation in Europe and the United States* (Ithaca, NY: Cornell Univ Pr, 1985)

Brimmer, Andrew F. 'Prospects for Commercial Banks in International Monetary and Capital Markets' (paper delivered at *Financial Times* conference on World Banking, January 1974)

Brown, Michael E., *et al.* (eds.) *The Perils of Anarchy* (Cambridge, MA: MIT Pr, 1995)

Brooks, Richard O. and Thomas M. Hoban *Green Justice* (Boulder, CO: Westview 1996)

Broz, J. Lawrence *Rent-seeking and the organization of the fiscal-military state: Central banking in England and the United States, 1694–1834*, working paper series/Center for International Affairs; paper no. 94-1 (Cambridge, MA: Center for International Affairs, Harvard Univ, 1994)

Burlando, R. and J.D. Hey. 'Do Anglo-Saxons free-ride more?', *Journal of Public Economics* 64/1: 41–60 (April 1997)

Bureau of National Affairs, Report For Executives 'Fed Unlikely to End Foreign Bank Activity in US in Light of FDICIA, Official Says' (10 June 1992)

Burk, Robert Fredrick *The corporate state and the broker state* (Cambridge, MA: Harvard Univ Pr, 1990)

Burley, Anne-Marie, and Walter Mattli 'Europe Before the Court,' *International Organization*, 47/1: 41–76 (Winter 1993)

Burns, Arthur 'Maintaining the Soundness of Our Banking System', address at the 1974 American Bankers' Association Convention, Honolulu, HI 21 (October 1974)

Burton, Thomas M. 'Methods of Marketing Infant Formula Land Abbott in Hot Water', *Wall Street Journal*, 25 May 1993

Busch, Marc L. and Reinhardt, Eric R. 'Nice strategies in a world of relative gains: The problem of cooperation under anarchy' *Journal of Conflict Resolution* 37/3: 427–446 (September 1993)

Buxbaum, Richard M. and Klaus J. Hopt (eds.) *Legal Harmonization and the Business Enterprise* (Berlin, New York: Walter de Gruyter, 1988)

Byman, Daniel L. and Kenneth M. Pollack 'Let Us Now Praise Great Men: Bringing the Statesman Back In', *International Security* 25/4: 107–146 (Spring 2001)

Cafruny, Alan W. *Ruling the Waves* (Berkeley, CA: Univ of California Pr, 1987)

—— 'The Political Economy of International Shipping: Europe *versus* America', *International Organization* 39/1: 79–119 (Winter 1985)

Cairncross, Francis *Costing the Earth* (Boston: Harvard Business School Pr, 1991)

Cameron, David R. 'British Exit, German Voice, French Loyalty', paper prepared for delivery at the Annual Meeting of the APSA, Washington, DC (September 1993)

Canzoneri, Matthew, Wilfred Etheir, and Vittorio Grilli (eds.) *The New Transatlantic Economy* (Cambridge, UK: Cambridge University Press, 1996)

Caporaso, James A. 'Toward a sociology of international institutions', *International Social Science Journal* 45/4: 479–490 (November 1993)

—— *Theories of political economy* (Cambridge, UK: Cambridge Univ Pr, 1992)

—— 'International relations theory and multilateralism', *International Organization* 46/3: 599–632 (Summer 1992)

—— 'Functionalism and Regional Integration' (Sage professional papers in international studies, no. 02–004, c 1972)

Cappelletti, Mauro, Monica Seccombe, and Joseph Weiler (eds.) *Integration Through Law: Europe and the American Federal Experience* (New York: W. de Gruyter 1985, 5 volumes)

Carlisle, Rodney *Sovereignty for Sale* (Annapolis, MD: Naval Institute Pr, 1981)

Cary, William L. 'Federalism and Corporate Law: Reflections Upon Delaware', *Yale Law Journal* 83/4: 663–705 (March 1974)

Cassing, James, Timothy McKeown, and Jack Ochs 'Political Economy of Tariff Cycle', *American Political Science Review* 80/3: 843–862 (September 1986)

Caves, Richard E. *American industry: Structure, conduct, performance*, Foundations of modern economics series, 7th edn. (Englewood Cliffs, NJ: Prentice Hall, c 1992)

—— 'Canada's Tariff Structure', *Canadian Journal of Economics: 278–300* (May 1976)

Center for American Studies (Brussels) *Federalism: A US–European Comparative View* (19 May 1984) including chapters by Stephen Prer and P.L. Kelley

Cerny, Philip 'Globalization and the Changing Logic of Collective Action', *International Organization* 49: 4: 595–625 (Autumn 1995)

Chandler, Alfred Dupont, with the assistance of Takashi Hikino *Scale and Scope* (Cambridge, MA: Belknap Pr, 1990)

Chapman, Paul K. *Trouble on Board: Plight of the international seafarer* (London: ILR [*sic*] Pr, 1992)

Charnovitz, Steve 'Environmental and Labour Standards in Trade', *The World Economy* 15/3: 335–356 (May 1992)

Charny, David 'Competition Among Jurisdictions in Formulating Corporate Law Rules: An American Perspective on the "Race to the Bottom" in the European Communities', *Harvard International Law Journal* 32/423: 430–434 (1991)

Chemical Manufacturers' Association 'Searching the Stratosphere: Industry's Contribution to Scientific Understanding of the Ozone Depletion Issue' (Washington, DC: CMA, 1991)

Chernow, Ron *The house of Morgan* (New York: Atlantic Monthly Pr, c 1990)

Chinitz, Benjamin and Raymond Vernon 'Changing Forces in Industrial Location', *Harvard Business Review* (January–February 1960)

Cho, Mildred K., Drummond Rennie, Ryo Shohara, and Anna Schissel 'Policies on Faculty Conflicts of Interest at US Universities', *JAMA* 284/17: 2203–2208 (1 November 2000)

Choi, Dosoung, Sreenivas Kamma, and Joseph Weintrop 'The Delaware Courts, Poison Pills, and Shareholder Wealth', *Journal of Law, Economics, and Organization* 5/2: 375–393 (Fall 1989)

Choi, Stephen J. and Andrew T. Guzman 'Choice and Federal Intervention in Corporate Law', *Virginia Law Rev.* 87: 961–992 (2001)

Choucri, Nazli (ed.) *Global Accord* (Cambridge, MA: MIT Pr, 1993)

Chubb, John 'The Political Economy of Federalism', *American Political Science Review* 79: 994–1015 (1985)

Clendenning, E.W. *The Eurodollar Market* (Oxford, UK: Oxford Univ Pr, 1970)

Cnossen, Sijbren 'The Case for Tax Diversity in the European Community', Special issue of the *European Economic Review* 'Tax Harmonization in the European Community 34/2–3: 471–480 (May 1990)

Coase, Ronald 'Notes on the Problem of Social Cost', chapter 6 in *The Firm, The Market, and The Law* (Chicago: Univ of Chicago Pr, 1988)

—— 'The Problem of Social Cost', *The Journal of Law and Economics* vIII: 1–44 (October 1960)

Cohen, Benjamin J. 'Crossing frontiers', in *The Political economy of global interdependence* (Boulder, CO: Westview Pr, 1991)

—— *In Whose Interest* (New Haven, CT: Yale Univ Pr, 1986)

—— *Organizing the World's Money* (New York: Basic Books, 1977)

Cohen, Jeffrey E. *The Politics of Telecommunications Regulation: The States and the Divestiture of AT&T* (Armonk, NY: ME Sharpe, c 1992)

Collis, David John *Developments in corporate strategy* (Boston, MA: Harvard Business School; 93-065, 1993)

Conybeare, John A.C. 'Voting for Protection: An Electoral Model of Tariff Policy', *International Organization* 45/1: 57–81 (Winter 1991)

Cook, Arthur E. *A History of the United States Shipping Board and Merchant Fleet Corporation* (Baltimore, MD: Day, 1927)

Cooper, Richard N. 'Economic Interdependence and Foreign Policy in the Seventies', *World Politics* 24/2: 160–181 (January 1972)

—— *The Economics of Interdependence* (New York: McGraw-Hill, 1968)

Costigliola, Frank 'The Other Side of Isolation: Establishment of the First World Bank, 1929–1930', *Journal of American History*, 61/3: 602–660 (December 1972)

Coughlin, Cletus C. 'Domestic Content Legislation', *Economic Enquiry* 23: 437–438 (July 1985)

Council on Scientific Affairs 'The Worldwide Smoking Epidemic: Tobacco Trade, Use and Control', 263 *Journal of the American Medical Association* 3312 (27 June 1990)

Cowles, Maria Green 'Setting the Agenda for a New Europe', *Common Market Studies* 33/4: 501–526 (December 1995)

—— 'The Politics of Big Business in the European Community: Setting the Agenda for a New Europe', Ph.D. dissertation (American Univ, 1994)

Craig, Gordon and Alexander George *Force and statecraft*, 2nd edn. (Oxford, UK: Oxford Univ Pr, 1990)

Crandall, Robert W. *Changing the Rules: Technological Change, International Competition, and Regulation in Communications* (Washington, DC: Brookings Institution, 1989)

Cranford, John R. 'State Banks: A History of Resilience', *Congressional Quarterly Weekly Report* 49/14: 843, 845, 848 (6 April 1991)

Cromer, Esme *From This Day Forward* (Stoke Abbot: Thomas Harmsworth, 1991)

Cuming, Ronald C.C. (ed.) *Perspectives on the Harmonization of Law in Canada* (Canada: Univ of Toronto Pr, c 1985)

Currie, Brainerd *Selected Essays on the Conflict of Laws* (Durham, NC: Duke Univ Pr, 1963)

Curzon, Gerard *Multilateral Commercial Diplomacy* (London: Michael Joseph, 1965)

Dahlstrom, Robert and Arne Nygaard 'An Empirical Investigation of Ex Post Transaction Costs in Franchised Distribution Channels' *Journal of Marketing Research*, 36: 160–170 (May 1999)

Daines, Robert 'Does Delaware Law Improve Firm Value', *J. of Financial Economics* 62: 525–558 (2001)

Daines, Robert and Michael Klausner 'Do IPO Charters Maximize Firm Value?' *J. Law, Economics & Organization* 17/1: 83–120 (April 2001)

Dale, Richard *International Banking Deregulation* (Oxford, UK: Blackwell, 1992)

—— *The Regulation of International Banking* (NJ: Prentice-Hall, 1984)

Daly, Herman 'Against Free Trade: Neoclassical and Steady-State Perspectives', paper presented to Working Conference on International Trade Agreements and the Environment, Kennedy School of Government, Harvard (29 April 1994)

De la Rue, Sydney *Land of the Pepperbird* (New York: G.P. Putnam's Sons, 1930)

Dempsey, Paul Stephen 'Compliance and Enforcement in International Law—Oil Pollution of the Marine Environment by Ocean Vessels', *Northwestern Journal of International Law and Business*, 1986: 6: 459–561

Derthick, Martha and Paul J. Quirk 'Why the Regulators Chose to Deregulate', in Noll (ed.) (1985)

Dertouzos, Michael L. *et al. Made in America: Regaining the Productive Edge*, MIT Commission on Industrial Productivity (Cambridge, MA: MIT Pr, 1989)

DeSombre, Elizabeth R. *Domestic Sources of International Environmental Policy* (Cambridge, MA: MIT Pr, 2000)

Deutsch, Karl *Political Community in the North Atlantic Area* (Princeton, NJ: Princeton Univ Pr, 1957)

Dollar, David and Jeff Frieden 'The IPE of Financial Deregulation in the United States and Japan', Conference on Structural Change in the American Financial System, Rome (October 1988)

Dominguez, Kathryn M. *The role of international organizations in the Bretton Woods system*, NBER working papers series; working paper no. 3951, Cambridge, MA: National Bureau of Economic Research (1992)

Doner, Richard F. 'Bankers and Bureaucrats: Capital and the Role of the State in Thailand', *Journal of Asian Studies* 49/4: 998–1000 (November 1990)

Dornbusch, Rudiger, John Makin, and David Zlowe *Alternative Solutions to Developing-Country Debt Problems* (1989)

Dotto, Lydia and Harold Schiff *The Ozone War* (Garden City, NY: Doubleday, 1978)

Dowling, Michael and Alfred Leidner 'Technical standards and 1992: Opportunity or entry barrier in the New Europe?', *Columbia Journal of World Business* 25/3: 5 (1990)

Doyle, Michael W. 'Metropole, Periphery, and System: Empire on the Niger and the Nile', in Peter Evans *et al. States Versus Markets in the World-System* (Sage, 1985)

Doz, Yves and C.K. Prahalad *The Multinational Mission* (Simon & Schuster 1999)

Drezner, Daniel W. 'Globalization and Policy Convergence', *International Studies Review* 3: 53–78 (Spring 2001)

—— 'Bottom Feeders', *Foreign Policy* (November/December 2000)121: 64–70

Dunning, John H. *Theories and Paradigms of International Business Activity* (Elgar 2002)

Dye, Thomas *American Federalism: Competition Among Governments* ( Lexington, MA: Lexington Books, 1990)

Easterbrook, Frank H. and Daniel R. Fischel *The Economic Structure of Corporate Law* (Cambridge, MA: Harvard Univ Pr, 1991)

Eden, Lorraine 'From Silent Integration to Strategic Alliance: The Political Economy of North American Free Trade' (Ottowa: Centre for Trade Policy and Law, 1992)

Ehrenfeld, John (ed.) 'Dimensions of Managing Chlorine in the Environment', *Report of the MIT/Norwegian Chlorine Policy Study* (Cambridge, MA: MIT Center for Technology, Policy, and Industrial Development, March 1993)

Eichengreen, Barry and Jeffrey Frieden (eds.) *The Political Economy of European Monetary Unification* 1: 31 (Boulder, CO: Westview, 1994)

Emery, Sidney W. 'The Effective United States Control Fleet', *United States Naval Institute Proceedings* 96: 160 (May 1970)

Enright, Michael J. *The determinants of geographic concentration in industry*, Working paper, Division of Research, Harvard Business School; 93-052 (1993)

Erickson, Christopher L. 'Labor Costs and the Social Dumping Debate in the European Union', *Industrial and Labor Relations Review* 48/1: 28–48 (October 1994)

Erroco, Luca and Alberto Musalem 'Offshore Banking: An analysis of micro- and macro-prudential issues', IMF Working Paper WP/99/5 (January 1999)

Esty, Daniel and D. Geradin 'Regulatory Co-opetition,' *J. of International Economic Law* 3/2: 235–255 (2000)

—— (eds.) *Regulatory Competition and Economic Integration* (Oxford, UK: Oxford Univ Pr, 2001) including chapters by Barenberg, Bebchuk, Bercusson, Bratton, Charny, Deakin, Demaret., Engel, Faure, Ferrell, Fox, Govaere, Hertig, McCahery, Macey, Revesz, Rose-Ackerman, Shavior, Trachtman, and Vogel

European Bank for Reconstruction and Development (EBRD) *Environments in Transition* (Winter 1993)

—— 'Environmental Standards and Legislation in Western and Eastern Europe Towards Harmonisation; Draft Report Task IV(b): Water Sector Case Study' (April 1993)

European Commission 'Report on US Barriers to Trade' (Brussels, annual)

—— 'Communication on Maritime Industries: Industrial Policies in a Competitive Environment,' (c 1992)

—— 'Harmonization of Company Law in the European Community: Measures Adopted and Proposed' (1989)

—— *Commission of the European Communities v. Kingdom of Denmark*, Case 302/86: ECR 4607 (1988)

—— *Completing the Internal Market* (Luxembourg: Office for Official Publications of the EC, 1985)

—— 'European Economic and Monetary Union' (Brussels: 1981)

European Round Table 'Foundations for the Future of European Industry' (10 June 1983)

Evans, Carol 'International Strategic Alliances', in *Multinationals and the National Interest* (US OTA 1993)

Evans, Peter, Dietrich Rueschemeyer and Theda Skocpol *Bringing the State Back In* (Cambridge, UK: Cambridge Univ Pr: 1985)

Evans, Peter, Dietrich Rueschemeyer and Evelyne Huber Stephens (eds.) *States Versus Markets in the World-System* (Sage, 1985)

Fairlamb, David 'Beyond Capital', *Institutional Investor*, August 1994

Farman, J.C., B.G. Gardiner, and J.D. Shanklin 'Large Losses of Total Ozone in Antarctica Reveal Seasonal $ClO_x/NO_x$ Interaction', *Nature* 315: 207–210 (May 1985)

Farrar, Donald E. 'Commercial Banks, Trust Departments and Concentration of Power: A Legacy of Glass-Steagall', Washington, DC: US SEC *Capital Market Working Paper #5* (1981)

Fay, Stephen *Portrait of an Old Lady* (New York: Viking, 1987)

Federal Reserve Bank of New York series on comparative banking regulation (c 1988)

—— *Quarterly Review* Winter 1987–1988

Federal Reserve Board of Governors and Secretary of the US Department of the Treasury *Report to Congress on Capital Equivalency* (19 June 1992)

Fehrenbach, T.R. *The Gnomes of Zurich* (London: Leslie Frewin, 1966)

Felando, August 'Harmony Between Tuna Fishing and the Environment of the Eastern Pacific Ocean', paper presented to the World Conference of Tuna Fishing Countries, Tokyo, 3–6 December 1991

Fernandez, Raquel 'The Scope for Collusive Behavior Among Debtor Countries', *J. of Development Economics*: 297–313 (1990)

Fforde, John *The Bank of England and Public Policy 1941–1958* (Cambridge, UK: Cambridge Univ Pr, 1992)

Fields, Karl J. *Enterprise and the state in Korea and Taiwan* (Ithaca, NY: Cornell Univ Pr, 1995)

Finger, J.M., H. Keith Hall, and Douglas R. Nelson 'The Political Economy of Administered Protection', *American Economic Review* 72: 452–466 (June 1982)

Finlayson, Jock A., and Mark W. Zacher 'The GATT and the Regulation of Trade Barriers', *International Organization*, 33/4: 275–314 (Autumn 1981)

Finnemore, Martha 'International Organizations as Teachers of Norms', *International Organization: 565–597* (August 1993)

Finnemore, Martha and Kathryn Sikkink 'International Norm Dynamics and Political Change', *International Organization* 52/4: 887–917 (Autumn 1998)

Fiorina, Morris P. 'Legislator Uncertainty, Legislative Control, and the Delegation of Legislative Power', *Journal of Law, Economics & Organization* 2 (1986)

—— 'Groups Concentration and the Delegation of Legislative Authority', in Noll (ed.) (1985)

Fischel, Daniel R. 'The "Race to the Bottom" Revisited: Reflections on Recent Developments in Delaware's Corporation Law' *Northwest Univ Law Review* 76/913: 919–920 (1982)

Flanagan, Robert J. *Bargaining without boundaries: The multinational corporation and international labor relations* (Chicago: Univ of Chicago Pr, 1974)

Flood, Mark D. 'The Great Deposit Insurance Debate', *Federal Reserve Bank of St. Louis Review* (July 1992)

Florida, Richard and Derek Davison 'Gaining from Green Management', working paper, Heinz Center, Carnegie Mellon University (November 1999)

Forsythe, Kenneth W. Jr. and Maury E. Bredahl 'Strengthening Import Regulations Segments World Markets', *Food Review* 15/1: 2–7 (January–June 1992)

Frank, Robert H., Thomas Gilvich, and Dennis T. Regan. 'Does Studying Economics Inhibit Cooperation?', *J. of Economic Perspectives*, 7/2: 159–171 (Spring 1993 and rejoinder 1996)

Frieden, Jeffry A. and David A. Lake *International Political Economy* (St. Martin's Pr, 2nd edn. 1991; 4th edn. 2000).

Frieden, Jeffry A. *Studies in international finance*, Foreign economic policy of the United States (New York: Garland Pub., 1993)

—— *Invested interests*, International Organization 45/4: 425–451 (Autumn 1991)

Friedlander, Ann F. *The Dilemma of Freight Transportation Regulation* (1969)

Friedrich, Carl J. *Constitutional Government and Democracy: Theory and Practice in Europe and America* (Waltham, MA: Glaisdell Publishing, 1968, 4th edn.)

Fry, Richard (ed.) *A Banker's World: The revival of the City 1957–1970* (London: Hutchinson, 1970)

Fung, Archon, Dara O'Rourke, and Charles Sabel *Can We Put an End to Sweatshops?* (Boston, MA: Beacon Press, 2001)

Gallarotti, Giulio M. 'The limits of international', *International Organization* 45/2: 183–220 (Spring 1991)

Garcia-Johnson, Ronie *Exporting Environmentalism* (Cambridge, MA: MIT Pr, 2000)

Garrett, Geoffrey 'Global Markets and National Politics', *International Organization*, 52/4: 787–824 (Autumn 1998)

——'Capital Mobility, Trade, and the Domestic Politics of Economic Policy', *International Organization* 49: 657–687 (1995)

General Agreement on Tariffs and Trade (GATT) 'United States—Restrictions on Imports of Tuna', Report of the Panel, GATT Doc. DS29/R (Geneva: GATT Secretariat, June 1994)

——'United States—Restrictions on Imports of Tuna', Report of the Panel, GATT Doc. DS21/R (3 September 1991)

——'Thailand—Restrictions on Importation of and Internal Taxes on Cigarettes', Panel Report (Geneva: GATT Secretariat, 7 November 1990)

George, Edward, Richard Roberts, and Christopher Arnander *Take Your Partners* (New York: Palagrave, 2001)

Gerschenkron, Alexander *Bread and Democracy in Germany* (Ithaca, NY: Cornell Univ Pr, 1943/[1989])

Gholz, Eugene 'Possible Futures of the International Patent Regime: Action in NAFTA, GATT, WIPO and the EC' (MIT Center for International Studies, mimeo, 15 September 1993)

Gilligan, Carol *In a Different Voice* (Cambridge, MA: Harvard Univ Pr, 1982)

Gilligan, Thomas W., William J. Marshall, and Barry R. Weingast 'The Interstate Commerce Act of 1887' (manuscript, Stanford Univ, November 1988)

Gilligan, Thomas W. *et al.* 'Regulation and the Theory of Legislative Choice: the Interstate Commerce Act of 1887', *Journal of Law & Economics*, 32: 35–61 (April 1989)

Gilmore, W.C. *International Efforts to Combat Money Laundering* (Cambridge, UK: Grotius Publications, 1992)

Gilpin, Robert *The Challenge of Global Capitalism* (Princeton, NJ: Princeton Univ Pr 2002)

——*The Political Economy of International Relations* (Princeton, NJ: Princeton Univ Pr, 1987)

——*US Power and the Multinational Corporation*, Political economy of international relations series (New York: Basic Books, 1975)

Globerman, Steven 'Trade Liberalization and the Environment', in Globerman and Michael Walker (eds.) *Assessing NAFTA* (Vancouver, BC: Fraser Institute, 1993)

Goldstein, Judith *Ideas, Interests and American Trade Policy* (Ithaca, NY: Cornell Univ Pr, 1993)

Goldstein, Judith 'The Political Economy of Trade' *American Political Science Review* (March 1986)

Goldstein, Judith and Robert O. Keohane (eds.) *Ideas and foreign policy* (Ithaca, NY: Cornell Univ Pr, 1993)

Goldthorpe, John (ed.) *Order and Conflict in Contemporary Capitalism* (Oxford, UK: Oxford Univ Pr, 1984)

Golub, Jonathan 'Globalization, Sovereignty and Policy-Making', in Holden (2000)

Goodman, John B. 'International Competition in Insurance', in David B. Yoffie (ed.) *Beyond Free Trade: Firms, Governments, and Global Competition* (Boston, MA: Harvard Business School Pr, c 1993)

Goodman, John B. and Louis W. Pauly 'The Obsolescence of Capital Controls?', *World Politics* 46: 50–82 (October 1993)

Gourevitch, Peter *Politics in Hard Times* (Ithaca, NY: Cornell Univ Pr, 1986)

—— 'The Second Image Reversed: The International Sources of Domestic Politics', *International Organization* 32: 881–892 (Autumn 1978)

—— 'International Trade, Domestic Coalitions and Liberty: Comparative Responses to the Crisis of 1873–1896', *Journal of Interdisciplinary History* (Autumn 1977)

Gowa, Joanne S. *Allies, Adversaries, and International Trade* (Princeton, NJ: Princeton Univ Pr, c 1994)

Graebner, Norman (ed.) *An Uncertain Tradition* (New York: McGraw Hill, 1961)

Graham, E. Monte *Fighting the Wrong Enemy* (DC: IIE, 2000)

Greve, Michael S. and Fred L. Smith (eds.) *Environmental Politics* (Praeger, 1992)

Grieco, Joseph M. *Cooperation Among Nations* (Ithaca, NY: Cornell Univ Pr, 1990)

Grieder, William 'The Global Marketplace: a Closet Dictator', in Nader (1993)

Grinspun Ricardo, and Maxwell A. Cameron(eds.) *Political Economy of North American Free Trade* (New York: St Martin's Pr, 1993)

Grossman, Gene M. and Alan B. Krueger 'Environmental Impacts of a North American Free Trade Agreement', *National Bureau of Economic Research* Working Paper #3914 (November 1991)

Grossman, Gene M. and Elhanan Helpman *Interest Groups and Trade Policy* (Princeton, NJ: Princeton Univ Pr, 2002)

Grotius, Hugo *The Rights of War and Peace* (1654 [trans.1901])

Guillén, A.M. and Matsaganis, M. 'Testing the "social dumping" hypothesis in Southern Europe', *Journal of European Social Policy*, 10/2: 120–145 (2000)

Gushee, David E. 'Stratospheric Ozone Depletion: Regulatory Issues', Congressional Research Service Issue Brief No. IB89021, updated 17 December 1990

Hall, Peter A. *Governing the economy* (Cambridge, UK: Polity Pr, 1986)

Haas, Ernst 'Turbulent Fields and the Theory of Regional Integration', *International Organization* 3/2: 173–212 (Spring 1976)

—— *Beyond the Nation-State* (Palo Alto, CA: Stanford Univ Pr: 1964)

—— *The Uniting of Europe* (Palo Alto, CA: Stanford Univ Pr: 1958)

Haas, Peter M. 'Banning Chlorofluorocarbons', *International Oganization*, v 46 n 1 (Winter 1992)

—— 'Knowledge, Power, and International Policy Coordination', *International Organization* 46/1: 1–390 (Winter 1992)

—— *Saving the Mediterranean* (New York: Columbia Univ Pr, 1990)

Haas, Peter M., Robert O. Keohane, and Marc A. Levy (eds.) *Institutions for the Earth: Sources of Effective International Environmental Protection* (Cambridge, MA: MIT Pr, 1993)

Hackett, D.P. 'An Assessment of the Basel Convention on the Control of Transboundary Movements of Hazardous Wastes and Their Disposal', *The American Univ Journal of International Law and Policy* v 5 (1990)

Haggard, Stephan *The Political Economy of the Asian Financial Crisis* (Washington DC: Institute for International Economics, 2000)

Haggard, Stephan and Beth A. Simmons 'Theories of International Regimes', *International Organization*, 41/3: 491–517 (Summer 1987)

Hahn, Robert and Albert McGartland 'The Political Economy of Instrument Choice', *Northwestern Univ Law Review* 83: 592–611 (1989)

Hammond, Thomas H. and Jack H. Knott 'The Deregulatory Snowball: Explaining Deregulation in the Financial Industry', *J. of Politics* 50/1: 3–31 (February 1988)

Harding, Alan and Peter Garside 'Globalisation, Urban Political Economy and Community Power', paper presented to the APSA conference 2–5 September 1993

*Harvard International Law J.* 'The US–EC Hormone Treated Beef Conflict', 30/549 (1989)

Heidenheimer, Arnold, Hugh Heclo, and Carolyn T. Adams *Comparative Public Policy: The Politics of Social Choice in Europe and America* (New York: St Martin's Pr, 3rd edn. 1990)

Helleiner, Eric *States and the Reemergence of Global Finance* (Ithaca, NY: Cornell Univ Pr, 1994)

Herrigel, Gary 'Democracy at Work: Changing World Markets and the Future of Labor Unions', *Industrial and Labor Relations Review* 46/4: 742–744 (July 1993)

Hertz, Noreena *The Silent Takeover: Global Capitalism and the Death of Democracy* (Cambridge, UK: Cambridge Univ Pr, 2001)

Higgonet, Rene *Eurodollars and International Banking* (New York: St Martin's Press, 1985)

Hilliard, Thomas 'Trade Advisory Committee: Privileged Access for Polluters', *Public Citizen's Congress Watch* (December 1991)

Hillman, Robert W. 'Cross-border Investment, Conflict of Laws, and the Privatization of Securities Law', special issue of *Law and Contemporary Problems* 55/4: 331–355 (Autumn 1992) on 'International Regulatory Competition and the Securities Laws'

Himmelberg, Robert F. (ed.) *Regulatory Issues since 1964: The Rise of the Deregulation Movement* (New York: Garland, 1994)

Hines, James R. 'Tax Policy and the Activities of Multinational Corporations', 401–445 in Auerbach (ed.) *Fiscal Policy* (Cambridge, MA: MIT Pr, 1997)

—— 'Altered States', *American Economic Review*, 86/5: 1076–1094 (December 1996)

Hines, James R., Jr. and Eric M. Rice 'Fiscal paradise', *Quarterly Journal of Economics* 109/1: 149–182 ( February 1994)

Hirschhofer, Harald 'The Role of the EC Commission in the Creation of a European Securities Trading Network' (mimeo c 1990)

Hirschman, Albert O. 'The Search for Paradigms as a Hindrance to Understanding', *World Politics* 22/3: 329–343 (April 1970)

—— *Exit, Voice and Loyalty* (Cambridge, MA: Harvard Univ Pr, 1970)

Hoberg, George, Jr. 'Technology, Political Structure and Social Regulation: A Cross-National Analysis', *Comparative Politics* 18: 357–375 (1986)

——*Pluralism by Design: Environmental Policy and the American Regulatory State* (New York: Praeger, 1992)

Hobson, J.A. *Imperialism: A Study* (London: Allen & Unwin, 1902/1968)

Hoffmann, Stanley 'The European Union', *Current* 365: 34–45 (September 1994)

——'Europe's Identity Crisis Revisited', *Daedalus* 123/2: 1–24 (Spring 1994)

——*Duties Beyond Borders* (Syracuse, NY: Syracuse Univ Pr, 1981)

——'An American Social Science: International Relations', *Daedalus* (Summer 1977) reprinted in *Janus and Manerva: Essays in the Theory and Practice of International Politics* (Boulder, CO: Westview Pr, 1987)

——'Obstinate or Obsolete', in *Daedalus* (Summer 1966)

Holden, B. (ed.) *Global Democracy* (London: Routledge 2000)

Homer-Dixon, Thomas F., Jeffrey H. Boutwell, and George W. Rathjens 'Environmental Change and Violent Conflict', *Scientific American* 16–23 (February 1993)

Hooks, Linda *Bank Failures and Deregulation in the 1980s* (New York, 1994)

Huberich, Charles Henry *The Political and Legislative History of Liberia*, 2 vols. (New York: Central Book Co. 1947)

Hudec, Robert E. *Enforcing International Trade Law* (Salem, NH: Butterworth *c.*1993)

——*Enforcing International Trade Law* (Butterworth, 1993)

Hufbauer, Gary Clyde and Jeffrey J. Schott *North American Free Trade*, 2nd edn. (DC: IIE 1993)

Hufbauer, Gary Clyde, Jeffrey J. Schott, and Kimberly Ann Elliott *Economic Sanctions Reconsidered*, 2nd edn. (DC: IIE 1990)

Huntington, Samuel P. 'One Soul at a Time: Political Science and Political Reform', *American Political Science Review* 82/1: 3–11 (March 1988)

——'The Marasmus of the ICC', *Yale Law Journal* (61, 1952)

——'Clientalism: A Study in Administrative Politics' (Ph.D. diss., Harvard Univ, *c.*1951)

Hurley, Edward Nash *New Merchant Marine*

Hutchison, Robert A. *Vesco* (New York: Praeger, 1974)

Huth, Paul, Christopher Gelpi, and D. Scott Bennett 'The escalation of great power militarized disputes', *American Political Science Review* 87/3: 609–624 (September 1993)

Inclán, Carla, Dennis P. Quinn, and Robert Y. Shapiro 'A Dynamic Study of the Origins and Consequences of Changes in US Corporate Taxation, 1981–1998', *American Journal of Political Science* 45: 179–201 (January 2001)

Ikenberry, G. John *The Challenge of Global Capitalism* (Princeton, NJ: Princeton Univ Pr, 2002)

——'Conclusion: An Institutional approach to American Foreign Economic Policy', *International Organization* 42/1: 219–243 (Winter 1988)

Ikenberry, G. John, David A. Lake, and Michael Mastanduno (eds.) *The State and American Foreign Economic Policy* (Ithaca, NY: Cornell Univ Pr)

Inkeles, Alex 'Convergence and Divergence in Industrial Societies,' in Attir *et al.* (eds.) *Directions of Change* (Boulder, CO: Westview Pr, 1981)

Inter-American Tropical Tuna Commission (IATTC) *Annual Report*, 1992

International Commission on Shipping (IConS), Hon. Peter Morris (ed.) *Ships, Slaves and Competition* (Charleston NSW, Australia: International Commission on Shipping, c 2001)

International Confederation of Free Trade Unions (ICFTU) 'Annual Survey of Violations of Trade Union Rights' (various years)

International Monetary Fund (IMF) *International Capital Markets*, various years 1986–1993

—— *Emerging Financial Centers* (January 1984)

International Organization of Securities Commissions (IOSCO) Report (10 August 1989)

International Transport-Workers' Federation (ITF) *ITF FOC Campaign History*, undated mimeograph (received 1992)

Irwin, Douglas A. 'The Political Economy of Free Trade' (mimeo, October 1992; Univ of Chicago Graduate School of Business)

Jaffee, Adam B., S. Peterson, P. Portney, and R. Stavins 'Environmental Regulation and the Competitiveness of US Manufacturing: what does the evidence tell us?', *J. of Economic Literature* 33: 132–163 (March 1995)

Jellife, Derrick B. 'Commerciogenic Malnutrition', *Nutrition Review* 30 (1972)

Johns, R. A. *Tax Havens and Offshore Finance*, Studies in International Political Economy series, general editor Susan Strange (St Martin's Pr, 1983)

Johnson, Walter 'Edward R. Stettinius, Jr.', in Norman Graebner (ed.) *An Uncertain Tradition: American Secretaries of State in the Twentieth Century* (New York: McGraw Hill, 1961)

Jones, Geoffrey *British Multinational Banking 1930–1990* (Oxford, UK: Clarendon Pr, 1993)

Joseph, James, and Joseph W. Greenough *International Management of Tuna, Porpoise, and Billfish* (Seattle, WA: Univ of Washington Pr, c 1979)

Joskow, Paul 'Asset Specificity and the Structure of Vertical Relationships: Empirical Evidence', *Journal of Law, Economics, and Organization* 4/1: 103–106 (Spring 1988)

—— 'Vertical Integration and Long-Term Contracts', *Journal of Law, Economics and Organization* (Spring 1985)

Joskow, Paul L. and Nancy L. Rose 'The Effects of Economic Regulation', in Richard Schmalensee and R.D. Willig (eds.) *Handbook of Industrial Organization* 2/25 (1989)

Joskow, Paul and Richard Schmalensee *Markets for Power* (Cambridge, MA: MIT Pr, 1983)

Joslin, David *A Century of Banking in Latin America* (Oxford, UK: Oxford Univ Pr, 1963)

Kahler, Miles 'Modelling Races to the Bottom' (mimeo c 1999)

Kahn, Alfred E. *The Economics of Regulation: Principles and Institutions* (John Wiley & Sons, 1970; reprinted MIT Pr, 1988 with foreword by Paul L. Joskow)

Kagan, Robert A. 'National Styles of Regulation', *Law & Society Review Ann* 21/5: 717–742 (1988)

Kamar, Ehud 'A Regulatory Competition Theory of Indeterminacy in Corporate Law', *Columbia Law Rev.* 98: 1908–1958 (1998)

Kane, Edward J. 'Competitive Financial Deregulation', in Portes and Swoboda (eds.) *Threats to International Financial Stability* (Cambridge, UK: Cambridge Univ Pr, 1987)

Kananneh, H. 'The Relationship of Bottle-Feeding to Malnutrition and Gastroenteritis in a Pre-Industrial Setting', *Environmental Child Health* (December 1972)

Kant, Immanuel 'Perpetual Peace', 'The Idea of a Universal History in a Cosmopolitical Plan', and *Groundwork of the Metaphysic of Morals*

Kapstein, Ethan B. *Sharing the Wealth* (W.W. Norton & Co, 1999)

——'Territoriality and Who is "US"? (response to John Gerard Ruggie)', *International Organization* 47/3: 501–505 (Summer 1993)

——'Between Power & Purpose: Central Banks and the Politics of Regulatory Convergence', *International Organization* (Winter 1992)

——'Supervising International Banks: Origins and Implications of the Basle Accord', *Princeton Essays in International Finance* No. 185 (December 1991)

——'Resolving the Regulator's Dilemma', *World Politics* (1988)

Katzenstein, Peter J. *The Culture of National Security* (New York: Columbia Univ Pr, 1996)

——*Small States in World Markets* (Ithaca, NY: Cornell Univ Pr, 1985)

Katzenstein, Peter J. (ed.) *Between Power and Plenty* (Madison, WI: Univ of Wisconsin Pr, 1977)

Katznelson, Ira and Helen V. Milner *Political Science: State of the Discipline* (New York: W.W. Norton, 2002)

Keck, Margaret and Kathryn Sikkink *Activists Beyond Borders* (Ithaca, NY: Cornell Univ Pr, 1998)

Kelly, Janet *Bankers and Borders* (Cambridge, MA: Ballinger, 1977)

Kenyon, Daphne A. and John Kincaid (eds.) *Competition Among States and Local Governments* (Washington, DC: Urban Institute Pr, distributed by Univ Pr of America, c 1991)

Keohane, Robert O. and Stanley Hoffmann (eds.) *The New European community: Decisionmaking and Institutional Change* (Boulder, CO: Westview Pr, 1991)

Keohane, Robert O. and Lisa Martin 'Institutional theory, endogeneity, and delegation', mimeo for Progress in International Relations Theory (Scottsdale, AZ: 15–16 January 1999)

Keohane, Robert O., Michael McGinnis, and Elinor Ostrom 'Proceedings of Conference on Linking Local and Global Commons', Harvard CFIA (1993)

Keohane, Robert O. and Craig Murphy 'International Institutions', in Mary Hawkesworth and Maurice Kogan (eds.) *Encyclopedia of Government and Politics*, II (Routledge 1992 and 2003)

Keohane, Robert O. (ed.) *Neorealism and Its Critics* (New York: Columbia Univ Pr, 1986)

——*After Hegemony* (Princeton, NJ: Princeton Univ Pr, 1984)

Keohane, Robert O. and Joseph S. Nye, Jr. *Power and Interdependence* (Boston, MA: Little Brown, 1977; revised and expanded in 3rd edn., Addison-Wesley Publishing, 2000)

Kerr, Clark *The Future of Industrial Societies: Convergence or Continuing Diversity?* (Cambridge, MA: Harvard Univ Pr, 1983)

Key, Sydney J. and Hal S. Scott 'International Trade in Banking Services: A Conceptual Framework' (Washington, DC: Group of Thirty Occasional Paper #35).

Khor, Martin 'How the South is Getting a Raw Deal at the WTO', in Sarah Anderson (ed.) *Views from the South* (San Francisco, CA: International Forum on Globalization, 1999)

Kindleberger, Charles *The World in DePrion, 1929–1939* (Berkeley, CA: Univ of California Pr, 1974)
——'Formation of Financial Centers', Princeton Essays in International Finance No. 36 (1971)
——*American Business Abroad* (New Haven, CT: Yale Univ Press 1969)
King, Gary, Robert O. Keohane, and Sidney Verba *Designing Social Inquiry* (Princeton, NJ: Univ Pr, 1994)
Kingdon, John W. *Agendas, Alternatives, and Public Policies* (Boston, MA: Little, Brown, 1984)
Klein, Naomi *No Logo* (New York: Picador USA, 2000)
Kogut, Bruze *International Strategic Management* (Thomson 1998)
Korten, David C. *When Corporations Rule the World* (Bloomfield, CT: Kumarian Pr, 2nd edn., 2001)
Kramer, Ludwig 'The Single European Act and Environmental Protection', *Common Market Law Review* 24: 659–688 (1987)
Krasner, Stephen *Defending the National Interest* (Princeton, NJ: Princeton Univ Pr, 1978)
Krasner, Stephen (ed.) *International Regimes* (Ithaca, NY: Cornell Univ Pr, 1983)
Kratochwil, Friedrich V. *Rules, Norms, and Decisions* (Cambridge, UK: Cambridge Univ Pr, 1989)
Kreps, David M. *Game theory and economic modeling* (Oxford, UK: Oxford Univ Pr, 1990)
Krieger, Joel *Reagan, Thatcher, and the Politics of Decline* (Oxford, UK: Oxford Univ Pr, c 1986)
Krueger, Anne O. 'The Political Economy of the Rent-Seeking Society', *American Economic Review* 64: 292–303 (1974)
Krugman, Paul *The Great Unraveling: Losing Our Way in the New Century* (W.W. Norton, 2003)
——*Strategic Trade Policy and the New International Economics* (Cambridge, MA: MIT Pr, 1986)
Krugman, Paul and Maurice Obstfeld 'Importance of Regulatory Asymmetries' and 'Regulating Banking', *International Economics* (1988)
Krugman, Paul with Alasdair Smith *Empirical Studies of Strategic Trade Policy* (Chicago, IL: Univ of Chicago Pr, 1994)
Kuhn, Thomas S. *The Structure of Scientific Revolutions* (Chicago, IL: Univ of Chicago Pr, 1970)
Kupchan, Charles A. *The End of the American Era* (New York: Knopf, 2002)
Kurzer, Paulette *Business and Banking* (Ithaca, NY: Cornell Univ Pr, 1993)
Laffont, Jean-Jacques and Jean Tirole 'The Politics of Government Decision-Making: A Theory of Regulatory Capture', MIT Department of Economics Discussion paper #506, 1988; revised in *Journal of Law, Economics and Organization* (1991)
Laird, Sam 'Nontariff barriers of developed countries, 1966–86', *Finance & Development* 26/1: 12–14 (March 1989)
Lang, Tim and Colin Hines *The New Protectionism* (London: Earthscan, 1993)
Langevoort, Donald C. 'Schoenbaum Revisited: Limiting the Scope of Antifraud Protection in an Internationalized Securities Marketplace', special issue of *Law*

*and Contemporary Problems* 55/4: 241–261 (Autumn 1992) on 'International Regulatory Competition and the Securities Laws'

Larson, Henrietta, E.H. Knowlton, and C.S. Popple *History of Standard Oil Company* (New Jersey 1927–1950)

Lasswell, Harold D. *Politics: Who Gets What, When, How* (New York: McGraw-Hill, c 1936/1956)

Lawrence, Robert 'Japan's different trade regime', *Journal of Economic Perspectives* 7/3: 3–20 (Summer 1993)

Lawrence, Robert *et al. A Vision for the World Economy* (DC: Brookings Institution, 1996)

Lax, David and James Sebenius *The Manager as Negotiator* (New York: Free Pr, 1986)

LeBor, Adam *Hitler's Secret Bankers: The Myth of Swiss Neutrality During the Holocaust* (Secaucus NJ: Birch Lane Pr/Carol Publishing Group, 1997)

Leonard, H. Jeffrey *Pollution and the Struggle for the World Product* (Cambridge, UK: Cambridge Univ Pr, 1988)

Leonard, H. Jeffrey and Christopher J. Duerksen 'Environmental Regulations and Manufacturers' Location Choices', *Columbia J. of World Business* 52–68 (Summer 1980)

Leone, Robert A. *Who Profits* (New York: Basic Books, 1986)

Lepgold, Joseph and Miroslav Nincic *Beyond the Ivory Tower* (New York: Columbia Univ Pr, 2001)

Levine, Michael and Jennifer Forrence 'Regulatory Capture, Public Interest, and the Public Agenda', *Journal of Law, Economics and Organization* 6(0): 167–202 (1990)

Levinson, Arik 'Environmental Regulations and Industry Location', in *Fair Trade and Harmonization*, J. Bhagwati and R.E. Hudec (eds.) vol. 1 (Cambridge, MA: MIT Pr, 1996)

Levy, Marc 'European Acid Rain', in Hass *et al.* (1993)

Lieber, Robert J. (ed.) *Eagle Rules* (Prentice-Hall 2002)

Lindblom, Charles *Politics and Markets* (New York: Basic Books 1977)

Lipson, Charles. *Standing guard: protecting foreign capital in the nineteenth and twentieth centuries*, Studies in international political economy (Berkeley, CA: Univ of California Pr, c 1985)

——'The Transformation of Trade: the Sources and Effects of Regime Change', *International Organization*, 36/2: 417–455 (Spring 1982)

Lissakers, Karin *Banks, borrowers, and the establishment: A revisionist account of the international debt crisis* (New York.: Basic Books, c 1991)

Litfin, Karen *Ozone Discourses* (New York: Columbia Univ Pr, c 1994)

Lizondo, J. Saul 'Foreign direct investment', in *Readings in international business: a decision approach*, Robert Z. Aliber and Reid W. Click (eds.) (Cambridge, MA: MIT Pr, 1993), 85–112

Locke, John *Second Treatise on Civil Government* (1690)

Locke, Richard M. and Kathleen Thelen *The Shifting Boundaries of Labor Politics* (Cambridge, MA: Minda de Gunzburg Center for European Studies, Harvard Univ, c 1993)

Locke, Richard M. and Michael Piore *Remaking the Italian Economy* (Ithaca, NY: Cornell Univ Pr, 1997)

Long, Larry W. 'Public Relations', *Public Relations Review* 13/2: 3–14 (Summer 1987)
Lowenkopf, Martin *Politics in Liberia* (Stanford, CA: Hoover Institution Pr, 1976)
Ludlow, Peter *Beyond 1992* (Brussels: Center for European Policy Studies, 1989)
—— *The Making of the European Monetary System: A Case Study of the Politics of the European Community* (London: Butterworth Scientific, 1982)
Lukauskas, Arvid 'Regulating Unfair Trade' (book review), *Political Science Quarterly* 109/2: 383–386 (Summer 1994)
Luttwak, Edward 'From Geopolitics to Geo-Economics', *National Interest* (Summer 1990)
MacArthur, John R., Jr. *The Selling of Free Trade* (Berkeley, CA: Univ of California Pr, September 2001)
McCauley Robert N. and Rama Seth 'Foreign Bank Credit to US Corporations: The Implications of Offshore Loans', *FRBNY Quarterly Review* (Spring 1992), 17: 52–65
McChesney, Fred S. *Money for Nothing* (Harvard 1997)
—— '"Pay to Play" Politics Examined, With Lessons for Campaign Finance Reform', *Indep. Rev.* 6: 345 (2002)
McCraw, Thomas K. 'Regulating Big Business: Antitrust in Great Britain and America, 1880–1990' (book review), *Journal of American History* 80/1: 287–289 (June 1993)
—— 'The Corporate State and the Broker State: The Du Ponts and American National Politics, 1925–1940', *The Journal of Interdisciplinary History*, 21/4: 714–717 (Spring 1991)
—— *The Essential Alfred Chandler* (Boston, MA: Harvard Business School Pr, 1988)
—— *Prophets of Regulation* (Cambridge, MA: Harvard Univ Pr, 1984)
McCray, Sandra B. 'State Regulation of Banks in an Era of Deregulation' (Washington, DC: Advisory Commission on Intergovernmental Relations, c 1988)
M'Gonigle, R. Michael and Mark W. Zacher *Pollution, Politics, & International Law* (Berkeley, CA: Univ of California Pr, 1979)
McGoodwin, James R. *Crisis in the World's Fisheries* (Palo Alto, CA: Stanford Univ Pr, 1990)
McGuire, Therese J. 'Federal Aid to States and Localities and the Appropriate Competitive Framework', in Kenyon and Kincaid (eds.) (1991)
McInnis, Daniel, see Greve and Smith (1992)
MacKenzie, Deborah 'Now it Makes Business Sense to Save the Ozone Layer', *New Scientist:* 120/1636: 25 (29 October 1988)
McKenzie, Richard and Dwight Lee *Quicksilver Capital* (New York: Free Pr, 1991)
McKeown, Timothy 'The Politics of Corn Law Repeal and Theories of Commercial Policy', *British Journal of Political Science* 19: 353–380 (July 1989)
—— 'Hegemonic Stability Theory and 19th Century Tariff Levels in Europe', *International Organization* 37/1: 73–91 (Winter 1982)
Magee, Stephen and Leslie Young 'Endogenous Protection in the US, 1900–1984', and 'Comment' by J. Peter Neary, chapter 4 in Robert M. Stern (ed.) *US Trade Policy in a Changing World Economy* (Cambridge, MA: MIT Pr, 1987)

Magee, Stephen, William Brock, and Leslie Young *Black Hole Tariffs and Endogenous Policy Theory* (Cambridge, UK: Cambridge Univ Pr, 1989)

Magnuson, Warren, US Senate Committee on Interstate and Foreign Commerce (CIFC), Subcommittee on Merchant Marine and Fisheries, *Hearings on Ship Transfers*, 85th Congress, 1st session, S. 1488 (1957)

Majone, Giandomenico 'The Rise of the Regulatory State in Europe', *West European Politics* 17/3: 77 (July 1994)

—— 'Deregulation or Reregulation? Policymaking in the EC since the Single Act' (mimeo c 1993)

—— 'Environment and Trade in the European Community' (mimeo outline of a public lecture, Harvard Univ, Center for European Studies, 25 March 1993)

—— 'The European Community Between Social Policy and Social Regulation', paper presented to the 1992 Annual Meeting of the American Political Science Association, 3–6 September 1992

—— 'Regulatory Federalism in the European Community', paper prepared for delivery at the 1991 Annual Meeting of the American Political Science Association (29 August–1 September 1991)

—— (ed.) *Deregulation or Reregulation: Regulatory Reform in Europe and the US* (New York: St Martin's Pr, 1990)

Malloy, Michael P. 'US International Banking and the New Capital Adequacy Requirements: New, Old and Unexpected', 7 *Annual Review of Banking Law*, 75: 88–105 (1988)

Mansbridge, Jane, *Beyond Self-Interest* (Chicago: Univ of Chicago Pr, 1990)

Manzetti, Luigi 'The Politics of Privatization and Deregulation in Latin America', *Quarterly Review of Economics and Finance* 34 (1994)

March, James G. and Johan P. Olsen *Rediscovering Institutions* (New York: Macmillan–Free Pr, 1989)

—— 'The New Institutionalism: Organizational Factors in Political Life', *American Political Science Review* 78: 734–749 (September 1984)

Marinaro, Frank J. 'Banking Law: The Clash Between the McFadden Act and a National Banking Market', *Annual Survey of American Law* 1990/2: 203–238 (Summer 1990)

Mark, D. Harmon 'Britain In and Out of the Exchange Rate Mechanism of the European Monetary System', paper prepared for delivery at the Annual Meeting of the American Political Science Association (Washington, DC, September 1993)

Marks, David, with John R. Ehrenfeld, Gordon E. Forward, Gunnar Larsson, and Juan Rada World Economic Forum Summit, 'Extended Producers' Responsibility Laws: An Approaching Tidal Wave of New Recycling Regulation?' (Cambridge, MA: MIT Univ Pr, 1993)

Marks, Stephen V. and John MacArthur 'Empirical Analyses of the Determinants of Protection,' *International Trade Policy*, John S. Odell and Thomas D. Willett (Ann Arbor: Univ of Michigan Pr, 1991)

Martin, Lisa *Coercive Cooperation* (NJ: Princeton Univ Pr, 1992)

Masten, Scott and Stephane Saussier 'Econometrics of Contracts: An Assessment of Developments in the Empirical Literature on Contracting', *Revue d'Economie Industrielle* 92: 215–236 (2000)

Mattli, Walter and Tim Büthe 'Setting International Standards', *World Politics* 56/1 (October 2003)

May, Ernest R. *American Imperialism* (Chicago, IL: Imprint Publications, 1991)
Mayer, Don and David Hoch 'International Environmental Protection and the GATT', *American Business Law Journal* 1: 2 (September 1993)
Mayer, Martin *The Bankers: The Next Generation* (New York: Truman Talley, 1997)
Mazey, Sonia and Jeremy Richardson *Lobbying in the European Community* (Oxford, UK: Oxford Univ Pr, 1993)
Meadows, Donella H., Dennis L. Meadows, and Jorgen Randers *Beyond the Limits* (Post Mills, VT: Chelsea Green Publishing, 1992)
Mearsheimer, John J. *The Tragedy of Great Power Politics* (New York: Norton, 2001)
—— 'The False Promise of International Institutions', *International Security* 19/3: 5–45 (Winter 1994/1995)
Mennis, Bernard and Karl P. Sauvant *Emerging forms of Transnational Community* (Lexington, MA: Lexington Books, c 1976)
Mill, John Stuart *A System of Logic* (1843)
Milner, Helen *Interests, Institutions and Information: Domestic Politics and International Relations* (Princeton, NJ: Princeton Univ Pr, 1997)
—— *Resisting Protectionism* (Princeton, NJ: Princeton Univ Pr, 1988)
Mitchell, Ronald 'Regimes Do Matter', APSA convention paper (September 1993)
—— 'Intentional Oil Pollution of the Oceans', in Hass *et al.* (1993)
Mitrany, David *The Functional Theory of Politics* (London: St Martin's Pr, 1975)
—— *A Working Peace System* (Chicago: Quadrangle Books, 1943)
Mokhiber, Russell and Robert Weissman *Corporate Predators* (Common Courage Pr, 1999)
Molina, Mario J. and F. Sherwood Rowland 'Stratospheric Sink for Chlorofluromethanes: Chlorine Atomic Catalyzed Destruction of Ozone', *Nature* 249: 810–812 (1974)
Moran, Theodore H. *Beyond Sweatshops* (Washington, DC: Brookings Institution Pr, 2002)
—— *Foreign Direct Investment and Development* (Washington, DC: Institute for International Economics, 1998)
—— *Multinational Corporations and the Politics of Dependence* (Princeton, NJ: Princeton Univ Pr, c 1974)
Moravcsik, Andrew 'A New Statecraft? Supranational Entrepreneurs and International Cooperation', *International Organization* 53/2: 267–306 (Spring 1999)
—— *The Choice for Europe* (Ithaca, NY: Cornell Univ Pr, 1998)
—— 'Taking Preferences Seriously: A Liberal Theory of International Politics', *International Organization*, 51/4: 513–553 (Autumn 1997)
—— 'Negotiating the Single European Act: National interests and conventional statecraft in the European Community', *International Organization* 45/1: 22–23 (Winter 1991)
Morrisette, Peter M. 'The Evolution of Policy Responses to Stratospheric Ozone Depletion', *The Univ of New Mexico Natural Resources Journal* 29 (Summer 1989)
—— 'Lessons from Other International Agreements for a Global $CO_2$ Accord', Discussion Papaer ENR91-02, Resources for the Future (October 1990)

Moschel, Wernhard 'International Restraints of Competition', *Northwestern Journal of International Law and Business* 10/1: 76–83 (Spring 1989)

Mosley, Layna 'Room to Move', *International Organization* 54/4: 737–773 (Autumn 2000)

Moss, David A. 'Kindling a Flame Under Federalism', *Business History Review* 68/2: 244 (22 June 1994)

—— 'Kindling a Flame Under Federalism', mimeo paper presented at a seminar led by Claudia Goldin at Harvard University (April 1993)

Muller, Mike 'The Baby Killers' (London: War on Want, mimeo, March 1974)

Murphy, Craig *International Organization and Industrial Change* (Cambridge, UK: Oxford Univ Pr, 1994)

Murphy, Dale D. 'Culture Conflicts: *Sports Illustrated* and US–Canadian Trade', Council for US–Canadian Business Understanding (2000)

—— 'Comparative (Regulatory) Advantage: Firm–State Relations in the Global Economy', International Studies Association conference paper, Minneapolis, MN, Daniel Verdier discussant (1998)

—— 'Asset Specificity and International Cooperation: Lessons from Transaction Cost Economics', paper for panel, International Studies Association conference, San Diego, CA, David Lake discussant (April 1996)

—— 'Open Economies and Regulations: Convergence and Competition among Jurisdictions', Ph.D. dissertation, MIT Department of Political Science (Kenneth A. Oye adviser, 1995)

—— 'Open Economies Competition For Comparative Regulatory Advantage', MIT Center for International Studies working paper (available upon request to permanent email: dale@alum.mit.edu; November 1993)

—— 'Many Cooke's Make Light Work: Regulatory Convergence in Banking Capital Standards', mimeo MIT Political Science Department (1991)

Murphy, Dale D. and Kenneth A. Oye 'Interjurisdictional Harmonization and Divergence Across Open Economies', American Political Science Association conference paper (Chicago, IL, August 1995)

Myers, Ransom A. and Boris Worm 'Rapid worldwide depletion of predatory fish communities', *Nature* 423/6937: 280–283 (15 May 2003)

Nader, Ralph *et al. The Case Against 'Free Trade': GATT, NAFTA, and the Globalization of Corporate Power* (San Francisco: Earth Island Pr, 1993)

Nader, Ralph, Mark Green, and E. Joel Seligman *Constitutionalizing the Corporation* (Washington, DC: Corporate Accountability Research Group, 1976)

Naess, Erling *Autobiography of a Shipping Man* (1977)

—— *The Great PanLibHon Controversy* (1972)

Nash, Gerald D. 'Origins of the Interstate Commerce Act of 1887', *Pennsylvania History* 24 (1957)

National Academy of Sciences (NAS) *Policy Implications of Greenhouse Warming* (1991)

—— *Petroleum in the Marine Environment* (1975)

National Research Council, National Academy of Sciences, and Committee on Reducing Porpoise Mortality from Tuna Fishing *Dolphins and the Tuna Industry* (Washington, DC: National Academy Pr, 1992)

Naylor, R.T. *Hot Money and the Politics of Debt* (Montreal: Black Rose Books, 1987 and 1994).

Nicolaidis, Kalypso 'Mutual Recognition: The New Frontier of Multilateralism?', *Project Promothee Perspectives* n. 10 (Paris, 1989)

Nivola, Pietro S. *Regulating unfair trade* (Washington, DC: Brookings Institution, c 1993)

Noll, Roger 'Economic Perspectives on the Politics of Regulation' (1989), in Richard Schmalensee and R.D. Willig (eds.) *Handbook of Industrial Organization*, volume II (1989)

Noll, Roger (ed.) *Regulatory Policy and the Social Sciences* (Berkeley, CA: Univ of California, 1985)

Nollen, Stanley D. and Dennis P. Quinn 'Free Trade, Fair Trade, Strategic Trade, and Protectionism in the US Congress, 1987–1988', *International Organization* 48: 491–525 (Summer 1994)

Nordlinger, Eric *On the Autonomy of the Democratic State* (Cambridge, MA: Harvard Univ Pr, 1981)

North American Free Trade Agreement (NAFTA) 'NAFTA Supplemental Agreements on Labor and the Environment', 'Agreement on Environmental Cooperation', and 'North American Agreement on Labor Cooperation' (13 August 1993)

North, Douglas 'Institutions', *Journal of Economic Perspectives* 5/1: 97–112 (Winter 1991)

Northrup, Herbert R. and Richard Rowan *The ITF and Flag of Convenience Shipping* (Univ of Pennsylvania, Wharton Industrial Research Unit, 1983)

Noyes, Dan 'Toxics 'R Us: the Booming Global Business of Hazardous-Junk Dumping', *Mother Jones* 15/7: 56–61 (November–December 1990)

Nye, Joseph S., Jr. *The Paradox of American Power* (Oxford, UK: Oxford Univ Pr, 2002)

——'Redefining the National Interest', *Foreign Affairs*, 78/4 (July/August 1999)

Oates, Wallace and Robert Schwab 'The Allocative & Distributive Implications of Local Fiscal Competition', in Kenyon & Kincaid (eds.) (c 1991)

——'Economic Competition Among Jurisdictions', *J. Public Economics* 35 (1988)

O'Connor, William E. *International Cooperation vs. Nationalism in the Economic Regulation of the World's Airlines* (dissertation, American Univ 1970)

*Ocean Development and International Law* 'The Tuna-Dolphin Controversy in the Eastern Pacific Ocean', 25: 1–30 (1994 )

Odegard, Peter H. *Pressure Politics: The Story of the Anti-Saloon League* (New York: Columbia Univ Pr, 1928/[1966])

Ogus, Anthony *Regulation: Legal form and Economic Theory* (Oxford: Clarendon Pr, 1994)

Organization for Economic Co-Operation and Development (OECD) 'Maritime Transport', 1973: 88–103 (1974)

——Working Group on Accounting Standards 'Consolidation Policies in OECD Countries: Report' (1986–1988)

Olson, Mancur *The Logic of Collective Action* (Cambridge, MA: Harvard Univ Pr, 1965/1971)

Oster, Sharon *Modern Competitive Analysis* (Oxford, UK: Oxford Univ Pr, 2nd edn. 1994)

Oster Sharon M. and John M. Quigley 'Regulatory Barriers to the Diffusion of Innovation: Some Evidence from Building Codes', *Bell Journal of Economics* 8: 361 (1977)

*Oxford Economic Papers* on 'Public Economics in the European Community', 42/1: 1–292 (January 1990)

Oye, Kenneth A. *Economic Discrimination and Political Exchange* (Princeton, NJ: Princeton Univ Pr, 1992)

—— *Cooperation Under Anarchy* (Princeton, NJ: Princeton Univ Pr, 1986)

Oye, Kenneth A. and James H. Maxwell 'Self-Interest and Environmental Management', *J. of Th. Politics* 6/4: 192–221 (1993)

Oye, Kenneth A., Robert Lieber, and Donald Rothchild (eds.) *Eagle in a New World* (New York, NY: HarperCollins, 1992)

Paarlberg, Robert L. *Fixing Farm Trade* (Cambridge, MA: Ballinger, c 1988)

Paine, Lynne Sharp *Pfizer: Global Protection of Intellectual Property* (Boston, MA: Harvard Business School Case Services, 6 April 1995)

Palan, Ronen 'Trying to Have Your Cake and Eating It: How and Why the State System Has Created Offshore', *International Studies Quarterly* 42 (1998)

Palast, Greg *The Best Democracy Money Can Buy* (Plume, 2003)

Panetta, Leon *et al.* 'America's Living Oceans', Pew Charitable Trusts (May 2003)

Pareto, Vilfredo *Manual of Political Economy* (New York: A.M. Kelley, 1927)

Pashigian, B. Peter 'Environmental Regulation: Whose Self-Interests Are Being Protected?', *Economic Inquiry* 23: 552–584 (October 1985)

——'The Effects of Environmental Regulation on Optimal Plant Size and Factor Shares', *Journal of Law and Economics*, 27/1: 1–28 (April 1984)

Pauly, Louis W. *Who Elected the Bankers* (Ithaca, NY: Cornell Univ Pr, 1997)

——'Foreign Banks in Australia: The Politics of Deregulation' (Australia: Macquarie Univ, 1987)

—— and Simon Reich, 'National Structures and Multinational Corporate Behavior', *International Organization* 51/1: 1–30 (1975)

Pearson, Charles S. (ed.) *Multinational Corporations, Environment, and the Third World* (Durham, NC: Duke Univ Pr, 1987)

Peltzman, Sam 'The Economic Theory of Regulation after a Decade of Deregulation', in *Brookings Papers: Microeconomics*, 1–59 (Washington, DC: Brookings Institution 1989)

—— *Political Participation and Government Regulation* (Chicago: Univ of Chicago Pr, 1998)

Perot, H. Ross and Pat Choate *Save Your Job, Save Our Country* (Hyperion, 1993)

Phillips, Kevin *Wealth and Democracy* (New York: Random House/Broadway Books, 2002)

Pincus, Jonathan J. *Pressure Groups and Politics in Antebellum Tariffs* (New York: Columbia Univ Pr, 1977)

——'Pressure Groups and the Pattern of Tariffs', *Journal of Political Economy* 83: 757–778 (1975)

Piore Michael J. and Charles F. Sabel *The Second Industrial Divide* (New York: Basic Books, 1984)

Plank, S.J. and M. Milanesi 'Infant Feeding and Infant Mortality in Rural Chile', *WHO Bulletin* No. 48 (1973)

Polanyi, Karl *The Great Transformation* (Boston, MA: Beacon Pr, 1944/1957)
Polsby, Nelson W. *Political Innovation in America* (New Haven, CT: Yale Univ Pr, 1984)
Pool, Ithiel de Sola, Raymond A. Bauer, and Lewis A. Dexter *American Business and Public Policy: The Politics of Foreign Trade* (Chicago, IL: Aldine, 1963)
Pool, Ithiel de Sola *Technologies without Boundaries* (Cambridge, MA: Harvard Univ Pr, 1990)
Porter, Gareth 'Trade Competition and Pollution Standards', *J. of Environment and Development* 8: 2, 133–151 (1999)
Porter, Michael *The Competitive Advantage of Nations* (New York: Free Pr, 1990)
—— *Competitive Strategy* (New York: Free Pr, 1980)
Porter, Michael and Claas van der Linde 'Green *and* Competitive', *Harvard Business Review* (September–October 1995: 120–134; and November–December 206–208)
Portes, Richard and Alexander K. Swoboda (eds.) *Threats to International Financial Stability* (Cambridge, UK: Cambridge Univ Pr, 1987)
Post, James E. 'Nestlé Boycott', case materials (Graduate School of Business, Stanford Univ, 1981)
Powell, Lewis 'Attack on American Free Enterprise System', mimeo (23 August 1971)
Prakash, Aseem *Greening the Firm* (Cambridge, UK: Cambridge Univ Pr, 2000)
Prakash, Aseem and Jeffrey Hart *Responding to Globalization* (London: Routledge: 2000)
Prosser, Dean 'Interstate Publication', *Michigan Law Review* (1953)
Puchala, Donald 'Of Blind Men, Elephants and International Integration', *Journal of Common Market Studies* 10/3: 267–284 (March 1972)
Putnam, Robert D. *Bowling Alone* (New York: Simon & Schuster 2000)
—— 'Diplomacy and Domestic Politics: The Logic of Two-level Games', *International Organization* 42/3: 260–427 (Summer 1988)
Putnam, Robert D. and Eva Cox *Democracies in Flux* (Oxford, UK: Oxford Univ Pr, 2002)
Quinn, Dennis P. and John T. Woolley 'Democracy and National Economic Performance', *American Journal of Political Science* 45: 634–657 (July 2001)
Quinn, Dennis P. 'The Correlates of Change in International Financial Regulation', *American Political Science Review* 91: 531–551 (September 1997)
Quinn, Dennis P. and Carla Inclán 'The Origins of Financial Openness: A Study of Current and Capital Account Liberalization', *American Journal of Political Science* 41: 771–813 (July 1997)
Quinn, Dennis P. and Thomas M. Jones 'An Agent Morality View of Business Policy', *Academy of Management Review* 20: 22–42 (January 1995)
Quinn, Dennis P. and Pietra Rivoli 'The Effects of American- and Japanese-Style Employment and Compensation Practices on Innovation', *Organization Science* 2: 323–341 (November 1991)
Rampton, Sheldon and John Stauber *Trust Us, We're Experts* (New York: Penguin Putnam, 2001)
Rauscher, Michael 'On Ecological Dumping', *Oxford Economic Papers* 46/SPEISS: 822–841 (October 1994)
Rawls, John *A Theory of Justice* (Oxford, UK: Oxford Univ Pr, 1982)
Rees, Joseph *Hostages of Each Other* (Chicago, IL: Univ Chicago Pr, 1994)

Regens, James L. 'Acid Rain Policymaking and Environmental Federalism: Recent Developments and Future Prospects', *Publius* 19/1: 75–91 (Summer 1989)

Reinhardt, Forest Lee 'Forest products firms and their timber suppliers: essays in economic organization and behavior', Ph.D. thesis (Cambridge, MA: Harvard Univ, 1990)

Revesz, Richard L. 'Rehabilitating Interstate Competition: Rethinking the "Race-to-the-Bottom" Rationale for Federal Environmental Regulation', 67 *New York Univeristy Law Review* (1992)

Richardson, Louise Mary 'Managing allies and being managed by alliances: Suez and the Falklands', Ph.D. thesis (Cambridge, MA: Harvard Univ 1989)

Risse, Thomas, Stephen Ropp, and Kathryn Sikkink (eds.) *The Power of Human Rights* (Cambridge, UK: Cambridge Univ Pr, 1999)

Ritchie, Mark 'Agricultural Trade Liberalization', in Nader (1993)

Roberts, Richard and David Kynaston *City State* (London: Profile Books: 2001)

—— (eds.) *The Bank of England* (Oxford, UK: Oxford Univ Pr; 1997)

Rodrik, Dani *Has Globalization Gone Too Far?* (Washington, DC: Institute for International Economics 1997)

Rogowski, Ronald *Commerce and Coalitions* (Princeton, NJ: Princeton Univ Pr, 1989)

Romano, Roberta 'Less is More: [Institutional Activism]', *Yale Journal on Regulation* 18: 174–251 (2001)

—— 'The Political Economy of Takeover Statutes', *Virginia Law Review* 73/111 (1987)

—— 'Law as a Product', *Journal of Law, Economics, and Organization* 1/2: 225–283 (Yale Univ: Fall 1985)

Rosenau, James N. (ed.) 'Toward the Study of National-International Linkages', in *Linkage Politics* (New York: Free Pr, 1969)

Rosenberg, Alexander *Philosophy of Social Science* (Boulder, CO: Westview, 1988)

Rowat, Malcolm D. 'Protectionist Tilts in Antidumping Legislation of Developed Countries and the LDC Response: Is the "Race to the Bottom" Inevitable?', *JWT* 26/6 (1990)

Rowlands, Ian H. *The Politics of Global Atmospheric Change* (Manchester, UK: Manchester Univ Pr, 1995)

Ruggie, John Gerard *Constructing the World Polity* (London: Routledge, 1998)

—— 'Trade, protectionism and the future of welfare capitalism', *Journal of International Affairs* 48/1: 1–11 (Summer 1994)

—— 'Territoriality and beyond', *International Organization* 47/1: 139–174 (Winter 1993)

—— 'International Regimes, Transactions, and Change: Embedded Liberalism in Postwar Economic Order', *International Organization* 36/2: 245–281 (Spring 1982)

—— 'International Responses to Technology', *International Organization* 29/3: 557–583 (Summer 1975)

Ruggie, John G. and F. Kratochwil 'The State of the Art on the Art of the State', *International Organization* (1987)

Ruttenberg, Stanley, testimony, US House Committee on Merchant Marine and Fisheries, SMM, *Energy Transportation Security Act of 1974*, HR-8193, 93d Congress, 1974

Sabel, Charles F. 'Studied Trust', *Human Relations* 46/9: 1133–1171 (September 1993)

Sachs, Jeffrey 'New Approaches to the Latin American Debt Crisis', Princeton Studies in International Economics #174, 1989
—— *Development Economics* (Oxford, UK: Blackwell, 2003)
Salvatore, D. *Protectionism and World Welfare* (Cambridge, UK: Cambridge Univ Pr, 1993)
Sampson, Gary P. *Trade, Environment and the WTO* (DC: Johns Hopkins Univ Pr, 2000)
Samuelson, Paul 'The Pure Theory of Public Expenditures', *Review of Economics and Statistics* 36: 387–389 (November 1954)
Sandholtz, Wayne and John Zysman '1992: Recasting the European Bargain', *World Politics* XLII/1: 95–128 (October 1989)
Sartori, Giovanni 'Concept Misinformation in Comparative Politics', *American Political Science Review* 64: 1033–1053 (1970)
Sauvant, Karl *et al.* at UNCTAD *World Investment Report* (www.unctad.org/wir/, annual esp. 2000, 2001)
Savage, James G. *Politics of International Telecommunications Regulation* (Boulder, CO: Westview, 1989)
Schattschneider, E.E. *The Semisovereign People* (New York: Holt, Rinehart and Winston, 1960)
—— *Politics, Pressure and the Tariff* (New York: Prentice-Hall, 1935)
Schenk, Catherine R. 'The Origins of the Eurodollar Market in London (1955–1963)', *Explorations in Economic History* 35: 221–238 (1998)
Schlefer, Jonathan 'History Counsels "no" on NAFTA', *New York Times* (14 November 1993)
Schmertz, Herb *Good-Bye to the Low Profile* (Boston: Little-Brown, 1986)
Schmidheiny, S. *Changing Course* (Cambridge, MA 1992)
Sebenius, James K. 'Designing Negotiations Toward a New Regime: The Case of Global Warming', *International Security* 15/4: 110–150
—— *Negotiating the Law of the Sea* (Cambridge, MA: Harvard Univ Pr, 1984)
Sesser, Stan 'Opium War Redux', *New Yorker* (13 September 1993)
Shelanski, Howard and Peter Klein 'Empirical Research in Transaction Cost Economics', *Journal of Law, Economics, and Organization* 11: 335–361 (October 1995)
Shepherd, William G. *Public Policies Toward Business* (Richard D. Irwin, Inc., 7th edn. 1985)
Shepsle, Kenneth A. 'Comment' in Noll (ed.) (1985)
Shepsle, Kenneth A. and Barry R. Weingast 'The Institutional Foundations of Committee Power', *American Political Science Review* 81: 929–946 (September 1987)
Shiva, Vandana 'Biodiversity and Intellectual Property Rights', in Nader (1993)
Shoch, James E. 'Party Competition, Divided Government, and the Politics of Economic Nationalism', Ph.D. diss., MIT Political Science Department, 1994; Suzanne Berger, advisor
Shotwell, James T. *The Origins of the International Labor Organization*, vol I: 471 (1934)
Sikkink, Kathryn 'Codes of Conduct for Transnational corporations: The Case of the WHO/UNICEF Code', *International Organization* 40: 4 (Autumn 1986)
Silber, W.L. 'The Process of Financial Innovation', *American Economic Review* [Papers and Proceedings] 73/2: 89–94.

Silverman, Brian, Jack Nickerson, and John Freeman 'Profitability, Transactional Alignment, and Organizational Mortality in the US Trucking Industry', *Strategic Management Journal* 18: 31–52 (Summer 1997)

Simmons, Beth 'Why Innovate? Founding the Bank for International Settlements', *World Politics* 45/3: 361–405 (April 1993)

Sinn, Hans-Werner, including 'Tax Harmonization and Tax Competition in Europe', Special issue of the *European Economic Review* 'Tax Harmonization in the European Community', 34/2–3: 489–505 (May 1990)

Sitkoff, Robert H. 'Corporate Political Speech, Political Extortion, and the Competition for Corporate Charters', *Univ of Chicago Law Review* 69: 1103–1166 (Summer 2002)

Skalaban, Andrew 'Policy Cooperation Among the States: The Case for Interstate Banking Reform', *American Journal of Political Science* 37/2: 415–428 (May 1993)

—— 'Interstate Competition and State Strategies to Deregulate Interstate Banking, 1982–1988', *The Journal of Politics* 54/2: 793–810 (1992)

Skocpol, Theda and Edwin Amenta 'States and Social Policies', *American Review of Sociology* 12: 131–157 (1986)

Skolnikoff, Eugene *The Elusive Transformation* (Princeton, NJ: Princeton Univ Pr, 1993)

Skowronek, Stephen *Building a New American State* (Cambridge, UK: Cambridge Univ Pr, 1982)

Smith, Adam *The Wealth of Nations* (Chicago: Univ of Chicago Pr, 1776/[1976])

Smith, Mark. A. *American Business and Political Power* (Chicago: Univ of Chicago Pr, 2000)

Smouts, Marie-Claude 'Some thoughts on international organizations and theories of regulation', *International Social Science Journal* 45/4: 443–452 (November 1993)

Snidal, Duncan 'The Limits of Hegemonic Stability Theory', *International Organization* 39/4: 579–614 (Autumn 1985)

Sobel, Andrew C. 'Regulatory Change and Convergence Upon a Global Securities Market', paper prepared for the 1992 Annual Meeting of the APSA, 3–6 September 1992

Solingen, Etel 'Between markets and the state: scientists in comparative perspective', *Comparative Politics* 26/1: 31–52 (October 1993)

Sorsa, Piritta 'GATT and Environment', *World Economy* 15/1: 115–133 (January 1992)

Spann, Robert and E.W. Erickson 'The Economics of Railroading: The Beginning of Cartelization and Regulation', *Bell Journal of Economics* 1 (1970)

Spar, Debora L. *The Cooperative Edge* (Ithaca, NY: Cornell Univ Pr, 1994)

Spar, Debora L. and David Yoffie 'Multinational Enterprises and the Prospects for Justice', *J. Int'l Affairs* 52/2: 557–581 (Spring 1990)

Sprague, Irvine H. *Bailout: An Insider's Account of Bank Failures and Rescues* (New York: Basic Books, 1986)

Spulber, David *Regulation and Markets* (Cambridge, MA: MIT Pr, 1986)

Stigler, George 'The Theory of Economic Regulation', originally published in *Bell Journal of Economics and Management Science*, Spring 1971: 114–141; and his Supplementary Note, 1975

Stigler, George (ed.) *Chicago Studies in Political Economy* (Chicago, IL: Univ of Chicago Pr, 1988)

Stiglitz, Joseph *Globalization and Its Discontents* (W.W. Norton, 2002)

Stith, Clark D. 'Federalism and Company Law: A Race to the Bottom in the European Community', *Georgetown Law Journal* (1991)

Stone, Alec 'What is a supranational constitution? An essay in international relations theory', *Review of Politics* 56/3: 441–475 (Summer 1994)

Stone, Peter H. 'For Bankers, Persistence Pays Off (Interstate Bill)', *National Journal* 26/36: 2034–2036 (September 1994)

Storper, Michael 'Oligopoly and the Product Cycle', *Economic Geography* 61/3: 260–283 (July 1985)

Strange, Susan *Retreat of the State* (Cambridge, UK: Cambridge Univ Pr, 1996)

—— 'States, Firms and Diplomacy', *International Affairs* 68/1: 1–15 (London, 1992)

—— 'Cave! Hic Dragones: A Critique of Regime Analysis', in Krasner (1982)

—— *International Economic Relations of the Western World 1959–71/2: International Monetary Relations* (Oxford, UK: Oxford Univ Pr, 1976)

Strunk, Norman and Fred Case *Where Deregulation Went Wrong: A Look at the Causes Behind Savings and Loan Failures in the 1980s* (Chicago: US League of Savings Institutions, 1988)

Subramanian, Arvind 'Trade Measures for Environment: A Nearly Empty Box?', *World Economy* 15/1: 135–152 (1992)

Summers, Lawrence, internal World Bank memo, reprinted in *Economist*: 66 (8 February 1992)

Sutton, John *Sunk Costs and Market Structure* (Cambridge, MA: MIT Pr, 1990)

—— 'Explaining Everything, Explaining Nothing? Game Theoretic Models in Industrial Economics; Does Oligopoly Theory "Explain" the Behavior of Industry?', *European Economic Review* 34/2–3: 505–513 (May 1990)

—— 'Endogenous Sunk Costs and the Structure of Advertising Intensive Industries (Explaining Industrial Structure)', *European Economic Review* 33/2–3: 335–345 (March 1989)

Swank, Duane *Global Capital, Political Institutions and Policy Change in Developed Welfare States* (Cambridge, UK: Cambridge Univ Pr, 2002)

Swire, Peter P. 'The Race to Laxity and the Race to Undesirability', Symposium on Constructing a New Federalism, *Yale Law and Policy Review*, 14: 67 (1996)

Tait, Joyce and Les Levidow 'Proactive and Reactive Approaches to Risk Regulation: The Case of Biotechnology', *Futures* (April 1982)

Taylor, Andrew 'What Opponents Seek (Opponents of Interstate Branch Banking)', *Congressional Quarterly Weekly Review* 52/8: 462 (26 February 1994)

Tedlow, Richard S. *Keeping the corporate image: Public relations and business, 1900–1950*, Industrial development and the social fabric; v. 3 (Greenwich, Conn.: JAI Pr, c 1979)

Tiebout, Charles 'A Pure Theory of Local Expenditures', *Journal of Political Economy* 64/5: 416–424 (October 1956)

Tobin, Glenn 'Global Money Rules: The Political Economy of International Regulatory Cooperation', Ph.D. dissertation, Harvard Univ Kennedy School of Government (1991)

Tobin, Glenn 'International Efforts to Regulate Banking and Securities Markets', Kennedy School of Government, Working Group on the Politics of Money, Finance and Debt (draft, 6 November 1990)

——*National Rules and International Money* (draft mimeo, May 1990)

——'International Capital Adequacy Negotiation (A Case Study)', Center for Business and Government, John F. Kennedy School of Government (Cambridge, MA: Harvard Univ, February 1990)

Tosini, Suzanne C. and Edward Tower 'The Textile Bill of 1985: The Determinants of Congressional Voting Patterns', *Public Choice* 54: 19–25 (1987)

Trachtman, Joel 'International Regulatory Competition, Externalization, and Jurisdiction', *Harvard International Law Journal* 34/1: 47–104 (Winter 1993)

——'Conflict of Laws and Accuracy in the Allocation of Government Responsibility' (mimeo, 27 July 1993)

——'Recent Initiatives in International Financial Regulation', *Northwestern J. of International Law & Business* 12: 241 (Fall 1991)

——'GATT Dispute Settlement Panel', *American Journal of International Law* 86/1: 142–151 (January 1992)

Trigilia, Carlo 'Small-Firm Development and Political Subcultures in Italy', *European Sociological Review*: 161–173 (December 1986)

Tucker, Robert C. (ed.) *The Marx–Engels Reader* 2nd edn. (Norton, 1978)

Uimonen, Peter 'Trade policies and the environment', *Finance & Development* 29/2: 26–28 (June 1992)

UK House of Lords, Select Committee on Science and Technology, study on ship safety (February 1992)

UN Centre on Transnational Corporations (CTC) *Transnational Banks and the International Debt Crisis* (UN, 1991)

——*Environmental Aspects of Transnational Corporation Activities in Pollution-Intensive Industries in Selected Asian and Pacific Developing Countries*, ESCAP/UNCTC Publication Series B/15 (New York, 1990)

Underdal, Arild *The Politics of International Fisheries Management* (New York: Columbia Univ Pr, 1980)

United Nations Environment Programme (UNEP) *OzonAction*, Industry and Environment Programme Activity Center (various issues)

US Advisory Committee on Intergovernmental Relations and The Urban Institute, Conference on 'Interjurisdictional Tax and Policy Competition', 23–24 March 1988 (funded by the J. Howard Pew Trust)

US Department of State Dispatch 'Gist: High-Seas Driftnet Fishing', 3/42: 783 (19 October 1992)

US Department of State 'International Narcotic Control Strategy Report' (US GPO: March 1991)

US Department of Transportation, US Coast Guard *Background Summary Regarding the International Conference on Tanker Safety and Pollution Prevention*, London, 5–17 February 1978, and *Final Regulatory Analysis and Environmental Impact Statement, Regulations to Implement the Results of the International Conference on Tanker Safety and Pollution* (1979) (Washington: Coast Guard).

US House, Committee on Merchant Marine and Fisheries *Study of Vessel Transfer, Trade-in and Reserve Fleet Policies*, 85th Congress 1st session, 1957

US House, testimony on the Riegle-Neal 'Interstate Banking and Branching Efficiency Act of 1994' (HR 3841)

US House, Hearings on *The Energy Transportation Security Acts* of 1974 (HR 8193) 1977 (HR 1037)

US House of Representatives, Committee on Interstate and Foreign Commerce, R.L. McCarthy (of DuPont) 11–12 December 1974

US International Trade Commission (ITC) *Tuna: Current Issues Affecting the US Industry* (August 1992)

—— 'The Effects of Greater Economic Integration within the European Community on the United States: Report to the Committee on Ways and Means of the US House of Representatives and the Committee on Finance of the US Senate on Investigation No. 332–267 Under Section 332 of the Tariff Act of 1930', July 1989; and idem 'Third Follow-Up Report' (March 1991)

—— 'Tuna: Competitive Conditions Affecting the US and European Tuna Industries in the Domestic and Foreign Markets', Report to the Committee on Finance, US Senate, and the Committee on Ways and Means, US House of Representatives, Washington, DC (December 1990)

—— 'Pros and Cons of Initiating Negotiations with Japan to Explore the Possibility of a US–Japan Free Trade Area Agreement: Investigation No. TA-332-255' (September 1988)

—— 'US Global Competitiveness: Oilseeds and Oilseed Products, Report to the Committee on Finance, US Senate' (December 1987)

US Senate, Committee on the Environment and Public Works, Subcommittees on Environmental Protection and Hazardous Wastes and Toxic Substances, 100th Congress 1st session 1987, *Ozone Depletion, the Greenhouse Effect, and Climate Change*

US Senate 'Corporate Rights and Responsibilities: Hearings Before the Senate Committee on Commerce', 94th Cong., 2d Sess., 241 including statement by Harvey J. Goldschmidt (1976)

US Senate, CIFC Subcommittee on Commerce, *Investigation of Federal Maritime Administration, Transfer to Foreign Flag*, S.173, 83d Congress, 2d session (1954)

US Senate, CIFC *Merchant Marine Study and Investigation*, 81st Congress, 2d session, pursuant to S. 50 and S. 2786 (27 February 1950)

US Senate, Committee on Government Operations, Permanent Subcommittee of Investigation *Hearings on Sale of Government-Owned Vessels*, 82d Congress (February 1952)

US Trade Representative, Interagency Task Force Study (15 October 1991)

Vandermeersch, Dirk 'The Single European Act and the Environmental Policy of the European Community', *European Law Review*, vol. 12 (December 1987)

Vanderwicken, Peter 'Why the News is Not the Truth', *Harvard Business Review* (May–June 1995)

Verdier, Daniel *Democracy and International Trade* (Princeton, NJ: Princeton Univ Pr, 1994)

Vernon, Raymond, Debora Spar, and Glenn Tobin *Iron triangles and revolving doors: Cases in US foreign economic policymaking* (New York: Praeger, 1991)

——'Behind the scenes: how policymaking in the European Community, Japan, and the United States affects global negotiations (environmental protection)', *Environment* 35/5: 12–29 (June 1993)

Vernon, Raymond, *Big Business and the State* (Cambridge, MA: Harvard Univ Pr, 1974)

—— *The Economic and Political Consequences of Multinational Enterprise* (Boston: Harvard Univ, 1972)

—— *Sovereignty at Bay* (New York: Basic Books 1971)

—— *America's Foreign Trade Policy and the GATT*. Essays in international finance; no. 21. Princeton, NJ, International Finance Section, Dept. of Economics and Sociology, Princeton Univ (1954)

Victor, David 'Tradeable Permits and Greenhouse Gas Reduction' (Cambridge, MA: Kennedy School of Government Discussion Paper E-90-16, 1990)

Vietor, Richard H.K, *Contrived Competition: Regulation and Deregulation in America* (Boston, MA: Belknap Pr of Harvard Univ, 1994)

Vietor, Richard H.K., Forest Reinhardt, and Peggy Duxbury 'StarKist' (Boston, MA: Harvard Business School Case Services, 1994)

Vogel, David and Robert Kagan (eds.) *Dynamics of Regulatory Change: How Globalization Affects National Regulatory Policies* (Berkeley, CA: Univ of California Pr, 2002)

Vogel, David *Trading Up* (Cambridge, MA: Harvard Univ Pr, 1995)

—— 'The European Community and the Harmonization of Regulatory Policy: Implications for Sustainable Development Under NAFTA' (mimeo, 1993)

—— 'Environmental Protection and the Creation of a Single European Market', paper prepared for delivery at the 1992 Annual Meeting of the American Political Science Association, the Palmer House Hilton, 3–6 September 1992

—— *Fluctuating Fortunes: The Political Power of Business in America* (New York: Basic Books, 1989)

—— *National Styles of Regulation: Environmental Policy in Great Britain and the United States* (Ithaca, NY: Cornell Univ Pr, 1984)

Vogel, Steven *Freer Markets, More Rules* (Ithaca, NY: Cornell Univ Pr, 1996)

Waitzer, Edward J. 'Securities Regulation in Canada and the US (Mergers and Acquisitions)', *The National Law Journal* 9: 30 (18 May 1987)

Wallerstein, Immanuel *The Capitalist World Economy* (Cambridge, UK: Cambridge Univ Pr, 1979)

Wallis, John Joseph and Douglass C. North 'Measuring the Transaction Sector in the American Economy, 1870–1970', 1: 378–444 in Steven G. Medema (ed.) *The Legacy of Ronald Coase in Economic Analysis* (UK: Elgar, 1995)

Walt, Stephen M. 'Politicians and professors: A double standard (honesty and deceit) (Washington Report)', *Bulletin of the Atomic Scientists* 43: 3–5 (July–August 1987)

Waltz, Kenneth *The Use of Force* 4th edn. (Lanham, MD: Univ Pr of America, c 1993)

—— *Theory of International Politics* (Reading, MA: Addison-Wesley, c 1979)

—— *Man, the State and War* (New York: Columbia Univ Pr, 1959)

Walzer, Michael *Thick and Thin: Moral Argument at Home and Abroad* (Notre Dame, IN: Notre Dame, 1994)

Weatherstone, Dennis 'An American View of Europe's Consolidation in 1992', remarks before the Swiss–American Chamber of Commerce (Zurich, 20 June 1988), reprinted in *American Banker* (24 June 1988)

Weaver, Paul *News and the Culture of Lying: How Journalism Really Works* (New York: Free Pr, 1994)

Weiner, Myron *The Child and the State in India* (Princeton, NJ: Princeton Univ Pr, c 1991)

Weiner, Sanford and James Maxwell 'The Political Economy of the CFC Phaseout', in 'Dimensions of Managing Chlorine in the Environment', *Report of the MIT/Norwegian Chlorine Policy Study*, John Ehrenfeld (ed.) (MIT Center for Technology, Policy, and Industrial Development, March 1993)

Weingast, Barry R. 'Regulation, Reregulation, and Deregulation', *Law and Contemporary Problems* 44/1: 147–177 (Winter 1981)

Weinstein, James *The Corporate Ideal in the Liberal State 1900–1918* (Boston, MA: Beacon Pr, 1968).

Wells, Louis T. (ed.) *Using Tax Incentives to Compete for Foreign Investment* (World Bank 2001)

—— *The Product Life Cycle and International Trade* (Cambridge, MA: Harvard Univ School of Business Administration, 1972)

Wendt, Alexander *Social Theory of International Politics* (Cambridge, UK: Cambridge Univ Pr, 1999)

—— 'Anarchy is What States Make of It', *International Organization* 46/2: 391–425 (Spring 1992)

—— 'The Agent-Structure Debate in International Relations', *International Organization* 41/3: 335–370 (Summer 1987)

Whalen, Gary 'The Securities Activities of the Foreign Subsidiaries of US Banks', *Economics Working Paper* 98-2, Office of the Comptroller of the Currency (February 1998)

White, Eugene *The Regulation and Reform of the American Banking System, 1900–1929* (Princeton, NJ, 1983)

Williamson, Oliver E. *The Mechanisms of Governance* (Oxford, UK: Oxford Univ Pr, 1999)

—— 'The New Institutional Economics', *J. of Economic Literature* 38: 595–613 (September 2000)

—— *Economic Institutions of Capitalism* (New York: Free Pr, 1985)

Willoughby, Malcolm Francis *Rum War at Sea* (Washington, DC: GPO, 1964)

Wilson, James Q. (ed.) *The Politics of Regulation* (New York: Basic Books 1980)

Wilson, John S., mimeos accessed online September 2002 at www.worldbank.org, including 'World Bank Research in Progress on Standards' (c 2002), 'The Economic Benefits of Removing Technical and Regulatory Barriers' (1998), 'Triennial Review of the Agreement on Technical Barriers to Trade' (1997), and 'International Trade: Standards, Technical Regulations, and Global Reform' (1997)

Winham, Gilbert R. *The evolution of international trade agreements* (Toronto; Buffalo Univ of Toronto Pr, c 1992)

Winston, J.R. *Lloyds Bank 1918–1969* (Oxford, UK: Oxford Univ Pr, 1982)

Winter, Ralph K., Jr. 'The "Race for the Top" Revisited', *Colum. L. Rev* 89: 1526 (1989)

—— 'State Law, Shareholder Protection, and the Theory of the Corporation', *J. of Legal Studies* 6/2: 251–292 (June 1977)

World Resources Institute *World Resources* annual yearbook

Wright, Quincy 'Etudes des mesures internationales les plus aptes à prévenir la pollution des milieux maritimes', Institut de Droit International, 53 *Annuaire* 255 (1969 II)

Wriston, Walter *The Twilight of Sovereignty: How the Information Revolution is Transforming Our World* (New York: Scribners 1992)

Yamamura, Kozo (ed.) *Policy and trade issues of the Japanese economy: American and Japanese perspectives*, publications on Asia of the School of International Studies, Univ of Washington; 36 (Seattle, WA: Univ of Washington Pr, c 1982)

Yandle, Bruce 'Bootleggers and Baptists: The Education of a Regulatory Economist', *Regulation* (May–June 1983)

—— 'Intertwined Interests, Rent Seeking, and Regulation', *Social Science Quarterly* 65/4: 1002–1012 (December 1984)

Yarbrough, Beth V. and Robert M. Yarbrough 'Regionalism and layered governance', *Journal of International Affairs* 48/1: 95–117 (Summer 1994)

—— 'Preferential trade agreements and the GATT', *KYKLOS* 47/2: 179–96 (Summer 1994)

—— 'Cooperation in the liberalization of international trade', *International Organization*, 41/1: 1–26 (Winter 1987)

Yoffie, David B. *International trade and Competition*, 2nd edn. (New York: McGraw-Hill c 1994)

Yoffie, David B. (ed.) *Beyond Free Trade* (Boston, MA: Harvard Business School Pr, c 1993)

Yoffie David B. and Helen Milner 'Between Free Trade and Protectionism' (Cambridge, MA: Harvard Business School Division of Research, November 1987)

Young, Oran R. 'International Regimes: Problems of Concept Formation', *World Politics* 32/3: 331/356 (April 1980)

Zysman, John *Technology and trade*, BRIE working paper 67 (Berkeley, CA: Univ of California Berkeley Pr, 1994)

Zysman, John and Laura Tyson (eds.) *American Industry in International Competition* (Ithaca, NY: Cornell Univ Pr, 1983)

Xing, Yuqing and Charles D. Kolstad 'Do Lax Environmental Regulations Attract Foreign Direct Investment?', *Environmental and Resource Economics*, 21/1: 1–23 (2002)

# Index